THE SECRET LAND

THE ORIGINS OF ARTHURIAN LEGEND
AND THE GRAIL QUEST

PAUL BROADHURST

WITH
ROBIN HEATH

CŒLIFER ATLAS

PRIMVM MOBILE
CRISTALLINE
FIRMAMENT

Hic canet errantĕ Lunam, Solisq; labores
Arcturŭq;,,pluuiasq; hyad.gĕinosq; triões

I.D.

FIRST PUBLISHED
IN NOVEMBER 2009
by

BOX 888
Launceston, PL15 7YH
Cornwall, United Kingdom

www. mythospress.co.uk

ISBN NO. 978-0-9513236-5-6

THE SECRET LAND
© Paul Broadhurst

THE QUEST FOR THE
PREHISTORIC ARTHUR
© Robin Heath

Book & Cover Design by Gabriele Trso, Cornwall
Printed by TJ International, Padstow

ACKNOWLEDGEMENTS

This book has not been produced by a large company. It has been written and published from a Cornish cottage, mostly to the flicker of candles burning at both ends. As it is also printed in Cornwall this makes it a purely Cornish project, which is fitting under the circumstances. Very few people have been involved in this study of the secret landscape, by its very nature.

Special thanks to my partner Gabriele Trso for her research work, which has added great depth to the book, as well as her inspiration, editorial and production skills which have resulted in not just a book, but a work of Art. The research was illuminating and the sense of discovery exhilarating. Without the insights provided by Robin Heath and Tricia Osborne this book would lack the rigour of scientific discipline. Thanks, too for their input and observations of a more esoteric kind.

Others who helped with ideas and conversation during the quest were also instrumental, each in their own way, and include David Elkington, Charles Thomas, Roslyn M. Frank, Graham King, Kevin Gibbs, Irene Earis, Roger Irving-Little, Anthony Holloway and Roger Toy.

This book is dedicated to
The late John Michell
He was rarely early
But we wish he could have
Stayed a little longer

Paul Broadhurst

Completing a book demands much of many people. I would like to thank Paul for his original impetus, his enthusiasm and his insightful vision; to Gabriele for her tenacity, patience and artistic flair while laying out the book; to my partner Tricia for needed critical proof reading, and for her loving support. In addition, I would like to thank Irene Earis for her commentaries on the emerging material. My sole regret is that a copy of the finished book cannot now be placed in the hands of our late friend John Michell, who loved the history and landscape of both Cornwall and Wales.

Robin Heath

An important note about

TRUE NORTH

Readers need to be aware that the North-South grid lines on maps do not correspond to the direction of True North. These grid lines are for the convenience of mapmakers and do not occur in Nature. Throughout this book True North (currently marked by the Pole Star in the tail of the Little Bear, Ursa Minor) is referred to, having been recognised in all ages as the central point around which the visible universe appears to revolve.

For further details see page 302.

'Now where heaven reaches its culmination in the shining
Bears, which from the summit of the sky look down on all
the stars and know no setting and, shifting their opposed
stations about the same high point, set sky and stars in
rotation, from there an insubstantial axis runs down through
the wintry air and controls the universe, keeping it pivoted
at opposite poles: it forms the middle about which the starry
sphere revolves and wheels its heavenly flight, but is itself
without motion and, drawn straight through the empty
spaces of the great sky to the two Bears and through the very
globe of the Earth, stands fixed, since the entire atmosphere
ever revolves in a circle, and every part of the whole rotates
to the place from which it once began, that which is in the
middle, about which all moves, so insubstantial that it
cannot turn round upon itself or even submit to motion or
spin in circular fashion, this men have called the axis, since,
motionless itself, it yet sees everything spinning about it.'

Manilius, Astronomica
1st Century AD

***Other Titles
by Paul Broadhurst***

The Green Man and the Dragon

The Dance of the Dragon

The Sun and the Serpent

Tintagel and the Arthurian Mythos

Secret Shrines

***Other Titles
by Robin Heath***

*Alexander Thom:
Cracking the Stone Age Code*

Sun, Moon & Earth

Powerpoints

The Measure of Albion

Stonehenge

Sun, Moon & Stonehenge

THE SECRET LAND
CONTENTS

	LIST OF ILLUSTRATIONS	8
	INTRODUCTION	10
1	ARTHUR THE BEAR KING	13
2	SKY BEARS AND STAR LORE	29
3	RETURN OF THE GOD KINGS	41
4	HUNTING THE BEAR	53
5	THE LAIR OF THE BEAR	67
6	ISLAND OF THE KINGS	79
7	THE GEOMETRY OF TIME	91
8	THE LIONS OF LYONESSE	105
9	A LION'S TALE	115
10	THE WILD HUNT	127
11	MERLIN'S MENAGERIE	143
12	THE CALL OF THE WOLF	159
13	GUARDIANS OF THE SECRET LAND	171
14	THE HEARTLAND	189
15	GODDESS OF THE UNDERWORLD	209
16	LORD OF THE HUNT	227
17	STAR-GOD OF PARADISE	243
18	THE TREE OF KNOWLEDGE	263
19	ARTHUR'S DESCENT INTO THE OTHERWORLD	275

THE QUEST FOR THE PREHISTORIC ARTHUR

	INTRODUCTION	291
1	THE BEAR IN THE LANDSCAPE	293
2	ARTHUR, ARTH FAWR AND ALIGNED SITES	303
3	ARTHUR AND NORTHNESS	309
4	REVEALING THE PREHISTORIC ARTHUR	321
5	CORRIDORS OF POWER	333
	APPENDICES I TO VI	
	THE BOTTREAUX FAMILY	344
	DRAKE AND THE ELIZABETHANS	345
	THE HUNT OF VENUS	348
	RECENT ARCHEOLOGICAL DISCOVERIES AT THE GREAT BEAR OF TINTAGEL	349
	THE KING OF LOSTWITHIEL	350
	A FLIGHT TO THE EAST?	350
	BIBLIOGRAPHY	353
	INDEX	356

LIST OF ILLUSTRATIONS

This book, by its very nature, is highly illustrated. Almost a hundred and fifty of these have been meticulously prepared by Gabriele Trso, whose talents for the visual arts are quite extraordinary. Without her dedicated labours THE SECRET LAND would have lacked the essential empathy between the written word and the landscape that expresses that indefinable Spirit of the Land. The maps of the giant effigies discovered during this quest are especially captivating; it is not easy to present them in a book as they appear on a map. In this she has exceeded beyond expectations. Thanks to Graham King of the Museum of Witchcraft, Boscastle for the colour picture of The Wild Hunt. Vivienne Shanley for the Egloskerry Dragon, King Arthur's Hall and the Tintagel Solstice Axis. Gabriele Trso for the Bear and Ragged Staff, The Great Bear Axis, King Arthur's Hall/ Lundy Axis, The Pipers, The Horn of Cornwall and Merlin and the Great Bear by kind permission of Michael Godwin and Roger Toy from King Arthur's Great Halls at Tintagel. Robin Heath for the Cornish and Welsh Lundy/Stonehenge Triangle, The Great Bear and the Pole Star, The Seven Stars of the Great Bear at Tintagel and the Lundy Island North-South Axis. His graphics shine new light on the achievements of our ancestors.

THE SECRET LAND
ORIGINAL PHOTOGRAPHY BY PAUL BROADHURST

1. ARTHUR THE BEAR KING
The Great Bear of Tintagel 17
The Lady of Vinca 20
Shaman in Bearskin 26
Ursa Major by A. Dürer 28

2. SKY BEARS AND STAR LORE
Bear Boy 30
The Bear and Ragged Staff 35
Constellation of the Great Bear 40

3. RETURN OF THE GOD-KINGS
The Franks Casket 44
William, Duke of Normandy 47
Viking King with Bear Pelt 51

4. HUNTING THE BEAR
St Nectan's Kieve 52
Glastonbury Tor 54
The Great Bear looking at Tintagel 56
Egloskerry Agnus Dei 57
Boscastle Harbour 58
Willapark, Boscastle 59
Pentargon Caves 60
Minster Church 61
King Arthur's Stone, Slaughterbridge 66

5. THE LAIR OF THE BEAR
St Piran's Well, Trethevy 70
Rocky Valley Maze 71
Tintagel Island 78

6. ISLAND OF THE KINGS
Sheep grazing at Tintagel 80
Rock-cut tunnel at Tintagel 83
King Arthur's Cups and Saucers 85
Nordic Kingship Inauguration 86
King Arthur's Footprint 88

Merlin's Cave 89
King Arthur's Head 90

7. THE GEOMETRY OF TIME
Tintagel Green Bishop 92
Tintagel Island font 93
Tintagel Churchyard monolith 95
Tintagel Island Plateau 96
The Great Bear and the Pole Star 97
The Great Bear's Polar Axis 102
Minster Cross 100
The Cheesewring 102
The Tintagel Solstice Axis 103
The Seven Stars of the Great Bear
  over Tintagel 104

8. THE LIONS OF LYONESSE
The Bodmin and Lostwithiel Lions 107
The Great Lion of Bodmin 111
Bodmin Obelisk 111
Lanivet Cross 112
Lanivet Viking Memorial 113

9. A LION'S TALE
The Constellations of Leo Major & Minor 115
The Lostwithiel Lion 117
Lion tin-stamp 118
Cardinham Cross 119
Lanlivery lion carving 120
Ygdrassil Tree 121
Beheading Game at Lanlivery 123
Widecombe roof-bosses 124
The Black Prince 126
Restormel Castle 126

10. THE WILD HUNT
Lostwithiel 'Green Bishop' 130
Lostwithiel Gargoyle 132

Lostwithiel Font   135
Lostwithiel Bear   136
The Horn of Cornwall   141
Odin as Lord of the Underworld   142

11. MERLIN'S MENAGERIE
Bodmin Font   145
St Kew with Bear   149
The Little Pig of Helland and Blisland   153
The St Mabyn Bear   154
The Little Pig and Castle Killibury   158

12. THE CALL OF THE WOLF
King Arthur's Hall   161
The Lundy and King Arthur's Hall axes   162
The Nine Maidens   163
The Great Dog of St Columb   164
Bench-end in St Columb Church   166
Lantern Cross at St Mawgan   168
Arundell Memorial Brass   168
Wolf Crest of the Arundells   169
St Columb Carnival Bears and Lions   170

13. GUARDIANS OF THE SECRET LAND
The Great Dog and Canis Major   176
Jack of Tilbury   178
Lanherne Cross   181
The Flaming Dogs of St Newlyn East   186
Lanherne and St Mawgan Church   188

14. THE HEARTLAND
Prior Vyvan's tomb   191
The Great Hare of Bodmin Moor   195
King Arthur's Quoit   196
King Doniert's Stones   197
St Cleer Holy Well   198
The Cheesewring   198
The Rillaton Cup   200
The Tinners's Hares or Hunt of Venus   205
Cornish Mummers   207
Moon-gazing Hare of Bodmin Moor   208

15. GODDESS OF THE UNDERWORLD
The Darley Oak   211
Lewannick Font   212
The Egloskerry Dragon   213
Mary Magdalene   216
Launceston Church   217
Launceston Castle   218
Lostwithiel 'Green Goddess'   221
Alchemical Salamander   222
Dog biting Hare on Lostwithiel Font   227
Portal Stones, Stowes Hill   223
Pointer Stone at Stowes Hill   224
Daniel Gumb's House   226

16. LORD OF THE HUNT
The Cosmic Wheel, Hallstatt   232
The Giant of St Winnow   233

Puck   234
Druid's Hill, Boconnoc   235
The Boconnoc Giant   240
'Old Father Time' from Bradoc Church   241

17. STAR-GOD OF PARADISE
Starry Crown from Tintagel Church   248
Corona Borealis   248
The Owl of St Veep   249
St Winnow Church   250
Punchbowl Inn sign   252
Grylls-Bere Coat of Arms   253
St Nectan's Chapel   255
Boconnoc Obelisk avenue   256
Head of Horned God   259
St German's Hunting misericord   260
Adam and Eve   262

18. THE TREE OF KNOWLEDGE
The Tristan Stone   272

19. ARTHUR'S DESCENT INTO
      THE UNDERWORLD
Inscribed stones on Lundy Island   280
Lundy Island   283
Knights Templar Rock   286

THE QUEST FOR THE PREHISTORIC ARTHUR

PHOTOGRAPHY AND GRAPHICS BY ROBIN HEATH

1. THE BEAR IN THE LANDSCAPE
The Great Bear and True North   292
A Bear for all Seasons   297
The Day, the Year and a Circumpolar
      Star Clock   298

2. ARTHUR, ARTH FAWR AND ALIGNED SITES
Geodetic connections between major
      prehistoric sites   305
N/S alignment between Bryn Celli Ddu
      and Morte Point   306
The Stonehenge Triangle   307
Culmination of the Moon at Carn Ingli   308

3. ARTHUR AND NORTHNESS
Carreg Coetan Arthur   312
Major Moon Standstill at Coetan Arthur   313
Arthur's Quoit   318
Two Precision Instruments   320

4. REVEALING THE PREHISTORIC ARTHUR
A Fearful Symmetry   324
The Arthur Triangle   326
The Geodetic Habits of the Celtic Monks   327

5. CORRIDORS OF POWER
The Lundy Axis   336
The King Arthur's Hall Axis   337
King Arthur's Hall   338

INTRODUCTION

ost people, as soon as they cross the border into Cornwall, feel as if they are entering a different land. There is a subtle shift in perception, a vague feeling of expectation and adventure in the air. What is it about the place that lifts our spirits and calls out to some half-forgotten instinct lingering at the edge of our consciousness?

Is it the wildness of the wave-lashed rocks that surround it on all sides, or the thought of standing on a lonely cliff awed at the sheer vastness of a setting-sun sky which appeals to our romantic nature? Could it be the power of the granite tors, studded with oddly-sculpted shapes that look like giant faces frozen by the wind? Or is it some old memory stirring, a memory of when the land was different, when time was of a different order, when life was seen through different eyes? Why do we love the salt air and the sound of the rolling tides, or want nothing more than to sink down on a grassy cliff or meadow surrounded by wild flowers, listen to the silent sounds of nature and drift off into a dream?

Cornwall has always been a place on its own. Its history and the forces that have shaped it have set it apart from the rest of Britain. As the last refuge of the indigenous British when waves of invaders drove them down into the far west, it still preserves something of those ancient, far-off days. Maybe it is this we sense, a reminder of how things used to be, before the hurly-burly of modern influences disturbed its timelessness.

As Cornwall is virtually an island, surrounded by the sea and cut off from the mainland by the River Tamar which runs almost from the north to the south coasts, it has always welcomed those from other lands. Classical writers have left their impressions from those days, and it is clear that the old Cornish (British) people had frequent contact with seafarers from around the world, including Phoenician, Greek, Roman, Spanish, Irish, Viking and Norman. Often, they lived amongst the population or formed trading colonies. The Romans themselves, unlike elsewhere in Britain, never sought to subdue the Cornish, happy to maintain a productive relationship that was mutually beneficial.

The rocks and soil of a place give it a special character, just like those distinctive old trees bent by the prevailing wind. The lush and secret valleys of the deep coombes seem trapped in a web of timelessness. Even in the midst of the twenty-first century when time seems to be running out, there are spots where it appears to stop altogether. Then the spirit of the landscape speaks to our inner ear and reminds us that we may be passing through, but the land is always here.

This book, I hope, will help to explain something of the strange attraction of this old land and why it can affect us so deeply. Yes, it is the landscape of rocks and sea, the moors and the tree-covered lanes that evoke in us that feeling of stepping through into another world, as well as the legendary places with their potent energy where our imagination is released to roam free wherever it will. It is freedom that is our goal, our minds purified by the ocean breeze that keenly blows through its dark and dusty corners. Then we see that the land, the sky, is alive. While the human world rushes frantically about its business the spirit within the land, slumbering for so many ages, opens one eye narrowly and wonders: why can't you see that you are not just children of the Earth, you and the Earth are One...

What are we to make of the discoveries presented in this book? A series of giant effigies carved, as if by a God's hand, in the country between the precipitous cliffs of Tintagel in the north of the county and the gentler terrain of the south, with the eldritch wilderness of Bodmin Moor at its heart? Is it all some strange fantasy, a product of that imaginative side of the mind?

Anyone reading the following pages will probably experience a gamut of emotions ranging from initial disbelief and bewilderment to incomprehension and amazement, eventually culminating in the realisation that there are indeed great mysteries concealed in the very shape and character of the land itself.

As we walk or drive along a curiously-shaped road that has its own strongly distinctive atmosphere how could we ever know we are travelling along the back of a huge earthly image of a Great Bear that represents one of the most important constellations in the night sky?

What visionary impulse caused people in some remote time to try and reflect Heaven on Earth in such a manner? Why did they create myths like those of King Arthur, whose name means *Great Bear*, which would always be associated with the place even if it be thousands of years into the future? Lions, a gigantic dog, even a great god-giant are all to be found here, each one having its own legendary attributes linked to the earliest traditions and folklore of mankind.

The circumstantial evidence that these giants in the landscape, each one a wondrous work of art, have meaning and purpose beyond any aesthetic value is overwhelming. Every one of us is drawn to live in, or habitually visit, a place because of some inexplicable magnetic quality that attracts us through our instinctual senses. There is an interaction, an energetic exchange between us and that particular place. Who can explain it? Like the cycles of Life and Death, there is no explanation, these things simply *are*.

In previous cultures these matters were of abiding importance. Every tree, rock, river and spring of pure water were sources of the spirit within Nature. Every phase of the moon or repeating cycle of the sun or stars had a special meaning and influence. It is likely that people then had more finely-tuned senses for such things; today there is too much noise and activity to distract us from the real environment that sustains earthly life. Some say the fairies fled when television arrived, imprisoning our imaginations and numbing our sensibilities. Others note a gradual decline in our ability to attune to the landscape since the Industrial Revolution, when people abandoned the age-old ways.

But just because we live in a different world today does not mean we are any less human than our forebears. All these instincts and memories are stored away and can still be awakened. Yet the real memory of our long sojourn on this planet is in the very land under our feet. As we walk the old roads and pathways our pilgrimage becomes a sort of personal Grail Quest, if, that is, we are really dedicated seekers of the truth.

Gaze upon these extraordinary works of art and the way they stamp the county with an especially magical character; marvel at the ingenuity of those old myth-makers who created the legends; stand under the stars with a sense of wonder and childlike awe. For the true Grail is not any physical object, but a state of mystical consciousness, of being one with Nature. This can be attained by anyone who walks the Grail path with a pure heart and an enquiring mind, and has the courage to ask the right question.

Paul Broadhurst
August 1st 2009

1

ARTHUR THE BEAR KING

intagel, that atmospheric storm-blasted headland off the north coast of Cornwall, is, according to immemorial British legend, the birthplace of King Arthur. It was a Welsh monk, Geoffrey of Monmouth, soon to be a bishop, who first immortalised it in written form in *The History of the Kings of Britain*, a collection of mythic tales and fabulous history published in about 1135. However, there is little doubt amongst historians that he drew much of his material from an oral tradition of great antiquity, stories told and retold by generations before him around the fires of pre-Norman Britain. He claimed that he gleaned much of his information from a book in the 'ancient British tongue' lent to him by Walter Map, Archdeacon of Oxford. But this book, or a copy of it, has unfortunately never been found, and it could be that Geoffrey was using a literary pun, common in manuscripts of the time, to refer indirectly to this oral background of the native British tradition. The *History* contains strong elements of the world of Celtic magic; included within the main body of the book is another work, the *Vita Merlini*, a collection of writings about the Life and Prophecies of the Druidic sage Merlin.

Geoffrey's proper name was *Grufydd ab Arthur*, or Geoffrey, son of Arthur, and, being of Welsh (or some say Breton) descent, we might expect him to have claimed that Arthur's birth took place in either of these regions for reasons of patriotism. But Geoffrey was unequivocal: King Arthur was conceived and born at Tintagel. Two hundred years before the publication of Geoffrey's book, which was destined to become one of the greatest 'best-sellers' of all time, another Welsh chronicler, Nennius, also wrote of the exploits of King Arthur in his *Historia Brittonum* of about 800 AD. These tales spoke of Arthur as an almost supernatural being, a god-like folk hero from the mists of Britain's past, and called him the *Bear of Britain*. Before him, an even earlier writer, Gildas, in *The Ruin and Conquest of Britain* used the same title, *the Bear*, to refer to an illustrious leader, although he does not name him, in the only surviving record of Britain in the sixth century.

That King Arthur was known as *The Bear* in antiquity is not surprising—the name itself means *Bear*. The Brythonic language (a latinised version of the old British tongue) is still in use today in modern Welsh, where *Arth* means *Bear*. In Irish, the word is *Art*.

Both Geoffrey and Nennius, drawing on very early sources which almost certainly derive from the previous Bardic traditions of the Druids, thus establish two important ideas associated with King Arthur and the ancient lore of the British Isles. The first is that he was born at Tintagel (and no other place has ever claimed this distinction, making it unique) and the second is that he was known as *The Bear*. The Tintagel legend is well-known, Arthur's association with the Bear perhaps less so. Yet both these ideas are linked in such a remarkable way that everyone, Arthurian scholar or casual visitor, will surely be amazed when they realise that both these legends convey an extraordinary and ancient truth.

Living in the rugged wild country of North Cornwall close to Tintagel for more than thirty years, I had first been drawn to the area by its strangely potent aura. There was a feeling that there were somehow secrets hovering just out of reach, something unsuspected by the crowds of tourists who flock there every summer. Yet the popularly held image of King Arthur was radically different from that portrayed in these few original accounts. Since they were written, the Arthurian legends had, over the centuries, become hopelessly entangled with medieval romances overlaid with questing knights, stories of love and treachery and the inevitable end of a golden age, when order had turned into chaos. Historical evidence has shown that if King Arthur had really lived in the fifth or sixth century as we have been led to believe, then the usual image of shining knights had nothing whatsoever to do with the reality of these times and they were much more likely to have dressed in leather and animal skins than suits of gleaming armour.

Despite this, the Tintagel area has a haunting, irresistible quality, as if underlying the original legend is something of great significance, something unspoken, hidden from our normal senses; a feeling that whispers to the inner ear on a full-moon night with the sea-silvered waves murmuring their mermaid voices, or whistles through your very being during a winter storm in Merlin's Cave. This great sea-cave through which the waves crash at full tide is directly below the vertiginous castle ruins on the island above, and a place of spine-tingling elemental power. Its connection with the wizard Merlin is often thought to be the product of highly imaginative poets and authors, yet I was to discover that there are indeed great truths behind the persistent legends. It is only after all these years I now realise that all this was not just my own vivid imagination or poetic flight of fancy, for Tintagel is at the core of a mystery so ancient and remarkable that it truly deserves its place in history.

During these thirty or so years I have spent a great deal of time exploring the surrounding landscape, peering into its hidden nooks and crannies, endlessly poring over maps, and some of these mysteries had already revealed themselves, leading to a book, *Tintagel and the Arthurian Mythos*, written some fifteen years ago. But one wild and windy autumn day as the rain spattered against the windows I found myself lost in reverie whilst absent-mindedly pondering a map of the area, when an extraordinary image grew before my eyes. Slowly at first, it began to emerge from the shapes outlined on the unfolded and rather dog-eared map before me, and then, suddenly, like a lightning bolt from the dark Cornish skies, it manifested in front of my eyes for the very first time.

Set out in front of me was the startling image of a giant Bear, engraved in the landscape around Tintagel. It was formed by the ancient roads that meandered their way along the dramatic coastal road over-looking cliffs and sea, and others that wove their way inland down steep narrow wooded lanes of immense antiquity worn into the living rock.

At first I thought it a mirage, a trick of the mind, or simply a coincidence that such an amazing image could occur—especially here, at the very centre of Arthurian tradition. At that time I knew vaguely that the name Arthur was associated with *The Bear*, but had never taken it very seriously, assuming it was probably a tribal reference to his supposed size or strength. But as I squinted at the map this gigantic effigy seemed to come alive before my eyes, assuming an even greater significance. The great beast appeared to be endowed with features that could surely be no accident. To begin with, the Bear's gaze was firmly fixed on Tintagel Island, which is almost entirely surrounded by the Atlantic Ocean, and where, according to the legend, King Arthur had been conceived and born. It was here that a castle had been built in the thirteenth century, the ruins of which still perch precariously on the edge of the cliffs. The muzzle of the Bear appeared tethered to an ancient earthwork known as Bossiney Mound, the site of another earlier castle and of likely prehistoric origin. This earthen mound was known locally as the site of *King Arthur's Round Table*, which was said to lie within it, magically re-appearing every Summer Solstice.

The Bear's 'eye' seemed to be marked by the tiny hamlet of Trethevy, once a medieval manor, but with much older roots. Here was an ancient chapel opposite a Holy Well, and even a Roman milestone, very rare in this part of Cornwall. On the bridge of his snout, the outline forming a distinctive kink where the valley plunges steeply, were the famous Rocky Valley labyrinths, prehistoric maze-like patterns cut into the cliff next to a ruined mill. Crowning his head was the old picturesque port of Boscastle, and yet another castle had been built here on a mound overlooking the collection of cottages built around a natural inlet. This had been very important in antiquity, the only safe harbour for many miles along this notoriously dangerous coast, and had also been the headquarters of the Norman Bottreaux family, the likely builders of Tintagel Castle.

The Bear's back, beautifully drawn by a steep winding road as if to resemble rumpled fur, led to the lonely site of Minster Church, set deep in its sylvan woodland dripping with moss and lichen, once a thriving monastery and medieval healing shrine. Close by, also on the Bear's back, was a small collection of cottages and farms known as *Treworld*. As the prefix *Tre* in Cornish means habitation or dwelling-place, this curious name appears to have been anglicised to mean *Place of the World*. Excavations had revealed a medieval settlement at exactly this spot. Further along the Bear's back was the old church at Lesnewth, which these days seems very isolated, but in former times was an important administrative centre for the whole area known as the *Hundred of Lesnewth*.

Part of the Bear's body also seemed to be visible, with its great front paw firmly placed on the town of Camelford, long associated with Arthurian tradition. The old name for the river that flows through it was *Cam-Alan* (meaning the crooked River Alan) and this is exactly the name that appears in some of the old Arthurian accounts. On his great shaggy leg was Slaughterbridge with its medieval bridge over the same river, famous in Cornish legend as the place where King Arthur was mortally wounded before being taken to the Isle of Avalon, that otherworldly realm where he waits until the time is right for his inevitable return. Here, close to the Elizabethan manor house of Worthyvale lies a megalithic stone engraved in Latin commemorating a Roman general, but known locally as *King Arthur's Stone*. The rest of the Bear's body appeared indistinct, as if growing out of the land itself.

Perhaps the most striking feature of all struck me as located within the Bear's Head itself. Here was one of the most impressive of all Cornish sites, known as *St Nectan's Kieve*, a waterfall that tumbles down a steep ravine into a smooth naturally hollowed-out stone bowl, or *kieve* in Cornish, and then through a circular hole worn through the rock. It is a place that creates a unique and powerful effect upon the observer. This peculiar feature had, however, always struck me as somehow distinctly *un*-natural, for I could never imagine how a waterfall could cut its way through a curtain of solid rock without the assistance of the hand of man. Consequently it had always looked to me like some sort of Druidic sculpture, deliberately created to enhance the dramatic effect of this stunning natural location.

Standing there, especially after wet weather when the rushing waters become a torrent, is a profound experience, for the sound is amplified by the steep chasm into which the waterfall tumbles. One can easily become lost in this awesome natural power which overwhelms the senses. One Cornish story speaks of this as the place where the Knights of the Round Table pledged themselves to the quest for the Holy Grail. In the context of the newly-revealed Great Bear, it seemed like nothing less than the Bear's throat. It was certainly located in just the right place. With its potent atmosphere, the splash and roar of its ever-flowing waters as they pour into the cavernous twilight of the rock-hewn chasm, it seemed full of mystery; a place where the land has the power to speak directly to us across the countless centuries, of which our current age is but the unthinking blink of an eye.

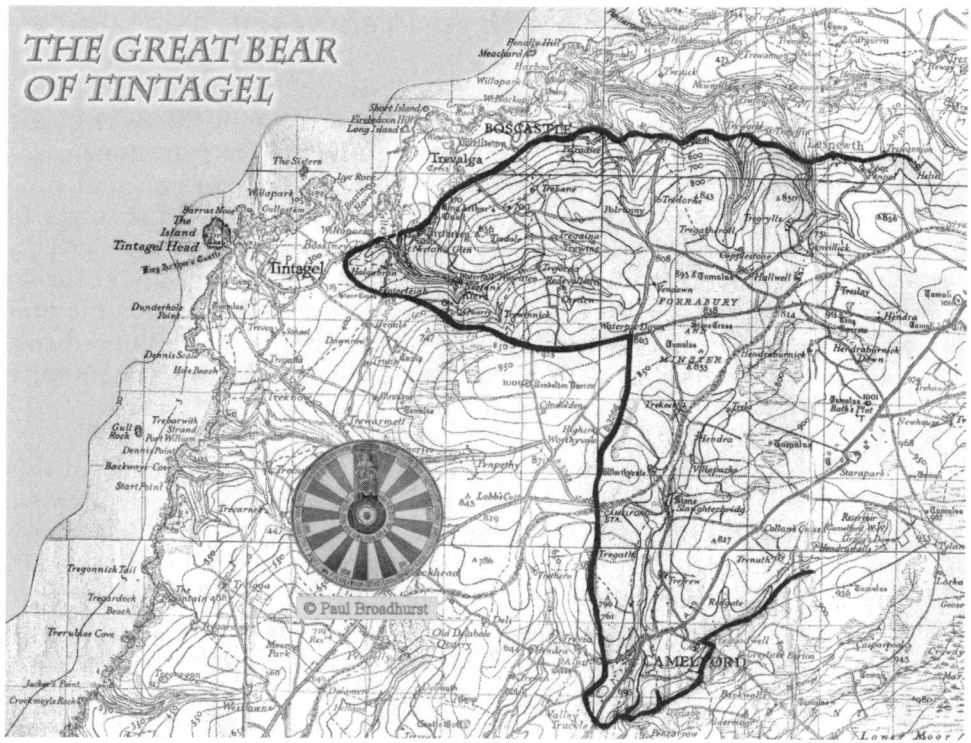

THE GREAT BEAR
OF TINTAGEL

© Paul Broadhurst

The Great Bear of Tintagel

Ancient roads create the outline of a huge Bear looking straight at Tintagel Island, where according to the old British legend, King Arthur, whose name means *Great Bear,* was born. Directly above the Bear's head is the harbour village of Boscastle, the abode of the Bottreaux family who were related to William the Conqueror and the likely builders of Tintagel Castle.

Above that is Pentargon Cove, a Cornish name meaning *Arthur's Head.* The Bear's eye appears marked by an ancient Holy Well and chapel at Trethevy, once a monastic settlement, and his snout is tethered to the old mound at Bossiney (not marked on these old one-inch to the mile maps which have been joined together to include the whole figure; paper stretching over the years means that the grid lines on the left do not match perfectly) whilst the Bear's back, complete with rumpled fur, is delineated by old hollow ways worn in the rock which lead past two important churches, Minster and Lesnewth. Also on the Bear's back is Treworld. The Bear's paw stands on Camelford, with its shaggy leg on Slaughterbridge, the traditional site of King Arthur's last battle.

The Bear's throat is marked by St Nectan's Kieve, one of Cornwall's most spiritually potent places, where a waterfall plunges into a smooth rocky basin and then through a curious hole in the rock. This striking feature almost seems as if it were purposefully designed to be a living sculpture in keeping with the symbolism of a great Mother Bear, especially when its waters roar through the steep chasm. Further along the valley that leads towards the sea are the Rocky Valley Mazes, situated on the bridge of the Bear's muzzle.

The Bear Myth in Prehistory

This discovery of a giant effigy of a Bear etched into the landscape around Tintagel prompted me to explore the meaning of the Bear in the pre-Christian era, for it seemed likely that any beliefs or traditions associating the Bear with kingship would come from a far more ancient time than the traditional Arthurian period. This is assumed by historians to have been in the so-called Dark Ages of the fifth and sixth centuries AD, a time when the Romans had retreated from Britain and it was under threat from invading Saxons. It is called 'Dark' because this period was inevitably one of confusion as the land reverted to its tribal kings and overlords. The greatest of them is said to have been King Arthur, who eventually succeeded in uniting the country against its foes.

Before exploring in greater detail the actual sites involved in this giant effigy, we should therefore focus our vision on a time for which we have no written records. Nevertheless, there is a great amount of evidence to show that the Bear Cult of prehistoric times was not only widespread across the ancient world, but of crucial importance to the way people interpreted the world around them. The conclusions we draw will have profound implications for our understanding of these early times. As I found myself immersed in this quest to discover the true significance of Bear mythology I slowly realised that none of this was a trick of the mind. There really was a Great Bear in the Cornish landscape, and it must have been of immense importance to the people who sculpted and carved it into the land. How they might have done it was unclear at this time. The questions that currently absorbed my attention were why was it there, and what did it mean?

It soon became clear that for many millennia before the modern era the Bear represented the timeless principles of cosmic order and was at the centre of a world-view that, quite literally, revolved around the Great Bear in the sky. This was because to our distant ancestors the starry heavens represented the source and continuity of all life. Consequently the mythologies associated with the constellations were amongst the earliest stories ever told.

Even today, when the great majority of the human race hardly ever look upwards to the night skies, most people would recognise the constellation of the Great Bear, or *Ursa Major*, as it is called in Latin, as it circles endlessly around the North Star. In fact it is one of the few constellations bright enough to be visible to those in cities. Stargazers use it to find the pole star by projecting an imaginary line from the two bright stars opposite its 'tail', *Merak* and *Dubhe*, which point to *Polaris*, the Pole Star, marking the axis of the heavens around which the whole visible universe apparently turns. This has obvious and deep significance, but it is also a practical method of determining direction, used throughout history by seafarers and travellers. The Great Bear is one of a group of circumpolar constellations that include *Draco*, the Dragon, *Ursa Minor*, the Little Bear, *Cepheus*, the King, and *Cassiopeia*, the Queen. Because at northern latitudes they are visible at all times, weather permitting, these star groups have always possessed the reputation of being timeless and indestructible, things that exist in a higher order of time and space beyond those of the earthly realms.

It is almost impossible today to put ourselves into the mind-set of ancient people, but we can at least recognise that they saw in the world around them a sentient universe, one that had intelligence and meaning. The stars may have been just as significant to them as the animals on which they depended for their survival, and it is natural that they would have projected their earthly experiences onto the star-patterns they saw, imbuing them with the stories and characteristics of the creatures on Earth. Many of the constellations appear to us to bear little resemblance to these animals, yet still these old tales persist, even if much adapted and fragmented. The seven stars that are the most recognisable feature of the Great Bear are, however, just part of a larger constellation which actually does look something like a representation of a Bear with its limbs outstretched. The legends and lore associated with this particular pattern are amongst the earliest myths ever, for if we can readily recognise it today we can perhaps imagine how significant it was to people who slept under the stars themselves and gathered around fires to share ancestral stories. Because of this, in the Northern Hemisphere the Great Bear was a central feature in the original Myth of Creation.

The earliest hunter-gatherers, at one with the natural world, were probably the first to venerate the Bear for many reasons. Both lived and hunted in the same places, sharing the forests and rivers, and frequently came into contact with each other. It would also have been apparent that the Bear was the closest of animals in biology, behaviour and appearance, and that both showed respect for one another, for Bears will only attack humans when provoked.

However, the lore of Bear-worship suggests an even deeper relationship, for the Bear was believed to be the great primeval ancestor of humanity. This is where the expression *forebears* originates. Its intelligence and behaviour were the most human-like of all animals, with its omnivorous diet and, despite its heavy build and lumbering gait, surprisingly athletic qualities; it is adept at both climbing and swimming. They are typically solitary animals, and like the lions of the jungle regions were also known as the King of Beasts. These Lords of the Forest, with finely-tuned senses of smell and hearing that could detect movement at a great distance, were endowed with almost supernatural powers, continuously aware of everything that happened within their territory. Here we can perhaps sense many of those qualities that made early people associate the Bear with kingship.

The Bear's human-like qualities extended to standing on two legs, using its paws to gesture, and exhibiting particularly soulful expressions as if thinking or deliberating, just like people. The naturalist Anton Benedikt Reichenbach, in 1847, noted that the 'Bear's face, hearing and sense of touch are all refined'. He also observed that the individuality and character of different Bears reflects the diversity of humans. Female Bears were unique in that they suckled their young by holding them to their breasts, even further confirming our common origins in the mind of the prehistoric observer. A most poignant example of this is a number of figurines from prehistoric times showing the image of a Bear Goddess nursing an infant. One in particular, known as *The Lady of Vinca*, found in former Yugoslavia and dating from 4,800 BC, is probably the earliest known representation of a 'Madonna and Child'. This still has echoes today,

The Lady of Vinca, prehistoric sculpture of a Mother Bear nursing an infant, ca. 7000 years old

for the Ainu tribeswomen of Hokkaido in Japan still nurse Bears, believing them to be gods visiting the Earth. Bears' reproductive behaviour can also be similar to humans, and a twelfth century Bestiary records that Bears *do not love each other as four-footed creatures do, but rather embrace in the same manner as men and women*.

But perhaps the most intriguing thing of all was that during the winter, the Bear 'died' by going into a cave, where its heartbeat virtually stopped, until resurrected to life in the following spring. In this way the Bear became a living metaphor of the cycle of life. On the one hand it reflected the dying Sun of the winter which was reborn in springtime, emulating the annual round, on the other it echoed the path of the human soul, which died on earthly levels only to be reborn in the future. Perhaps we can sense here that the Bear was one of the earliest religious prototypes, which sacrifices itself only to be born again when the springtime Sun returns bringing light, life and renewal. It is perhaps not surprising that, for example, the Ojibway Indians of the Great Lakes region thought that Bears were transformed humans; messengers of the wheel of eternal life.

Just as amazing to our forgotten ancestors would surely have been the nightly perambulations of the starry Bear in the heavens. Those omnipresent Seven Stars that guarded the Gate of Heaven, the Pole through which new souls were believed to come to Earth, and old souls ascend to Heaven, acted out their role every night as cosmic guardians. The Great Bear, in its nocturnal travels, appears to run on all fours when it is nearest the horizon, and then gradually rises up on its hind feet as it begins to ascend back into the sky. At certain times of the year this signals the approach of dawn, as if honouring the great turning point of the heavens and the rebirth of the Sun each morning.

The worship of the great starry Bear of the northern hemisphere included other celestial phenomena that would have seemed supernatural to our forebears. The *Aurora Borealis*, or Northern Lights, the heavenly display of shimmering, multicoloured luminescence that is such a striking feature of polar regions would also have been of relevance to the myths. These colourful displays must have dramatically emphasised the cosmic nature of the heavenly Bear and the region of the sky which is its abode.

During the Ice Age, when Bear mythology was probably first developed, these aerial displays of stellar and associated phenomena were even more impressive than today due to the cold, clear conditions that prevailed. As we trace the Cult of Bear worship from these times to the present day, we will become ever more aware that these ideas were at the root of humanity's relationship with the natural world, and guided it towards an ideal of heavenly order represented by the Bear, just as a king is responsible to bring order and stability to his land. It is no coincidence that King Arthur was later believed to live in exactly the same region of the sky as the Bear, or that his name in the Celtic language is derived, in Welsh tradition, from *Arth Fawr*—the Great Bear. The seven most prominent stars of the constellation were also called *Arthur's Wain* or *Chariot*, as they were believed to transport the King endlessly around the central point of the universe.

The Cult of the Great Bear

A great deal of physical evidence for the primeval worship of the Bear has been found across the world, indicating how widespread it once was. There are many examples to underline this, but a couple will suffice to emphasise the great antiquity of the Bear Cult in the pre-Christian era.

In Campbell and Loy's *Humankind Emerging* the 80,000 year-old site of Drachenloch in Switzerland, a Neanderthal religious cave sanctuary, was found to contain bones and ashes on a 'sacrificial altar':

'The most famous example of what has been claimed to be Neanderthal hunting magic is the so-called Bear cult. It came to light when a German archaeologist, Emil Bachler, excavated the cave of Drachenloch between 1917 and 1923. Located 8,000 feet up in the Swiss Alps, the 'lair of the dragons' tunnels deep into a mountainside. The front part of the cave, Bachler's work made clear, served as an occasional dwelling place for Neanderthals. Farther back, Bachler found a cubical chest made of stones and measuring approximately 3.25 feet on a side. The top of the chest was covered by a massive slab of stone. Inside were seven bear skulls, all apparently arranged with their muzzles facing the cave entrance. Still deeper in the cave were six bear skulls, seemingly set in niches along the walls. The Drachenloch find is not unique. At Regourdou in France, a rectangular pit, covered by a flat stone weighing nearly a ton, held the bones of more than 20 bears'.

We may reflect on the fact that 80,000 or so years ago prehistoric man arranged seven bear skulls (the number of prominent stars in the constellation) in a stone box deep within a cave in the Earth. For this star group is also, because of its shape, known by the name of various containers, including coffins and biers associated with death and resurrection. In *The Dawn of Art* Jean-Marie Chauvet describes how he found another example of this type of early religious behaviour, this time dated to 31,000 years ago, and tells of its powerful effect upon him and his companions:

'A little further on we were deeply impressed by what we discovered. In the middle of the chamber, on a block of grey stone of rectangular shape that had fallen from the ceiling, the skull of a bear was placed as if on an altar. The animal's fangs projected beyond it into the air. On top of the stone there were still pieces of charcoal, the remains of a fireplace. All around, on the floor, there were more than thirty bear skulls; now covered in a frosting of amber-coloured calcite, they were purposely set out on the earth. There were no traces of skeletons. This intentional arrangement troubled us because of its solemn peculiarity.'

What is being described here are examples of what must be amongst the earliest-known religious shrines on Earth. Other Bear artefacts are just as poignant as Chauvet's discovery. In 1995 a flute made from a hollowed-out bear femur was found in a cave once occupied by Neanderthal people in the Idrijca Valley in western Slovenia, dated to 43,000 BC. If indeed it was a flute (some archaeologists are not convinced) what strange and haunting music it must have made. In 1923 at Montespan in the Haute-Garonne region of France Count Bégouën and Norbert Casteret discovered a Paleolithic cave with a life-size clay model of a Bear that had been draped with a bearskin whose skull was found between the paws. Fifteen millennia before this Cave-Bear had been at the centre of some atavistic ceremony the like of which had probably been performed since the earliest ages of Mankind.

The ritualistic veneration of Bears obviously possessed a profound meaning for early humanity, and lasted for an immense period of time. Skulls and bones of *Ursus Spelaeus* (the Cave Bear) have also been found in five caves around Hallstatt in Austria, the site of an important centre of the La Tène Celtic culture on the shores of a deep forested lake, demonstrating the longevity of Bear worship even into the Iron Age. Also in Austria hundreds of Bear skulls and bones have been found in caves around Graz. At the Grottes de Regourdou near Lascaux in France mixed human and Bear bones have been found in profusion, suggesting some form of ritualistic ceremonies contemporary with the famous cave paintings. Other examples of Paleolithic art show people dancing with Bears. The physical evidence found (to mention but a few examples) suggests that the Cult of the Bear once lay right at the very heart of primitive religion.

Survivals of the Bear Cult

It is well-known that early Christianity absorbed many remnants of former nature worship, overlaying its new ethos on pagan rituals, legends and sites that were the focus of religious traditions for thousands of years before the modern era. Even the Christian myth of the sacrificial victim, destined to become the saviour of mankind, has its roots in the previous mythologies of various spiritual heroes which were widespread throughout the ancient world. In like manner, old goddesses and gods were assimilated into the new beliefs, often bearing the same names as before, only with the added prefix of 'saint' to identify them as now belonging to the new faith (in the New Testament 'saint' is merely a word that describes a follower of Christianity and not a particularly holy individual). The early Christian Saint Ursula (from *Ursus*, Latin for Bear) was known for rescuing no less than eleven thousand virgins from Bears—most likely this is a a reference to having saved their souls from the perceived evils of nature worship.

Others, such as St Korbinan, tamed Bears and frequently used them to carry their possessions or as companions on their pilgrimages. The ritualistic aspects of early Christianity can also be identified in relation to Bears. An Estonian legend recalls that Bears enter their dens on St Michael's Day (29th September) to begin their hibernation almost as if they are entering into some sort of mystical underworld initiation. It is clear that much of the Christian religion itself is firmly grounded in these old ways, including the sacrifice of Jesus Christ, the ritual drinking of his blood and eating of his flesh in the form of the 'host' which echoes the former sacrifice of humans and, before that, animals. As the most anthropomorphic of beasts, the Bear can thus lay claim to having been one of the earliest forms of ritual sacrifice.

Throughout Europe we come across other Christian saints whose legends strongly associate them with Bears. In some parts Bears are called 'Martins' after St Martin, whose feast day on 11th November marks the time when they start to retreat into their underground lairs, thereby symbolically descending into the Underworld. They later emerge, like so many of the classical gods, reborn in the spring. It is no accident of mythology that so many old deities, like Mithras, Dionysus and Jesus Christ, were all born in a cave at the time of the Winter Solstice. Although the nativity of Christ is popularly said to have taken place in a manger, in the Church of the Nativity in Bethlehem the exact spot is said to be located beneath the building in a subterranean chamber. Each religion absorbs the essential beliefs of its predecessors, even though it adapts them to the prevailing conditions of the time. In this way the religious impulse remains a central feature of our very being, inherited from our forebears since the dawn of mankind.

In regions where orthodox Christianity found great difficulty in overcoming the old beliefs and traditions such as Britain, people continued largely as before, even allowing for the fact that the great forests and wildernesses of prehistory were progressively tamed. These areas are often thought of as 'Celtic' nowadays, referring to the belief systems, mythology and folklore which retain a living body of ancestral memories—however much they appear to be half-forgotten—lingering under the conscious mind. It is often these very areas that are so deeply ingrained with Arthurian traditions. In the legends of areas like Cornwall, Wales, Brittany and other regions of Europe these stories preserve that unique Celtic character which can never have originated through the exploits of a particular historical character, however much they may have been overlaid in later times, for they are far too widespread and diverse. The truth is that we are dealing here with a multi-coloured fabric woven through the ages, a fabric which has accreted layers of meaning throughout the whole history of humanity. In trying to disentangle this complex skein of material we must follow the threads to see where they may have originated.

It is in areas such as Cornwall that we may hope to discover evidence of how and why these threads were woven, even if their origins are so remote from us today that they may have faded almost beyond recognition. Yet the material for this quest is, as we will discover, imprinted into the land itself and its dimly-preserved ancient traditions. But before embarking on this present journey of discovery we should familiarise ourselves further with the viewpoint of our ancestors, those who lived with the land and the heavens in a way that we can perhaps only barely imagine today.

The Shamanic Bear Hero

'The bear was honoured as the Lord of the Forest or the son of the supreme ruler, whose calling it was to uphold justice. Groups that were widely separated geographically shared the belief that a bear killed in the hunt would enter a new life.'

Bernd Brunner: Bears, a brief history (commenting on the American anthropologist Irving Hallowell's 1926 study Bear Ceremonialism in the Northern Hemisphere).

We find ourselves asking how is it possible to achieve an understanding of the prehistoric mind and its approach to the environment? How did ancient people actually think of the world around them? What guided their lives?

Fortunately there are fragments of these long-standing traditions still extant in certain regions which can give us a glimpse into this lost world. One area in particular is still a repository for a way of life that has all but vanished in the modern world, largely because of the strongly independent character of its people. This region today straddles the borders of different countries, overlapping with both France and Spain. The Basque territories of the Pyrenees still proudly maintain their ancient character in many respects, and preserve much of the old pre-Christian ways although these have often, quite naturally, become mingled with Christianity. In particular, the Basque people have kept their traditions of Bear lore where others have consigned them to the archaeological record of prehistory.

For 20 years, Roslyn M. Frank, Professor Emeritus of the University of Iowa, has conducted fieldwork amongst the Basque peoples and uncovered a large body of material that shows us exactly how important Bears were in the lives of the inhabitants of these 'Celtic' areas. In her paper *Hunting the European Sky-Bears*: *When Bears ruled the Earth and guarded the Gate of Heaven* she identifies a whole cycle of stories and ritual adventures of an archetypal hero called *Hartzkume*, or *Little Bear*, linked to the heavenly Bear constellations. This hero's encounters with other celestial beings form a body of lore and ritual practices that is very deeply-rooted in the human psyche, drawn from a time when star-lore was a complete group of tales that could be read in the night sky. As she observes:

'The identification of the stars of the Great Bear constellation with a bear and/or bear hunt has led it to being classified as belonging to the most ancient cognitive strata of star figures known to European peoples. It has also been assumed that scenes portrayed by certain other star figures were once associated with some half-forgotten sky text handed down to us, although incompletely, through Greek sky myths'.

Here, the Bear is identified as the foundation myth around which many other episodes of the later gods and goddesses revolve, known to us in fragmentary form from the Greek world. We will examine these shortly, but an important point is raised here in that much of this later mythology derives from a more ancient world-view. In the Basque tradition 'Little Bear' is the offspring of a Great Bear and a human female, and the stories and public performances narrate various episodes from his life, including encounters with 'a remarkable series of celestially-encoded characters'. Professor Frank found that this tradition was echoed across Europe in a cycle of folk tales and rituals associated with celestial Bears. Sometimes the central character is called John Bear, John Little Bear, or the Bear Son.

In these stories, the significance of the star groups of the Great Bear and the Little Bear, *Ursa Minor* (both of which exhibit a remarkably similar shape to the naked eye as if to reflect their familial associations) appear to have resulted from a time when earthly bears were venerated as divine beings. In these times the Bear Son or Little Bear, who was half-bear and half-human, acted as an intermediary between the heavenly

Indian shaman from the Blackfoot tribe dressed in a Bearskin, by George Catlin.

and earthly realms. This strongly suggests that the Bear constellations were behind the original European myth of origins that was transmitted from age to age, and represented the ultimate theme of cosmic order. It is this theme of a time when earthly affairs were ordered according to divine principles, and its eventual decline, which lies behind many of the Arthurian traditions of later ages.

It looks as though certain of the star-gods and goddesses may have been later additions to the original mythology, as guides and helpers for the Bear hero. In the stories of the Bear Son he has a collection of spirit animal helpers as he progresses on his ritual journeys, including his descent to Earth and his ultimate ascent back to the northern heavens (this aspect will assume greater importance in our own exploration in due course). In this way other constellations support him in his quest, and Professor Frank considers that they are likely to include the Apple Tree Serpent *Draco*, the Sky River *Eridanus*, the Lion-Cat *Leo*, the Hunting Dog *Canis Major* and the Hare *Lepus*. Other constellations such as *Ophiuchus* the Serpent-slayer and *Andromeda*, the chained princess, along with her rescuer *Perseus*, as well as the figure of *Hercules*, may, she believes, have originally formed part of the same cycle of stories.

Most of these constellations are non-zodiacal, for they derive from a far earlier vision of the heavens than the later solar-centred system, when the Sun's passage through the star-groups became more prominent and eventually succeeded in overshadowing the more ancient traditions. The word *zodiac* means 'circle of animals' and it seems likely that the term may have originally applied to an earlier and endlessly revolving round of animals long before it became linked with the traditional signs of the zodiac along the ecliptic which we are more familiar with today.

The ceremonials of the Basques show a deep understanding of the interconnectedness of everything in the Cosmos, and chart the Bear Son's birth, youth, adulthood, death and eventual resurrection when he returns to the stars. These folk traditions were structured around Bear ritual and the hunting that accompanied it, not only amongst the Basques, but among many other indigenous cultures. Vestiges of the Paleolithic Bear Cult are in fact very widespread, and have been discovered in Britain, France, Spain, Austria, Switzerland, former Yugoslavia, Bulgaria, Romania, Poland, Scandinavia, Russia, Finland, Alaska, Lapland and throughout the Northeast coast of America to mention but a few. The similarity of many of these rituals and beliefs is striking, particularly those of the

North American tribes like the Munsee-Mahican Delawares, who link the Bear constellations with their *Ceremonies of World Renewal* that symbolise re-creation. In these a shamanic healer, often dressed in a bearskin and wearing talismans from his animal spirit helpers, re-enacts the sacred stories which reflect the cosmic drama taking place in the heavens and the cycles of death and rebirth.

Further research from other investigations shows that episodes from these ritual performances were far more common than we might think. For example, 221 variants of the descent of the Bear Son into the Underworld (the earthly plane) had been documented in Europe as far back as 1910. In 1959, 57 versions of the tale were noted in Hungary. 1992 saw the publication of a study that listed 120 variants across Scandinavia. Similar studies showed other examples, including 'Fairy Tales' in France and Latin America, these latter apparently introduced by Spanish migrants.

The evidence leaves no doubt that throughout the Northern Hemisphere there once existed a cosmology of great antiquity where a half-human, half-bear hero enacted ritual dramas which were linked to the stories associated with the northern sky constellations, in particular those of the Great and Little Bear.

Could this explain the existence of a giant effigy of a Great Bear at Tintagel, linked to a hero-figure that later became known as King Arthur the Bear, harking back to a Golden Age when cosmic order prevailed? Is this giant physical imprint actually a tangible psychological and spiritual footprint of our own collective journey? If it derives from prehistoric times as the evidence suggests, and survived into the Dark Ages, the so-called Age of Arthur, then it must also have been at the core of the Neolithic and Bronze Ages. These were the times when the builders of the megaliths covered the land with standing stones, circles and great monuments, the only real physical evidence from an era whose beliefs and traditions, although of immense antiquity, are lost to us. This is an important subject to which we will return, for it will reveal significant clues to help us understand some of the reasons why they were originally built. These discoveries will probably prove astonishing to many, and introduce a new dimension in understanding a possible unified *raison d'être* behind the construction and location of prehistoric sites.

Professor Frank's own estimate of exactly when the Bear Cult became formalised into recognisable ritual after its beginnings as a shamanic way of life in the Mesolithic or Upper Paleolithic eras is approximately 4000 BC, a time that coincides with the rise of the megalith builders. Her research suggests this shows significant *'Bronze Age connections, and reveals relationships between the John Bear stories of the megalithic culture'*.

So was this the time when the Bear myth was at its height, when there was a massive cultural shift which saw the construction of thousands of stone circles and associated monuments? Did the age of settlement and the cultivation of crops that arose after the hunter/gatherers of Paleolithic times see a different emphasis placed on the Bear cult?

Once, people had hunted the Bear in the heavens to guide them on their travels, just as they had hunted the Bear in the forests and wildernesses of an untamed land. Now a different evolutionary period beckoned, one where settlement and tribal territories provided a new focus. This may have been a distinct break with the ways of the past, even if the changes took place over a long period, yet it was a natural development that created a new relationship between humanity, the land and the sky.

The move towards a more settled agricultural way of life brought to an end the continuous migrations of previous ages, and the forests began to be cleared for cultivation and husbandry, while the selected place of habitation was ringed by hills and landscape features that defined the tribal lands where the stars, Sun and Moon rose as if they were created out of the very Earth itself. The eternal guardian of the heavens, the Bear, would still have been central to their religious beliefs as the great presiding ever-present deity of the night skies, but now it was honoured in a different way reflecting the shifting patterns of life. We should not be surprised, then, if we detect in the building and arrangement of the earthworks and megalithic structures which exemplify this era a preoccupation with the constellation of the Great Bear and the central axis which determines its motion.

2

SKY BEARS AND STAR LORE

To the ancients the Cosmos must have been a vast riddle, explicable only in code and symbolism in a time long before words were invented. The only way they could begin to explain this riddle was through a series of stories drawn from their own experience and projected onto the wider world. This is the root of all mythology, and has given rise to a body of lore that has now degenerated into what we may often today call fairy tales or what is generally spoken of as 'myth', meaning something that is either simplistic or untrue. Yet the word *myth* in its original meaning conveys exactly the opposite, and the more we find out about the true origins of the idea, the more we become aware of the great depth of meaning concealed within it. Unfortunately there remains a considerable reluctance in the modern world to place any value on the myths and legends of antiquity, judging them to be no more than the childlike imaginings of primitive and superstitious savages. Consequently this current quest involves stripping away the accretions of millennia to reveal the true essence hidden within the stories. In this, the story of the Bear, and its more recent incarnation, the Bear-King Arthur, has much to tell us. These traditions of our own land coupled with the accounts from the Basque territories and the northern regions of Europe and America preserve the core of what was once a widespread system of belief.

Before humanity lost its sacred connection with the Bear and became afraid of its powers there was universal admiration for this extraordinary beast and its superhuman qualities. As Professor Frank found, the Bear of the forests was the earthly companion of the Great Bear in the sky that guarded the axis of the universe, the protector of celestial harmony. Not only did the Heavenly Bear perform the nightly ritual, with the aid of his fellow spirit animal helpers, of remedying the cosmic imbalance of Light and Dark, it was believed to engage in ritual combats by entering the Underworld in order to bring this heavenly order down to the Earth. Just as a shaman would engage in spirit flight, ascending and descending between Heaven and Earth via the hole in the sky, the Bear Son would enter the earthly plane through the Pole linking the heavenly and terrestrial realms. This was the same axis by which human souls were believed to enter and leave the physical world, and so the Cosmic Bear was believed to be the special guardian of humanity itself.

The uncanny ability of the Bear to listen and react to conversation with its human-like ears, facial expressions and ability to stand upright and gesture, as well as its considerable manual dexterity, all confirmed in the ancient mind that the earthly Bear was the primeval ancestor of humanity. They were thought to be so intelligent that they could comprehend human language almost before it was spoken.

Bear hunters had always noticed how a Bear's body, deprived of its fur coat, is extraordinarily similar to that of a human, and that female Bears in particular exhibit breasts and hips just like their human counterparts. They also suckle their young by holding them to their breasts. Even the footprints are similar. That indigenous people believed the Bear to be their sacred ancestor there is no doubt. One elderly informant in the French Basque village of Sainte-Engrâce stated categorically that '*The Basques used to believe that humans were descended from Bears*' and his son refused to eat a Bear's flesh because of its similarity to that of a human being. The Tlingit tribe of the Yukon stated '*Grizzlies are half-human*'. According to the Yavapi of Arizona '*Bears are like people except they can't make fire*'. Many tribes would not eat Bear meat because it was like eating '*a person's relative*'.

These once abundant animals are now extinct in many of the areas where they lived alongside humans for so many thousands of years. Yet they still haunt our imaginations, especially in childhood where the 'Teddy Bear' now fulfils the role of protective guardian and totemic companion. Why are children so enamoured of Bears unless they have some deep atavistic power over the human psyche? There can be no other explanation than we feel comforted and safe with them. Bears are otherwise often much misunderstood in the modern world, for they are essentially peaceful creatures that can be friendly to humans. There are in fact numerous legends and stories of Bears adopting human children and bringing them up as their own offspring, and also of humans who possess Bear-like characteristics; even so-called 'Bear-people' with hairy bodies. One account by the Irishman Bernard O'Connor, physician to the King of Poland in the seventeenth century, records how he came across a 12-year old boy in Warsaw who made bearlike sounds and could approach Bears without fear. Because of his powers he was respected as an almost mythical being. The supposed ursine origins of others is remembered in names throughout Europe and North America such as *Bearsson, Peter Bear, Sun Bear* etc. and another entire class of royal names like that of *Magnus Bearfoot*, who was King of Norway in the early twelfth century, the significance of which we will explore soon.

Medieval engraving of a 'Bear Boy' from Central Europe. There have been many examples throughout history of people becoming like a Bear after living with them.

The Healing Power of Bears

Amongst their many supernatural and divine powers, and besides the shamanic rituals performed by humans to restore the order of the natural world, Bears were also known as great healers. At the dawn of time the first shaman was a Bear—it could shape-shift into human form and perform all kinds of magic. Shaman healers would wear Bearskins, Bear tooth or claw necklaces, and have all manner of Bear accoutrements in their medicine bag. They danced Bear dances and sang Bear songs throughout their ceremonies. Professor Frank noted that even until the end of the twentieth century Bear paws were kept to ward off the evil eye in Basque households. Sick children would be placed on a Bear's back, and 'Bear Doctors' would call at houses where illness prevailed in the belief that they would protect all within from harm. Their mystical powers were invoked by ancestral stories that began 'It was in the time when the Bear was Lord'.

Because of its guardianship over the entrance and exit to the heavenly realms, the Bear was also endowed with the power to judge souls. Basque tradition tells that as the Bear presides over the axis which joins Heaven and Earth, it later became a companion to the Christian St Peter, standing at the Gate of Heaven alongside him to ascertain whether those about to enter were worthy. These northern regions encircled by the two sky bears eventually derived their name, the Arctic, from the Greek word for Bear, *Arktos*. In the old British language the original root was *Bera* or *Bher*, which meant both bright and brown, no doubt alluding to the respective starry and earthly qualities of what was believed to be the spiritual guardian of mankind.

The Celtic root *Arth* can also be found hidden within the word *Earth*, indicating the Bear's deep connections with the natural world. Other likely derivations are indicated in the related words *Heart* and *Hearth*, the latter referring to the sacred focus of the home, connected to the heavens via a chimney. This ancient idea gave rise to many aspects of folklore, including one where the spirit of the Winter Solstice (now known as Santa Claus or St Nicholas) descends into the house at the time when the Sun is reborn. The shamanic origins of many of these traditions are deeply rooted in human experience and are so powerful in the collective psyche that they persist even into times when the original meaning appears all but lost.

The etymology of the old British language gives many other clues to how important the Bear was in antiquity. In *Spurrell's English-Welsh Dictionary*, which preserves many now-lost elements of the Celtic languages, there is a long list of Bear-related words, and it may be useful to refer to them here, not only because the book is now difficult to obtain, but for the insights it provides into how prevalent these ideas once were. Amongst them are *Arth*, *Eirth* or *Arthod*, meaning bear; *Arthaido*, bear-like; *Arthal*, to growl; *Arthan*, bear's cub; *Arthen*, young she-bear; *Arthio*, to bark or growl; *Arthog*, bearish; *Aruthr*, marvellous, wonderful, prodigious and strange; and *Aruthro*, to wonder, to marvel, and also to terrify. We can see in these last two examples the striking similarity with the name *Arthur*, and one other reference is of particular interest too. *Alban Arthuan* (white bear-cub) is the old Druidic name for the Winter Solstice, and links the idea of the birth of a saviour-god, which still lives on in Christianity, with the Bear cosmology of deep antiquity.

The Greek Bear Myth

Referring to the great mythological body of lore from prehistory, many have noted how later legends appear to have been little more than a desperate gathering of the fragments of those former times, reinterpreted for their own changing cultural background. Commenting on this, one of the authors of the influential *Hamlet's Mill*, Giorgio de Santillana, who spent many years studying the mythologies of this star-lore, reminds us how the classical world gathered their own legends from far more ancient times:

> 'The dust of centuries had settled upon the remains of this great world-wide construction when the Greeks came upon the scene. Yet something of it survived in traditional rites, in myths and fairy tales no longer understood... Yet its original themes could flash out again, preserved almost intact, in the later thought of the Pythagoreans and of Plato.'

The ancient Greeks must indeed have inherited a great amount of their mythology from earlier cultures, (even Aristotle said that the gods were originally stars) adapting them according to their own background, for their story of how the Bear constellations originated shows significant correspondences with the previous prehistoric traditions. It is set in the forests of Arcadia, where the Moon Goddess Artemis, along with her band of nymphs, roamed the mountains at night hunting the wild creatures that lived there. Because she ruled the night, she could also see into people's dreams, and on one occasion she heard a maiden, *Callisto*, (whose name means *the most beautiful*), the daughter of one of her nymphs, whisper in her sleep. She told of how unhappy she was living with her father, King Lycaon, and her fifty brothers, who treated her cruelly. Artemis sent Callisto's mother to ask her to join the band of huntress nymphs as long as she would forsake all worldly passions and dedicate herself solely to the service of the goddess.

On the night of the full moon Callisto walked out into the forest where she was greeted by the goddess and her companions, and was handed a bow and quiver full of silver arrows with which to go hunting. She spent some years living in the glades and forests, until one fateful day she lay down for a rest.

It was here that Zeus found her, after having watched her from a distance all day. His wife Hera was away and Zeus being a notorious philanderer wondered how he could approach her, especially as she could run as fast as a deer. He decided to magically transform himself into Artemis, and, by this subterfuge, as soon as he was close enough forced himself upon her. Callisto, sworn to chastity in service of her goddess, was so ashamed she never told her companions what had happened. But one day whilst bathing with them she could not hide the fact that her belly was getting bigger, for she was pregnant. Artemis ordered her to leave, having broken her vows.

Callisto, broken-hearted, was forced to live on her own in the wildwood until she gave birth to a boy. But Zeus' jealous wife Hera found out and her screams of indignation echoed through the mountains of Arcadia. She vowed revenge. By her magic, Hera decided she would put a stop to all this. As Callisto was suckling her young son her voice gradually turned into a growl and her arms began to grow furry. She was soon transformed completely into a Bear.

Realising that her son needed the company of humans, she left him at her father's door, but was spotted by the cook who went to the King and explained that she had seen a Mother Bear carrying the child from the woods. King Lycaon called him *Arcas*, which means *Child of the Bear*.

Zeus, unhappy at these developments, changed himself into a rough farmer and descended to Arcadia, asking for food at the palace. But Lycaon had heard that gods were in the habit of occasionally visiting places in disguise, and became suspicious. He decided to make a dish of human meat to test his visitor's powers and see if, with his godlike powers, he would recognise it. The meat was to be that of Arcas.

Zeus immediately knew something was wrong and, enraged, hurled thunderbolts at the King and his sons, reducing them to ashes. Realising what had happened, he magically restored his own son Arcas to full health and took him to the home of Maia, the mother of Hermes. He also restored Lycaon to life again only to change him into a wolf, destined to roam the forests as a scavenger. Arcas eventually became King of Arcadia, the enchanted land of forests and wild animals and the domain of Pan, the great god of Nature.

Many years later when King Arcas was hunting near the temple of Zeus he came across a huge female black Bear that looked at him oddly. As he drew his bow, the Bear moved towards the Temple of Zeus, for it was Callisto, hoping to give him a sign so that he would spare her. Zeus, watching everything, immediately intervened, grabbing Callisto by her short tail, stretching it and hurling her into the heavens where he spread her stars out in the shape of the Great Bear. To make sure she would not suffer the loneliness of her earthly life, Arcas was also thrown into the sky where he became the Little Bear, the constellation of *Ursa Minor*, which closely replicates the shape of its mother. The King too was banished from the Earth, where he became the constellation of *Lupus*, the Wolf.

As Hera saw the new stars in the sky she suffered yet another fit of jealous rage. As the Bear was in the greatest place of honour as the highest and brightest group of stars in the sky she ordered that the Bears would never bathe in the waters of the sea. And this is what happened; for they revolve continuously around the Pole (above about 30 degrees North) and never sink or rise from the sea like other constellations.

In this myth of how the Great Bear and the Little Bear were origi- nally created there are powerful echoes of the former prehistoric beliefs. *Artemis* is the most ancient of Greek goddesses, a queen of the stars with the prefix *Art* and the she-bear as her symbol. The focus of the story is that of hunting, the greatest preoccupation of early peoples. The transforma- tion of people into Bears also echoes the shamanic traditions that were central to their existence. The Bear Son is the offspring of a human female and a god, just as in the Basque stories. And the testing of Zeus, who is presented with a dish of human/Bear meat surely refers to the rituals of sacrifice that were once common in the rites of Bear worship. Finally the two Bears, once human, are transposed into the heavens, where they be- come eternal guardians of the universe.

At Brauron near Athens is the only known site dedicated exclu- sively to Greek Bear worship. Here was the famous Temple of Artemis Brauronia, (which may be literally translated as the *Bear sister of Apollo*) where Bear Maidens performed the sacred rituals associated with the Greek tradition. These days it seems a remote place, set in a marshy valley overlooked by low hills, yet it was one of twelve ancient communities of the Attic confederation and provides a link with the legends of a consider- ably greater antiquity. A Christian chapel to St George has been built on a low mound from which issues a spring of clear water, probably because there was once a cavern behind it, now marked by a small shrine. Both St George and Bears are associated with such caves, the former having a penchant for dragons, the latter choosing it for their deathly sleep prior to rebirth. The roof of this Bear-cave collapsed during the fifth century BC.

The ceremony of the Brauronia was celebrated every four years, when pre-pubescent girls aged between five and ten dressed in saffron robes symbolising Bear skins performed various rites which included dancing as if they were Bears. Although nothing else is known about these rituals, Artemis was a protectress during childbirth, and so we can perhaps see here the connections between the Greek pantheon and the Callisto legend of earlier star-lore and the process of childbirth that links the two. Amongst the remains of this sanctuary are the columns of a Doric temple and a sacred pool where a variety of votive offerings were found. In the adjoining apartments, which had no less than nine dining rooms, were inscriptions that identified it as the *Parthenon of the Arktoi*, or Bears. The entire complex is aligned slightly East of North, towards the area of the sky where the constellation of the Great Bear can be seen as the heavenly vault darkens at certain times of the year.

These fragments of Bear-worship are informative, for as the old stories lost their original meaning and star-lore gave way to a Sun-oriented zodiacal system where the veneration of Bears was gradually eroded, much of the prehistoric tradition was lost. Besides the European and Basque memories that lived on in some remote areas, the former sacred creatures were increasingly hunted, not for their divine powers, but for their meat and fur, and to eradicate them from the countryside because of the perceived threat they held for humans. As seems to be the case with the gods and goddesses of previous ages, they eventually became objects of popular ridicule. This degeneration reached its peak in the late medieval period, when Bears were trapped, shot, imprisoned and subjected to torture. Bear-baiting became a common pastime, and, as a poignant reminder of their one-time cosmic function, they could be seen at fairs throughout Europe where they were made to dance around a pole just as their heavenly counterparts still danced around the Pole

The Bear and Ragged Staff — a totemic and heraldic device based on the Great Bear that appears 'chained' to the Pole around which the heavens seem to revolve.

of Heaven every night. In Elizabethan Britain they were still a common feature of public celebrations, with Bear-Parks and Bear-Pits throughout the land, with their sacred character perverted to a mere blood sport.

Remnants of their former veneration are these days few and far between, and bears have now disappeared from the British landscape altogether, hunted to extinction many centuries ago, although there were still wild Bears in Britian until the 'Arthurian' era of the sixth century. The official insignia of the county of Warwickshire is the *Bear and the Ragged Staff,* a distant echo of the Bear dancing around the Pole. Interestingly, the Earls of Warwick were often referred to as Bears and known as 'Kingmakers' because of their royal influence in those days. Throughout Britain many pubs still remind us of the importance of The Bear in their name, and almost every town in Britain probably has one called *The Seven Stars,* where it is always appropriate to raise a glass or two in honour of its truly ancient origins.

There is only one place in the country where a Bear ritual is still performed, and that is the Cambridgeshire town of Whittlesea. Recent years have seen a revival of this custom, which has many overtones of the significance of Bears that we might expect. Here, a man dressed as a 'Straw Bear' dances through the streets, visiting houses and bestowing benevolence on the inhabitants. This has all the trappings of an ancient fertility rite, with the straw probably indicating the Bear's blessing for a coming good harvest, for in early times it was closely bound up with the fertility of the Earth as well as that of humans as the presiding deity of childbirth. If we harboured any doubts of the one-time cosmic significance of such folk rituals, which were probably once much more widespread, we should note that this event takes place every year on *Plough Monday*. Here is a graphic example of how the emphasis shifted from the preoccupations of Paleolithic hunters to those of Neolithic settlers, now increasingly concerned with cultivating the land. This reinforces the idea of the Bear's powers over the fertile Earth, linking it with the star-group of the Heavenly Bear and the alternate name for the same constellation, the Plough, as it reflects the changing patterns of human evolution.

The Star Bear

The constellation known variously as The Great Bear, The Plough or the Big Dipper has, throughout history, been of prime significance all over the world, and not just in the regions where the Bear became a symbol of heavenly rulership. Its mystical powers are in evidence amongst the oldest civilisations on Earth, from the 6000 year-old Vedas of India to the Egyptian Book of the Dead, two of the earliest sacred texts in existence. So it may shed more light on our quest to briefly examine what other, non-European cultures, thought of these powers. We will discover that they held the constellation in similar high regard for its role in human affairs.

To begin with, it is instructive to learn that in India, from the most ancient times, the seven stars of the Great Bear were known as the seven *Rishis*, or Sages, great beings who presided over the wheeling constellations, and consequently the different ages of humanity. The Indo-European languages that are spoken today are based on Indian Sanskrit, so it may come as little surprise that the word *Rishi* comes from a Sanskrit root meaning *Bear*.

The Babylonians called the Great Bear the *Mother Bond of Heaven*, whilst the Greeks also spelled it *Omphaloessa*, referring to its function as the umbilical cord that joins Heaven and Earth, the source of earthly life, attached forever to the heavenly womb. Here are more references to the Bear constellation as the mother of humanity, and it is certain that during prehistoric ages when the cult of the Great Goddess was central to the religious impulse, the Bear was conceived, as remembered in the Greek myth, as a Mother Goddess.

In Egyptian star-lore the constellation was not known as the Bear, for there were no such creatures in Africa. Instead it was called the *Adze*, the tool used for cultivation in the same way as the star-group became known as the Plough in later times. At another time it was also depicted as the *Bull's foreleg*, being the strongest part of the Bull which

pulled the other constellations around the Pole. Some sources call it the
Leg of the Ox, which is tethered to the heavenly plough when the cow-
goddess Hathor ruled the heavens. In the Denderah Zodiac at the Temple
of Hathor the leg is shown 'chained' to the hippopotamus goddess, who,
like the Bear, is a deity of childbirth. The shape of the Seven Stars gave
rise to a remarkable object known as a *Pesh-en-kef*, a magical tool that
was of crucial significance in the rites attending birth and death. A small
model of the adze-shaped constellation was fashioned out of meteoric iron
(which itself was thought to possess mystical properties, having fallen
from the heavens). This was used to sever the umbilical cord at birth,
ritually enacting the cosmic belief that human souls came into incarnation
from the central axis of the universe. At death this celestially-encoded
tool was used in the 'Opening of the Mouth Ceremony' where the soul of
the deceased was released back to the stars by ritually applying it to the
lips. Numerous examples of these implements have been discovered, one
being found hidden in a shaft of the Great Pyramid.

Despite the fact that these traditions appear very different from
those beliefs of our prehistoric ancestors in Britain and Europe, it is
remarkable how similar the essential elements are. In all these traditions,
the constellation known to us as the Great Bear has been seen as the
ultimate guide and protector of human souls when they are born and when
they die. In between, the earthly Bear is a sort of shamanic figure who
has the powers to heal and bring heavenly order into the physical world.
The nurturing and child-bearing aspects of the Bear indicate that in those
early times, it was seen as a primal Mother Goddess who is responsible for
the fertility and health of her children, the human race.

As mythologies developed along with more structured civilisations
the function of the constellations changed too. With the rise of the Osirian
mythos the northern axis remained as the eternal centre of the wheel of the
'imperishable stars' that neither rise nor set. This corresponded with the
Judgement Hall of Maat, the Goddess of Truth, Justice and cosmic order
(interesting that one of the traditional Irish names for the Bear is *Math*,
and that both these names appear connected to the Latin *Mater*, meaning
Mother, and *Matter*, denoting physical existence). At this time the Great
Bear was known as *the bier* or *coffin* of Osiris, or the Ark that contained
his resurrected body. The stars of the Little Bear were thought to be the
mourners of Osiris' sarcophagus as they followed it on its infinite journey
to eternal life, freed from the wheel of incarnation.

We may note here that the word *Ark* is related to the Greek *Arktoi*,
meaning Bears, and that this has spawned another group of words, just
like that of *Art*, including *Arch* (a physical representation of the Arch of the
Heavens), *Arch*angel (meaning chief, principal or high angel) and *Archi*tect
(originally applied to the Creator God, but now meaning to intelligently
design). The Royal *Arch* and the Great *Archi*tect are both significant terms in
Freemasonry, which *Arc*ane knowledge derives from Egyptian cosmology.

And let us not forget *Arc*adia, the mythical realm of the Bear King.

In Europe, as the Bear myth waned, the constellation became the vehicle for the god-kings of popular mythology, sometimes called *Charles'* or *Charlemagne's Wain*, or in Britain, *Arthur's Wain* or *Chariot*, which accompanied them on their nightly rides across the sky.

So who exactly was King Arthur in the stellar scheme of things? Was he the constellation of the Great Bear itself? This seems unlikely, since the most ancient myths invariably speak of the constellation as predominantly female, the ancestor and mother goddess of humanity that presides over childbirth and the protection associated with mother-hood. Could he then be the Little Bear, associated in the European Bear Cult with the Bear Son, the result of the union of the Father-God Zeus with the Mother-Goddess in the form of Callisto, who becomes the Great Sky-Bear? This would appear more likely in that the Bear Son has the power to ascend and descend the *Axis Mundi* as a shamanic being, half-god, half-human, echoing many of the early mythological exploits of Arthur, who was said to be able to enter a revolving castle of glass. But there is also another constellation that is a strong candidate for the original proto-type of King Arthur, and he is indeed a King, who circles the Round Table of the Heavens and is also known as the guardian of the Bears. He is the Cosmic Bear-King known as *Arcturus*, or *Boötes*.

The Great Bear King

The Great Bear and the Little Bear have been locked into human consciousness since the very beginning; this much is apparent. It is not surprising that aspects of their heavenly character are so persistent that they have come down to present times, even if the details may vary oc-casionally due to different cultural backgrounds. Besides the underlying theme of the current quest to trace the original meaning behind the idea of Arthur, the Bear King, we perhaps appreciate by now that all this is part of a bigger story. As we focus on the way Bear mythology has become an integral part of our language and traditions the more we can see how it is truly one of the seminal concepts behind human civilisation.

We have seen how the root words *Ark* and *Art*, both referring to very ancient words for the Bear, have become incorporated into many everyday expressions. Yet the extent of this is surprising when we look at the myths. The Arcadian tradition, which refers to a long-lost 'Golden Age', comes from a time when the gods and goddesses lived in Arcadia, the Kingdom of the Bear. This, in the Greek story, is located in the Peloponnese, where a central mountain called 'Wolf Mountain' symbolised the Axis Mundi linking Heaven and Earth. The Arcadian tradition became assimilated into the Western Mystery Schools at an early date, for many sacred landscapes that mirrored the heavens were enshrined in esoteric knowledge as localities where the heavenly myths were enacted on the Earth.

Because of this, there is an entire clan of words surrounding the Bear. Even the Biblical story of the *Ark* of the Covenant is derived from the same root, being the box containing the Ten Commandments which represent the agreement between God and Humanity. In many traditions the shape of the Bear constellation is often seen as a container wherein lies the destiny of the world. The Bear has even made it into modern scientific jargon, for when a surveyor or astronomer is establishing co-ordinates in order to fix a position, he uses *bearings*, which are measurements taken in relation to True North—the realm of the Bear.

This idea of True North, the Kingdom of the Bear, being the central point from which everything is measured, is an intriguing one. The more we study it the clearer it becomes that this particular place was considered as a cosmic omphalos. Some scholars believe that Maat, the goddess of heavenly order, gave her name to *Mathematics*. It is interesting too that *Arc*, meaning part of a circle, is the shape made in the heavens by the ever-circling stars of the Bears. Measurement has always been connected with rulership, and it is the Bears that seem to rule the heavens due to their guardianship of the Pole. Their links with human and earthly fertility are profound when we realise that the spiralling of the universe was often conceived as a threaded axis along which the galaxies move. This is where the term *Nut* comes from, as in *Nut* and *Bolt*. Nut was the Egyptian Sky Goddess, and in German *nut* in this context is replaced by the actual word for *mother, Mutter*. The sexual metaphor is evident, with the German for the male part of the arrangement being *Schraube*—literally *screw*. Hence the Nut or Mother is like a wheel, with a hole at the centre through which the spiral progresses, a metaphor that exactly describes the changing motions of the heavens as they circle around the central point.

So the Bears guard the sacred centre, but who guards the Bears? The guardian is one of the most mysterious figures in the heavens, known variously as the *Bear-Keeper, the Bear-King, Arcturus* or alternatively the Wagoner or Driver of the Wain, *Boötes*.

The knee of the Bear King is marked by one of the brightest stars in the northern hemisphere, the golden yellow Arcturus, and the constellation that is named after it lies between the Great Bear and Virgo, both Mother Goddesses of fertility. The curving Tail of the Great Bear points directly to this prominent star and then leads on to *Virgo*, the ancient zodiacal goddess of Corn with her bright star *Spica*, the *Ear of Wheat*. A popular phrase to remember this is 'Arc to Arcturus then speed on to Spica!'. When the Bear became a Plough symbolising the cultivation of the Neolithic era Arcturus changed into Boötes, the Driver of the Oxen who tills the heavenly fields in order that the rotation of the heavens shall never cease.

But it is in his later incarnation as Arcas, the Bear King of Arcadia, we should look for guidance. The very word Arcadia evokes visions of a pastoral paradise with groves of ancient oaks, tumbling waterfalls and mountain glades where shepherds tend their flocks. It is the land of Pan, the Green Man of Nature whose enchanted music floats through the consciousness of humanity, beguiling us with its power to soothe the savage breasts of both humans and wild animals. Arcadia remains a lost dream of paradise hovering somewhere just beyond our vision. Perhaps it is for this reason that it was adopted by the Mystery Traditions of antiquity as a timeless land that somehow exists alongside our mundane world. In this land King Arcas taught the arts of civilisation, showed the shepherds how to grow corn and make bread, and introduced the wheel, thus inventing the chariot or wain—with his own chariot flying through the air drawn by dragons (probably a reference to *Draco*, the Dragon, who winds himself around the Little Bear).

Arcturus, the great civiliser of humanity, seems to be the link between the wild hunter/gatherers of the Mesolithic/Paleolithic eras, the old nomadic cultures of the earliest times, and the settled Neolithic and Bronze Age peoples. These were the new myth-makers, who, no longer following the old paths, established tribal territories where they erected megalithic monuments reflecting the movements of the stars. Was this the earliest form of King Arthur's legendary Round Table that later became enshrined in Celtic tradition? As we will discover, Arcas and Arthur, the Bear Kings who created a great cultural flowering in their respective realms, were the guardians of a wisdom that still haunts the human imagination, and still has surprises in store for us today. The stories of the stars that became transposed into mythological heroes have been with us from the very beginning, whether we see them as goddesses and gods or the Ladies and Knights of the Round Table. The quest is still the same; to discover our own true nature.

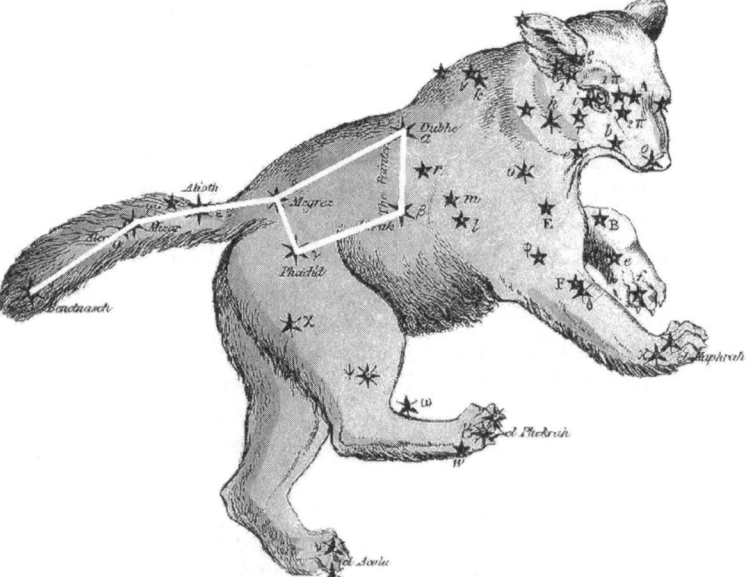

The constellation of the Great Bear, according to Urania's Mirror published in about 1825. The distinctive shape of the brightest seven stars is here emphasised; it is one of the most easily recognisable star patterns in the sky and has been used for navigation, surveying and astronomical observation since humans first walked the Earth.

For a detailed explanation on how the Great Bear functions as a star-clock and indicator of the seasonal cycles, see The Visual Astronomy of the Great Bear on pages 295 - 302.

3

RETURN OF THE GOD KINGS

he mythology of the Bear is, as we have seen, one of the most ancient and deeply-rooted beliefs since humanity first appeared on the Earth. The protectiveness and guardianship of the starry Bear in the heavens and its earthly counterparts, who exhibited the same qualities towards their offspring (and people, according to the widespread beliefs), resulted in a universal reverence and veneration of its gentleness, as well as its terrible ferocity when challenged. This selfless courage and uncompromising strength epitomises the nature of the beast, and it is clear why the Bear was such a powerful symbol of sovereignty, a word which alludes to a supreme female power, but also includes within it the word *reign*, implying the idea of kingship.

Yet kings did not always rule. In the earliest times society was matriarchal, with lineage being traced through the female instead of the male. This persisted until Celtic times, and within the legends that come down from this time it is easy to see that the male figures derive their power from goddesses in their various guises.

The legends and stories of King Arthur are no exception to this, and Excalibur, the source of his own power, has to be returned to the Lady of the Lake when he is mortally wounded, before he is ferried to Avalon by three otherworldly females who are probably an echo of the triple goddess of prehistory, epitomised by the Maiden, Mother and Crone. Merlin, too, is taught his magic by a female and is eventually entranced and imprisoned by one. In ancient lore, the female was definitely more powerful than the male.

Exactly when the patriarchal influence became dominant is difficult to ascertain, but it was probably during the Iron Age when warlike tendencies overshadowed the former more settled and stable cultures of the Bronze Age. Yet as we have discovered, these ancient ideas are not easily eroded—they tend to adapt themselves to the prevailing customs, living on in a myriad of ways. The goddesses of the past are not dead, just slumbering, like the giant Bear at Tintagel, beyond the limits of our conscious mind.

Our brief look at the mythic power of the Bear throughout antiquity will soon lead us back to where we began, with the great landscape effigy of a Bear looking purposefully at Tintagel Island, where according to the Celtic tradition immortalised by Geoffrey of Monmouth, Arthur the Bear King was born. But before we focus our attention on Tintagel itself, and the surrounding features that are significantly located within the body of the Great Bear, it is necessary to take a look at the legacy of these ancient traditions and those that inherited them. One of the keys to understanding the enigma of King Arthur is to recognise that instead of *Arthur* being simply the name of a particular historical character, as is popularly believed, it is in reality a title of kingship that was used throughout the Celtic world. Because of this there were many 'Arthurs' across Europe and beyond, fragments of whose lives are remembered in myth and history and often rationalised into a body of lore that presents insurmountable practical problems unless this is taken into account. As such it is understandable that the everlasting question of where King Arthur came from cannot otherwise be answered satisfactorily.

Was King Arthur from Cornwall, Wales, Brittany, Scotland, or even the countries of central Europe and parts of Russia, all places where his exploits are remembered? How could he possibly have fought all those battles in one lifetime unless he was truly superhuman and lived for an inordinate amount of time? The truth is his adventures and exploits are attached to these places because all these kings and tribal leaders shared the same name, or variations of it, and have become grouped together over time to present a *confusion of King Arthurs*, to employ an apposite collective noun. Each one inherited a tradition of kingship that was enshrined in ancient custom.

And what of Tintagel? When Geoffrey wrote the story of Arthur's birth down the place was already remembered as once being a highly significant royal centre in ancient times. Archaeology has since confirmed this. 'Royal' graves of the fifth or sixth centuries, although empty, have been excavated in Tintagel Churchyard overlooking the Island, and a large amount of very fine pottery has been recovered, proof that important celebrations were held there in the so-called 'Dark Ages'.

In *Tintagel and the Arthurian Mythos* I suggested that the Island had been a ritual centre of power since prehistoric times, and that the Celtic legend was a memory of far greater antiquity than generally supposed. Because of this, the building of a Norman castle there in the thirteenth century by Richard of Cornwall was not for normal defensive purposes, for there was nothing to defend other than a barren and windswept plateau of no strategic use. Archaeologists such as Professor Charles Thomas, one of the leading authorities on Tintagel, agree; there was no apparent reason to build a fortified castle there. Not so much as an arrowhead or any other weapon has ever been found on the Island, despite many excavations.

So why did Richard build a castle in one of the most remote and inaccessible places imaginable? Was he intending to hold court there? If so he would have surely become a social outcast, for few were likely to visit such an outlandish place, far from the trappings of civilisation. So wild and extreme is its location that in Elizabethan times it found what was probably its ideal purpose for the times, as far as such buildings go, when it was used as a prison. In fact there is no record of Richard or those that followed him even visiting the place at all. If we are perplexed by such a grandiose scheme to build on a precipitous island that was threatened only by the ferocious winter storms, then we must look elsewhere for an explanation. This naturally leads to the question of who the Normans really were, and why they showed such a great interest in the native British legends and landscape.

History, as we perceive it, is rarely the whole truth. When William the Conqueror won the Battle of Hastings in 1066 and the Anglo-Saxon King Harold Godwinson was famously shot in the eye with an arrow we are told that the foreign invaders brutally set about vanquishing the nation without regard for its former ways. Yet Harold and William had formerly been on friendly terms, with William knighting Harold and inviting the King to accompany him on a campaign. In fact at that time they were friendly rivals, for William was a legitimate heir to the throne of the House of Wessex, his wife Matilda being descended from Alfred the Great as well as a niece of the French King Henry.

All is not quite as simple as we commonly believe where kingship is concerned, and few understand the mindset and motivation of the characters involved. It is important, however, to realise that the Normans, that is the *Norse-Men* or *Men of the North*, were a dynasty of royal families of Scandinavian, Danish and Norwegian extraction whose Viking forces had been trying to claim Britain for centuries. One of the reasons for this was that they considered themselves to be the true and rightful kings of the British Isles.

Those interested in the labyrinthine politics of the time will find much of interest in *The God-Kings of Britain* by Hugh Montgomery, himself a descendant of the Norman nobles who accompanied William during the invasion. Here there is only space to point out that the Normans believed themselves to be the inheritors of a wisdom tradition stretching back to deep antiquity. They had, at various times, been kings or overlords of an even greater area than that ruled by the Western Roman Empire of the Carolingians. The Duke of Normandy, Rollo, the founder of the Norman dynasty, was descended from the great Norse family of the Ulvungars, and was eventually and reluctantly granted his lands by Charles the Simple, King of the West Franks. According to the thirteenth century chronicler Snorre Sturleson, Rollo was the son of a Norwegian king who came from a long line of Viking royalty stretching back to Rhoes, King of the Visigoths at the beginning of the fourth century. He is known to have

fought alongside the Romans, with Constantine the Great holding him in
high esteem. His full name in old Norse was Rhoes the *Weoôlgeot*, which
translated means he was a direct descendent of the god Odin. This is where
the term *Goth*, meaning God, comes from, and Rollo himself was King of
the 'Odinpeople', the descendants of the old Gothic kingdom which was
eventually destroyed by the Roman Emperor Aurelius in 270 AD.

When Rollo invaded Normandy in December 876 these 'Odinpeople' were caught between their old Norse religion and the Christianity
favoured by the Franks. Yet the extraordinary thing to our modern eyes is
that apparently there was no real conflict between them, for the Norsemen
achieved a remarkable synthesis of the two. There seemed to be no clash
of ideologies, probably because their old God Odin was believed to have
been hung on a tree and pierced in the side by a spear, almost exactly
the same as Jesus Christ. Artefacts like the Franks Casket in the British
Museum show images from both Pagan and Christian traditions side by
side. The ivory carvings are not only of exquisite craftsmanship that rivals
anything of its time, but depict images of the blacksmith god Weiland
in his forge holding up a chalice or grail directly alongside a depiction of
the Nativity of Christ.

*Carved ivory panels on the front of the early eighth-century Franks Casket showing both Christian and
Pagan influences. On the left is the blacksmith god Weiland in his smithy, apparently just having fashioned
a Grail-like cup. On the right we find the scene of the 'Adoration of the Magi', with three wise men following
the bright star to Jesus' birthplace. These scenes are eloquent testimony that for many centuries Christianity
and the older religions which preceded it existed alongside each other in a perfectly harmonious manner.*

The evidence of the Franks Casket and other Viking and Norman
relics clearly show that both religions co-existed side by side. Indeed,
it seems they sensed that they were merely varying interpretations of
universal mythologies, and in fact complemented rather than challenged
each other. The politics of course were a different story. Rollo himself
was baptised twice, according to the chronicles, once in 896 and again in
912, when he took the Christian name Robert.

The rivalry between the Normans and the Anglo-Saxons for the British throne had been going on since at least the time of Aethelred II (978-1016), and probably right back to Rollo's time. The intermarriage of all these families presents an almost impenetrable spider's web of influence and intrigue, yet it is clear that the Normans, as we have come to know them, were of a strongly pagan background deriving from the pre-Christian worship of Odin, Thor and a mystical inheritance stretching back to ancient times. They were descended from a line that practised polygamy and it would have been natural for them to have been guided in many of their actions by the beliefs of their ancestors. Coming from the cold northern regions it seems impossible they would have been unaware of the significance of the totemic mythology of the Bear and its connection with kingship and Arthurian tradition.

Another important factor to take into consideration is their intimate connection with very ancient Cornish (British) families. Since the Saxon incursions of the Dark Ages, the native Britons had been relentlessly pushed westward until most of the country had become a series of Saxon kingdoms. Old maps show the region called Cornwall extending throughout the Westcountry, which at that time included the prehistoric temples of Stonehenge and Avebury. This was still the case even later in Geoffrey of Monmouth's time, when the whole region formerly occupied by the Celtic tribe of the Dumnonii was called *West Wales* or *Cornwales*. Cornwall, as we know it today, became ever more isolated from the English kingdoms and was, along with Wales, the last refuge of the old British traditions that had come down from the earliest times. Both these regions had in their name the word *Wales*—an Anglo-Saxon term that, ironically, meant 'foreigners' (in essence a term of derision), and symbolically excommunicated the ancient British from their own land.

The final reckoning came when Athelstan defeated the remaining British/Cornish at the Battle of Hingston Down in about 936 AD, where the Cornish army included a strong Viking contingent. For many years the Saxons had been trying to rid Cornwall of its independent Bishops and replace them with their own, thereby destroying the last remnants of Celtic Christianity—a form of religion unique to the Celtic regions which preserved strong elements of former Druid beliefs. Up until now they had failed, but this time the invasion resulted in their takeover of the old monasteries and the destruction of their libraries which preserved much of the ways of pre-Roman/Saxon Christianity, a very different form than that which was now to be imposed for political reasons. This assault on the proudly-guarded ways of the West Britons triggered a mass exodus of ancient families across the channel to Normandy and Brittany, the latter being so-called because of the large number of old British families who made it their home. Brittany was 'Little Britain' whilst 'Great Britain' signified the mainland, the ancestral homeland of the exiles. One area of Brittany in particular was called *Cornwaille* in memory of the place so many of its inhabitants had come from.

It would be a mistake, however, to assume that the population of British/Cornish in the northern and eastern areas of France was simply the result of the Saxon invasions. There was a long-standing history of Westcountry families, especially the indigenous Cornish, going to live in Brittany and Normandy since prehistoric times. The legends of the early saints give a clear insight into the manner in which ancient people moved freely from one land to another, for they were inveterate travellers and it was often easier and safer to travel across the channel than to risk the bandit-infested roads of the Westcountry.

These saints—really religious initiates of the Druidic tradition—were renowned for travelling within the 'Celtic Triangle' of Ireland, Wales and Brittany, with Cornwall at its centre. St Samson, for instance, one of the best documented, was originally from Wales, spent many years in Cornwall and then founded a monastery at Dol in Brittany. These connections, especially between Cornwall and Brittany, have always been deep. Even until fairly recent times Cornish and Breton fishermen could converse freely in their respective languages as if they were one; which of course they were, the old once-universal Celtic/British language. One of the first Cornish saints was St Corentin or Cury, who is thought to have settled at Menheniot. He was consecrated Bishop of Cornwall by St Martin of Tours. Born in Brittany he died in 401.

The region of Northern France known as Armorica, like Wales, shared many Celtic saints and for the Normans Cornwall was also the most accessible and sympathetic area of Britain, as well as conveniently close to their estates and homes in Normandy and Brittany. They left a considerable legacy with more than a hundred churches still standing in the county which incorporate Norman craftsmanship. One sometimes gets the impression that they must have employed virtually every stonemason in the Duchy.

By the time Athelstan finally destroyed much of the old British culture, raiding monasteries and burning the manuscripts that were the heritage of the West Britons, the Cornish already had an extensive network of family members and friends in Normandy and Brittany. When they were forced across the channel they would certainly have found a warm welcome as balm for being exiled from their homeland. What should such exiles do in these circumstances? It would have been natural to keep the memories of their old land alive by perpetuating the mythologies of the places they once lived, and to cherish the idea of one day returning. These old Cornish families, the remnants of the British noble families, also intermarried with the local inhabitants and these alliances between the Cornish, Breton and Norman dynasties created a lasting bond of familial loyalties. They saw themselves as the guardians of a Wisdom Tradition of great antiquity, and they felt that their destiny lay in reclaiming Britain together with a restoration of the old beliefs that were so inextricably bound up with the landscape. It is no accident or quirk of history that the most significant landscapes associated with the legends of King Arthur and Merlin are those of Cornwall, Brittany and Wales, for these are exactly the areas where the guardians of the old traditions lived.

Genealogy was of prime importance to these old families, for who you were and where you came from were the essence of your character and destiny. This spiritual dimension was paramount, for each person had their own fate, and in a time when life was short a belief in a greater purpose was a powerful guiding force. The loyalties to one's ancestors and living relatives were part of a system of faith that formed a spiritual quest to fulfil one's true destiny. The intermarriage that took place between Vikings, Saxons, Celts and the native British thus laid foundations that created bloodlines of powerful significance.

When William the Conqueror's half-brother Robert de Mortain was given Cornwall for his loyalty to the King he rode into Cornwall flying the banner of St Michael, the old patron saint of Cornwall and Brittany, and claimed the traditional power centres that had been renowned since Druidic times. At Launceston, the capital, he began to build a new castle on the steep conical mound that had once been the core of a long-extinct volcano. At St Michael's Mount he did the same, and he also claimed Tintagel, the birthplace of Arthur, as part of his legacy. The 'invasion' of Britain and the Westcountry was in truth more a 're-invasion' as far as the Normans were concerned, as they reclaimed the land from those who sought to destroy the original native traditions and way of life.

William, Duke of Normandy, holds court with Bishop Odo and his brother Robert de Mortain, who took over Cornwall when the Normans and ancient British families, who had strong family ties, returned to claim their homeland.

Despite the inevitable bloodshed and tyranny that such wars bring, the Norman takeover was accompanied by a great flowering of church, cathedral and castle building throughout Britain. It was also the time of a great renaissance of the old British legends. It is usually the main task of invaders to ruthlessly eradicate all traces of the former traditions of the vanquished and replace them with their own, as was the case with the Saxons. Yet this is patently not the case with the Normans, and we must ask why. It was his fellow Norman Churchmen who commissioned Geoffrey of Monmouth to write *The History of the Kings of Britain* in which the exploits of Arthur and Merlin were set down for all time. In the ensuing years a further series of remarkable chronicles concerning King Arthur appeared, commissioned this time by various influential families in France, notably the Champagne family who had intermarried with the Norman dynasty. All these referred to the old British legends (*Parzifal*, for instance, by Wolfram von Eschenbach, was based on a Welsh/ancient British tradition), and resulted in a body of literature that preserved these old beliefs, adapting them for a new age in such a way that they struck a chord so ancient and powerful they still fire our imaginations to this day.

The most westerly lands of the British Isles, especially those areas we now call Cornwall and Wales, were steeped in the religion we call Celtic Christianity. This was a pure form of early religion that derived from Druidism and had little to do with that promulgated by the Roman Church, which was more a political tool of power and oppression designed by Constantine the Great. Whilst the Norman dynasty presided over a renaissance of the old British ways, it had been the Saxons, in league with Rome, who had done everything in their power to wipe them out. This religion was far more Druidic than orthodox Christian and preserved many centuries of wisdom from times when mankind was at one with the natural world. It was deeply rooted in the knowledge of the movements of the heavenly bodies and the mysterious progression and transformation of the human soul.

The Romans had been here before, of course, not as a Church but as a military force (although they never conquered these westerly lands — archaeology suggests they were here for trading purposes, notably in tin and other metals). During that time, Roman commentators like Ammianus Marcellinus noted that the Druids, the inheritors of the native British traditions, were a caste of lawgivers, scribes and natural scientists 'uplifted by searching into secret and sublime things'. Caesar, who did his best to eradicate all remnants of the old Druidic ways wherever he went, was nevertheless obliged to admit to their deep learning in his war chronicles *De Bello Gallico*; writings which give a clear insight into the nature of British society before it became subject to almost total annihilation. Amongst these are tantalising glimpses of the former ways, for they were, according to Caesar, 'occupied about things divine':

> 'As one of their leading dogmas, they inculcate this; that souls are not annihilated, but pass after death from one body to another, and that they hold that by this teaching men are much encouraged to valour, through disregarding fear of death. They also discuss and impart to the young many things concerning the heavenly bodies and their movements, the size of the World and of our Earth, natural science, and the influence and power of the immortal Gods.'

Caesar also stated that although the Celtic territories throughout Europe were subject to Druidic influence, the Druids had originally come from the British Isles. Like William Blake almost two millennia later, he claimed that Britain was the source of these traditions from the most remote times, a belief that has been especially persistent. From these fragments we can perhaps begin to piece together a vision of the ancient British beliefs before their attempted destruction by a series of ruthless invaders, first the Romans and then the Saxons.

The core of these beliefs was drawn from former prehistoric times when people lived close to Nature, and it was to be preserved at all odds. This is what the surviving West Britons were motivated by as they fought to protect their ancestral homeland, its sacred sites, places of power and the traditions attached to them. This was their true spiritual heritage, and with the coming of the Normans an opportunity presented itself to reclaim this lost way of life. Under this dynasty, and their alliances with the old Cornish families, a great renaissance took place under the guise of the Arthurian and Grail legends. As we are beginning to realise, the stories and knightly escapades of the romances are in essence a retelling of stories of far greater age, dressed up in the fine clothes and shining armour of a time when the battles and crusades of the medieval period were the overriding fashion.

As the modern writer Pete Jennings has observed in *Heathen Paths*, the 'Viking raids' of 787-1066 were really a 300-year guerrilla war by pagan freedom fighters against the encroaching tyranny of Catholic France. Furthermore, they were merely a sea-based continuation of wars that had been waged between 690-786. This view of history means that the Vikings were not really the ruthless invaders we have been led to believe, for they fought for 500 years to preserve the old ways against Catholicism, a theme that will recur as our story progresses.

Were the Viking incursions, including the Battle of Hastings, a sort of Holy War against papal influence? Hugh Montgomery has suggested that the story of Harold being hit in the eye by an arrow is a reference to the Norse God Odin, who lost his eye as payment for occult knowledge, and that other 'sacrificial' kings such as Rufus the Red were also victims of a spiritual battle between orthodox beliefs and those of a much older way of thinking.

Warriors of the Bear

Soon after the founding of the Norwegian kingdom over 1000 years ago a fearsome band of warriors styled themselves on the Cult of the Bear. They were dedicated to the supreme god Wotan (or Odin, as in common parlance the *W* was often missed out, and *t* and *d* are interchangeable according to dialect) and called themselves *Berserkers*, meaning 'clothed as a Bear'. Indistinguishable from ordinary mortals in everyday life they were said to perform amazing feats when taken over by the Bear Spirit such as walking through fire, swallowing red-hot coals or ripping shields apart with their teeth.

In one account known as *Heidrek's Saga* there were twelve
Berserkers who possessed magic swords, and here we may note an
interesting correlation with King Arthur and his Knights of the Round
Table. Their tremendous strength was greatly feared and their tempers
notoriously prone to fiery awakening. Even in the eleventh century many
members of Viking families considered themselves to be descended
from Bears, including the Earl Siward of Northumberland, whose father
was said to have had Bear's ears. The Danish King Svend Estridson
(1047-1074) also believed himself to have Bear ancestors.

Bear traditions were exceedingly important to the Norman/Viking
way of thinking and permeated their whole culture, even though this is
rarely mentioned today by historians. But scratch the surface and the
paganism of their culture is exposed. Even the Saxons were once steeped
in the old ways, for their hero Hereward the Wake is recorded as killing a
Bear in order to gain the friendship of Vikings, ironically in this case, to
fight against the Normans. In this he may have been allying himself with
the Berserkers, for he is certainly credited with Berserker-like behaviour
in incidents where he defeated large groups of Normans single-handed.
Another great Anglo-Saxon hero, *Beowulf*, was also styled on a Bear, so
named because he was a *Bee-Wolf*, a reminder of the Bear's overriding
passion for honey.

Bear lore was in this way an important aspect of Anglo-Saxon
culture as well as that of the Vikings, whose royal families had intermarried down the centuries, both coming from central and northern European
stock. In the *Anglo-Saxon Chronicle* the Royal House of Wessex and North-
umbria are claimed to have descended from Odin, who is often linked
with biblical characters leading back to Adam. Other independent records
also claim a genealogy derived from both Norse and Christian anteced-
ents. All this speaks of an original Viking/Saxon fusion of ideas, religion
and common ancestry that is very different to the 'pigeon-holing' that
has often been the case amongst historians who tend to over-analyze and
place different cultures in boxes of their own making. This amalgamation
of Christian/Pagan heritage can be seen in art, language, jewellery and
religious objects like the Franks Casket. Both were dynamic and adventurous cultures at the forefront of new technological achievements of weap-
onry and ship design, a far cry from the stereotyped barbaric warriors
or comic-book characters so often portrayed. The Prior of St Fridswides,
John of Wallingford, even complained that the Vikings were scrupulous in
their hygiene and grooming, in order that they would appear attractive to
high-born English ladies who they hoped to seduce.

The shamanistic elements of the Bear Cult of these times echo
the older, prehistoric experience of Bear magic. In *Hrolf's Saga* a warrior
called Bjarki (a Bear name) assumes the shape of a Bear in battle, and in
the same story the Berserker Bodvar falls into a deep trance and projects
himself as a Bear to engage in warfare. This, it seems, refers directly to the

shamanistic origins of the Viking Bear Cult, for dressing in a Bearskin and allowing oneself to be overcome by the beast within, or being 'possessed' by the spirit of the animal, is a very ancient form of magic extending back to the times of Paleolithic and Mesolithic hunters. In a faint echo of this idea, the Guards at Buckingham Palace still wear Bearskin hats today as they protect British royalty. Some researchers have speculated that the use of ritual, dance, alcohol and psychoactive drugs were part of the warrior Bear cult, all designed to release the ferocious strength of the Bear. Others point out that the name Odin means 'frenzy', indicating that the very name of the God may be associated with Bears. In all these examples we can see that the power of the Bear was central in a culture that had its roots deeply embedded in the natural world.

A Viking King is attended by two of his men in a stained-glass window at Crantock Church on the North coast of Cornwall. He is wearing a winged dragon helmet, probably a reference to the Pendragon dynasty to which King Arthur belonged. Around his neck is the pelt of a Bear, endowing him with its great strength and wisdom. Although this window is Victorian, it shows that even at this late date the connections between King Arthur and the Bear were understood as a shamanic inheritance from our forebears.

St Nectan's Kieve in a nineteenth century engraving. The waterfall rushes down a narrow gorge to tumble into a smooth bowl-like basin and then emerges through a hole in a curtain of rock. Positioned where it is in the head of the Great Bear of Tintagel it seems an extraordinary simulacrum of the Bear's Throat. At certain times of the year the sound of the rushing waters echoing around the chasm creates a roaring effect, very like that of a Great Bear.

4

HUNTING THE BEAR

ince the beginning of this quest we have found ourselves exploring some hitherto neglected aspects of our remote, and not quite so remote, past. The significance of the Bear in ancient ritual and cosmology and its connections with the concepts of sovereignty and kingship deriving from early shamanistic practices now provide us with firm ground on which to pursue our quarry from a different perspective.

Ever since coming across the area around Tintagel I felt that I was being drawn inexorably into some mysterious realm where the so-called 'real' world and another intangible yet powerful presence, perhaps the *Genius Loci* of the land itself, resides. This special atmosphere undoubtedly has an effect on the imagination, and may help to explain why so many of those of a poetic or artistic disposition down through the ages have been drawn into its mystery. Tennyson, and his contemporary the wonderfully eccentric Vicar of Morwenstow, Robert Stephen Hawker, sensed it too. Hawker had spent his honeymoon at Tintagel immersing himself in its potent aura, and upon meeting Tennyson for the first and only time, they had sat on the cliffs for hours talking of King Arthur. They were both seminal in the Victorian Arthurian Revival that introduced the legends to the popular culture of the day, and laid the foundation for our own perceptions, Tennyson with his *Idylls of the King* and Hawker with *The Quest for the Sangraal*, both magnificent evocations of this part of the wild and windswept Cornish coast.

My own initiation into this area may, I realised many years later, have been something more than mere serendipity. It was as a mystically-inclined seventeen year-old, a product of the hedonistic and mind-awakening era of London in the late 1960s, that I arranged to visit a friend, Jamie Arnott, who was spending the summer in the harbour village of Boscastle, just three miles along the coast from Tintagel. In those days of lost innocence we hitch-hiked everywhere without any concern or fear for our well-being.

As fate would have it, another friend said, 'I'm going to Glastonbury then—let's meet up!' So we set a date and agreed to meet—where else in that mystic era—at the Tor. When? At midnight.

In due course I set off, and after a catalogue of the usual hitch-hiking adventures which included travelling in the back of a van full of offal on its way to a dog's home, eventually arrived in Somerset on a windy night. An obliging motorist went out of his way to drop me at the foot of the Tor, which loomed like a vast black pyramid against the flying moonlit clouds.

Unable to see my way I scrambled up the steep hill, slipping on the wet grass, until I reached the tower of the ruined St Michael's Church scraping the steel-grey sky. It was twelve o'clock and I shouted for my friend David. My voice echoed around the Tor, mingling with the wind that swirled about the hill. I felt uneasy and intimidated by its looming presence, and, perhaps rather naively, expected someone to shout back. But it was a forlorn hope. The place was deserted. I slowly realised that David probably had no intention at all of keeping this surreal appointment. Cold, wet and hungry, my only option was to seek shelter on the tree-lined lower slopes of the Tor, where, amongst the groaning branches silhouetted against the sky I unrolled my sleeping bag and tried to get some sleep. There was little hope of this, however, as I gradually slid down the slopes of the hill until finally coming to rest in the roots of a large tree. A fitful night followed, full of creaks, moans and other unidentified noises, with now and then an hour or so's sleep punctuated by strange and disturbing dreams. When dawn finally came I felt the hot breath of a snorting animal in my face and, startled, awoke to find a cow eating my mud-encrusted sleeping bag. I rolled it up as fast as I could and fled.

The following morning I arrived in Boscastle and was sure I had stepped into another world. Ancient cottages clustered around the narrow streets, golden sunlight sparkled on the languid waters of the old harbour, small fishing boats headed out to sea on the brimming tide and I sensed for the first time that inexpressible magic of the place. It was as if somehow the mind had been washed clean and one was looking at the world with the uncluttered eye of a child. It seemed an impossibly romantic place, as if it were somehow out of time. I was entranced, and have lived in North Cornwall ever since.

This personal interlude is mentioned because, many years later, I realised that something unspoken may have happened to me whilst on the Tor that night. Both Glastonbury and Tintagel share a common link in the Arthurian tradition—Tintagel as the place of the King's birth and Glastonbury, the Isle of Avalon, as his final resting place. These two locations thus mark the beginning and the end of the career of the legendary King around whom so much mythology has been woven down the ages. It was, then, at the very least, a curious coincidence that my introduction to this particular part of Cornwall was preceded by a strange sort of initiation on the Tor. Some twenty years later I was to return to Glastonbury whilst following the St Michael Line, as recounted in *The Sun and the Serpent*, and realised that the Tor is indeed the focus of powerful spiritual energies which have been recognised since prehistoric times, much like Tintagel itself.

In the years that followed I explored the hidden corners of this prescient landscape in an effort to discover the sources of its strange power. Little did I realise then that I may have been unconsciously responding to an impulse to immerse myself in much more than just the natural beauty of one of the most extraordinary landscapes in Britain. Only now do I see that it is a landscape that conceals, in its lanes, hills and spiritually potent places, an amazing message from the distant past.

Walking The Bear

Many visitors to this area of North Cornwall come to walk its countryside, with stunning views of the sea along its renowned cliff path between Boscastle and Tintagel, and the faery-haunted glades and meadows of the more intimate country inland. Walking along the outline of the Bear adds another dimension; not only can one experience the sensuous pleasures of the land itself, full of unexpected vistas and other surprises, but you can also meditate on why this giant figure should exist as a pattern in the landscape. For it is largely elevated above the surrounding area, and consequently does indeed seem to grow from the land, with its great head almost as if sculpted from the rock and earth that gives it shape.

The map on which I originally noticed the outline of the Bear and its associated sites was the old two-and-a-half-inch to the mile map 1325 from the Pathfinder series, for it was the only one on which the entire figure can be seen to exist as a whole. The more recent Explorer map 111 has most of the figure, but misses out the lower part of his leg, and others too, including the Landranger series, need to be joined together to appreciate the full effect. On the whole I prefer to work with the old one-inch to the mile maps, which are more informative and colourful than modern ones. They also preserve something of the old character of the landscape before new roads and developments changed it for ever.

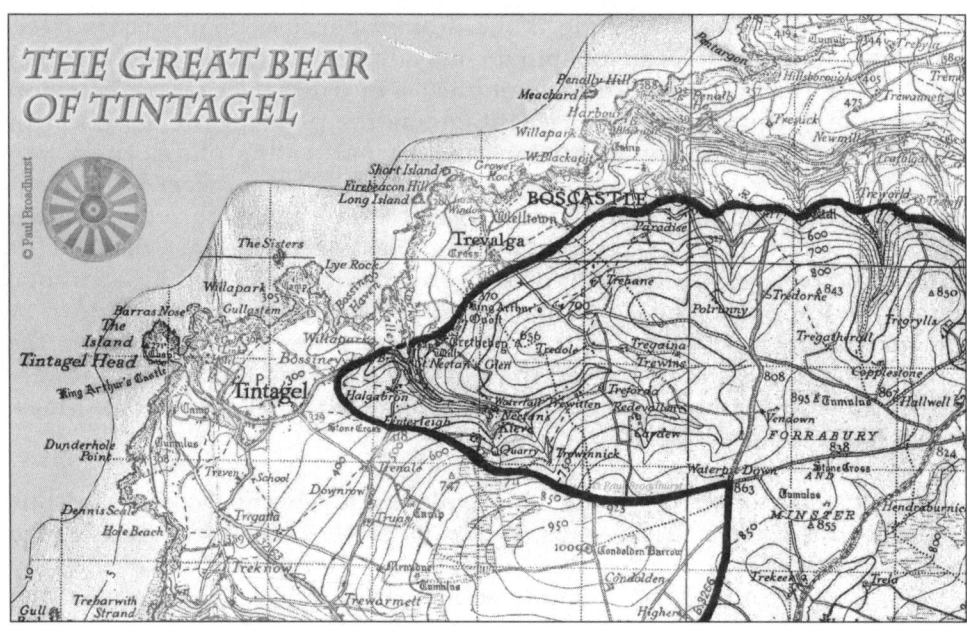

Looking at this map we can immediately see that the village of Boscastle is positioned right above the Crown of the Bear's Head as if implying a certain spiritual power. The site of the old castle, now a flat-topped grassy mound with cottages built into its side, with many incorporating stone from the original building, is an atmospheric place built on a spur above the valley along which the River Jordan flows. It was once the site of the abode of the Bottreaux family, and it is thought that *Bottreaux Castle* became Boscastle, giving the place its modern name. In 1873 Sir John Maclean noted that 'the sites of the outer and inner walls are very distinguishable' but this is not the case today. However, it is easy to visualise the castle looking down on the valley below, for it was of classic Norman circular design, but apparently not built with defensive purpose in mind. As Maclean observed 'we apprehend, however, that the castle could never have offered much resistance to an enemy, being commanded by higher ground on three of its sides'. This presents us with an enigma. If it was not built with defence in mind, we are left wondering why they chose this particular spot.

In the time of Henry VIII, the chronicler Leland noted on his travels through Cornwall that 'The Lord Bottreaux was lord of this town, a man of old Cornish lineage'. Their French name, however, refers to their Norman descent for they came from Brittany and spoke the same language as the Cornish; in fact some historians have speculated that they were originally Cornish themselves as Leland claimed, having been forced to move across the channel by Irish incursions. Certainly their ancestor Nicholas fought alongside William the Conqueror during the 'invasion' of Britain, for they were, like him, also descended from the Viking Rollo, the first Duke of Normandy.

Right from the beginning the Bottreaux family were deeply involved at the highest echelons of royal power. In the early years their name is variously spelled as *de Botherel*, *Bottril* or *Boteril* but later became the *Botreaux* or *Bottreaux* family as it is commonly spelt these days. They owned many manors throughout Cornwall and further afield and served as 'Sheriffs of Cornwall, knights of the shire, keeper of the keys to the king's castles and guardians of the priories' as local historians Rod and Anne Knight note in *The Book of Boscastle*. They were also involved in the affairs of national government and William Bottreaux II was in personal service to the King as well as Sheriff of Cornwall from 1205-09. A century or so later William Bottreaux IV performed military service overseas for the King and was again appointed Sheriff from 1320-23 and Governor of Tintagel Castle. His son Reginald, Sheriff at the time of the Black Prince, held 12 manors in Cornwall and a document from an inquiry at Launceston shows that he and his family were considered a different race altogether from the 'Englishmen' or Anglo-Saxons who were recorded in the area. Was this a reference to their ancient British or Norman background?

Further evidence of the importance of the Bottreaux family is that many of them were buried in the Priory at Launceston, the capital of Cornwall, and instructions were left that an armed man should ride before the body, to be rewarded with food and lodging for life by the monks; a quite striking example of the high esteem in which they were held. They were likely to have been members, or at the very least, affiliated to, the Knights Templar during their heyday, since one of

The Lamb of God - a symbol used by the Knights Templar - in Egloskerry Church.

the churches they were responsible for, at Egloskerry near their old manor of Penheale, has a remarkable tympanum of an *Agnus Dei*, or Lamb of God, the Templar insignia. Above the now blocked-up north door is also the only extant Cornish example of an Ouroborous, a dragon biting its own tail, resembling a figure-of-eight or the sign of infinity. We will in time come to discover that these symbols are not casual adornments but possess a definite meaning and purpose, and that the Bottreaux family were deeply involved in the Mystery Wisdom of the old British ways.

It is also extremely likely that the Bottreaux family were the ones who actually undertook the building of Tintagel Castle, probably during the time of Richard of Cornwall (historians now think it was built around 1230 although previously it was assigned to Earl Reginald almost a century earlier in the reign of Henry I). Should it be the case that the Bottreaux family were the builders of Tintagel Castle then it seems interesting that they chose to live in Boscastle rather than Tintagel or its environs, although Boscastle's natural harbour may help to explain this as it is the only safe port for some 40 miles along this part of the treacherous Cornish coast.

We will return to this intriguing family again in due course when looking at the apparent role such ancient families played in the guardianship of the Cornish landscape, but it may be of passing interest to note that the last of the Bottreaux, William X, who had travelled to both Rome and Jerusalem and was killed in the Battle of St Albans in 1462, left a daughter who married Sir Robert Hungerford, who inherited their estates. Curiously the most ancient hostelry in the Berkshire town of Hungerford is *The Bear*, where I once happened to stay many years ago. One of those coincidences, I expect. For now, though, we will continue 'walking the Bear' and focus on the places themselves and the things we can experience at first hand. It should, I hope, be a pleasurable and illuminating quest.

The village itself is justly famous for its quaint and picturesque qualities—the upper part for the medieval cottages that appear to grow organically from the very earth itself and the lower harbour area for its unique jetty and its generally dramatic aspect, especially during stormy weather. In the past, when it was a busy harbour, the village was also known for its collection of at least 18 public houses! The entrance to the harbour is dominated by a large rock outcrop known as *Profile Rock* or more commonly *Queen Victoria's Head* due to its resemblance to the doughty monarch, but before the Victorian Age it must have been called something similar, for it does indeed look like a mature female head crowned with a pinnacle of rock. Was it called Queen Bess's Head during the Elizabethan era, or by other appropriate names at different times?

Low Tide at Boscastle in the old days when it was the only safe haven along this part of the danger-ous North Cornish coast. Situated on the 'Crown' of the Great Bear it was the headquarters of the Bottreaux family who were probably responsible for the building of Tintagel Castle under the orders of Richard of Cornwall. The rocky outcrop on the right is called 'Queen Victoria's Head' and looks un-cannily like a mature female head from certain angles. It stares across the harbour entrance towards Tintagel, just three miles away.

Those who come here to visit the famous Museum of Witchcraft located in the harbour often comment that it looks very much like the presiding Goddess of the Land, some incredibly ancient female deity that guards the Bear's head. She stares across its mouth in the direction of Tintagel towards a white tower built originally as a watchtower by Revenue men looking for smugglers, and now used as a coastwatch lookout.

This tower stands on the living rock within a prehistoric enclosure known as Willapark (from the Brythonic Celtic words *whyllas* and *parc* meaning enclosed lookout) which is marked with earthworks and Bronze-Age barrows, one of the finest places in the county for observing sunsets over the Atlantic Ocean. As with so many other such sites in the West-country it is often described as an Iron Age Hillfort, but there is little evidence for this, and it was probably originally far older, having been adapted throughout the ages. People have been living here for many thousands of years, and their works are everywhere. Nearby are a group of rare surviving early medieval strip-fields or lynchets known as *The Stitches* which are still farmed today. Cyrus Redding observed in 1842 that these cliffs were the haunt of the red-legged chough, believed by Cornish folk to embody the spirit of King Arthur. The whole place has a timeless quality that can induce a dreamlike state of otherworldiness, of drifting off into a quieter, simpler world.

At certain states of the tide, though, the dreamer may be awoken by a great roar. Is this the Bear stirring? Well, those of a more imaginative disposition may think so, for it can sound uncannily like one at times. About an hour on either side of low tide a huge rumbling snort can be heard, accompanied by a waterspout and clouds of white spray that can gush right across the inlet on a good day. This is Boscastle's Blowhole, sometimes called *The Devil's Bellows*, caused by the pressure of water building up in a seacave that runs from the cliff into the harbour.

All these curious and historical features are of particular interest to us because the village, with its castle mound and prehistoric settlement is located directly above the 'Crown of the Bear'. Forrabury Church, near to the steep cliffs and close to the area known as *Paradise* directly on the Bear's head, has prehistoric associations too, for alongside it is a long raised earthwork of surprising dimensions. What its exact age and function was no-one knows, but it is highly unusual and is probably the *bury* in *Forrabury*. The evocative name Paradise comes from a monastic settlement of Cistercians who once had a walled garden here (which was traditionally called *Paradise* in reference to the Garden of Eden) where they grew healing herbs; a 'physick garden' through which flowed the River Jordan. Old stories tell of the white-robed monks sometimes appearing as ghostly figures on the cliffs close by.

As we can see, Boscastle is an interesting place full of many different layers of history. When we move outside the village other sites also suggest it once had a special significance beyond that of merely a natural harbour. For instance, about half-a-mile from the village is a cliff penetrated by deep caves that used to be visited for their geological interest. They can still be accessed by boat, but be warned; the scree cliff face is highly dangerous to the inexperienced rambler. However, the point is that this place is known as *Pentargon* — Cornish for *Arthur's Head*. To find such a place located just above the Bear's head is yet another of those curious 'coincidences' that will accompany this entire quest.

The caves at Pentargon — Cornish for Arthur's Head, *coincidentally located above the head of the Great Bear. (From an old postcard by local photographer Richard Webber).*

The Bear's Back

To begin with we find ourselves almost at the crossroads at the top of the village opposite the site of an ancient chapel to St James, once the personal chapel of the Bottreaux family (various stones from this can be seen leaning against the cottages on the hill). Following an old trackway called *Butt's Lane*, where local men used to practice their archery skills as a legal requirement a few hundred years ago, we drop down to a duck pond and an enormous clump of *Gunnera Manicata*, a sort of giant wild rhubarb, making the place seem like a scene from Alice in Wonderland. Close by a footpath leads across a field, past the most famous tree in Boscastle—

known as *The Fairy Tree* or *The Bell Tree*—actually an unusual form of Lime, with twisted branches that hang down to the ground, beloved of generations of children who love to climb up into its hollow interior. The path leads across the fields of Home Farm to a stile. This road then takes us to one of the most powerfully atmospheric churches in the whole of Cornwall, surrounded by ancient oak woods and much visited in the spring when it is literally smothered in daffodils and wild garlic.

Or rather, it is the sequestered site that is so atmospheric. For Minster Church itself has undergone extensive renovations since the roof collapsed one Sunday evening in the 1860s. The barrel vault roof with its ornate images, along with the beautifully carved bench ends, the box pews and the singers' gallery were all burnt, sold or given away, thus depriving us of its true ancient

Minster Church, which sits on the back of the Great Bear. Set in its secluded woodland dell it is a very atmospheric place, once the site of an important monastery that grew up around the hermitage of a Celtic Saint.

character. Yet still there is some indefinable presence within—it is like a silence so profound that one can actually hear it, especially during the hours of darkness.

Sunk in its wooded dell, it is a very ancient site, believed by some historians to have been founded by an early Celtic saint around 500 AD who lived in a rock-cut cell. Close by was a healing well, the site of which is believed to have been rediscovered on the lower slopes to the North of the church. It became the Mother Church of Boscastle and gave the place its earliest recorded name—*Talkar* or *Talkarn*—meaning *rock chapel*. The details of this saint are very hazy, but according to Victorian hagiographers (who used their fertile imaginations to add dramatic effect when nothing else was available) she was a Welsh Princess called *Madryn*, or *St Merthiana* or *Materiana* as she is known today. She is also the patron saint of the church on the cliffs overlooking Tintagel Island, and the presiding presence of the whole area in which the figure of the Bear is found. Could it be a coincidence that her current name includes the word *Mater*, Latin for *Mother*, implying that her name is merely a latinized version of a former Mother Goddess? If so, then what we know about the Bear Goddess of prehistory and this misty Celtic figure chime perfectly. These two churches have the distinction of being the only ones in Britain named after this particular saint.

The original church was built in about 1150 by William de Bottreaux whose father Nicholas had accompanied William the Conqueror, and was given to the Benedictine Order of St Sergius and St Dionysus of Anjou in France. It became an important priory or monastery with a healing shrine dedicated to the saintly Madryn that was very popular in the Middle Ages. Professor Charles Thomas has made a study of Minster (Latin for *monastery*) and concluded that it may have been a pilgrimage centre of some renown. Miraculous healings may have been part of its attraction, for in 1478 William of Worcester refers to two that he knew of, so it seems they may have been a regular occurrence. Pilgrims from Ireland, Wales and France would land in Boscastle Harbour to walk along the old trackway alongside the River Valency to visit the sacred place.

In passing, it should be mentioned that this valley has a very inspirational effect on many people. Thomas Hardy famously used to walk along it almost every day whilst he was restoring the nearby church of St Juliot's on the other side of the valley, courting his future wife Emma here and incubating his future novels that were to bring him fame and fortune. And one of the country's favourite pieces of music — *The Lark Ascending* by Ralph Vaughan Williams was composed whilst he was walking alongside the mellifluous stream. The shrine was destroyed during the Reformation, and the miraculous bones of St Madryn lost forever. All that remains of the shrine today is its granite lid lying just behind the font bearing signs of its possible later use as a threshold stone.

There are other curiosities at Minster. The graveyard outside has two striking trees, remarkable for their tortuous shapes. They seem to be dancing in the potent energy of the place, frozen in arboreal rhythms. The old monastery orchard and gardens can also be discerned buried under centuries of growth leading down to the river, and this is where the masses of wild garlic have come from that have spread over the whole area. An inexplicable carving of a pair of scissors which has baffled many historians can be seen on the tower. And if one examines the oldest, eastern part of the building, you can see where a former vicar (an amateur archaeologist) excavated underneath the area where the altar now stands, and by the looks of it put the stones back in a very hurried fashion. Did he find anything in some old crypt? We will probably never know.

As we leave Minster, we might wonder at its location, for it seems remote even today. For the villagers of Boscastle to walk the three or so miles to it for religious services in the past and the fact that it was an important monastery until the Dissolution, it must surely have had a certain significance that belies its apparent isolation. R. S. Hawker was deeply moved by the place, and penned a poem that captures some of its indefinable mystery:

The Minster of the Trees! A lonely dell
Deep with grey oaks, and 'mid their quiet shade
Grey with the moss of years: the cloister lowly laid
Where passing monks at solemn evening made.
Their chanting orisons; and as the breeze
Came up the vale, by rock and trees delay'd
They heard the awful voice of many seas
Blend with the passing hymn – thou Minster of the Trees.

Following the crumpled furry back of our beast along sunken leafy lanes we are led to the delightful tiny hamlet of Treworld. Archaeological excavations here have revealed the outlines of an early medieval farmstead which may signify that it was once more important than appears today. But what is of interest is the name. In this part of Cornwall, almost on the borders with England, many of the names are composites of the old Celtic tongue and the more recently introduced English. If this is the case then we have a very interesting name indeed, for *Tre* in old Cornish means dwelling or farmstead, and *world* would seem to refer to the Earth itself. Situated directly on the back of the Bear this gives the place a certain cosmological dimension in terms of the Bear guarding the Pole of the Heavens, as if the world itself is supported, or its balance maintained, by the Bear. Such a thought may seem somewhat obscure at this point, but later in this quest will assume a quite extraordinary significance. For the moment, though, we will contain our enthusiasm to learn why this should be so and carry on walking along a road that may seem narrow and tranquil today, but in the past was something of a bustling thoroughfare.

This is no mere idle fancy, for this winding lane was once the main road to our next port of call, Lesnewth. Down a steep hill and across a ford, we come to a Holy Well in a meadow on the right, and then follow the splashing roadside stream to the church with its small gathering of cottages and farms. It seems very peaceful nowadays, but Lesnewth was once the administrative centre for the entire area, known as the Hundred of Trigg Minor (a Hundred was a sort of Anglo-Saxon parish). There is very little now to remind us of its glory days, for the church has been heavily 'restored'. Charles Henderson, in his *Cornish Church Guide*, commented on this when he wrote 'Prior to the deplorable restoration of 1866 the church was a Norman cruciform building of great interest...' However, today the whole place gives the impression of a sleepy hamlet where nothing ever happens. How different it must have been centuries ago when the Courts of Justice and all the other accoutrements of local power resided here.

Towards the East this road crosses a junction and then gradually diminishes until it terminates at Helsett Farm, creating the effect of the figure of the Bear appearing spontaneously from the marshy downland. It is as if this effigy is sufficiently demonstrated, or that the Bear is, in some indefinable way, growing out of the very land itself.

One other feature in this immediate area is of interest, brought to my attention by local farmer Kevin Gibbs. It is a rough, triangular, currently neglected, privately owned piece of tree-covered land on which rise a number of springs. However, it bears the hallmarks of having been an important place and an ancient stone cross of extreme age, judging by its appearance, once stood by its boundary, now re-erected about half-a-mile away. A public footpath crosses the land, also indicating that it was notable in the distant past. Its name gives the clue: *Halwell* is one of the many names that occur where a *Holywell* was once located. Close examination of this site reveals that two springs in particular rise from this piece of ground. One is pure, clear water, and the other is chalybeate or iron-bearing, colouring the water dark red and staining the rock down which it cascades. This would perhaps not be so worthy of note if the two springs did not rise just a few feet from each other. This is a remarkable geological occurrence.

The only other place to my knowledge where a similar feature is found is at the foot of Glastonbury Tor where the 'Red Spring' of the famous Chalice Well and the nearby 'White Spring' converge. In Arthurian tradition, the Red Spring symbolises the Holy Blood of Christ and is connected with the legend of Joseph of Arimathea, who is reputed to have brought the Holy Grail, the receptacle that caught the blood of Christ, to Britain. Here, intriguingly, we have a close parallel to the famous Glastonbury springs, again linked with Arthurian tradition, but this time connected with the Bear. In fact its position is made even more remarkable in that the springs are located in exactly that area of the Bear's effigy where we might expect the heart to lie. Here the red waters gushing from the depths of the Earth appear to symbolise the lifeblood of the land in a potent symbolic allusion. Does this highly unusual feature symbolically represent the life force of the land? Is this the Heart of the Bear?

The Bear's Paw

Before moving on to explore the Head of the Bear and its important associations with Tintagel and its environs, we will take a brief detour to examine what looks like a giant shaggy front leg with its paw resting on the town of Camelford. Indistinct though it may appear at first, it is just possible to see this shape, which we might be inclined to dismiss were it not for the significant Arthurian connections located here.

Tracing the leading edge of the Bear's leg we follow the road from the crossroads at Waterpit Down along the B2366 towards Camelford, past a dwelling known as *King's Acre*, that only a few short years ago had its garden ringed with worn granite boulders that looked as if they may have come from a stone circle or other megalithic site. One has to allow a little imagination when coming to the town itself, for the roads have changed drastically during recent times. However, it seems that there is a giant paw resting on Valley Truckle, with its furry outline continuing along from Tregoodwell (yet another old Holy Well by the side of the road) towards Davidstow, with views of nearby Roughtor with its Neolithic and Bronze Age settlements.

Camelford derives its name from the River Camel, and old Cornish traditions have linked it strongly with the Arthurian tales. This is not surprising since *Cam*, in the old British language, means *crooked*, and the old name for the river was the *Alan*. The two together create the name *Camalan* and, according to Sir Thomas Malory's *Morte d'Arthur*, Camlann is the traditional site of the final defeat of King Arthur by his treacherous half-brother Mordred.

Located right in the middle of this great Bear's leg is the place known as Slaughterbridge (still in the parish of Minster), long believed to be the actual site of this battle. In fact the area around the bridge over the River Camel is full of ancient remains, with a medieval village called Old Melorne, whose remnants can still be seen in an overlooking field, and also the site of a genuine battle believed to have taken place between the Celts and the Saxons around 825 AD. In fact some historians think that there may have been more than one battle here during the Dark Ages, and Leland in his day noted that here 'pieces of armour, rings, and brass furniture for horses are sometimes digged up...'

Close by is an uprooted megalith that has been used at one time as a footbridge over the river, known variously as *King Arthur's Stone* or *King Arthur's Grave*. A later chronicler, Richard Carew, observed in Elizabethan times that '...*upon the River Camel was the last dismal battle strooken between the noble King Arthur and his treacherous nephew Mordred wherein one took his death and the other his death's wound. For testimony whereof the old folk hereabouts will show you a stone, bearing Arthur's name...*'. Carew thought he could make out an inscription that spelt *Atri*, which he felt was a corrupted form of Arthur. In fact it bears a memorial inscription in Latin, appropriately to a Roman soldier named 'Latinus, Son of Magarius' which we could hardly expect countryfolk of that era to understand. But it could well be much older, for there is a long tradition of megaliths being re-used as memorials and early Christian crosses. Its size would certainly appear excessively large for the gravestone of a Roman soldier compared to other known examples.

Another interesting fact is that the Elizabethan Manor of Worthy-vale (once the property of the Bottreaux family), where the stone is found, was called in the Domesday Book *Guerdevalan*, a name that sounds suspiciously like the word *Avalon*, the otherworldly place where King Arthur was supposed to have been taken. One day, so the story goes, his wounds will be healed from his battle with the dark Mordred, and he will return to restore his rightful realm.

With all these curious facts emerging to mark this spot as one of the most important in Arthurian legend, it does indeed appear significant that it is located on the front leg of our giant Bear. We might even begin to suspect that the story of King Arthur's battle at this place could be a later version of a folk memory of something far, far older.

King Arthur's Stone at Slaughterbridge, on the leg of the Great Bear. It is inscribed with a memorial to a Roman soldier named Latinus, but Cornish tradition says it marks the site of King Arthur's last battle.

5

THE LAIR OF THE BEAR

s we leave Paradise, the old monastic site on the Crown of the Bear's head, we walk along the coast road between Boscastle and Tintagel with occasional dramatic views of the edge of the towering cliffs and ocean beyond. A glance backwards and the white tower of *The Lookout* on Willapark stands in solitary isolation on the summit of its rockfast prehistoric enclosure. In front of us lies one of the most striking landscapes in Britain, densely packed with breathtaking natural features and ancient sites that have given rise to a rich tapestry of legends.

Walking the Bear's head is a journey through the pages of history, with each age leaving its mark. This faded palimpsest of the past goes back beyond the Victorian and medieval tales of the birth of King Arthur, who rose to become the figurehead of a Golden Age and its eventual demise, to a world of Celtic magic, here still within our reach. Some of the places we are to encounter have the power to strip away the flashy veneer of the modern world revealing memories of what may seem like an impossibly distant time. Yet strangely, we can often find ourselves slipping into that dreamlike state where the past, present and even the future all seem to co-exist together. This is the power of the land, to awaken us from our deep sleep.

The first place we come to on the upper brow of the Bear is the Elizabethan Welltown Manor, its entrance marked by the base of an old granite signpost. This fine private house still retains its oak beams and circular stone staircase. It featured in the Victorian novel *John Herring* by the prolific author and eclectic vicar Sabine Baring Gould, a friend of Hawkers, some of whose family lived in Boscastle. It was the home of a well-known local family, the Tinks, and the initials *B T* can still be seen over the doorway in memory of Benjamin Tink who built it. One of the bells in Forrabury Church is inscribed *John Tink 1812*. This unusual house is one of a collection of Elizabethan houses within the environs of the Bear, along with Reddevallen, the one-time Manor House of nearby Trevalga.

These Elizabethan links are interesting, as it was during this age that there was a great flowering of Arthurian ideals initiated by such luminaries as Edmund Spenser, Philip Sydney and Elizabeth's astrologer the magus John Dee, who claimed to speak with angels and wrote a number of books calling for a renaissance of the Arthurian spirit. In the days when Science and Magic were seen as one and the same his many varied interests included star-gazing and navigation; he counted amongst his circle Francis Drake, John Hawkins and Walter Raleigh, fellow Arthurians who laid the foundation for what they thought of as another Golden Age and the re-creation of the British Empire last seen during King Arthur's reign. Sir Francis Drake in particular is to feature significantly in the unfolding story that follows; his association with the area is of considerable interest.

Trevalga, where we find ourselves next, is one of the most unspoilt villages in the whole county, and looks likely to remain so at a time when local families who have often been here for generations find it almost impossible to live in the place of their birth due to a recent explosion in the price of property. Trevalga is like an oasis in this desert of accommodation, and is largely protected from the developers due to a strange twist of fate. It was bequeathed as a Trust by the last Lord of the Manor, Gerald Curgenven on his death in 1959 and is managed in the traditional manner where those who have connections with the area are favoured above the estate agent or summer rent. It is today owned by Marlborough College, the famous public school in Wiltshire. If this seems a little odd, then here we have an even more curious fact; Marlborough College grew up around the site of a prehistoric mound, one of those artificial flat-topped conical hills that are such a notable feature of the ancient landscape. They were in effect the centres of power where laws were proclaimed and kings enthroned and often date back to the prehistoric era. It is sometimes assumed that the Normans were responsible for the Motte and Bailey structures on which their castles stood, yet it is often the case that they simply adapted existing mounds which pre-dated their arrival.

This one in particular, though, has an intriguing connection with our own quest. In old British lore, this mound, which has very ancient oaks growing around its summit and can still be visited, is reputed to be the burial place of Merlin. In fact it is known as Merlin's Mound, and originally gave its name to the town of Marlborough, *Merlin's Barrow*.

How could a remote outpost of the Cornish countryside have such a mythic resonance with a far-away Wiltshire town close to Avebury, the greatest Neolithic Temple complex in Britain? This cannot be easily answered, yet we have noted before how 'Arthurian' landscapes appear to have links that go far beyond the realities of the everyday world. One possibility is that a certain strata within society is initiated into the mysteries that lie beyond the veil of the mundane levels of existence, understand the innate power of the ancient legends and seek to perpetuate them in the same manner as the dynasties of Normans and their successors. As we continue this quest we will become increasingly aware of a great deal of circumstantial evidence showing that certain families saw themselves as guardians of some ancient wisdom of which the ordinary world is almost entirely unaware.

We have seen how these landscapes draw creative personalities to them because of their inspirational energy. Trevalga is no exception to this, and the formerly well-known literary figure, man of letters and amateur archaeologist J.D. Cook, who was born in Camelford, settled here. He is buried in St Materiana's churchyard at Tintagel.

Trevalga Church is a delight for those who love old churches and stands more or less in a farmyard, along with a wheel-headed cross that could be as early as the eighth century. It is dedicated to St Petroc, one of the early fathers of Celtic Christianity, who came from Wales and founded religious communities at Padstow and Bodmin. His emblem was the stag (often associated with Merlin in the form of a White Hart) and his legend tells how he was awoken by an angel and commanded to go on a mission to Brittany, leaving his sheepskin mantle and staff guarded by a wolf. Perhaps it is not surprising that St Petroc's legend has these sha-manic overtones, for he was more a Druidic than Christian priest, coming from a background of deeply-rooted Celtic mysticism.

The lane from the village leads to a crossroads that marks its edge, and, crossing the road outlining the Bear's brow, runs up a steep and narrow hill past a converted chapel to the Old Rectory, where there is a Holy Well that has been recently restored. In a field opposite is a slate standing stone, rare in this vicinity. Could this area have been an old sacred site that marked the Bear's eye, with its monolith looking right over the coast down below? From this spot you can see both Tintagel and Boscastle, the only place in the area where one view encompasses the whole length of the Bear's head. Or could it mark the Bear's third eye, its organ of spiritual perception?

If this is the case, then the real Bear's eye could well be located further along the road, at the hamlet of Trethevy. Here is an impressive collection of ancient monuments that retain an atmosphere of extreme age. By the side of the main road are the sad remains of a fallen megalithic dolmen known as *King Arthur's Quoit*. Close by is an old crossroads around which congregate a very interesting group of buildings. Immediately, one comes across castellated walls which create the boundary between the lane and the gardens of a former monastic foundation, later a manor house. This area is haunted, quite literally, by the ghosts of the past. For many years I used to visit friends living further along in St Nectan's Glen and would walk back down Genver Lane, a very ancient trackway, in the dark. Personally, I never encountered anything more than a rather spooky incident where a dog barked frantically at some unseen presence. How-ever, on more than one occasion these friends were sure someone was walking towards them—only when they said 'Good Evening', and the figure walked right through them, leaving a distinct chill in the atmosphere, did they realise it was some sort of apparition. Trethevy is well-known for such strange phenomena, and many who live in the area have had similar ghostly experiences.

The old manor house is largely medieval, with a Holy Well overshadowed by an ancient walnut tree outside the entrance. In the bathroom is a curious thick slate set in the wall, with a 'squint' hole opposite. This is said to be the place where monks would lie to perform an uncomfortable penance for some misdemeanour, with a viewing hole so that the Prior could ensure they were indeed 'suffering' sufficiently. There is also a local story of a former tenant hanging himself in the house, and it certainly does have a strange feeling inside. A few years ago it was a plant nursery, and whilst strolling around the gardens you would come across the highly unusual sight of a Roman milestone standing amongst the greenery. The existence of this (and another at Tintagel Church) can only mean that the area was of considerable importance to the Romans, with the road to Tintagel prominently marked. Why? There were no metals to trade, and the land has always been impoverished and unproductive compared to other areas. There must have been some other good reason beyond trade and commerce.

Almost opposite the old manor house is one of the gems of the area—a tiny chapel dedicated to St Piran. Walking through its door is like stepping through time, for it has the feeling of a primitive Celtic chapel, with little adornment and an aura of simple sanctity. Its old stone walls have seen many changes through the ages, having at one time even become a pigsty! It was given back to the Church in 1941, when it had a massive greenstone altar slab and the remains of stone seats around the walls. There is little doubt that this was the original chapel for the monks, since the field behind has always been known as Chapel Field. It is a place to

sit quietly and meditate, perhaps wishing for insights ourselves as we are here positioned right on the Bear's eye, looking directly at Tintagel Island.

Opposite the chapel is a highly unusual pyramid-shaped Holy Well surmounted with an iron cross, also dedicated to Cornwall's patron St Piran. To one side of it are the remains of an early building butted up against it made out of massive upright slates, one with a small window cut into it. Could this have been part of the collection of buildings from the monastic settlement, or was it an early well-chapel? If so, it is unique in Cornwall.

St Piran's Well at Trethevy. This curious pyramid-shaped building stands above a spring that has quenched the thirst of pilgrims bound for Tintagel since ancient times.

Beyond Trethevy the road turns and descends rapidly, making a fierce hairpin bend. This creates a distinctive 'kink' in the outline of our Bear due to the steeply-inclined valley along which the River Trevillet flows.

But those with an eye for ancient features will note the remains of an older route, now overgrown, which looks as though it may have been the original track before the road was modernised. Here is a place to pause a while before following a footpath down to the river, where there is a small bridge by Trevillet Mill overhung by ivy-covered cliffs. It is a particularly magical area that leads to another, ruined, mill. A few feet away are two notable rock-cut carvings of labyrinths believed to be from the Bronze Age. These are the famous Rocky Valley Mazes, a seemingly inexplicable mystery, first discovered by Dr Sidney Madge in 1948 when they were covered in vegetation.

They depict the classic 'Cretan' labyrinth that occurs worldwide, as shown on coins excavated from Knossos (except in reverse) and have long been one of the great curiosities of the area. What they are doing on a Cornish rock face nobody knows. Some say they are evidence of direct contact with the Mediterranean (not so far-fetched as one might imagine, for large quantities of fine pottery from this area have been excavated on Tintagel Island). Others point out that they are part of the long-standing tradition of 'Troy-towns' or maze patterns that go back deep into British folklore. Still others, especially witches and practitioners of magic, say they are magical tools that symbolise the brain with its two halves, and that by tracing the pattern with your finger, or 'finger-walking' as it is known, you can achieve a heightened state of consciousness as if balancing the left-hand and the right-hand sides of the brain. But why here? It seems an unlikely spot, sunk in the penumbral twilight of this lonely dell.

One of the Rocky Valley Mazes, an ancient symbol that some authorities have suggested might be linked to the circling motion of the Seven Stars of the Great Bear.

One visitor to these maze patterns was Geoffrey Russell, who had experienced a mystical revelation concerning the same labyrinthine designs. He likened the symbol to a type of mandala, which when used for meditation may allow the mind to access a state of quiescence so it could penetrate the veil of the invisible realms. He thought it connected to one of the earliest accounts of King Arthur, *The Spoils of Annwn*, written in about 1200 but, like other such works, drawn from the Dark Ages which in turn derived from earlier material. In this, King Arthur and his fellow companions enter the Underworld to search for a wonder-working cauldron, the earliest mention of a miraculous vessel that later became the Holy Grail. Another author, Geoffrey Ashe, suggested, in *The Ancient Wisdom*, that the seven coils of the maze represented the circling path of the Seven Stars of the Great Bear, with the Pole at its centre. This idea has evidently been current for a very long time, for the Masonic writer Gerald Massey, in *The Natural Genesis*, also claims that the spiral maze is an analogue of 'the seven encirclers of the Great Bear'. Of course the most famous legend attached to labyrinths such as this come from ancient Crete, where Theseus bravely entered the lair of the Minotaur—half man, half beast—to do battle, and then find his way out again by following Ariadne's thread. This, it seems, is an allegorical story of how we must go deep within ourselves to conquer the animal instincts that lurk at the very threshold of our consciousness, and then re-emerge transformed.

Another writer on mystical matters, Walter Johannes Stein, summed this idea up succinctly in *The Death of Merlin; Arthurian Myth and Alchemy*: *'The labyrinth was thus a temple representing the convolutions and windings of the human brain, to remind the beholder that without the thread of intelligence, without logic, escape from the labyrinth was impossible. Only Theseus, the man of intelligence, could, with the aid of the Ariadne thread of logic, overcome the animal man, the Minotaur.'*

The location of the Mazes seems highly significant in this case. They appear as if positioned virtually on the outline of the Bear. This might lead us to consider that they do indeed pinpoint a particular place of spiritual power, the bridge of the Bear's snout which could be interpreted as its organ of smell. It is a strange thought, but bears are renowned for their sensitivity in this respect; they can detect the smell of humans and animals from a very great distance. This is probably their most developed sense. Or is it a place where we, as humans, can synchronise ourselves to the breathing rhythms of the Great Bear, the Earth Mother, in the same way that using the Mazes might create a sympathetic link between the circling rhythms of the Great Bear in the sky?

The path alongside the river leads to an area well-known for its mystical presence where many people claim to have seen faeries and other elemental nature spirits. The tumbling waters have sculpted hollow bowls in the rock down which the torrent pours, leading to a narrow inlet pounded by the sea. It is a wild place where the waves crash against the rocks uncompromisingly, and the Atlantic is at its most dramatic. It is awe-inspiring but awesome, like the character of this entire coast. Beautiful, but terrifying. A few years ago it claimed a sacrifice—an onlooker, lost in the power of the ocean, was snatched by a wave in a split second as his friends cried out. He was never seen alive again.

Walking the road to Tintagel we are led up the other side of the steep hill from Rocky Valley to Bossiney. If we were to take a detour to Bossiney Haven, with its beach and towering cliffs, we would pass close by the remains of a medieval village, now just an area of overgrown hummocks. Further along towards the sea is a petrifying well, where the mineral-rich waters can 'fossilize' a piece of cloth.

Bossiney appears at first to be just a fairly ordinary collection of cottages and houses on the outskirts of Tintagel, but its history is of special interest. For nearly four hundred years until the reform act of 1832 it was a borough, returning two members of Parliament (voted for by its half-dozen electors!). Leland noted that the ruins of a 'great numbre' of houses could be seen in his day, for Bossiney was a place of far greater importance in the past.

These M.P.s were inaugurated on the summit of the ancient earthwork known as Bossiney Mound at the western end of the village, just visible from a gateway where the road forks. Today it is in a private garden, planted with trees and flowers, with an old well known as Jill Pool forming a trickling stream at its farthest side. An ancient and impressive stone bowl graces the garden, looking for all the world like a giant grail. Some of the Mound has been removed at some time in its history, but with the coming of the Normans it was a classic *Motte and Bailey*, probably with wooden palisades. It thus became the symbolic power centre of the area, and the meadow in front served as the village green where almost anything could be bought and sold — including slaves. During the time of Richard, Earl of Cornwall (around 1250), he granted rights and privileges to this small borough equal to those of Cornwall's capital at Launceston. This seems highly unusual, to say the least, and indicates the one-time importance of this out of the way place.

On old maps, next to Bossiney Mound is a 'court' in that Gothic lettering used to denote places of antiquity. This refers to the Elizabethan Court House, now Tintagel Pottery. A stone carved with a Celtic-style head is built into one of its corners, and may well come from an earlier building on the site. Its use as a court probably derives originally from the Mound itself, for such sites are known as centres of ritual where laws and judgements were proclaimed. This is undoubtedly why M.P.s were elected on its summit (a custom that carried on until quite recent times with the Liberal M.P. John Pardoe, who represented the constituency of North Cornwall for a number of years.) But by far the most famous M.P. for Bossiney was Sir Francis Drake, who built Borough House on the opposite side of the road. Its immensely thick walls have had, over the last six centuries, an interesting collection of visitors. At one time it was owned by the playwright J.B. Priestley, who was so deeply fascinated by the mysterious properties of time and human consciousness.

Why Drake chose to become M.P. for Bossiney, a poor and remote place in his day, is an interesting question. Was it because he wished to align himself with the Arthurian mythology that was enjoying such a renaissance in his time? Drake was an enigmatic character of many parts, and besides his exploits as an explorer and maritime adventurer became Mayor of Plymouth, performing many public-spirited works including the first constant supply of fresh water piped from Dartmoor, a considerable feat of civil engineering. But he appeared to have a great interest in matters mystical, too (see appendix II). Was Drake trying to conjure up the spirit of King Arthur? If so, he seems to have succeeded to a remarkable degree, for he somehow drew to himself the same heroic aura. His exploits at sea earned him a mythic immortality as a sort of maritime Arthur, who was in league with powerful forces. At the time of the defeat of the Spanish Armada it was commonly believed that the magic of the Merlin-like John Dee, Drake's mentor, had caused a sudden storm to blow up out of nowhere, scattering the Spanish fleet. Commemorative medals were struck to celebrate this mystic event. As a saviour of the nation, Drake has gone down in history as a heroic legendary figure who will one day return, just like King Arthur, when the country needs him.

It looks as if we can safely conclude that Drake's connection with Bossiney was more than sheer chance. As a Westcountryman he would have been aware of the famous legends of the area, particularly of King Arthur's birth at Tintagel. And, like King Arthur, the folklore surrounding him was to become something of an industry. The Spanish feared him as a magician who could command the winds by the Devil's aid and had a magic mirror (like Dee) to spy on their fleets. Local Devon folk told how he created fire-ships by magic to defeat the Armada, how he turned Buckland Abbey, a former Cistercian monastery, from a ruin to a mansion in just three days, and how a spirit warned him through his magic mirror of his wife's impending remarriage. After his death off Panama in 1595, various mementoes were brought home to Buckland Abbey, including his drum, which, it is said, will be heard to beat again upon his imminent return.

One of the other notable things about the links between Drake and King Arthur is his name: *Drake* is old English for *dragon*, and *Uther Pendragon* was Arthur's father, who famously sired the prince on Tintagel Island with the aid of Merlin as recounted by Geoffrey of Monmouth. A man like Sir Francis Drake must inevitably have seen himself following in the mythical footsteps of the old British legends, even so far as helping to create a revival in the new era of confidence and self-belief in national destiny that was at the heart of the Elizabethan Age.

Perhaps the most interesting thing about Bossiney Mound is an old legend attached to the place. Baring Gould, that indefatigable collector of folklore and local legends recorded that:

> 'According to Cornish tradition, King Arthur's Round Table lies deep in the earth buried under this circular earthen mound; only on Midsummer's night does it rise, and then the flash of light from it for a moment illumines the sky, after which the golden table sinks again. At the end of the world it will come to the surface again and be carried to heaven, and the saints will sit and eat at it and Christ will serve them.'

Like the mound at Boscastle it appears to have had little defensive function or superior position given the surrounding landscape. A story like this attached to Bossiney Mound holds another clue to the likelihood that it may have been there when the Normans arrived. In fact the legend itself seems a surprising reference to the Mound having orginally had a cosmological function. A wealth of evidence will underline this idea as we proceed on this quest, for *King Arthur's Round Table* is a metaphor for the stars that endlessly circle the Axis of the heavens—the North Pole around which the heavenly Great Bear revolves. But here is one of the first clues that the true origins of this legend is to be found in the skies. Our Bear in the landscape appears tethered to Bossiney Mound, situated at the very tip of his nose, as if it were an earthly counterpart of the still point of the heavenly realms.

This allusion to the Round Table being 'buried in the earth' might strike us as fanciful or meaningless superstition were it not for our understanding that it symbolically represents the localised 'Pole' of the landscape where Heaven and Earth come together. Local lore tells of this place having a castle on it long before the more famous 'King Arthur's Castle' was built on the Island, probably a folk memory of the early date of the Mound. This would naturally have been adopted by the Norman lords, very likely the Bottreaux family, who were well-versed in the mythical history of the area.

But why should the Round Table only rise on Midsummer's night? This is when the Sun is at its most powerful, a sort of Golden Age, before beginning to decline until its death at Midwinter. Here we have the crucial cycles of earthly life encapsulated in a very concise mythic formula: the Great Bear is the guardian of the Pole since the earliest Ages of mankind when the omnipresent circumpolar stars represented cosmic order and stability. Later, when a more Sun-oriented ethos took hold, the King who represented this orderly realm of the Round Table became a solar hero surrounded by his twelve knights, or zodiacal influences, each with their own characteristics. (In Geoffrey of Monmouths' account Arthur fights 12 battles, probably another reference to the Sun passing through the signs of the zodiac). As such, he reaches his prime, and is then 'wounded', with his virility and power declining until his 'death' at the Winter Solstice. The King is dead, Long Live the King! For he is to be reborn and return, the eternal cycle repeating itself until the end of time. Here we have a reference to the true origins of the Arthurian mythos—the endless round of the Earth spinning through the heavens, its central axis guarded by the Great Bear, and the birth, triumph and death of the Sun King lived out on Earth.

Bossiney Mound is a place of strong atmosphere, where history hangs in the air alongside a tangible feeling of spiritual energy. Those who are sensitive to such manifestations can feel this energetic influence, and when the dowser Hamish Miller measured the earth energies at this spot he concluded that it had the power of 'a large cathedral', with two massive 'dragon' currents crossing at its centre. Local writer and publisher Michael Williams, who used to live nearby, once put the legend of the Round Table to the test by visiting the Mound with a number of others on Midsummer's night. As they approached the small chapel built into its side they saw glowing lights shining eerily through the windows. As the place was locked and empty there seemed no other explanation than something mysterious had occurred. The experience had a deep effect on him, and since then he has spent much of his time exploring, writing and publishing books about legends and the supernatural.

As we leave this now innocuous-looking Mound that has such profound and hidden depths to it we begin to realise that this Bear in the landscape is no mere figment of our imagination, but a true mystery whose existence speaks of some ancient understanding where the patterns on the Earth symbolically reflect the patterns in the Heavens. As above, so below.

Following the Bear's outline from the tip of its nose towards where we would expect its mouth to be, we come to an ancient stone cross at Fenterleigh, a footpath that takes us towards Halgabron, and then through ancient woodland to yet another remarkable place. St Nectan's Kieve is one of the most strangely-beautiful and powerful of all Cornish sites. Everyone who visits it for the first time is invariably awed into silence as they stand at the bottom of the tree-covered gorge, looking up at a stunning sight. The waters of the River Trevillet pour over a rocky cleft to tumble in a spray of silver mist into a great rock bowl, or *Kieve* in Cornish, whose sides have been smoothed by the power of the water. This is dramatic enough, but then the water brims through a large hole in the rock, just wide enough for someone to climb through. In fact some do as part of a rite of rebirth, such is its symbolic power, although it is not recommended since it can be very dangerous. It has the appearance of being a natural formation, yet it is impossible to imagine how a river could create such a unique feature. Could it be a sort of elemental sculpture purposefully designed to enhance and amplify the Voice of the Bear?

It is little wonder, then, that the place has gathered around it some interesting legends. One is of the eponymous saint himself, which is probably a later version of the Celtic river god *Nechtan* who also occurs in other regions. An earlier version is spelled Knighton. He is reputed to have made his sanctuary above the mystic waterfall in this secluded spot in about the sixth century. Here he built a tower in which hung a silver bell with which he communicated with the monks of Tintagel. He died at a time when the Celtic faith was being eradicated in favour of the newer Roman version of Christianity, and on his deathbed prophesied that one day the older, simpler faith of his forebears would return. After his death, he was interred in an oak chest underneath it, along with his silver bell, which, so the story goes, can still be heard at certain times.

The story of St Nectan reminds us that these old saints are often little more than a folk memory of former gods and goddesses deriving from the old Celtic and Druidic traditions. In regions such as Cornwall these beliefs were never really forgotten for they lingered on in local lore and customs for many centuries. Even in Victorian times such stories, known as drolls, were told around the hearth, much as they had been for thousands of years. The tales of faeries, giants, King Arthur and the Celtic saints were a direct link with the old natural philosophy and embodied the immemorial traditions of the landscape. And, as we are in the process of discovering, they often have more than a grain of truth in them. The idea of St Nectan communicating with the monks of Tintagel is strangely echoed by an interesting fact that can be seen on the Ordnance Survey map; the waterfall, Bossiney Mound and Tintagel Castle are all in direct alignment (or communication), with both the waterfall and Castle being exactly a mile from the Mound. Both these qualities, straightness and measurement, relate to rulers and hence to the concept of rulership.

What might St Nectan's Kieve represent in the body of our Great Bear? As we stand there, lost in the roaring sound of the rushing waters resonating throughout the rocky chasm, there can only be one conclusion: this is the 'throat' of the Bear. Its roaring is created by the river that cascades over the waterfall into the ravine that amplifies the sound, and then runs down through the haunted valley eventually to pass within yards of the Rocky Valley Mazes. Its roaring is perfectly in synchrony with its environment, for as the Goddess of the Earth it is governed by the weather patterns of the atmosphere. On a wild stormy day it can be intimidating, such is the sound that echoes so powerfully through the gorge. On a gentler summer's day it can be mesmerisingly peaceful, with a gentle stream whispering out of the hole in the rocky curtain.

This is a place of otherworldly manifestations. It is very common for people to photograph strange light effects, especially the phenomenon known nowadays as 'orbs'; bright globes of light that manifest only in the camera, as if they are beyond the range of normal sight. Some appear to have 'spirit faces' in them when enlarged, as if denizens of other realms are looking out at us from a different dimension. Hooded figures are also reported, both at the waterfall and amongst the gnarled trees of the Glen. The whole area is infested with tales of apparitions, ghostly occurrences and strange happenings.

Is this the place where the Earth Mother, the terrestrial version of the Great Bear of the heavenly realms, speaks to us? Many people find this place deeply moving and in recent years it has become a focus for earth-honouring rites and also as a place of healing. It is important to emphasise that such a natural shrine should be treated with the utmost reverence and respect, for as the old Cornish legends remind us, to do otherwise is to invite the displeasure (and perhaps even worse) of the unseen realms.

After this collection of truly extraordinary sites located in and around the head of our Bear, many of them delineating its shape, the road outlining the lower regions of the head has little further of interest except that its shape suggests a furry jowl. Our next task is to explore the place that this giant image is staring so intently at — Tintagel itself.

Tintagel Island, joined to the mainland by a narrow isthmus. Every high tide the sea rushes into Merlin's Cave on the landward side of the Island. Its unique situation has contributed to its all-pervading mystery down through the centuries. Famous as the place of King Arthur's conception and birth, and thought to have been the site of a royal citadel from Celtic times, it was here that a castle was built in the thirteenth century by Richard of Cornwall. The evocative ruins of this castle are visited by hundreds of thousands of people every year who seek to immerse themselves in the legend of Arthur. What gives this legend such a power over the human imagination? The existence of a giant landscape effigy of a Great Bear looking straight at it provides a mysterious connection between the landscape here and the constellation of the Great Bear that endlessly circles the Pole Star.

6

ISLAND OF THE KINGS

hrough the soft-focus lens of history Tintagel Island appears as a place shrouded in mystery, its beginnings lost in a world of ancient magic. We have already seen how Geoffrey of Monmouth, the chronicler of its legend, was commissioned by Norman churchmen to preserve what remained of the old British lore. Such was the apparent interest in the Celtic traditions that Alexander, Bishop of Lincoln, urged him to finish his work on the *Prophecies of Merlin* before embarking on *The History of the Kings of Britain*, the book revealing the legendary history of the British race which included the story of King Arthur's birth. Before Geoffrey little was accessible in written form to historians, and Henry of Huntingdon records his astonishment at finding a copy of *The History* at the Norman Abbey of Bec in 1139, for he had never before come across such a work.

The question we need to address is why did these influential Normans wish to preserve for all time ancient legends that would otherwise undoubtedly have been lost? This was a time when the once-vibrant oral traditions of the Celtic world were in decline, and had they not been written down these stories may have been consigned to the realms of superstition, and forgotten forever.

The answer can only be that the Normans considered themselves to be a part of this tradition. Certainly they did everything they could to maintain and transform it for a new age. Geoffrey was only one of a series of authors who were to rewrite the Arthurian legacy for a time when kings and knights were clad in shining armour and travelled extensively on their various crusades. A new era beckoned, and yet they wished to associate themselves and their reign with a world that had long since vanished.

The story of King Arthur's birth and subsequent career is one shot through with ancient magic and mysterious happenings, all firmly rooted in an age when magic was no mere superstition but a natural part of life. It was also the motive force behind the stories passed on from generation to generation. Even so, the story of Arthur's birth has dramatic elements that grip the imagination. It was during an Easter banquet that Uther Pendragon, the King of Britain, had fallen in love with Ygerne, the wife of Gorlois, Duke of Cornwall, whose stronghold was on Tintagel Island.

While Gorlois was fighting a battle some way off, Uther demanded of the wizard Merlin a way to satiate his passion, and, somewhat reluctantly, Merlin agreed to help. With the aid of a shapeshifting magic potion he transformed Uther into a likeness of Gorlois. In this guise, he was welcomed back to the castle by Ygerne while the real Gorlois lay wounded on the battlefield. That night he lay with her, and Arthur was conceived. Yet as a child he was to mysteriously disappear, for Merlin, as part of his bargain with Uther, laid claim to him.

To the Normans and the old British families who had reclaimed their homeland after centuries in exile, it looks as though it was of the utmost importance for them to revive their ancestral legends, for they represented the very roots of their native traditions (it is worth mentioning in passing that the name *Ygerne* sounds as if it is of Viking origin, whilst *Gorlois* sounds Norman). Both the Celts and the Vikings, as well as the Normans who were their descendants, considered their ancestral inheritance as paramount. Who they were and where they had come from was a matter of the most profound significance, and their allegiance to the Arthurian ethos was a crucial part of their makeup. This is a tradition that has never died. In the time of Elizabeth I her advisor and consultant John Dee produced a genealogy 'proving' that she was descended from King Arthur's lineage. The majority of the English kings, especially the Plantagenets and Tudors, believed they had Arthurian blood flowing in their veins, and this is still the case today, for the current royal family is the latest in a long line of those who consider themselves descendants through intermarriage. If and when Prince Charles becomes Charles III he will become part of the myth, for his middle name is Arthur.

Sheep graze amongst the misty ruins of Tintagel Castle at the turn of the nineteenth century. How local people got them there is a mystery; even human visitors risked their lives as they were forced to clamber up the steep and treacherous slopes by holding on to clumps of grass.

As the mist clears a little around Tintagel Island we can begin to see why the Normans/West Britons may have felt their destiny to be linked to the myth of King Arthur. As far as we know up to a hundred or so years elapsed between the publication of Geoffrey's book and the building of the Castle on the Island.

During this time there had been a great flowering of Arthurian literature. Many of these writings, like Geoffrey's, were saturated with Celtic magic and were firmly based on earlier traditions. Wolfram von Eschenbach's *Parzival*, for instance, was drawn from an old British (Welsh) manuscript where the hero embarks on a quest to discover the meaning of the Grail and travels through a magical landscape full of strange beasts, characters and situations. It is a world of the wondrous that interweaves with the everyday.

Facts are few and far between here. But one thing we do know is that during the time of Earl Richard of Cornwall, the younger brother of King Henry III, a castle was built at Tintagel. The truly curious thing about this is that, like the mounds at Bossiney and Boscastle, it had little defensive function. After all, what would you be defending? A windswept rock that was virtually inaccessible, where, under siege, you were sure to be starved out in a very short time? It was certainly never used as a fort or castle in the conventional sense.

The only credible explanation is that at a time when the Arthurian ideals were probably the most powerful driving force of the European royal dynasties, an impressive statement was to be made concerning the Norman links with King Arthur and everything he stood for. Tintagel Castle was thus a potent symbol of the connections between their dynasty and a world of far greater antiquity, a magical thread of kingship and royalty that ran through from prehistory to medieval times.

Tintagel is indeed an island, with the tide cutting it off from the mainland twice a day as the sea crashes through Merlin's Cave directly beneath the Great Hall, and this gives us many clues as to its former significance as a 'sacred Island' of Celtic tradition. One is the existence of a tiny eleventh century chapel, now roofless and ruined, known as St Julitta's Chapel. This saint, who was called 'St Ulette alias Uliane' in William of Worcester's travel diary of 1478 is thought by some to have been one of the many children of the Welsh King Brychan who may have founded a religious settlement here in the fourth or fifth century. The early date of the existing remains indicates that before a single stone was laid to build Tintagel castle the Island was already considered a sacred place. Even after the castle had long decayed the chapel was consecrated once a year by a priest from Bodmin Priory (which also had jurisdiction over Bossiney Mound), who was forced to scramble up the steep and dangerous grassy slopes at the risk of life and limb. This was a custom that may have continued right up until the nineteenth century, when the flamboyant Vicar of

Tintagel, Parson Kinsman, delighted in entertaining visitors to the spectacle of himself dressed in exotic flowing gold and scarlet robes, reading psalms to the wheeling seagulls as he officiated at services within its
crumbling walls.

As the fabric of this ancient building slowly dissolves back into
the elements from which it is made, the old chapel raises a question that
is difficult to ignore. Why was the Island considered a holy site? Ralegh
Radford, who was the first to conduct detailed excavations in the 1930s
thought that the chapel was all that remained of an important early Celtic
Christian monastery flourishing between the sixth and ninth centuries.
This idea is currently out of favour (historians are not immune from
the fads of fashion that reflect the preoccupations of the time), yet the
remains of the large number of buildings found show that it was indeed
an important place long before the Normans arrived. The existence of
these extensive remains was reinforced when, in the long dry summer of
1983, fires raging in the tinder-dry grass revealed the foundations of up
to a hundred other buildings, causing archaeologists to completely review
their opinion that the Island had been only sparsely settled in ancient
times. The prevailing view today is that it was a unique centre for some
sort of seasonal rites connected with kingship. Charles Thomas, probably
the leading archaeological authority on the history of the Island, suggests
it was 'between AD 400 and 700 the focus of something most unusual,
attracting a suite of objects unique in post-Roman Britain and Ireland,
possibly in Atlantic Europe north of Iberia'.

He came to this conclusion after examining thousands of very fine
quality potsherds dug up by Radford, many with a distinctive cross motif
classified as from the medieval period. Coming across them in tea-chests
in the storerooms of the County Museum he was astonished to discover
that these fragments were not from this period at all, but from the fifth
and sixth centuries, or the 'Dark Ages' hundreds of years before medieval times. They were unique to the site, thereafter called 'Tintagel Ware',
and from North Africa or the Mediterranean area. Many of the fragments
were from amphorae that had held the finest commodities. We are presented with two possibilities: either they were from a shipwreck, and the
locals had enjoyed a great celebration of their good fortune or they were
brought from the centres of the classical world for some prestigious event,
such as the coronation of a king, that warranted such quality goods.

The idea of jars of wine, oil and other luxuries surviving a shipwreck on the wild North Coast of Cornwall, however, seems a little far-
fetched. As Charles Thomas suggests, it is more likely that Tintagel Island
was a ceremonial centre well-known throughout the ancient world for its
connection with kingship. This might also explain the mystery of why
two Roman milestones from the third or fourth centuries were set up on
the road leading to it. We can only conclude that the Island was a unique
centre of ritual and celebration for many centuries before the Castle was

built, and because of the existence of the early chapel its purpose was also connected with a sacred function. This makes perfect sense from the available evidence and would explain why the Normans strove to create a tangible link with its past. The only likely reason that encompasses all the known facts is that Tintagel was a place where kings were inaugurated. Kings in those days were not conceived of as mere mortals, for they ruled by divine right as God-Kings. Could this explain why Tintagel was known to our ancestors as a legendary centre of kingship and why it had a sacred character? Other evidence as well suggests that the Island was believed to have a certain power beyond its serendipitous location.

Earth Rites

There are a number of curious features about the Island that hold more clues to its true character. Besides the extensive remains of the many buildings hidden under its thin topsoil, two wells on the summit (one natural and the other dug into the rock) and a ruined bread oven, other, more intriguing features vie for our attention. One of the most curious of all is a rock-cut tunnel on the western edge of the plateau, first noted by Leland in 1538, who described it as 'the ruins of a vault'. Richard Carew later noted it as 'a cave reaching once, by my guide's report, some farre way underground.'

Two very unusual properties of the tunnel are that its walls and roof are shaped like Gothic arches, and that it is cut into the rock in an exaggerated sinuous manner. Both these factors rule out its possible use as a mine or other similar working, for no-one would ever cut a serpentine tunnel through rock when a straight one would suffice. It would simply be too much of a demanding task unless there was some overriding reason. One can clearly see the tooling marks on the walls, and examination reveals it has been cut with great precision. The sloping floor appears to have been designed to collect water that drips from the roof, and, indeed, it originally had a pool at its lower end which was drained some years ago because of its inconvenience to visitors. It has also been suggested that the lower opening in this area may have been closed, making it a true cave, as suggested by Carew's observations.

Those who are interested in the mystical properties of such subterranean structures, usually known as *fogous* (Cornish for cave) may however be inclined to disagree with the current archaeological view that it was designed as a food store.

The rock-cut tunnel on Tintagel Island. What are its mysterious origins? Is it a food store or a place of underground initiation?

Other examples such as Boleigh at St Buryan or Pendeen at St Just (even though they are built structures rather than rock-cut tunnels) appear to have been made for less mundane reasons. In this case it is not only a long way from the castle, but it is also exceedingly damp in winter and would appear to have been less than ideal for use as a store. Its true purpose may have been very different, for many sensitives and dowsers report a concentration of spiritual or earth energy within it, which heightens the effects of meditation and other consciousness-raising techniques. The use of bells, bowls and other resonant instruments likewise have been found to have similar effects.

Is it possible that this subterranean structure was created for ritual purposes, much like the other Cornish fogous which are believed to have had such a use? There is a long tradition of caves being used for sensory deprivation and the enhancing of spiritual awareness stretching far back in time. They have always been known as places of initiation where people can connect with the Earth Spirit as if within a womb. The symbolism of rebirth in this case would be very profound indeed, for in the Celtic shamanic tradition Druids and their acolytes were often obliged to spend long periods within caves, undergoing mystical experiences and emerging with refined spiritual vision. Later monastic regimes also continued this practice with monks committing themselves to crypts, caves and other dark places within the Earth where their inner visionary powers were awakened. Many Celtic saints such as St Samson were said to have tamed a dragon within such a place. On one level this is a reference to the spiritual energies of the Earth which were allegorically spoken of as dragons or serpents. On another it speaks of the transformation that occurs when one gains mastery over the lower self. Was this the real purpose of this intriguing feature? As a place of initiation into the mysteries of a culture that was deeply rooted in a world of Celtic magic? Was it a gateway to the Otherworld?

All over the Island are a number of apparently natural cave-like openings that often give the impression of having been purposefully enhanced, places where one can sit and contemplate the endless rhythms of the sea, Sun, Moon and stars. These rocky places of shelter would have afforded perfect spots to enter into the natural meditation that comes from being in the midst of Nature. So many of these 'hermit caves' exist that it is easy to imagine a community of contemplative monks, or before that, Celtic mystics or Druids, using these places as a centre, a sort of mystical college, much as Ralegh Radford envisaged.

One of the most interesting of these is a rocky alcove to the South of the plateau evocatively called *King Arthur's Seat*. Whilst at first appearing natural, it has some unnatural features too. To its western side a small window appears to have been cut through the rock so that a view of the ocean and the setting Sun can be seen. Sheltered from the prevailing wind it is a favourite place to rest and escape the rain on a wet day when no-one else is around. In fact it is surprisingly comfortable, allowing one to stretch out lengthways and look across the yawning chasm that separates the Island from the mainland and the old Church of St Materiana on the cliffs opposite.

Carved into its floor is a peculiar series of shallow depressions colourfully known as 'King Arthur's Cups and Saucers'. Whilst it would be a wonderful flight of fancy to imagine King Arthur having a cup of tea with his Queen there, they are so unusual as to tempt us to believe that they have some less prosaic function. They are reminiscent of a type of prehistoric rock-art known as 'Cup and Ring' marks (although  in this case, without the 'rings'). These occur across Europe, and although it seems that no-one knows why they were made, it has been speculated that they might represent certain star formations, or even 'stone' maps.

However, having spent some time sheltering in this dramatically-situated alcove during wet weather, I noticed that when these 'cups and saucers' were full of water they may have had another previously unsuspected use. They are situated in such a way that when the Moon is visible it can be reflected in the water, and such is the energetic nature of the place that one can easily fall into a trance-like meditation whilst gazing at it. This is very similar to a magical technique known as scrying— the origin of crystal-ball gazing—when a small pool of water or other liquid was used as a focus for the mind in order to access the subconscious levels. John Dee and his mediumistic accomplice Edward Kelley famously used this method to communicate with 'angels', employing a scrying-glass instead of liquid. The results were recorded in *'A true and faithful Relation of What passed for many yeers between Dr John Dee and Some Spirits'*, published posthumously in 1659.

Dee's motivation for this was pure research—to understand the laws of Nature and the underlying principles of Creation. The scrying instrument Dee and Kelley used was a speculum, or polished mirror of black obsidian, but pools of water had also been used by ancient astronomers to measure the declination of stars on their nightly journey across the sky. These shallow depressions, filled with water, would have made perfect 'magic mirrors' for observing the Moon and stars that rose in the South, such as those of Orion and Sirius, reflected in the dark liquid. And besides this reflective star-gazing, who knows, there may even have been other, more magical applications, as Dee claimed.

Footprints of the God-Kings

A short step away from this rocky cleft, if it is possible to tear oneself away from its mesmerising situation, we find probably the most important of all the features on the Island. Cut into the bedrock on the very summit of the plateau is a worn hollow known as *King Arthur's Footprint*. It is just the right size for a well-built man to place his right foot in and proclaim himself the rightful King of Britain. Missed by most people who walk past it without recognising its importance, it is a highly significant clue to the true history of Tintagel.

Of course anything with the epithet King Arthur attached to it has many historians and archaeologists running for cover, all too quick to denounce it as mere folklore. This has certainly been the case in the past, with these 'Arthurian' artefacts consequently ignored, or at the very least unrecognised as genuine clues to the Island's past. Yet here, as we place our foot tentatively in this rocky hollow we are following in the wake of a custom that reaches back far into prehistory. All over the Celtic world there exist many examples of these 'footprints'—sometimes cut into the living rock, sometimes carved into boulders or slabs of stone. They are all connected with ancient rites of kingship.

The inauguration of a Nordic king, who by placing his foot on a sacred stone invokes the power of the Earth and by holding his sword upward draws down the magical powers of the Heavens, thus becoming the Axis Mundi of his Kingdom, symbolically connecting Heaven and Earth.

These 'footprints in stone' are amongst the most telling from the ancient world as far as kingship is concerned, for they represent the tradition of the king being 'married' to the land which he vows to serve. In a rare record of the sort of ritual that accompanied this, Martin Martin, in *The Western Isles of Scotland* of 1716, quotes from an ancient manuscript which preserves something of the real significance of such sacred stones. Describing the ceremony of Proclaiming the Lord of the Isles, during which a bishop and a number of priests were present, along with the chieftains of all the principal families and the chief lawgiver, he writes:

'There was a square stone 7 ft or 8 ft long, and the track of a man's foot thereon, upon which he stood, denoting that he should walk in the footsteps of his predecessors. And that he was installed by right in his possession. He was clothed in a white habit, to show his innocence and integrity of heart, that he should be a light to his people, and maintain the true religion...

Then he was to receive a white rod, intimating that he had the power to rule, not with tyranny and partiality, but with discretion and sincerity. Then he received his father's sword, or some other sword signifying it was his duty to protect and defend them from the incursions of their enemies in peace and war, as the obligation and customs of his predecessors were.'

The symbolism of a new king placing his foot in a mark that has been hallowed by many centuries of tradition can hardly be overestimated. Both feet and footwear have a strong mystical significance beyond their everyday function. They symbolise uprightness, a firm foundation upon which to act, and are the only part of the body that is in almost continuous contact with the Earth itself. This idea is behind the ancient measurement of the 'royal foot' to which many other such measures are related. It also refers to the concept of pilgrimage, for as all pilgrims know, each journey commences with a single step, and this includes the road to becoming the leader of a tribe or nation. Interestingly, throughout the Celtic world a golden sandal was a universal mark of kingship.

This long-standing tradition of Celtic inauguration stones is of prime significance in understanding the Island, for it stamps it with a character that would give us a strong hint of its ancient function even had the legend of King Arthur never been preserved. The Druidic-like rite described by Martin was widespread in the ancient world, and certainly there are many examples of such stones extant, the most famous being the Stone of Destiny, or *Lia Fail*. The legends surrounding this particular coronation stone have dominated the concept of kingship in the British Isles for many centuries. It was said to have been of heavenly origin before becoming the pillow on which the biblical prophet Jacob slept when he had a dream of angels descending and ascending between Heaven and Earth in Genesis 28:12 (this sounds very like a polar myth, where human souls enter and leave the earthly sphere along the Pole, as if in this case the stone itself represents the centre of the world).

It was on this stone that the first kings of Israel were crowned at the Temple of Jerusalem before it was reputedly brought by the prophet Jeremiah from the Holy Land to Ireland, and placed on the Hill of Tara, the Druidic centre of ancient Ireland. It was reputed to cry out when the right king was crowned, and became the focal point for the entire tradition of Irish sovereignty. Later the Stone of Destiny spent some time on the holy island of Iona, before reaching Scotland where the Kingdom of Dalriada was established. Its use as a ritual coronation stone continued when the first king of a united Scotland was inaugurated on it in 850 AD, and then moved near Perth to become the Stone of Scone. In 1296 Edward I of England took the stone to Westminster Abbey, where it was built into the Coronation Throne. Every English monarch except Queen Mary I has been crowned on it since, although it has now been returned to Scotland after many adventures, including having been stolen by Scottish radicals.

King Arthur's Footprint *on the summit of Tintagel Island with St Materiana's Church visible on the horizon. Anyone gathered on the cliff top opposite would have had a magnificent view of kingship rituals taking place, and it is likely crowds of onlookers participated in this way whilst the King and his attendants performed the sacred ceremony.*

This collection of amazing legendary adventures is amongst the most famous examples of how significant these 'Stones of Destiny' from the ancient world were, and dozens of others still exist, many with footprints like that at Tintagel. Yet the one on the Island, in the context of Arthurian lore, holds a special place. For a start, anyone placing their foot in the sacred hollow would be facing due North, which, as we will see, is of deep symbolic significance, for this is the direction of the source of their power. Located on the highest point, any ritual taking place there could be observed in great detail by considerable numbers of people gathered on the cliffs opposite. You only have to stand on the mainland and observe anyone close to the footprint to see everything with remarkable clarity. It is the ideal place to conduct such a ritual, with its backdrop of natural splendour, separated from the mainland yet visible to all. There is no other place like it in Britain.

Merlin's Cave

As we descend the hundreds of steps that lead down from the Island we can also see how it is gradually crumbling away, for in recent times major works have been necessary to stabilise the cliffs which are continually undergoing erosion. In fact it was far more extensive in the past, and much of its castle walls and other features have vanished, collapsing onto the boulder-strewn seashore below. Crossing the modern bridge (large elm trees provided access in medieval times until they too collapsed, leaving the Island virtually inaccessible unless you were of a very adventurous spirit) we come to the Cove below, with its waterfall and gaping chasm beneath the Great Hall of the castle ruins. This is Merlin's Cave, on a stormy day one of the most awesome places imaginable. Above the entrance can be seen the remains of the Island's short industrial history, when it was mined for wolfram and silverlode. A small railway used to run across the top of the cave, and a now bricked-up entrance once provided access to a labyrinth of tunnels dug into the living rock.

The miners who ex-
plored the interior of this place
must have thought that they
had come across something
out of the drolls and legends
of Cornish folklore, for they
reported magnificent crystal
caves glittering in the flickering light of their lamps, and it
was common for them to take
home trophies of the exceptionally clear quartz crystals—
some as big as a fist—known
as *Tintagel Diamonds*. Many
of the old Tintagel families

still retain these crystals as prized possessions, brought from the Island
by their grandfathers from the subterranean realm of Merlin's and King
Arthur's secret caves.

But we cannot leave the Island without treading the smooth slate
pebbles on the floor of Merlin's Cave and immersing ourselves for a short
time in its powerful atmosphere. It is a striking natural cathedral of a
place running right underneath the castle, where, on a wild day, the wind
tears through, whipping the sea to a frenzy. It is no wonder it is associated with the Druidic seer Merlin, for it gives a powerful impression of
ancient elemental magic.

This is another place where many people report psychic experiences, from feelings of light-headedness to full-blown mystical illumination.
Certainly it is one of those locations where one is immersed in the rhythms
and powers of Nature to such a degree that ordinary thinking is temporarily
suspended. It can be an awesome, terrifying place at certain times. Veins of
quartz run through the rock and gulls roost in the crevices far above, their
calls echoing around the walls and mingling with the rushing sea. But be-
ware in case you go into too deep a trance. If the tide is on the turn the cave
can flood with an alarming suddenness. You should only venture in when
the tide is at its lowest, or on its way out. Those of a foolhardy disposition
may take note of the following cautionary tale:

In the 1980s a Continental couple intent on seeing the legend-
haunted cave arrived one late afternoon, looked down to the Cove and
although the tide was coming in, judged that they could make it in time.
They rushed down to the beach and managed to enter the cave just
before a great wave poured over the pebble bank at its entrance, flooding
it completely within a few seconds. Unable to wade against the pressure
of the incoming sea they clambered up to a rocky ledge as the sea rose.
As darkness fell, one can only imagine their feelings as the tide rose relentlessly and waves lashed the slippery rocks to which they desperately

clung. Climbing ever higher to avoid being swept away by the crashing waves, they were forced to hang on for dear life high up near the roof. That surely must have been the longest night of their lives.

When dawn broke the following day they were still miraculously alive, and crawled, bruised, battered and soaking, from their rocky lair to emerge safely onto the beach. It is probably fair to guess that they were never the same again.

The message is that unless you wish to become a Druid sacrifice yourself, take extreme care when approaching Merlin's Cave, for, like the Island itself, it can be a dangerous and intimidating place under certain conditions. It may be best to invoke the spirits of the old wizard and legendary king themselves, asking for guidance and protection in probably much the same way that countless generations in the past must have done, who were perhaps more attuned to the formidable powers of Nature and the vicissitudes of human existence.

But as we finally leave the Island and its environs, one last message from Nature looms out from the weather-worn rocks to sear itself into our imagination. Climbing the steep steps to the upper ward of the castle, situated precariously on the mainland cliff, we are confronted by yet another striking feature. Here, gazing out from the cliff face of the Island is the extraordinary image, hundreds of feet high, of a giant king's head reclining in the rock. His bearded chin and regal nose can leave us in no doubt that this is a simulacrum of the 'once and future king', inexplicably carved by the natural forces that have always shaped the destiny of Tintagel. Closer examination reveals that his 'eye' appears to be closed, as if sleeping. As he stares, eyeless, towards the mainland, we may allow a strange thought to flit through our minds:

When will he awake?

7

THE GEOMETRY OF TIME

'Arthur was the spirit guardian of those islands, the keeper of the Bear and also the leader of the bear hunt. His legendary adventures were ritually enacted as the tribes moved around the central pole of their territory, imitating the revolutions of the Great Bear around the pole star. Their totem was the bear; the image of their chief god was Arcturus and the Great Bear constellation, and the title assumed by their leader was *Arth Fawr* or *Arthur*.'

New Light of the Ancient Mystery of Glastonbury
John Michell

aving explored various aspects of the Island, we are not, however, quite finished with Tintagel. In fact we are about to discover other elements of its stunning natural location that are undoubtedly among the most significant reasons for its ancient fame. These will prove a revelation to those who are inclined to think that legends such as that of King Arthur are little more than meaningless superstition. Nothing could be further from the truth.

Treading the path towards St Materiana's Church on the cliffs opposite, we can hardly resist a backward glance at its flat-topped plateau and note once more how any ritual taking place at King Arthur's Footprint would be clearly visible to anyone assembled here. Can there be any doubt that such rites would have been attended by large numbers of observers, separate from the proceedings but still caught up in the drama of the moment? Below the plateau is the jagged western entrance to Merlin's Cave, and beyond is the headland known as *Barras Nose*, with its prehistoric earthworks and enclosure.

This place too has had an interesting part to play in the recent history of Britain with regard to the defence of the realm. For it was here that a nationwide idea took root that has protected the coast and countryside from a new type of invader—the rapacious developer. After the building of *King Arthur's Castle Hotel* (now called *Camelot Castle*), the opulent Victorian landmark that so dominates the skyline of Tintagel, it was suggested that a similar establishment be erected at Barras Nose directly opposite the Island, so that fashionable tourists could gaze down on the ruins whilst elegantly sipping cocktails as the Sun went down over the ruins of the legendary King's domain.

Such was the public outcry at this suggestion that local people banded together to protect their heritage from the developers, organising a campaign that was to become far greater than they could have possibly envisaged. They were so successful that it created a groundswell of opinion that the coastline of the Westcountry, and eventually much of Britain itself, should be saved from inappropriate building which would ruin its natural character. From this remote headland, staring across to the place of Arthur's birth with all its associations with the protection of the land, the National Trust was born.

Ahead we catch sight of Tintagel church rising from its ancient enclosure, a fairly plain building on the outside, built to withstand the mighty winter storms, but one of the most interesting on the inside. Step through its heavy oak door and the atmosphere within immediately strikes a chord with those sensitive to such things. The wind whistles around its old walls, and there is some fine stained glass, some of it made by the Rev. Kinsman, Vicar and Constable of the castle who was reputed to be, amongst other things, interested in alchemy. The windows behind the altar are also exceptionally fine but in this case relatively modern, a memorial to another incumbent, the Rev. A. C. Canner, a scholarly man who wrote one of the most informative guidebooks evoking old Tintagel. Unusually for such glass it combines a modern style with the timeless, with images of the Sun and Moon creating a feeling of cosmic balance and harmony.

Tintagel's 'Green Bishop', a reminder of the early Celtic Christian traditions that survived in Cornwall until relatively recent times.

The church (built between 1080 and 1150) has a number of treasures that are of interest to our quest, despite the usual Victorian restoration that ripped out its medieval benches and the wooden doors 'of great antiquity' and destroyed a series of ancient wall-paintings. Fixed to the wall of the south transept is a Roman memorial stone, a reminder that this place was notable even before the Dark Ages. It was discovered in 1899 by the antiquarian Rev. W. Iago when the slanting evening sunlight threw the lettering into sharp relief, and commemorates a Roman general called Licinius. He is believed to have married Constantia, sister of Constantine the Great in 313 AD, defeated Maximus in the same year and then become ruler of the Eastern Empire, warring with Constantine who was trying to impose the new state religion of Roman Christianity. Exactly what this memorial stone is doing here is a mystery. Was Licinius somehow associated with the place? He was certainly known to be a defender of the old pre-Christian religion, hence his antagonism to Constantine.

There is also an archaic greenstone font with a head at each corner and carved with serpents. At one time in its long history it has collapsed, damaging a corner and requiring it to be supported by four incongruous-looking pillars. An old oak chair, probably Tudor, stands just beyond the rood screen with two dragons on the armrests and a fine carving of an unusual version of the Green Man. Here, a figure wearing an early bishop's mitre is magically transformed into a writhing mass of foliage, a reminder that Green Men and priests once shared a common bond as guardians of the fertility of the land.

The oldest part of the building, thought to be pre-Norman, is its north-eastern corner, and one can see the more primitive style of its stonework, especially from the outside. A modern altar in the north transept, though, has built into it a rare clue to the importance of St Julitta's Chapel on the island. This is a finely-carved triangular stone recovered from the Island in 1855. Its six-leaved rosette motif is found across northern Europe and is particularly associated with Viking and Celtic areas, as well as being a characteristic feature of Visigothic art. But what strikes us is its fine quality, which would grace a cathedral or great abbey. It is an indication of the one-time importance of the lonely ruined chapel, the oldest building on the Island and a far cry from what we see today.

In what is the most spiritually potent part of the building, the Lady Chapel to the north of the main altar, is another important relic from the old chapel. Lying in a recess is an extremely ancient, worn, probably pre-Norman, font. This was manhandled down from the chapel to be used as a pig-trough in a farm close to what is now the King Arthur's Arms pub. It was rescued from this ignoble fate by a local man who added it to his collection of carved garden ornaments, and claimed it was the very font that King Arthur himself was baptised in! One of his descendants gave it to the church for safe keeping, and it now rests in this quiet corner with nothing to tell of its unique past. If only it could speak it would reveal many secrets of the tiny chapel on the Island and its true history. But it lies mute, an ancient grail which preserves many mysteries within its time-worn stone.

The old font from Tintagel Island. What stories it could tell...

Who was St Materiana? We have already touched on this during our visit to Minster Church, and speculated that because of her name she may have been a Christianised version of an earlier goddess. Forms of the name vary. In 1259 she was called *Merteriane*, with *Mertheriana* in 1277 and *Materiana* in 1317. The Latin root *Mater* in all these forms suggests she was a Mother-Goddess, for her name appears to derive directly from the Latin *Matronia*. Baring Gould and John Fisher, in their

Lives of the Cornish Saints say she was a Welsh princess called Madrun or Madryn, who lived at the time of King Vortigern (who features in the legend of Merlin's childhood), and who introduced the Saxons into Britain causing rebellion amongst his subjects. He was burned alive in about 464 AD when his wooden castle was set on fire, with Madryn escaping the flames and eventually seeking refuge in Cornwall.

We may be inclined to dismiss much of these popular traditions as no more than idle superstition, yet there is clearly a connection between the two churches dedicated to her in North Cornwall, and Wales, the land of her birth. The true nature of these links between the two countries (for they have always been thought of as separate to England, with their own language and customs) may come as something of a surprise to those who claim such legends are little more than fanciful tales, for many of them, as in the case of King Arthur, are cultural memories of great antiquity, preserving encoded truths.

We touch here on another important aspect of the old British/Welsh/Cornish legends, for in the earliest of all collection of writings of Arthurian lore known as the *Mabinogion*, Modron occurs as a goddess, whose son, Mabon, represents the golden-haired new-born Sun Child, a sort of Celtic Apollo. As we continue to explore these connections between the lands which became the last refuges of the native British race, such links will assume a significance beyond anything that may have previously been suspected.

But for the present let us leave the church of St Materiana, or Madryn, or Modron, and move outside, for the site on which it is built has much information to yield up. When the churchyard was excavated in 1990-1 the remains of what was thought to be an earlier church were found, as well as a series of empty slate-lined coffins of such unusual character that they were referred to as 'royal graves'. Alongside were traces of funerary feasts and a collection of pottery fragments from the fifth or sixth centuries, identified as coming from South-East Turkey or Cilicia. This was more evidence of a definite link between Dark Age Tintagel and the centres of the Classical world, this time the Byzantine Empire. It looks as though whoever was once buried in these graves had considerable international influence, confirming Tintagel as a powerful royal centre. The narrow slate-lined graves were built directly onto the rock some six feet below the present level. Some were aligned East-West, but an even earlier group was uncovered where the graves were arranged pointing to a particular focal point, a hollowed out socket cut into the bedrock.

Whatever had stood in this socket must have been of singular importance for these early graves to be arranged in such a manner. It may have represented the *Genius Loci* of the place, the original focus of a sacred site that was, many centuries later, to have a church built upon it. What could it have been? By great good fortune this ancient artefact still exists. Lying forgotten in the grassy churchyard for many years was the standing stone that fits exactly into this socket—the original 'sacred' stone of the site. It has now been re-erected in precisely the same spot as it was originally set up, except that it is now six feet higher due to the rise in soil level, a unique and tantalising vestige of the distant past half-hidden amongst the leaning gravestones.

Its exact age is a matter of speculation since it is impossible to date stones, but it is likely to be Bronze Age or even Neolithic. It certainly gives the impression of coming from the great age of standing stones, which could be anything from between 3000 and 5000 years ago. If so, it is a tangible link with these early times, and a signpost to the great antiquity of Tintagel and the church site.

The stone itself is of uncommon appearance, unlike anything found in the area. It is now covered in a layer of thick lichen but when it was newly erected after the excavations were completed in the early 1990s one could see the sparkling mica amongst the curious black-and-white granite from which it is made. It appears to be very unusual in its composition as well, for this is a type of rock that is not found locally.

Another interesting thing about this monolith is that it has been shaped to a rounded triangular form, again something not seen elsewhere. This three-sided shape is reminiscent of the 'Triple Goddess' of prehistory, where the female divinity was thought to have three distinct aspects. Even more curious is a smooth hole or depression in its lower area, where the stone is naturally darkened by its mineral content. It has been suggested that this may be a 'libation hole' where oil, milk, or some other liquid was applied as a sort of anointing ritual to consecrate it.

The monolith in Tintagel churchyard with its 'libation hole' clearly visible, just after re-erection. These days it is lichen-covered and more difficult to see.

The highly unusual nature of this stone, its location and the fact that it was honoured by the arrangement of primitive graves radiating from it inevitably leads us to conclude it must have been the most significant feature of the churchyard site in prehistoric times. Why? It was a question that puzzled me for years, until I happened to visit it with Robin Heath and his partner Trish one late autumn afternoon, when an interesting theory developed.

I asked Robin, one of the country's leading researchers into megaliths and astroarchaeology (the study of how archaeological monuments relate to the Sun, Moon and stars) and the author of many books for his advice because he had been involved in the subject for a long time.

Over the years he had conducted many landscape surveys, and immediately suggested from his previous experience what this stone may have been. He noticed that the monolith was positioned as a perfect sighting stone to view the sky against the backdrop of the horizontal plateau of Tintagel Island. From this spot it would be possible to observe circumpolar stars and other constellations that came closer to the Earth, rising and setting just above the level horizon formed by the flat-topped Island to the North. Normally it would have been impossible to create such a star observatory without raising earthworks to make an artificial horizon, due to natural undulations in the landscape. Such works were usually integral to ancient sites such as Stonehenge and Avebury in order to mimic a flat natural horizon, but here was a naturally-occurring landscape feature ideally suited to such a use.

This was the only place in the country where Nature had contrived to create a flat-topped island set against the most level horizon it is possible to get — the sea. After so many years wondering about its purpose, I found this an interesting idea, so I asked him which stars in particular may have been observed from this spot. He had no compass or theodolite at the time to take accurate readings, but knew from the position of the Sun in the sky. 'It looks like the Island, viewed from the stone, would have provided the perfect observatory for viewing the circumpolar constellations', he said. 'Especially the Great Bear'.

Perhaps one can imagine my reaction. Many years ago I had found the image of the Great Bear in the landscape, looking directly at Tintagel Island. Now one of Britain's leading experts was telling me that the Island and the church that looks across to it may have been designed as an observatory for exactly this constellation and its companions.

'If we come back later tonight we can confirm this with our own eyes', said Robin. So we did. Although there were clouds in the darkened sky, there was just enough clarity to confirm that the Pole Star was stationed above the Island, with the stars of the Great Bear circling slowly around it. The sighting stone in the churchyard had taken on a totally new significance, for amongst other things it may explain its curious triangular shape (three being a number associated with a primeval Mother Goddess) and I realised too that it may have represented the Polar Axis itself, which could be why those early graves were directed towards it.

In the old religion, souls came into earthly incarnation from the still point in the heavens, travelling along the axis, and returned to it upon death. And who guarded the point around which earthly life revolves? It was Arthur in his role as Arcturus, the Bear Keeper, and his Mother Goddess the Great Bear, as they took their places at the endlessly-revolving Round Table of the polar constellations. It is from this continuous motion of the heavens that the cycles of earthly time are created.

A further dimension to this train of thought revealed itself when I remembered that in archaeological excavations on the Island a series of post-holes had been discovered cut into the bedrock. They were irregular, and so were unlikely to have been for dwellings or tents. We wondered whether they may have been for the insertion of wooden posts that could have assisted in tracking the movement of stars as they moved around the Pole. We also noticed that not far away from the church-yard were a series of apparently natural stone platforms at the edge of the cliff, one of the best positions to see the Island, with the sea crashing around it and through the narrow western entrance to Merlin's Cave. Observing Tintagel from this angle brought the horizon of the sea closer to that of the Island, and made this theory even more tenable.

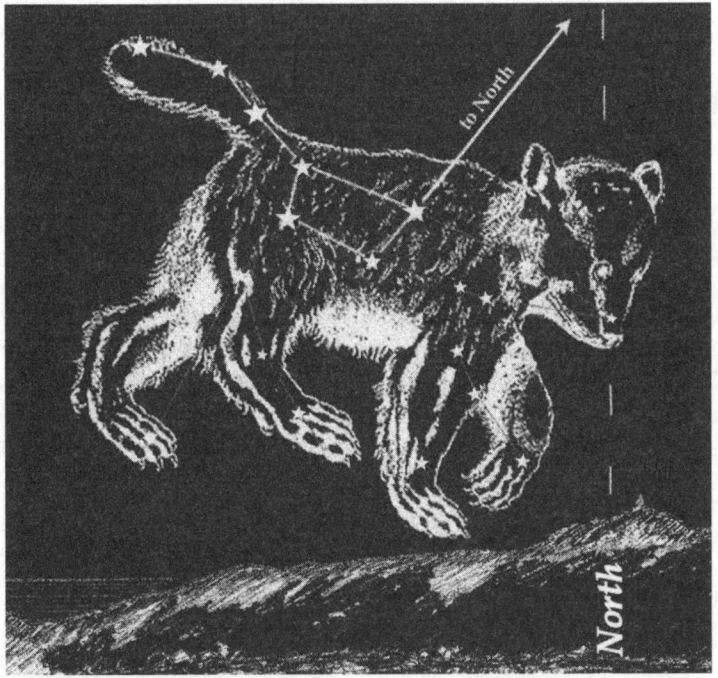

The Great Bear and the Pole Star. Navigators, astronomers and surveyors have always used the two bright stars furthest from the Bear's 'tail', Dubhe and Merak, to accurately locate True North. Was Tintagel Island a Star Observatory for the circumpolar constellations, especially The Great Bear?

The Great Bear's Polar Axis

These revelations about Tintagel as a possible observatory for the constellations surrounding the Pole Star were, though, only just the beginning of a journey to understand who might have laid all this out, and the ultimate question of why? At the time we felt we were just gathering fragments of a puzzle whose pieces were virtually lost to our sight. However, all that had been discovered so far had another extraordinary dimension to it that created a much bigger picture—and one that would make the hairs on the napes of our necks stand up in excitement.

Some years previously Robin had made a striking discovery concerning the way certain megalithic and other prehistoric sites in Britain were related to each other. Whilst researching his book *Sun, Moon and Stonehenge* he realised that Stonehenge, that most iconic example of the mysterious megalith-builders' art on Salisbury Plain and Britain's national temple for thousands of years, as well as other major sites, were linked together in a vast geometric pattern.

He got the idea that the famous bluestones, the stones that formed the original stone structure that was later enlarged into the sarsen circle must have been taken there for some highly significant reason. Analysis had shown in 1923 that these stones had come from the Preseli mountains of West Wales. The question that had always puzzled archaeologists was why should the builders have transported heavy stones from hundreds of miles away when they already had access to a plentiful supply of suitable ones much closer to the site?

In his 1956 book *Stonehenge*, Professor Richard Atkinson had noted that they belonged to the very earliest phase of Stonehenge due to the large amount of bluestone chippings found at the lowest levels of silting in the so-called 'Aubrey holes' and the original circular perimeter ditch. He concluded that an early proto-Stonehenge made from bluestones, and complete with lintels, was assembled almost contemporaneously with a large rectangle defined by sarsen stones whose four corners were laid at the perimeter on the original earthwork. This 'Station Stone' rectangle, whose sides were accurately in the ratio of 5 to 12, marked at that latitude the rising of the Sun and setting of the Moon at their most northerly positions.

Being aware of all this Robin drew a line between Stonehenge and the Preseli site and this revealed that the angle was the same as that of the diagonal of the 5 by 12 rectangle within Stonehenge itself. This was a breakthrough moment, for the two sites were copying the geometry of the Stonehenge Station Stone rectangle. Furthermore, he determined that Lundy Island provided the third corner of a huge geodetic triangle. Lundy Island is visible from the Preseli site in Wales, where one can still see abandoned megaliths lying rejected at the foot of the Carn Menyn outcrop that were presumably destined for the building of Stonehenge. It can also be seen from many locations in South and West Wales, and is similarly visible from many Cornish sites, including Tintagel and Boscastle.

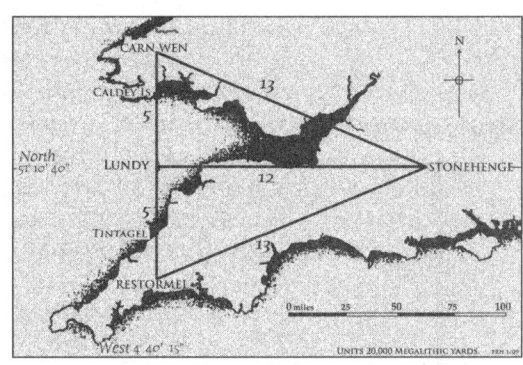

The next discovery was even more fascinating, for Lundy lies exactly due West of Stonehenge. When Robin drew a line connecting the two a great triangle appeared that had Stonehenge, the site where the original bluestones had come from, and Lundy Island all perfectly placed at its key points. Not only this, but because the North-South axis crossed the East-West axis it formed a right-angle on the island. He found that the old name for Lundy in Welsh was *Ynys Elen* — meaning *island of the elbow*, implying a right angle. This triangle drawn across the landscape had other properties too, for it was in the Pythagorean proportion of 5:12:13, exactly the same as the Station Stone rectangle at Stonehenge. Was the removal of the bluestones and their incorporation into the original design of Stonehenge undertaken to indicate this huge landscape triangle which Stonehenge marked at one corner?

He also discovered that encoded into this 'Stonehenge Triangle' were the relative motions of the Sun and Moon, and that the actual measurements of the sides were also significant. He later went on to explore all this in greater detail along with another pioneer researcher, the antiquarian scholar John Michell, in *The Measure of Albion*. Those interested in these discoveries concerning the reasons for the location of Stonehenge and how it is related to cosmology and the wider landscape of Britain are referred to these works as well as Robin's chapters at the back of this book.

Another aspect of this Stonehenge triangle was that it had a 'reflection' or mirror image that implicated Cornish sites, including Tintagel, Restormel Castle near Lostwithiel, and the prehistoric earthwork of Castle Dore near Fowey on the south coast. Surveying on site had shown that the causeway leading to Castle Dore was oriented towards the direction of Stonehenge. Many of these sites, he noted, had longstanding Arthurian connections.

We already know of Tintagel, but according to Geoffrey of Monmouth, Merlin was also said to have built Stonehenge, and King Mark, during the Arthurian period, was believed to have had his court at Castle Dore. Lundy too had a link, for an ancient stone in St Elen's churchyard on the Island — the site of an early Christian burial site — has a name some have thought to be *Vortigern* inscribed on it. King Vortigern is a

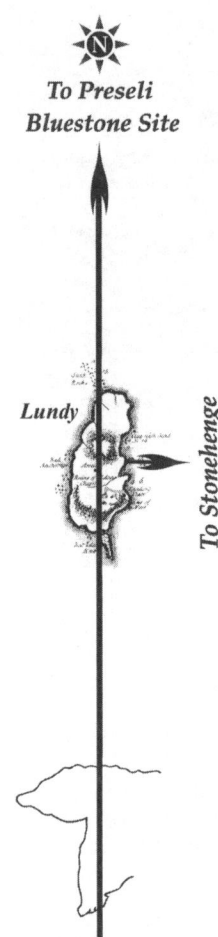

Lundy

To Stonehenge

**The Great Bear
of Tintagel**

seminal figure in the legend of the young wizard Merlin, who is summoned to his castle on Mount Snowdon to quell two fighting dragons. Restormel Castle had been the residence of the Dukes and Earls of Cornwall, who had modelled their reigns on Arthurian mythology. Yet most strikingly of all, from the point of view of the current quest, the North-South axis shared by both triangles ran right through the body of the Great Bear!

This information was almost too much to absorb. First the discovery of the shape of the Great Bear, then the realisation that Tintagel may have been purposefully designed as some sort of circumpolar observatory, and now the recognition that all this was part of a greater design linked to other Arthurian sites that included Stonehenge. Not for the first or the last time I asked myself if all this could be a projection of our minds. But any lingering doubts were to be dispelled as we examined the evidence even more closely.

The main axis leading from the Preseli bluestone area directly southwards through Lundy Island, when projected into Cornwall, runs through the very top of the Bear's head, close to the place known as Pentargon, Cornish for *Arthur's Head*. It then passes very close to the site of Minster Church outside Boscastle as well as the curiously-named hamlet of Treworld. Tregatherall Farm was the next point, where old carved stones have been found.

It then aligns with a massive, elaborately carved cross shaft—the biggest in the area—on Waterpit Down, and further on runs very close to the recumbent inscribed megalith known as *Arthur's Grave* at Slaughterbridge. Both these stones have been moved in the past. The former had been commandeered as a pivot-stone for a horse-driven threshing machine at a nearby farm before being re-erected in 1889 close to its original position, the latter had been used as a footbridge across the River Camel—however both

Minster Cross on Waterpit Down, before its restoration in the nineteenth century. Was this huge stone a marker for the Polar Axis?

are so large and cumbersome that by their very nature they are still more or less where they must have been originally set up. These huge stones marked this North-South axis line, and later, GPS readings taken on site confirmed this. In between these two stones was a place called *Grylls Rose*, notable in this context because North/South axes are known as *Rose Lines*.

This was followed by other developments. Just outside Boscastle was a previously unrecorded stone row of white quartz boulders at longitude 4°38'16", (map ref SX 137915) above Anderton Farm near St Juliot's Church (this name is a later version of St Julitta, the same saint to which the chapel on the Island is dedicated). This had been brought to my attention by local farmer Kevin Gibbs, who had realised they must have some special significance. These three stones are set into the side of a steep valley, with two white boulders earth-fast and with the topmost stone slightly toppled from its original position; they look rather like sheep in the distance, and are visible from a wide area including the hill above Boscastle. The shape of this upper stone is very like that of a giant white stone arrowhead that would have appeared starkly outlined on the horizon, before, that was, a stone hedge was directly built behind it. These stones appear on no map, and nobody except the local farmers such as Kevin seem to have noticed them, yet for us they were of great significance, appearing to delineate the eastern extremity of the body of the Great Bear.

The 'Arthur Stones'-previously unrecorded stone row with its top 'pointer' stone dislodged. (Photographed through the trees from the opposite site of the valley).

When we measured their azimuth we were convinced that this unknown stone row — which we tentatively named *The Arthur Stones* — were of considerable importance. Allowing for the movement of the top pointer stone over what might be many thousands of years, they point in the general direction of True North. The choice of pure white stones seemed to indicate that they were meant to be used at night. We also wondered whether, because of their angle of slope, they might have been designed to point to a particular star as it crossed the polar meridian. Later, a site visit revealed another stone in a hedge below the field which was aligned with the two earth-fast boulders. Theodolite readings gave this alignment as 350 degrees 61 minutes, almost ten degrees West of North. This meant that the stone row was pointing to the West of True North. With its steep slope, which must have been carefully selected as part of the design, it reminded us of a telescope angled towards a point on the horizon above. Did it once align to a particular star in the constellation of the Great Bear as it touched the Earth?

The Lundy axis followed the longitude 4°40'15" right from the Preseli Mountains, along the axis of Lundy, and then through the head of the Bear, and now we had found that the Tintagel area and its Great Bear were part of a countrywide geometric pattern over which the presiding spirits were King Arthur and Merlin. Were we uncovering some tangible truth behind the legends that concerned the northern constellations — the region of Arthur the Bear King? Had those ancient surveyors, whoever they might have been, left messages in the landscape that they knew someone might one day rediscover? Our heads were full of questions that at the time seemed bewildering and perplexing, yet the evidence was clear, demonstrable, and there for all to see.

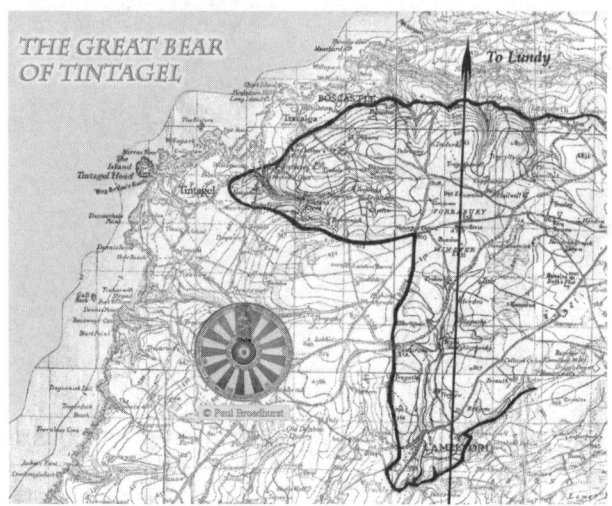

The Great Bear of Tintagel *and the North-South Polar Axis which links the Preseli Bluestone site, Lundy Island, Restormel Castle and Castle Dore, all highly significant sites in antiquity. The great stone at Slaughterbridge known as 'King Arthur's Stone' lies very close to this axis and may have been a marker.*

The Tintagel Solstice Axis

This revelation about the Polar Axis of the Bear was, however, only one aspect of the mystery concerning this giant figure and its links with Tintagel Island. Some years previously I had noticed a long straight road leading across the northern edge of Bodmin Moor towards the Neolithic and Bronze Age settlements at the foot of Roughtor. When extended on a map this line ran right through the Island. In the opposite southeastern direction it led to the rocky prominence known as Stowes Hill. Although irreparably damaged by quarrying due to the fine quality of the granite, this is where the towering top-heavy rock formation known as *The Cheesewring*, noted in local legend as a Druid focus of Sun worship, still remains one of Cornwall's most memorable sights. It stands

in a prehistoric enclosure that once contained many such monuments, now mostly fallen victim to the stone–cutters. Archaeological surveys have shown that this place, five or six thousand years ago, was a massive ritual complex, in effect the sacred centre of the whole area. The angle of this axis running from Tintagel to the Cheesewring coincides with the direction of the rising Sun at the Winter Solstice, the moment of the Sun's rebirth. In the opposite direction it delineates the Summer Solstice sunset.

The striking rock-pile known as 'The Cheesewring', a geomantic marker at one of Cornwalls greatest ancient ritual sites.

When this solsticial axis is seen in the light of the legend of Arthur as a solar hero, it can be understood that the tradition of Arthur's birth at Tintagel may be, in mythic terms, a half-remembered story of the rebirth of the Sun God, in this case laid out in the landscape. Midwinter is also the time that the legends place Arthur's symbolic drawing of the sword from the stone, so it appears as the most important time of the year around which everything else turns. Here we touch the dual aspects of the principles of ancient kingship, as the hub of the starry sphere, the central figure at

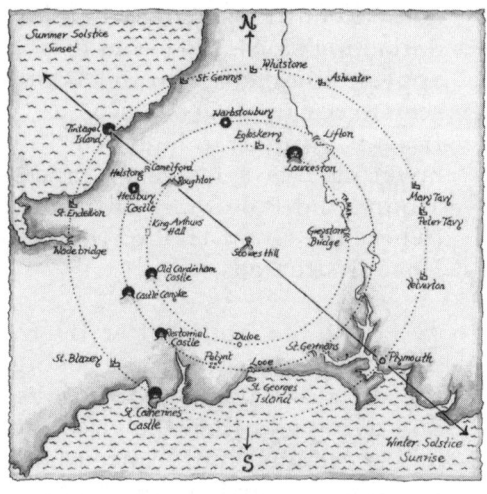

the Round Table, and as the divine representative of the powers of Light that return every summer. The legends also recall that Arthur's coronation takes place in high summer, that is, the Summer Solstice, and this is exactly what historians now believe may have happened on Tintagel Island, when new kings were crowned. The great quantities of 'Tintagel Ware' found on the Island are probably the physical remnants of one of these occasions, which would almost certainly have taken place at midsummer rather than in the depths of winter.

Geoffrey of Monmouth must have known something about this as he preserved the old Celtic traditions in his book. He recorded that at the very beginning of the mythical founding of Britain by Brutus, his general Corineus killed the last Cornish giant by hurling him from the cliffs at Plymouth Hoe. This event was commemorated in earlier times by two large turf-cut figures called Gog and Magog which were still in existence in Elizabethan times. It all sounds a bit far fetched, except that this solstitial axis, running south-east from Tintagel to Plymouth, when extended, leads directly across the Citadel on the Hoe. This is reputedly the site of these giant figures, linking it geographically and cosmologically with Tintagel. Thus the killing of the last giant and the birth of Arthur both appear to refer to the relationship between the Sun and the Earth, and the different mythic interpretations of the understanding of Nature's seasonal cycles during successive ages.

On another visit to Tintagel, this time armed with a theodolite, Robin conducted a survey from the sighting stone in the churchyard to the Island in its setting amongst the coastal cliffs, and we caught a momentary glimpse into the minds of the astronomer-priests who had used this location for stellar observation. We realised that an amazing sight would have confronted them, loaded with symbolic power, on the evening of the Winter Solstice. Assuming a clear sky, the last rays of the dying Sun would vanish below the south-western Atlantic at about 4:30 in the afternoon. Conditions being what they are at this time of the year, with rapidly darkening skies, the seven bright stars of the Great Bear would gradually appear shimmering in the sky above the Island. Its head would then be seen to rise up above Boscastle (where the cliff called Pentargon—*Arthur's Head,* is located) to later rear upwards to the East of the Island's plateau, hovering like a heavenly presence. During the night it would revolve around the Pole Star, positioned directly over the eastern promontory (where the Great Hall of the castle and the giant image of King Arthur's Head is situated).

In the hours after its first appearance the Bear would become more and more erect, as if being born from the Earth and flying up into the sky along the corridor of the Polar Axis. This cosmic spectacle of the Sun dying and then the Great Bear rising up above the Island must have had enormous significance to those whose lives were so closely bound up with the seasonal cycles and the events taking place in the skies. It is difficult to overestimate the sheer impact of such an event on anyone gathered at the sighting stone in the churchyard; it would certainly have been an unforgettable experience, and could well have given rise to the legend of Arthur, the Bear King, being 'born' at Tintagel.

So what exactly is Tintagel? It is difficult to come to any other conclusion than that it was a crucial part of a great ritual landscape that reflected the movements of the Heavens in a way that they could quite literally be brought down to Earth: a place where ancient kings assumed the role of an intermediary between the events taking place in the Heavens and the manner in which they were reflected on the landscape. Is it any wonder they were thought of as god-kings who channelled divine forces?

The Seven Stars of the Great Bear hovering over Tintagel Island at the Winter Solstice, viewed from the 'sighting stone' in the clifftop churchyard. Is this stellar phenomenon the origin of the legend of Arthur, the Bear King, being 'born' at Tintagel?

8

THE LIONS OF LYONESSE

here are certain places on the Earth where the land 'speaks' to each of us—places that seem to harbour ancestral memories that are normally beyond our reach. Whether these memories arise from our own individual natures or from what Jung would have called the 'collective unconscious' we cannot tell. Perhaps it is a mixture of the two. 'Have we been here before?' is a question that strikes many people as they experience that feeling of *déjà vu* in Cornwall. The recognition that greets us at particular locations awakens something deep within. It may crystallise as a feeling of romantic appreciation of the beauty of the landscape or a dreamlike yearning for the peace and tranquillity of by-gone days. Either way, it is an impulse that, I believe, guides our lives. These places beckon to us because they have something to say.

Out of all the places I have found myself two especially have this effect: Cornwall, where I have lived as an honorary Cornishman most of my life, and Somerset, both counties that were once part of the old Celtic territories of what was called West Wales, or, in those misty days before written history, Dumnonia. Because of this they both happen to be steeped in the old British traditions—Somerset especially is infested with dragons—and they are also two of the centres of gravity of the Arthurian mythos. When such places speak to us it may start as a barely-heard whisper, but that can soon develop into a quite insistent conversation, full of questions.

I found myself wondering about all these things after a brief stay in Somerton, the ancient capital of Somerset, a number of years after the initial discovery of the Tintagel Bear. Staying at *The Unicorn* in Somerton, I had visited nearby Dundon Hill, a prehistoric encampment, and later, wandering through the town, had lamented that the fine old hostelry of *The Red Lion* was boarded up and apparently totally neglected. As an aficionado of traditional pubs and inns I felt saddened that another remnant of the old British way of life was no more.

On my return to Cornwall a curious thing occurred. Leaving Somerton I had recalled that Katherine Maltwood, the visionary artist who had discovered the Glastonbury Zodiac, what she called *Glastonbury's Temple of the Stars*, had begun her own quest at this very place. It was here that she first found the giant figure that led to her eventual discovery of a series of others, which she believed represented King Arthur as a Sun King surrounded by his twelve knights, or astrological signs. Drawn in the landscape around Somerton, figured by old roads and trackways, she discerned the outline of a great lion. I had always thought that many of the images put forward by Maltwood required a certain amount of imagination from the observer to arrive at the conclusions she did, but the Lion is very convincing in its appearance.

Lying on the floor behind the letterbox in my cottage to greet me was a copy of the local daily newspaper, *The Western Morning News*. As I made a cup of tea and flicked through it, my eyes alighted on a review of a new book about the old capital of Cornwall, Lostwithiel, by local author Barbara Fraser. It began with a reference from the seventeenth century Cornish chronicler Richard Carew, who recorded in his *Survey of Cornwall* of 1602 that Lostwithiel was derived from two old Cornish words which meant *Lion's Tail*.

Lion's Tail? It seemed an unlikely tale in itself. But a glimmer of light came on in my head, and the series of coincidences suddenly came into sharp focus. *Somerton – The Red Lion – the lion of the Glastonbury Zodiac – the Lostwithiel book review which just happened to mention Carew's interpretation of the place name;* all these unlikely connections seemed to be saying something.

So later I got out an Ordnance Survey map of the area and stared at it intently just to see — what, exactly, I really had no idea. But after the Bear discovery I was alert to any possibilities, no matter how strange they may at first appear. After a while I went into a curious state of mind, a sort of unfocused trance-like meditation that I have come to describe as 'map-scrying', where the details of the map gradually seem to vanish, and the shape of the roads appear to rise above the mass of information printed on the paper. And then, just as I began to think that all this really was a series of meaningless coincidences, a recognisable shape appeared to grow out of the map. It was the outline of a Lion, apparently leaping from the flat landscape in front of me. Its tail seemed to be lying directly on Lostwithiel.

Just like before, at first I thought I had projected this image from my own imagination, inspired by the curious set of coincidences of the previous few days. But as I examined the figure more closely it became ever more alive. It did indeed look like a young lion which was literally leaping out of the map, and certain important features in the landscape were, just like the Bear, of notable interest. Its nose looked as though it was marked by an ancient church adjacent to Lanhydrock House, once a monastic settlement that was one of the oldest possessions of Bodmin Priory and now a much-visited National Trust property. In fact the whole shape of the head seemed to be well outlined by the roads bounding the

900-acre ancient estate. On its huge front paw was the summit of a low hill with a reservoir built into it, close to a ruined Neolithic 'burial chamber'. The Lion's hind legs were jumping from the town of Lostwithiel itself as if growing from the land, similar to the effect I had previously observed with the Bear. On its rump, where one might expect the tail to be attached to the body, was the ancient residence of the medieval Dukes and Earls of Cornwall—Restormel Castle, positioned on a prominence ringed by woodland and the remains of a royal Deer Park.

Mulling over the Lion's possible implications, something else occurred. Out of the corner of my eye I spied *another* lion—this time in the shape of a great dignified leonine head, much larger in scale than the other, which in comparison seemed even younger and more full of energy. The form of this massive head was especially remarkable in that it was perfectly formed and instantly recognisable, outlined in the main by the old A30 road, the ancient pilgrim's route leading down to the far west before it was bypassed in recent times. The artistic detail of this great head was captivating, for his eye was beautifully drawn, his nose was marked by Lanivet Church, another important monastic site, and he had a beard that grew from his lower jaw, joining the front paw of his younger compatriot and linking them together.

Located right on top of the Crown of the Lion's head was Bodmin Church, the biggest in Cornwall, with a ruined fourteenth century chapel behind it. Also on the Crown was the site of the former Bodmin Priory, for many centuries the most powerful in the county. In early times it had jurisdiction over Bossiney and Tintagel. The remains of an ancient chapel, the ruined Berry Tower, now in the middle of a cemetery, was north of the Priory site too, and along with Franciscan Friars at the site of Mount Folly in the town, this implied that this entire area had

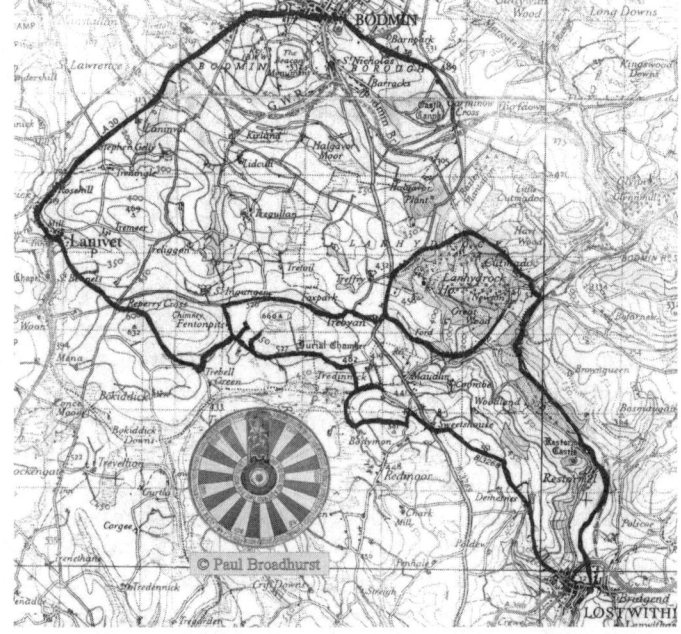

The Bodmin and Lostwithiel Lions - one with a great dignified head outlined by some of the most important religious centres in Cornwall. The other looks as if it is leaping from Lostwithiel, the one time Stannary capital of Cornwall. His head is marked by Lanhydrock Park and his 'tail' by Restormel Castle, the seat of the Dukes and Earls of Cornwall.

once been covered with a surprising concentration of religious houses. In the centre of the Lion's head was Bodmin Beacon, an open area with a massive obelisk at the edge of the built-up environs of the once county town, and on his neck was the enormous prehistoric 'fort' known as Castle Canyke, one of the largest in the area, nineteen acres surrounded by a vast ditch situated on the crest overlooking the Bodmin valley.

Two lions? I began to suspect that I could look at any random map and find dozens of them. But the more I looked the more convincing it became. Especially when I started to focus on the sites themselves. It seemed that here indeed were two lions adjacent to each other, one with a dignified, regal air about him and the other portrayed as a leaping image that spoke of the boundless energy of youth. I was also to find that some early star-maps do in fact have two lions instead of the one that has become universally famous as Leo. Besides *Leo Major*, there is *Leo Minor*, the Little Lion, which is positioned under the feet of the Great Bear and above its greater cousin. Although the two Lions in the landscape do not conform exactly to the constellations as represented on a star-map, it is nevertheless striking that they appear to symbolise their heavenly counterparts, and, even more remarkably, are set on the Polar Axis below the Great Bear, just as in the sky.

The Bodmin Lion

The head of this great Lion is, like the Bear, beautifully drawn in a simple linear style that largely follows the old pilgrim route through Cornwall. Because of this, before the new road was built travellers would have made their way along the outline of the head of this Lion on their way westwards. For thousands of years pilgrims and visitors alike would enter Cornwall's old county town at the site of Bodmin Priory. This was a Celtic settlement reputedly founded by St Guron, whose Holy Well can still be seen in the churchyard. Later it developed into an extensive Priory which covered many acres of what is now Priory Park, and was also a major pilgrimage centre that had grown, by the medieval era, from an isolated hermitage to the biggest monastery in Cornwall. As such, it retained much of its Celtic character and must have contained within its library many magnificent old books before the Saxon incursions under Athelstan destroyed them in an attempt to eradicate the old Cornish ways. In 932 Howel, the last Cornish king, was forced to surrender, thus sounding the death-knell for Cornish independence. As Pat Munn comments in *Bodmin Moor*, one of the most wide-ranging studies of the area, at this time '*Events quickened, now that the Cornish Church could be organised on diocesan lines and its people shunted on to the rails of the English political system, as the tenth century signalled a departure from ways Celtic*'.

In an effort to withstand the onslaught of the Anglo-Saxon attacks and their designs on the territories of the ancient tribe of the Dumnonii, the Cornish had enlisted the help of certain groups of Vikings to fight alongside them, and many of them appear to have settled in the county, helping to protect the land against their foes until the Battle of Hingston Down in 838, when Athelstan's precursor Egbert defeated the Cornish and their allies. Although Egbert was triumphant he never used his power to erode the Celtic culture in the same way as Athelstan. However he did ensure that the Hundred of Trigg Minor, which included Tintagel, was absorbed into his domain. (Bodmin was the capital of the *Hundred of Trigg Major*. Both once belonged to the *Hundred of Trigg* before being divided when Egbert took over the area, annexing the old place of Arthur's birth, which then became part of the *Hundred of Trigg Minor*).

The discovery of the Bodmin Gospels, a collection of writings from the mid-tenth to the mid-eleventh centuries, by an antiquarian bookseller in 1831 provides a number of insights into the time just before the Normans arrived. It seems clear from these writings that in most of Cornwall the old Celtic ways were still very strong despite English influence, which tended to be concentrated in the eastern part of the county (place-names reflect this, with Saxon words like *stow*, (holy place), *wic* (dwelling), *worthy* (enclosed homestead), *ham* (estate), *bury* (hillfort) and *coombe* (valley). The great treasures of Bodmin Priory included the relics of the Celtic Saint Petroc. These had apparently been rescued from Petrocstowe (Padstow) during a Viking attack in 981, along with the saint's staff and bell and the ivory horn that had once been given to him by the Cornish King Constantine. Petroc's totem animal was a stag, a symbol of the old religion, which is said to have sought refuge at the saint's feet during a royal hunt. He is reputed to have converted the King, who was chasing the stag, to Christianity.

The relics of Petroc, a Welsh (or some say Cornish) prince turned missionary who had lived in Ireland and was destined to become Cornwall's patron saint, guaranteed great profits for the monastery until a certain Canon Martin, who had already been disciplined for mismanagement, made off with them, taking them to Brittany. This very nearly caused what amounted to a national emergency, and such was the outcry that Henry II, who was overlord of Brittany, immediately despatched an armed party under the command of one of the Cardinham family (of which more later) to recover them. They were eventually returned in a new ivory casket that can still be seen in the church (although this too has been stolen in recent times and later found abandoned on a northcountry moor).

Petroc died in 564 whilst walking along the cliff path between Padstow and Little Petherick where he had set up a religious community. Such was his fame and the respect he commanded that he was said to have been mourned by an immense crowd of people who gathered on the surrounding cliffs. His cult eventually turned into a major religious movement, with dedications throughout England, Wales and Brittany.

St Petroc was not the only presiding spirit of Bodmin Priory, though, for in 1113, at least two decades before Geoffrey of Monmouth's book, another incident took place which again threatened international relations, but this time it concerned an altogether more legendary figure. Hermann of Tournai records in that year a group of monks from Laon were collecting funds for the rebuilding of their cathedral which had been destroyed by fire. As they crossed the Cornish border from Devon they had been told they were now entering 'the Land of Arthur', and were proudly shown rock formations called 'Arthur's Chair' and 'Arthur's Oven' (which although unknown today are amongst the earliest documented Arthurian sites).

They had with them miraculous relics of their own which had drawn a large number of Cornish folk hoping for cures and the answer to their prayers. In the midst of this throng the French launched into an animated discussion about King Arthur and Merlin, claiming that they had been French and not British at all. A man with a withered hand shouted out that far from being killed at the Battle of Camlann, the King was still very much alive. At this, uproar broke out and the church was very soon full of Cornishmen brandishing arms and threatening bloodshed. Only by the intervention of a diplomatic clerk, who managed to calm the seething crowd, was a potentially disastrous incident avoided.

Colourful though this account is, it reveals the passionate belief amongst the Cornish of the time that Arthur was not only somehow embodied within the land, but that his spirit was still very much alive. And, we must remember, this was some time before Geoffrey's book was published, creating a great renaissance of Arthurian lore. Can there be any doubt that the spirit of King Arthur lived on in the hearts and minds of the Cornish, and even with the Christian monks of Bodmin Priory, who also had a powerful bond with Bosinney and Tintagel and the old chapel of St Julitta on the Island? Perhaps they also harboured distant memories of how the Arthurian legends were literally impressed upon the landscape itself, and maybe even that this great Royal Lion that symbolised kingship was crowned with the Priory. The Celtic character was famously intransigent when it came to new or imposed ideas, for it clung to the old traditions tenaciously, and these often lingered on even until Victorian times in the 'fairy tales' and legends of giants as well as that of King Arthur. So could it be that they felt the land retained a power they may not have been able to fathom, but nevertheless were instinctively aware of?

Right in the centre of the Lion's head is a massive 144-foot high Egyptian-style obelisk. It was erected in 1856 as a memorial to Walter Raleigh Gilbert, a commander during the Sikh wars, and, as his name suggests, he was a descendant of Drake's old compatriot Walter Raleigh. His family lived at Priory House on the site of the old monastery, and a later member, Davies Gilbert, was a noted Cornish historian. As one of the old Cornish 'tribes' they may just have had an inkling that this site had an arcane significance connected with courage and fearlessness, the natural characteristics of any lion. (Perhaps these things persist in strange and unlikely ways in the collective consciousness, for the local football team is called the *Bodmin Lions*, whose ground is located in Priory Park!)

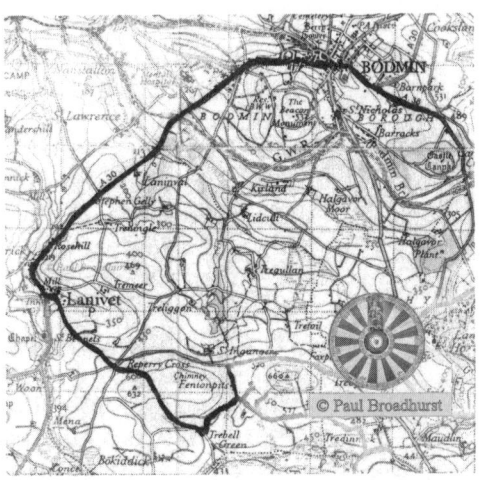

The Great Lion of Bodmin

Following the Lion's regal outlines away from the town we come to a place called Laveddon, exactly where his eye is positioned. This is an ancient place, within recent memory the site of a mill with a large pond. Water, curiously, often seems to be associated with eyes (as with St Piran's Holy Well on the eye of the Bear), perhaps, we might conjecture, because of its sparkling reflective qualities. As we come to the Lion's nose we find ourselves at another important site, a place known as the 'sacred centre of Cornwall'. An old Cornish saying records that Lanivet Church is 'in the middle of the county, North and South, East and West' and it does appear in many ways to represent the *omphalos* or navel of the county. Every country had its sacred centre in former times, from Delphi in Greece to Tara in Druidic Ireland. Located as it is at the mid-point on the old pilgrim's route of the Saint's Way which connected the north and south coasts, it was a focus for those travellers moving between Ireland, Wales and Brittany, and situated exactly half-way between the ports of Padstow and Fowey. At about fifty miles from Land's End and forty from the River Tamar it is symbolically the geometric centre of Cornwall and must have been very important too in pre-Christian times, for it has the Celtic prefix *lan*, meaning sacred enclosure. The earliest recorded name is *Lannived* in 1268, which may derive from *nived* or *neved*, meaning sacred grove.

Close by is St Benet's Abbey with its medieval house and tower, once a Benedictine Lazar House and hospital (*Benet* is a shortened Cornish version of *Benedict*). There was also an important Celtic monastery at Lamorick, right on the Lion's nose. This concentration of religious sites, like those of Bodmin, hints at an area with a special sanctity. The churchyard at Lanivet is notable for its magnificent elaborately carved crosses. One of these, standing behind the church in an open area of land, is said to precisely mark the exact centre of Cornwall, and is one of the most highly-decorated in

Bodmin Obelisk - situated in the centre of the Lion's Head.

the county. Amongst the designs is a symbol of two concentric circles with a dot in the middle, as if to signify a geometric centre. A similar motif is repeated on the front of the cross, this time with one circle, between the legs of what is surely one of the most curious images on any old cross, a figure with a 'halo' or aura around it, and what, some think, looks like a tail! The church's feast day on the last Thursday in April is probably derived from the Celtic festival of Beltane on May 1st, one of the most important times of the ancient calendar.

Lanivet Church was once a 'centre' then, in perhaps more ways than one. Half-way along the Saint's Way, as well as on the main pilgrim route to West Cornwall and St Michael's Mount, it was a meeting place for those travelling from England as well as the countries of the Celtic fringe. Such places were a great melting pot of many religions and different beliefs in a way that was unusual in the rest of Britain. The classical writers had noted that Cornwall in particular always extended a warm welcome to travellers no matter where they were from, being naturally inquisitive about other countries. Its strong maritime tradition meant that merchants and pilgrims had always mingled freely with the native population since the days of the Phoenicians and Greeks, who often established colonies and trading routes to acquire Cornwall's most important export of various metals, notably tin, which had dominated Cornwall's economy since the Bronze Age and was to continue to do so. Archaeological evidence also supports these connections with the classical world—not least the finds from Tintagel, linking it with the Mediterranean and the Byzantine Empire. A trading settlement from these times has also been unearthed at the mouth of the River Camel near Padstow, where pottery from North Africa, Turkey and Carthage was found.

It is perhaps no surprise to find near the porch of Lanivet Church a highly unusual coped stone tomb memorial elaborately carved from granite, believed to be of Viking origin. Arthur Langdon includes a description of this in his *Old Cornish Crosses*, and notes that on its richly ornamented upper surface are two curious animals joined together by the ridge that runs lengthwise along it. Whilst it is by no means unusual to find mythical beasts carved on old stones, it is rare to see them on such memorials, especially in Cornwall. We may be forgiven in this instance for wondering what they might have originally represented. Langdon points out that the style of carving is virtually identical to that found on the great cross-shaft on Waterpit Down near Boscastle (positioned on the Polar Axis) which we have already noted, as well as the old cross in Lanhydrock churchyard. These are all significant features in our quest so far, and may indicate that whoever carved these elaborate works of art were somehow involved in the mystery we are trying to unravel. Sometimes also called a 'hog's back' or 'boat-shaped' tomb memorial, this interesting object, along perhaps with the 'omphalos' cross, appears to come from a period of Christianity that pre-dated the influence of the Roman Church.

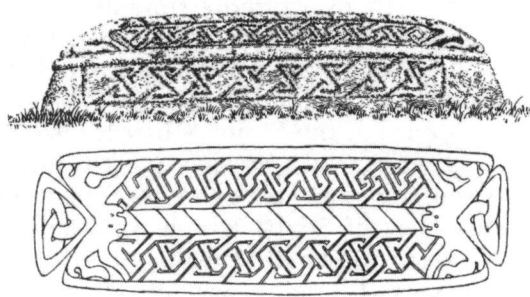

The Lanivet Memorial Stone

Could Lanivet's position, coinciding with the 'nostrils' of the Great Lion, mean that in very ancient times it was a place where the spirit or ether was somehow mystically inhaled, drawing certain influences into the Lion in a way that is difficult to imagine today? What does the Lion really represent? Lions have not roamed this land since prehistory, yet the legendary name for Cornwall was *Lyonesse*. Perhaps because of this there is a long-standing tradition that the lion was the original royal crest of the county, and this was why it was later adopted by the Dukes and Earls of Cornwall.

The Legend of Lyonesse

'a land of matchless grace was Lyonesse,
Glorious with rolling hills, rejoicing streams,
Hoar monuments upreared when Time was young,
Wide plains of forest, slopes of golden corn,
And stately castles crowning granite peaks'.

The Lady of Lyonesse
John Adams

Lyonesse was, according to one of the most persistent of Cornish traditions, the name of Cornwall during the time before a great flood caused an inundation that made St Michael's Mount an island. Then it was miles from the sea and in the middle of a dense wood, a fact demonstrated by the remains of petrified trees that can still occasionally be seen in Mount's Bay at very low tides. The Isles of Scilly were said to have been part of the mainland at that time, and William of Worcester recorded that no less than one hundred and forty parishes had been lost, and that fishermen often snagged their nets on old stone mullions and other remains of buildings on the sea bed, which in this area is very shallow. It is said that during the flood large numbers of people and animals perished, and that there was only one survivor, called Trevilian, who was carried to safety by the speed of his white horse, which leapt ashore at Perranuthnoe. In commemoration of this event, the Trevelyan family's coat of arms shows a horse rising from the waves.

Practically every Cornish historian or romantic poet has found themselves at one time or another writing about this fabled land, for the story tells of a remote time akin to the Golden Age of Arthurian lore, a halcyon age of peace and plenty. Yet as we can see, the story is more than just fable, for there is an entire body of evidence to show that one or even more major inundations have taken place in the past. Besides the physical evidence of the Mount's Bay forest (Victorian photographs of these petrified remains can be seen in the County Museum), the remains of walls and stone rows can still be seen vanishing into the shallow waters surrounding the Isles of Scilly, which was, before being drowned, one large island. Carew, from an old Cornish family and a friend of fellow Westcountrymen Drake and Raleigh, was also well-versed in these maritime observations, and declared:

> 'that such a Lionesse there was are proofs yet remaining... The space between the Land's End and the Isles of Scilly, being about thirty miles, to this day retaineth that name (of Lionesse), in Cornish Lethowsow, and carrieth an equal depth of forty to sixty feet, a thing not usual in the sea's proper dominion, save that about the midway there lieth a rock which at low water discovereth his head. They term it the gulf, suiting thereby the other name of Scilla. Fishermen also casting their nets thereabouts have drawn up the pieces of doors and windows. Moreover, the ancient name of St Michael's Mount was Cara Clowse (the hore rock in the woode), which now is at every flood encompassed by the sea, and yet, at some low ebbs, roots of mighty trees are seen round about it.'

The tradition of Lyonesse is also linked to the Arthurian period in another way, for in the legend of Tristan and Iseult, Tristan's father is the King of Liones (there is also a region of Brittany called *Leonais*, perhaps a memory from the settlement of the old Cornish families in that area). It also features prominently at the death of King Arthur, for in one version of the legend, after Arthur had fallen, Mordred pursued the remnants of his army into Lyonesse. Here the spirit of Merlin appeared and the land was suddenly sunk beneath the waves, drowning Mordred's forces. Arthur's knights, however, reached the Isles of Scilly and were saved, establishing a monastery on Tresco (where the famous sub-tropical gardens now exist amongst the remains of a Benedictine Abbey), and naming two islands within sight of it *Great Arthur* and *Little Arthur*. Tennyson referred to this belief when he set Arthur's final battle in Lyonesse.

The legend of Lyonesse harks back to a very remote time when Cornwall was a different land entirely, a legendary era that was closely linked with the Arthurian tales. It is as if both these fables are referring to a deeply mystical period long before the present Christian era when the totem animal of the realm was the Lion. As if in remembrance of this time, our Great Lion looks exactly due West, just like that equally ancient totem, the Bear. They are both set to stare forever towards the setting Sun and the direction of the great inundation remembered by the legend of Lyonesse.

9

A LION'S TALE

odern historians tend to scoff at Carew's idea that the name Lostwithiel was derived from the old Brythonic Celtic words for *Lion's Tail*, preferring instead to point out that a more believable alternative would be from *Lostgwdeyel*, meaning 'tail of the wood'. Under the circumstances that is understandable, but we have to ask whether Carew may have been aware of some tradition that caused him to suggest such an unlikely thing in the first place. In fact he tried to justify his statement by saying that the town was connected to the tail of the 'lion' in Restormel Castle as a reference to whichever Prince or Earl happened to be in residence at the time. Interestingly, in star-maps and heraldry, the lion is often shown with his tail turned up over his back, very much like our young Lion.

The area around Restormel Castle has long been important, according to ancient records. Camden, a contemporary of Carew, thought that it was the place named *Uzella* shown on the second century map by the Greek cartographer Ptolemy. A Roman hillfort above the site of the castle shows how significant it was in their day, and these earthworks were in fact called Uzella on the original Ordnance Survey map of 1813. Recent excavations have revealed that this hillfort was a centre of Roman metalworking.

Yet Carew's observation that Restormel was the 'Tail of the Lion' only appears to make any real sense if we take him literally at his word, even if he does excuse it by alluding to the Castle's royal owners. This may be entirely forgivable, for the heraldic insignia of the Earls of Cornwall was two lions, a coincidence that might

The constellations of Leo Major and Leo Minor, from Urania's Mirror. *These images appear to be symbolised on the Earth by the landscape Lions of Bodmin and Lostwithiel, two of the most ancient royal and religious centres in Cornwall.*

make us naturally wonder where this device originally sprang from. Was the lion simply a sort of totem animal adopted by them, much as Celtic tribes had their own animal guardian spirits chosen for their particular characteristics, in this case those of strength and courage? Or did they inherit them from an earlier time, as the legend of Lyonesse might suggest? If so then these symbolic lions come from a very remote period indeed, and it would be no great surprise that the Norman/Cornish Earls would wish to link themselves with their legendary roots, just as they had done with King Arthur.

The most interesting thing here, though, is how the two lions were apparently adopted by the Normans and then the Plantagenets to become the royal symbols for the entire English realm. Was this a deliberate act to associate themselves with the symbols of the original British race, before the country was overrun by Saxons and the Roman Church? Later, during the reign of Richard I, known universally as *The Lionheart*, another lion was added to the crest in his honour, bringing the new heraldic motif to the count of three, which it has remained ever since. Richard spent only six months in England during his ten-year reign, but nevertheless his various crusades were driven by a passion that echoed that of Arthur, and on his way to Palestine he presented his ally, Tancred, with what was said at the time to be King Arthur's famous sword.

The lions of Lyonesse and their apparent adoption by the royal dynasties points in a very convincing manner to the idea that English royalty really did consider themselves as god-kings who were descended from those who were initiated into an ancient Mystery tradition concerning the power in the land. Were they fully aware of the implications, or were they just bystanders in a drama that would inevitably play itself out, with these symbols merely an offshoot of necessary public relations? As we continue to explore the mystery behind the symbolism of the two lions, we will surely come to the conclusion that the royal families involved in this era of unprecedented change knew exactly why they aligned themselves to the old British mythology.

But let us now look more closely at the Lostwithiel Lion, for there is much to discover. The first thing we will notice is that it represents a new, vibrant and youthful energy very different to its companion at Bodmin. This, it would seem, is very much in keeping with the new thrusting prowess of the Norman dynasty and their determination to become the kings of the political jungle, whilst at the same time modelling their new empire on ancient tradition.

After the Battle of Hastings William had given Cornwall to his half-brother Count Robert of Mortain, who took his name from a village close to the Brittany/Normandy border. Robert, and in this case one of the three most powerful barons in Cornwall, Thurstan or Turstin (who had also been the first Norman Lord of Boscastle), dispossessed the previous Saxon

Lord of Lostwithiel, named Grim, and claimed the land for themselves. At the time of the Domesday Book in 1086 Lostwithiel was part of the Manor of Bodardle, and within the next few years the town soon started to grow. It was probably Baldwin fitz Turstin, son of the original Norman Lord of Bodardle, who created the moated circular earthwork on which Restormel Castle was later to be built in 1100. Whether the site was of pre-Norman origin is not recorded, but if their practice of re-using former earthworks, the old centres of power, was carried out in this case, then it may help to explain the significant location of the Castle.

For Restormel is not situated where it is by chance, or even particularly for the defensive reasons one might imagine. It is located according to a bigger plan, lying precisely on the same longitude as the centre of Lundy Island, and is consequently exactly on the North-South axis of the Great Bear/Lundy/Preseli meridian. Thus the Castle sits directly astride it, locking it into the wider geometry that includes Stonehenge. The conclusion can only be that the location of Restormel Castle was a deliberate act to mark this Polar Axis and use the place as a royal centre around which the local power, both political and geographic, revolved, seemingly as a metaphor for the heavenly realms. In this it appears to have been highly successful, for the area was, over the coming centuries after the Norman Conquest, to become the richest and most powerful in Cornwall.

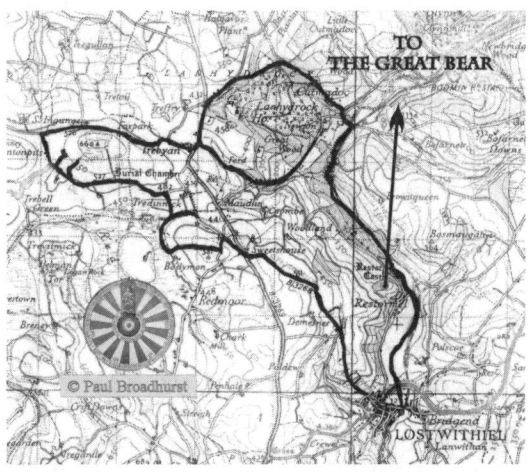

Restormel Castle, the ancient seat of the Princes and Earls of Cornwall, located at the 'tail' of the Lostwithiel Lion, and directly on the Polar Axis of the Great Bear.

The next owners of the castle after Turstin were the Cardinhams, who were descended from Bertrand de Dinant who had accompanied William to Hastings and married into the Turstin line. They were to become the most influential family in Cornwall, and the instigators of the development of Lostwithiel as a major port (during its heyday second only to Southampton along the entire southern coast of Britain). At that time East Cornwall and West Devon were amongst the most important sources of tin known to the western world, in the midst of an insatiable demand from the rest of Britain and Europe. Eventually, the Devon lodes were to become exhausted, leaving the Cornish to control the market. Bodmin was at the time the centre of the tin industry, and the *Via Regia*, or the Royal Way, connected the two towns (and our two landscape Lions) so that vast quantities of tin ingots could be exported from the quays that lined the banks of the River Fowey, then deep enough to be navigable to seagoing vessels.

Tin-stamp from Lostwithiel, bearing a lion that has remarkable similarities to the 'Lostwithiel Lion' in the landscape.

Manpower and other necessary expertise was imported from Brittany, and the Cardinhams built St Bartholemew's Church in the Breton style with lean-to aisles, one of only two in the county. Soon Lostwithiel had become an exceedingly rich and powerful place, with boats regularly docking from London, and the shipping of tin to Oléron, an island in the Bay of Biscay from where it would be despatched to La Rochelle, Bayonne, Bordeaux, Barcelona, Genoa, Messina and Levant, all places that were controlled by the great maritime merchants of the day, the Knights Templar. Because of the tin industry the Templars became a potent economic force in Cornwall, building a church at Temple on Bodmin Moor for the protection of travellers and overland pilgrims, and possessing many other churches and holdings throughout the county. Tin ingots were stamped with the rampant Royal Lion, which looks extraordinarily like our Lostwithiel Lion. In other areas further west the Templar motif of the Lamb of God was used. These symbols meant that each ingot could be assayed and easily identified. As well as becoming the jewel in the crown of the Cornish commercial ports, Lostwithiel also became a place of departure for crusaders on their way to the Holy Land.

The first Lord of Cardinham was Richard fitz Turold, who looked after Robert de Mortain's Cornish estates and had been a companion of William in the Battle of Hastings (he has been identified on the Bayeux Tapestry as a short stocky man holding two horses). He built a castle at the site of a prehistoric earthwork on a ridge overlooking what is now Cardinham Church, today called Bury Castle, just a few miles from Bodmin and Lostwithiel (this is probably where the name, whose earliest form was *Cardinan*, came from; *Caer*, the Celtic word for earthwork, and *Dinan*, the name of Richard's home in Brittany). This exposed position was not ideal, being high up on the fringes of Bodmin Moor, so he moved to a more sheltered spot at Trezance (Cornish for *Holy Place*). This was the site of an early chapel and Holy Well founded by the Celtic Saint Meubred, who is said to be buried at the nearby church.

Later they built another castle looking down the valley towards the church, but even this was eventually abandoned when the family inherited Restormel in the fourteenth century. They must have had strong Viking links, like William and Bertrand. Cardinham Church has one of the finest Celtic crosses in the country, dated to about 800 AD with Viking designs as well as elaborate knotwork patterns, a tangible clue to the Celtic/Viking alliance stretching over many centuries. This has an early inscription which, although now covered in lichen and indecipherable, reads *Arthi* according to the Bodmin antiquary Rev. Iago who examined it at first hand. This is a name that, considering our current interests, may strike us as especially intriguing. Does it mean *Bear* or is it a reference to

Arthur? The stone is situated outside the porch, and is aligned directly on its North/South axis, as we might perhaps expect if it refers to the circumpolar regions.

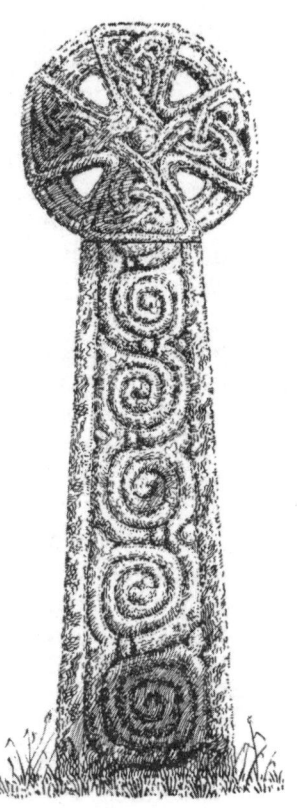

By 1186 Robert Cardinham was Lord of the Manors of Bodardle, Restormel and Cardinham, holding 42,000 acres of land between the river and Tywardreath, as well as all the navigable waters of the River Fowey. He also established a market by Royal charter. By the early thirteenth century Lostwithiel had become a major international port, its trade exceeding that of all the Cinque Ports together, and that did not even include the export of tin!

Richard, the son of King John, became Earl of Cornwall when he was 22 years old, after he had been on a crusade to the Holy Land. He was, partly through the dues received from Cornish tin and partly because of his shrewd business sense, to become the richest man in Britain, owning vast tracts of land and a great number of castles. Like his ancestors he must have been powerfully aware of the legends and traditions of ancient Britain, for he attempted to resurrect and transform the idea of King Arthur's Round Table for the first time in modern history. He summoned a full assembly of elected Knights of the Shires, the original model for what was to later become the first Parliament.

Cardinham Cross

It failed in this instance, but nevertheless remained as a template for the future democratisation of government. Richard of Cornwall's influence has thus had an incalculable effect on British history. He was elected King of the Romans (a sort of European Pope) at Aachen in Germany in a ceremony of great splendour, a reign that lasted 15 years. He also spent a brief spell in the Tower of London after being taken prisoner in 1264 at the Battle of Lewes.

Richard owned three castles in Cornwall, those of Launceston, Trematon and Tintagel, which he had ordered to be built at the place of Arthur's birth. He now sought to acquire Restormel and Lostwithiel, apparently wishing to establish it as the county town. So he bought the lands from Isolda de Tracy, and soon after, on 13th July 1269, he granted the town a charter which was still written including the old Viking terms; '...that our Burgesses may have there a Guild Mercatory and free and civil customs and Sake and Soke, and Thol and Thegn and Infangenethof.'

Barbara Fraser, in *The Book of Lostwithiel*, explains that 'By means of *Sake* and *Soke* they were allowed to hold their own Courts, and by *Infangenethof* were given jurisdiction over thieves caught in the borough. By *Thol* they were bound to pay duty on imports. And by *Thegn*, were allowed the status of freemen and landowners, but were bound to give military service to King and nobles on demand.'

This old charter shows how the Viking traditions were still strong even in the thirteenth century. But what is of particular interest here is the list of signatories; 'These being our witnesses – Robert de Esthall. Archdeacon of Worcester, our clerk, Reginald de Boterill, Philip de Bodrugan, and others.'

There is a familiar name here, for Reginald de Boterill was from the Bottreaux family who had their castle at Boscastle (then called Bottreaux Castle). He was the son of William I de Bottreaux and, because of his position close to the centre of royal power was consequently extremely likely to have been the actual man who took charge of building Tintagel castle at Richard's behest.

He was, therefore, by implication, privy to the belief system of the royal dynasty, who wished to restore the Arthurian realm not only by establishing a physical link with the place of his birth, but by having Richard's Cornish residence at another place of cosmological significance, Restormel Castle.

The Borough of Lostwithiel at that time included an area known as *Penknek* (later called Penknight) in the Parish of Lanlivery, just a few miles from the port town. This place had been a royal centre itself long before Lostwithiel had developed into the commercial hub of the area. Indeed, the town was at those early times just a chapelry to the church at Lanlivery. This place (there is also a *Lanlivry* in Brittany) has some further important clues to the nature of the beliefs of the Cornish Earldom. Next to the Crown Inn, the site of the old court and an unusual building of medieval longhouse design, is the fifteenth century church, very prominent in the landscape, having the tallest tower for many miles. Carved on it are two extraordinary designs, which, as far as I know, have

never been commented upon. These are of great significance in understanding the beliefs and attitudes of those times. One carving is of two lions with flowing manes and tongues protruding, holding what looks like a stylised plant (or is it a tree?) between them.

The Lanlivery Lions

This image is not just for decorative purposes; it is a message carved in stone. The two lions, as we know, are the royal symbol of the Earls of Cornwall, so in a way perhaps we should not be too surprised to find them here. But there may be another dimension to this if we are correct in speculating that these two lions could be ultimately derived from something that exists in the landscape. What came first? This is a reasonable question. As we peer into the past in an attempt to uncover whether these giant effigies were created by the Norman dynasties or merely mimicked as a sort of geomantic inheritance, all will become much clearer. This is a matter that will continue to occupy our investigations throughout this quest, yet all the evidence suggests that these beliefs are firmly based on a world-view of extreme antiquity, which is what ultimately gives them their power.

The protruding tongues are generally agreed by mythologists to represent the power of the Sun, for many Green Men and lions with their tongues sticking out can be seen in church carvings throughout Britain. Both encapsulate the Sun's strength, for the Green Man, in his most famous role, represents the spirit of spring and the returning light, whilst the lions are the symbol of the astrological sign of Leo, which rules high summer. Probably because of this, the sticking out of the tongue has in many different cultures always, it seems, been a customary way of banishing dark forces.

And what of the stylised plant or tree? Could it be the *Planta Genista*, the sprig of flowering broom adopted by the Plantagenets as their special emblem? It certainly possessed a mystical significance to them, for it had been the chosen badge of their line for centuries, even though it had only been used as their surname towards the end of their reign. Or could it be the Tree of Life that symbolises the Polar Axis? In both the Celtic and Viking traditions this symbol was paramount, being the great tree with its roots in the Earth that grows ever upwards towards the 'sacred centre' of the Heavens. In the Viking beliefs it is known as the sacred ash, or *Ygdrassil*, that links the three worlds; Heaven, the Earth and the Underworld. There are a number of other examples of two lions holding what is clearly a tree associated with this Bear/Lion axis in the landscape, many on Norman fonts and one example in particular over the door at Treneglos Church in North Cornwall. Here two lions guard a flourishing tree whose branches spread right over the leonine beasts.

The Ygdrassil Tree, symbolising the Polar Axis which connects the three worlds.

If this interpretation is valid, then here we may have a symbolic image that operates on a number of different levels, just as a true symbol should. On the one hand it is a motif of kingship, with the royal lions holding erect the Tree of Life, representing stability backed by the power of the Sun. It also symbolises the two Lions in the landscape, which, as we know, are to be found at the foot of the Tree or Polar Axis guarded by the Great Bear of Tintagel. As if to emphasise that these effigies are a symbolic reflection of the heavens, I also noticed when studying the map that the four major points within the body of the Lostwithiel Lion (Restormel Castle, St Bartholemew's Church, Lanhydrock House and the hilltop with a reservoir now built into it) closely replicated the shape of the four major stars in the constellation of Leo, except in mirror fashion.

The other carving, on the south-east corner of the tower facing the direction of the rising Sun, is even more striking. At first it appears quite alarming, for it depicts two figures holding what appears to be a decapitated head with very long hair. At the foot of the westernmost figure is what looks like a giant's head with curly hair and a beard rolling on the ground. These figures are notable in that they seem to exhibit a certain surprising cheerfulness under the circumstances.

What can this rather grisly, yet at the same time vaguely comic, image mean? A clue is concealed furthest away from the observer. Balancing the bearded head at the feet of the figure on the opposite side is a flaming image of the Sun.

The Beheading Game

I spent a number of years wondering about the meaning of this strange carving, so prominently displayed on one of the tallest church towers in the vicinity and closely linked to ancient royalty. Its situation opposite the two lions with the 'Tree of Life' indicates it has an important story to tell. Who commissioned these carvings? Was it the Cardinham family, the Lords of Restormel, who had been the local 'kings' of Cornwall in the fourteenth and fifteenth centuries? The church still belongs to the ancient Manor of Bodardle, as it was known in the Domesday Book, and was given along with its chapelries of Lostwithiel and nearby Luxulyan to the Priory of Tywardreath in about 1150. This was exactly the time when the Arthurian tales were enjoying a great revival throughout the land.

It was whilst researching another book, *The Green Man and the Dragon*, that I found myself reading the fourteenth century poem *Sir Gawain and the Green Knight*. Set in medieval times, it is acknowledged by scholars that this tale is derived from the Celtic world, and is firmly based on pre-Christian ritual concerning kingship. Here, Gawain (*Gwalchmai* in the old Brythonic language, meaning *Hawk of May*) represents the Sun God, a solar hero who finds himself at Christmas in King Arthur's

Court. Christmas is in fact the Winter Solstice, when the dying god of the old year is reborn. Just like the Sun, Gawain's strength grows towards noon, and is in decline afterwards.

King Arthur's foe is the Green Knight, a green-skinned giant who suddenly arrives unannounced at the King's court astride a green horse and brandishing a gleaming green steel axe. Yet for all his formidable appearance he comes in peace, for he holds a holly bough as a symbol of friendship. He issues a challenge to the assembled company: cut off his head with the axe and next year he will return the compliment. As Arthur is about to accept, Gawain steps forward, and with a mighty blow, strikes off the giant's head which rolls on the ground. However, nonchalantly, the giant picks it up and rides away, reminding Gawain that at the same time next year he must meet him in the 'Green Chapel' to pay with his own. After a series of adventures, Gawain does indeed appear to pay his debt a year later at the Winter Solstice, but is only symbolically killed, leaving him to live on and eventually discover the Holy Grail.

The elements of this ancient story incorporate many levels of understanding, and are known to have come down from very early times. They occur in at least eight other Arthurian texts, as well as a tale known as *Bricriu's Feast* from the Irish cycle of stories centred around the Celtic hero Cuchulainn, a Sun God with a shining halo of golden hair. Once we realise that this strange carving on the church tower is not meant to be alarming or threatening, we can begin to sense its real meaning. Here we have a representation of what was known in the Celtic world as *The Beheading Game*, a ritualistic way of understanding the Sun's cycle. The head of the old god, with his curly hair, staring eyes and straggly beard, lies at the feet of a figure who seems, along with his companion, to be triumphantly holding aloft the youthful head of the new-born Sun King. Kingship was always, in the ancient world, inextricably bound up with the old veneration for the Sun as the source of Light and Life. There are other motifs within this story too, which we become aware of when we understand the way puns were extensively used throughout the Celtic and medieval worlds. The *axe* of the Green Giant is a metaphor for the *axis* of the Earth, which, because the Earth is tilted away from vertical in relation to the Sun, causes the four seasons of spring, summer, autumn and winter to manifest.

As the tower is dated to the fifteenth century, this reinforces even more how the beliefs of the Earls of Cornwall were rooted in the Celtic ethos of far earlier times, and that they persisted for many centuries beyond the introduction of Christianity. It is often commented upon how the Christian religion in Cornwall never really supplanted the Pagan. The evidence of many remaining carvings from these times (where they have not been destroyed in Victorian restorations) speak of this. As repositories of the old British way of life such images often tell a tale of how the old customs survived whilst other regions were more subject to the controlling influence of the Roman church. Yet here in Cornwall Christian ideals were never really in conflict with those of other faiths to the same degree, primarily because of the legacy of Celtic Christianity which incorporated so much Druidic knowledge.

Pondering on the significance of Gawain, I noted that the Arthurian scholar John Matthews, in *Gawain, Knight of the Goddess*, had shown that he was 'once the most important knight at King Arthur's Court... a figure of great mythical, magical and historical importance' but that in later times his character had become greatly diminished as he became transformed, in Sir Thomas Malory's *Morte d'Arthur*, into a womanising villain. By coincidence, a few days after writing this section Gabriele and I found ourselves in the middle of Dartmoor and happened to come across the village of Widecombe. Intrigued by the size of the church, which was far larger than one would expect for such a remote and isolated place, we entered and spent some time admiring the magnificent collection of medieval painted roof bosses that are the notable treasures of the building. Numerous Green Men were in evidence, but three in particular which were aligned caught our attention. The central head looked Green Giant-like, and the two on either side were of ordinary human heads spouting foliage from their mouths. The Church guide stated that these two images were of Gawain!

But of course there is probably no such thing as coincidence—Gawain was shown here as a Green Man alongside what must be the Green Giant of Celtic folklore. The legend implies this too, as he takes the place of the giant exactly a year later, thereby fulfilling his obligations and initiating a new cycle of fertility. One can see how such a figure may have become stripped of his original nature in later times, and how his characteristic fertility was changed into womanising. Widecombe, was, we found, Templar territory because of its central position in the Dartmoor metal trade.

When Richard, Earl of Cornwall, died, his son Edmund took over the old Kingdom and set about continuing Lostwithiel's rise as a great commercial centre. For the 27 years that he was Earl the town became the undisputed capital of the county. He built the Great Hall—a scaled down copy of Westminster Hall in London—as the administrative centre of his realm and the meeting place of the Cornish Parliament, where the courts, offices and treasury were brought together for the first time. An entire complex was created, along with an Exchequer, Coinage Hall, assay buildings, smelting houses, strongroom and prison. There were also lodgings for various officials. The Hall, famous as the finest building in Cornwall (often referred to as the Royal Palace) still stands today, and is currently undergoing renovation. It fell into ruin in the seventeenth century and was eventually bought by the local Freemasons who used it as a meeting place. Costly repairs have, however, led them to consider that it would be better suited to community use, an ideal solution to protect its future. In consequence the Grade I listed building has recently been bought by a trust founded by the current Prince of Wales and Duke of Cornwall. So history, in its own curious way, turns full circle. On its gable end is the crumbling crest of the old Earls—two lions.

The scene at Lostwithiel during the peak of its success must have been one of great cosmopolitanism and vibrant commercial vigour. As the busiest port in Cornwall, as well as its first coinage town, there would have been a never-ending stream of vessels coming and going from many different countries, with wine, fish, meat, cheese, cloth, fruits, corn and every other commodity continuously being loaded and unloaded. And then there were the huge quantities of tin, bound for London and Europe, as well as the various fairs and markets with their colourful collection of shops and stalls. Add a mêlée of seamen, tinners, farmers, merchants and officials of all kinds, and the picture emerges of a thriving city port, the most important medieval town in the county; a sort of Cornish London. One can catch a flavour of what life must have been like, perhaps even today. Edmund himself described it as *The Fairest of Small Cities*.

Restormel's most well-known royal visitor after Edmund was Edward, known as the Black Prince because of the colour of his armour. He became the first Duke of Cornwall at the age of seven after his father, Edward III, created the Dukedom of Cornwall with his 'Great Charter' of 1337. He was also the Prince of Wales, as if uniting the two regions of the native British just as they had once been long ago.

On 20th August 1354 the Prince, with much ceremony and attended by an entourage of noblemen and knights, crossed the bridge into Lostwithiel to the sound of trumpeting heralds. People from across the county welcomed him, and he held court at Restormel for two weeks before moving on to Launceston. He visited the castle on only one other occasion in 1362, and gradually (due to a number of factors, including that Edward, unlike his predecessors, chose not to reside there, as well as the

Edward, the Black Prince, with his lion crest

deleterious effects of the Black Death) the prosperity of the town began to wane.

The Black Prince himself died of malaria in 1376, yet Lostwithiel's association with him, however brief and lacking the vibrancy of the time of his forebears, is compelling because of his great interest in following the ethos of Arthurian beliefs. His father Edward III had built a huge round hall at Windsor Castle to emulate the ideals of King Arthur, and created a new chivalric order, the Knights of the Round Table. He also set up the exclusive Noble Order of the Garter, a mystical fraternity that still exists today. Edward's reign thus reflected a high point during an era inspired by the Arthurian romances, as well as an attempt to recreate that long-lost Golden Age.

But the town's real ascendancy had been during the time of Richard and Edmund, and it was at this time that the architecture of the town was greatly enriched. The Church of St Bartholemew's was refurbished, adding a Breton-style octagonal lantern tower, unusual for Cornwall. It was probably around this time that a very mysterious object indeed was commissioned for the church, and one which will now focus our attention. This was a large octagonal font with some exceedingly curious images carved around it. One tableau especially is of great interest, described casually by earlier observers as 'a hunting scene'. But as we are about to discover, all is not as it first appears, for these old carvings are imbued with symbolism that when understood, preserve much encoded wisdom from the past.

Restormel Castle in the nineteenth century

10

THE WILD HUNT

n 1891, the Vicar of St Bartholemew's Church at Lostwithiel published a history compiled from the writings of previous chroniclers
who had passed that way during the centuries before, noting their
impressions and commenting on things that had caught their attention.
The list included Henry VIII's antiquary Leland, the Elizabethans Carew
and Camden and later writers such as Hals, Borlase, Lysons and Davies
Gilbert. It began:

> 'The Parish Church of Lostwithiel is dedicated in honour of St
> Bartholemew the Apostle and Martyr, and was probably built about the
> year 1190 by Robert de Cardinan (who was at that time Lord of the town
> of Lostwithiel and possessor of much property in the neighbourhood) on
> the foundation of an earlier church, which some people suppose to have
> been built in the days of the renowned King Arthur.
>
> As King Arthur was killed in a battle which was fought at a place
> called Slaughter Bridge, between Tintagel and Camelford, AD 542, this
> tradition places the original church at Lostwithiel amongst the earliest
> that were built here.'

The fact that King Arthur is mentioned right at the beginning of
this history is revealing, for it shows that even towards the latter nineteenth century he was still considered to be the presiding spirit of Cornwall long after his supposed death some fifteen hundred years before.
Even more interesting is that it connects King Arthur with the original
church on the site, and apparently shows a lingering memory of the direct
connection between Lostwithiel and 'Arthur's Grave' at Slaughterbridge.
As we have already discovered, Restormel Castle, the residence of Robert
of Cardinham, and the site of the church directly south of it, together with
Slaughterbridge, all lie on the great Polar Axis that runs from the Great
Bear of Tintagel through the 'tail' of the Lostwithiel Lion.

The church, it continued, once belonged to the Parish of Lanlivery,
which had been given to the monks of Tywardeath Priory by Baldwin,
son of Thurstan or Turstin, the original Norman owner of Restormel
and Lostwithiel. This links the town with the curious carvings on
Lanlivery Church depicting the two lions and the Beheading Game,
both vestiges of Celtic Sun lore. All this emphasises that the beliefs of

the Norman families, of which the Cardinhams were the most prominent, were, even in the fifteenth century when Lanlivery Church tower was built, still deeply rooted in Arthurian myth and the old Celtic traditions.

The Vicar who compiled this history may have been inspired by the discovery, in July the previous year, of two sepulchral vaults found behind walled-up arches near the porch (which can still be seen). Behind the walls were human bones, which he believed to be the earthly remains of Robert de Cardinan, who died between 1224 and 1234, and his wife Isolda fitz William. Did the spirit of Robert, the one-time 'king' of Cornwall, momentarily awaken, before his mouldering remains crumbled to dust?

The tower of the church is unusual for Cornwall, having been originally built during the thirteenth century and then later embellished by an octagonal lantern spire with gothic tracery and, in the north-eastern section, a distinctive Catherine Wheel. St Catherine, one of the favourite female saints of the Knights Templar, is said to have been roasted alive on a burning wheel, but as students of the esoteric traditions of the Templars have pointed out, there is another, more arcane interpretation of this symbol.

In this, the eight-spoked flaming wheel is a reference to the Sun's cycle and the old Celtic holy days. It is formed by the North-South axis of the spinning Earth crossed by the East-West axis, the line created by the spring and autumn equinoxes where the Sun rises exactly due East and sets due West, and overlaid by the positions of the rising and setting Sun at the so-called 'Celtic Quarter-days', marking the old festivals of Imbolc (Christian Candlemas), Beltane (Mayday), Lughnasadh (Harvest) and Samhain (All Saints). Because of its symbolic meaning, this eightfold pattern became one of the most important designs incorporated into Templar architecture as the ideal shape that reflected the pattern of earthly life (although St Catherine's wheel is often rationalised in iconography to six or even four spokes). The Templars understood that many of the images adopted by the Roman Church were merely age-old pagan ideas adapted and re-packaged for mass consumption, even if they were often stripped of their original meaning.

The influence of the Knights Templar can be seen everywhere in Cornwall (even though at least one author, Evelyn Lord, in *The Knights Templar in Britain*, completely omits the county!). They had a number of preceptories and commanderies, including an important one at Madron overlooking St Michael's Mount. Their great success was due to various factors, one being their maritime and trading skills and the invention of the first system of global banking which led to them controlling international commerce, and another was their understanding that all religions derive from the same principles of the laws of Nature. Because of this they are known to have blended Christian and Pagan beliefs, creating an inclusive religion that alienated few except the Roman Church. This is also ironically what ultimately led to their downfall, as their popularity and power grew to challenge the might of the Pope, who, along with the help of King Philip of France, who owed them vast amounts of money, conspired to destroy them on that famously 'unlucky' day of Friday the 13th of October, 1307. At dawn, across France, they were killed or imprisoned, later to be tortured into admitting a roll-call of crimes against the Church, not least those of practising various forms of paganism.

In Britain and Cornwall, however, most of them were allowed to continue under the protection of their fellow crusaders the Knights Hospitallers and the Knights of St John (otherwise known as the Knights of Malta), their influence gradually becoming absorbed into a more orthodox system. The Templar church of St Catherine, founded in 1120 on the main route into Cornwall just a few miles from Lostwithiel, continued under the new regime, as well as St Catherine's Castle built on the cliffs protecting the entrance to the port of Fowey.

However, just because the Templars were absorbed into these other Knightly orders does not mean that their beliefs in any way vanished—they were just driven underground. In places like Cornwall the old ways continued as they had done for many centuries, a blend of Pagan and Christian. The families that understood the essential truths of the Celtic and Viking ways of their ancestors continued to live according to these beliefs, as one can see in the remaining artefacts of these times carved in wood and stone. They were also, it is widely believed, in possession of profound knowledge concerning spiritual truths inherited from Druidic sources, which is why they had become so involved in the transmission of Arthurian mythology which concealed within it much of the old Wisdom Tradition. According to Wolfram von Eschenbach, the author of *Parzival*, they were nothing less than the keepers of the Holy Grail—that elusive and little-understood miraculous vessel, the fount of all true knowledge and wisdom.

So were the Cardinham family Templars? They certainly exhibited all the classic traits, having links with the Norman dynasty, living for a time at a place founded by a Celtic or 'Druidic' saint, and being the power behind the maritime success of Lostwithiel and its all-important tin trade conducted through the Templar ports in Europe and the Mediterranean. They also lived at Restormel Castle on the polar 'Tree of Life', creating a topographical and cosmological connection with the Arthurian legends of the Tintagel area, and were responsible for the building of the old Lostwithiel Church. An almost complete rebuilding in the fourteenth century replaced this, adding the tower, and later the unusual octagonal spire displaying the Catherine Wheel. What other evidence of their beliefs might we hope to come across? Are there any other 'messages from the past' that may lead us to understand what may have been the driving force behind their beliefs?

Just inside the main entrance to the church is one of the most extraordinary fonts in the country, carved out of a massive block of elvan stone from Pentewan near St Austell, and believed to date from the thirteenth century. This octagonal basin, in which perhaps forty generations have been baptised over the last 800 or so years, has some astonishing features, many of which are very surprising indeed to find on such a sacred vessel. The high relief of the carving emphasises its importance, since it has been cut from a piece of stone far larger than its eventual size, and consequently must have cost a great deal more than might be deemed necessary for a less monolithic task involving mere decoration. Each panel displays carvings that together create an amazing mix of Christian and apparently pre-Christian images.

One represents the Crucifixion, with the figures of St John and the Virgin Mary in the biblical scene where the saviour utters the words 'Woman, behold thy Son' and 'Behold thy Mother'(or could it be Mary Magdalene, for both St John and the Magdalene were central to Templar beliefs?) Another has an impressive Bishop's Head wearing an early form of mitre, but this is no ordinary representation for he is a 'Green Bishop' with sprays of foliage and flowers issuing from his mouth and ears, whose appearance seems very youthful. The Green Man was a Templar design inherited from the pagan world, thousands of which adorn churches and cathedrals across Europe and beyond. He is a symbol of the cycles of Life, Death and Rebirth in Nature, as well as that primal force behind everything that grows, the 'vital spark' of life.

The prominence of such images in ecclesiastical buildings throughout Europe is often greatly underestimated (there are literally hundreds of Green Men to every single image of Christ) and their position within the buildings is often telling. They are, for instance, frequently found directly above the Lady Altar in cathedrals such as Exeter (which had jurisdiction over Cornwall during this time), a significant location for the Templars who worshipped the Divine Feminine. This image had strong royal connotations, with the existence of many crowned Green Men or *Green Kings* reminding us that the king himself was a living symbol of fertility. A truly massive Green Man, painted and gilded, overlooks the entrance to the Coronation Chamber in the *Rathaus* at Aachen, where Richard of Cornwall (the builder of Tintagel Castle) was crowned King of the Romans in the thirteenth century.

The Lostwithiel 'Green Bishop'

It is, though, unusual to find a Green Man on a Cornish font, especially when he apparently represents a high-ranking member of the Church. We may recall a similar image on the oak chair in Tintagel Church, but otherwise they are uncommon. We have to ask the question that naturally arises from this mixture of the Pagan and Christian—did the Church of the twelfth and thirteenth centuries (and perhaps even later) have such strong links with the Celtic Christian tradition that a Bishop was considered to embody the spirit of Nature, a latter-day Druid priest who inherited his role from earlier times? The question almost answers itself, for the image is there before us, peering out with its emerging greenery for eight centuries. Two other panels are filled with gothic tracery, designs which we might more usually expect to find on such an artefact, providing a certain contrast to the other images which await our consideration.

Nothing could, however, prepare the unsuspecting visitor for what must be one of the most intriguing sights in any church. Exactly opposite the Green Bishop (and this position must be by deliberate design) is a fearsome grotesque head—almost ape-like—with beard, gaping mouth, staring eyes and two serpents draped over its pendulous ears. Such an apparently demonic image within the context of a Christian church, and especially on perhaps the most sacred object of all in which many thousands of souls have been baptised into the 'One True Faith' is utterly remarkable. Yet so embarrassing does it appear to be that it is rarely commented upon other than as a curiosity to be casually glossed over. It is possible to have a certain sympathy with this view, for what can one say about such an intriguing and highly unusual image? What could it possibly mean?

Besides its fearful demeanour there is one aspect of this grotesque gargoyle-like head that is the most prominent of all. Its forehead looms out in a very pronounced manner and is engraved with a seven-ringed spiral which has been stroked by generations of hands, smoothing the stone and giving it a darker colouration. Despite its appearance, this almost demon-like head has been for many centuries used as an object of veneration by those wishing to share its power.

I first came across this strange carving in the 1980s when researching *The Sun and The Serpent* with the dowser Hamish Miller. At that time we were tracking two major currents of earth energy through the Westcountry which were associated with what has become known as the 'St Michael Line'—an alignment of sacred sites dedicated to the Archangel Michael stretching across the length of southern Britain. What we discovered at the font intrigued us, for we found that at this exact spot two 'dragon' lines—one 'male' and one 'female', that we called Michael and Mary after the dedications of the churches they predominantly passed through—crossed here and appeared to focus down into the earth below. The font marked a powerfully energetic place, a highly unusual concentration of earth energy that could be detected and measured with dowsing rods. Dowsing, of course, is more commonly used for finding underground water than tracking currents of terrestrial energy, and this led us to consider the possible connection between the two. Fonts, after all, are

The Lostwithiel 'gargoyle'

nothing less than Holy Wells located within a church, and other researchers, including the pioneer dowser Guy Underwood, had noted how they were often positioned over a crossing of subterranean streams beneath the building. There are literally hundreds of Holy Wells in Cornwall, mostly named after the Celtic saints who venerated and used them for sacred purposes. They were renowned as places of spiritual power and used extensively for healing, divination and their inspirational virtues, and are amongst the oldest sacred sites on Earth. These were later adopted by the early Christian Church, which often built churches or chapels on or near them.

So here at least we had a partial explanation for some of the more unusual features of this weird head. The twin serpents draped over it, we surmised, could refer to the two 'serpent' or 'dragon' currents that we had found crossing at this exact spot. The spiral on its forehead could have spiritual implications, for it is located precisely where the 'third eye' — the pineal gland, known as the organ of spiritual perception — is found. This implies that the font and the water contained within somehow becomes 'charged' with energy that may enhance this faculty, especially as the forehead is so dramatically pronounced. And what of its grotesque features? Why would anyone wish to carve such an image on a sacred artefact? This is perhaps the most difficult question to answer. It is fair to say that in the past, people have largely been at a loss to explain this rather startling head.

Typical of these often rather desperate attempts to explain the apparently inexplicable, and in accordance with the narrow religious attitudes of the day, one observer read out a paper by a Dr Lanyon to the Archaeological Institution of Cornwall in Victorian times thus:

'The most prominent and grotesque figure on this font is a human head of large dimensions with a countenance much disturbed, and bearing the expression of extreme anguish. Two serpents are resting their heads wistfully on each ear, with their bodies writhing over the back part of the crown. This bas-relief, Dr Lanyon says, was intended to portray the once lovely countenance of man rendered hideous and disturbed by the sin of his first parents: the machinations of the Devil in the form of the Serpents being enough to justify the artist in giving to the face the utmost deformity of sin, and the misery which it entails.'

We may wince at this preoccupation with original sin displayed on a sacred object, but can also sympathise with the good doctor, under the circumstances, at any attempt to speculate what it may mean. However, I eventually realised that none of the above was likely to be true, and that there was another explanation altogether that made much more sense if one takes into consideration Templar beliefs. This produced a stream of thought that eventually led to what I believe may be the real meaning behind this curious, and somewhat alarming, image.

It was suggested to me by Robin Heath (who was for a number of years editor of the *Astrological Journal*) that it may symbolise aspects of the sign of Capricorn—the astrological sign that rules the energies of the Earth and the time of the Winter Solstice. Capricorn is usually depicted as a goat and in fact on closer examination, the head is indisputably that of a goat, with its long face, piercing eyes and beard. The image of the goat in Templarism is well-known because of its use for the portrayal of Baphomet, an heretical, Pan-like figure worshipped by the Templars (scholars have noted that the name *Baphomet* is a coded reference to the Hebrew word for *wisdom*). Probably because of the Templar heresy and the fact that they were driven underground, the goat was later to become an image of the Devil as a vehicle for Church propaganda that sought to stamp out the last remnants of pagan practice.

But why should such an arcane image appear on this font? The most likely answer is that whoever commissioned it (and it seems likely this was the Templar-inspired Cardinham family, perhaps even Robert himself who built the first church in about 1190) was deeply involved in the mystical qualities of pagan imagery as well as that of more orthodox Christian beliefs, and found nothing untoward in aligning the two, here, quite literally, by setting an image of Baphomet directly opposite that of the Green Bishop. The two serpents also support this hypothesis, since Baphomet is invariably shown with twin serpents coiling around a straight pole, a device known as the Caduceus. This is an emblem of the magical healing power of the serpent energies which coil around our inner Axis, or Tree of Life, to bring forth spiritual enlightenment.

It is also of interest that this image is virtually the only one on the font that has not been deliberately defaced, by, it is said, Cromwellian soldiers who were billeted in the church during the Civil War. According to the diarist Symonds, in 1644 the Parliamentary soldiers '*in contempt of Christianity, Religion and the Church... brought a horse to the font, and there, with their kind of ceremonies, did, as they called it, christen the horse and called him by the name of Charles, in contempt of his Sacred Majesty.*' Whoever was responsible for the damage caused to the other carvings, it does seem curious that they left the gargoyle, even though it would have been relatively easy to knock off its 'third eye'.

Another panel has a scene where a dog is sinking his teeth into an escaping rabbit or hare (another symbol that became associated with the medieval Devil because of its associations with fertility). There are two notable things about this, though, for the hare appears to be disproportionately large in relation to the dog, and another creature, which looks as if it might have been a lizard or salamander, has been completely chiselled away, so we will never know exactly what it represented. We will have to wait until a later chapter to discover the likely meaning of this particular scene, and the reader will probably be greatly surprised at the conclusions to be drawn.

However, adjacent to the goatish head is another panel containing two very lively lions, the royal symbol of the Earls of Cornwall (a previous commentator declared that these represented the ancient crest of the Cambrian and Cornish Kings, referring to the fact that the Kings of Cornwall were also the Kings of Wales until the death of Cadwallader in 689). Either way, these lions stamp the font with an image of royal approval. It looks as though the designers obviously wished to state their allegiance to the Norman and Plantagenet dynasties and thus cannot have been anti-royalist or heretical in the normal sense.

Finally we come to the most interesting panel of all. This, as we might expect by now, is rather casually dismissed as a 'hunting scene' and assumed to be a decorative feature depicting a medieval lord pursuing one of his favourite sports. But as we are about to learn, there are elements in this scene that point to a far deeper level of meaning. The scene is carved with an impressive vivacity and features a mounted knight or lord clad in light armour with a chain-mail hood and short jacket. A sword can also be seen, strangely carved in light relief. Because he is wearing what is known as a 'prick-spur' that was fashionable in the thirteenth century we can be reasonably sure that the font was carved about the time of Robert of Cardinham.

This rider is vigorously blowing a horn steadied by straps attached to his baldric, which runs around his shoulder and under his arm. On his left hand is what one observer in the past described as a 'well-fed' hawk. He also noted that due to the blast from his horn, the steed is *'taking fire thereat'* and *'trampling on the back of a dog, unfortunately in advance of his hoofs.'* This commentator, it has to be said, surmised that the font was carved during the time of... *King Arthur!*

So far, so good. This is undoubtedly a hunting scene, with a mounted and armoured falconer riding his steed. But as we have discovered, the images on this font have a deep mystical aspect that underlies what may at first appear to be a more prosaic interpretation. Pondering this, I began taking each thing in turn. I soon realised that this scene is not at all what it seems, having many different layers of meaning.

The horn, to begin with, may not be just an ordinary horn, for Cornwall has always been known as the 'Land of the Horn' supposedly because of its shape as a horn-shaped promontory jutting out into the Atlantic Ocean. 'Horn' and 'Corn' are in fact derived from the same Celtic root word, both of which mean 'abundance', as in *Cornucopia*, the *Horn of Plenty*. One of the oldest names for Cornwall, recorded in the Roman *Ravenna Cosmography*, was *Durocornovio*. The later Latin version was *Cornubia*, and the one in modern usage, *Kernow*, continues this theme. The Green Man (a modern term invented in Victorian times) was, in his Celtic incarnation, also named after the word Horn or Corn because of his associations with fertility and abundant growth, being variously known as Cernunnos, Cerne or Herne (linguistically, the letters *h* and *c* are interchangeable in Indo-European languages such as Brythonic Celtic).

Along with the curious image of the Green Bishop, might we begin to suspect that this horn-blowing figure is not just an ordinary hunts-man or falconer? And why is the falcon so large in relation to him and carved in such an unusual manner, from the rear instead of in profile, which would have created a far more impressive and realistic effect?

A number of thoughts occurred to me here. One was that Gawain, the Grail-seeker and nephew of King Arthur, was known in the old Brythonic language as the *Hawk of May*, and represented the Sun, as we found when looking at *Sir Gawain and the Green Knight* and the carving of the *Beheading Game* on Lanlivery Church. Could the hawk here represent the Sun? Another idea came from realising that this hawk also looked very like a heart in the peculiar way it was sculpted. In the esoteric tradition, the human heart and the Sun are always very closely linked, for the Sun is the 'heart' of our planetary system, and the human heart, the source of our earthly life, is our very own pulsing Sun within our physical bodies. Because of this, many religions actually use the symbol of the hawk to represent both the Sun God and the human soul, the most well-known being the Egyptian, where Horus the Hawk God is the Sun flying across the sky each day, and a hawk is also used to symbolise the *Ba*, or human soul, which flies away at death.

My conclusions were that each of these individual images that made up the hunting scene had mythical and mystical dimensions attached to them. But the greatest revelations were yet to come.

One winter's day we were sitting around the kitchen table, which was liberally covered with maps and photographs, involved in an animated discussion about some of the things that had surfaced so far in this quest. Gathered around the table and the coffee-stained maps were Gabriele together with Robin and Trish. We had just returned from a searingly cold and wet foray on Bodmin Moor, and were very pleased to be back thawing out in a warm dry place. On the table was a photograph of the hunting scene from the Lostwithiel font and a map of the Great Bear of Tintagel. Then, in walked my daughter Ellie who was visiting from London. I briefly explained what we were discussing, and she rather strangely, I thought, did not seem at all incredulous at what we had so far found. I showed her the Tintagel Bear, and then quite casually referred to the hunting scene on the font. Immediately, she said 'What's a bear doing on the font?' We all gaped. A bear? Where?

'There' she said, pointing to the scene and the four-footed creature leading the hunt. We were all totally dumbfounded. We had always glibly accepted the notion that the 'dog' leading the mounted hunter was just that, probably simply because it had been repeated so often and it made perfect sense that this should be so. Why should we have thought any different? But now we looked more closely and realised that Ellie (who was a student of zoology) was right. It was, without doubt, a Bear!

Something a little stronger than coffee was called for under the circumstances, as we realised that this four-footed creature was indeed no hunting hound, but quite obviously, now it had been pointed out to us, a genuine bear, with all the features one might expect, including a rather shaggy-looking body, thick-set head and pronounced rear quarters. No-one, including myself, who had spent a great deal of time closely examining these figures, had ever before noticed this truly extraordinary fact. It was a great lesson in how our perceptions are moulded by preconceived notions of what to expect, and how a fresh eye can spot things that should be blindingly obvious. Here, on this amazing font, so full of mystical symbolism, was apparently proof that the designers of this strange artefact knew all about the Great Bear of Tintagel, its Arthurian implications, and the fact that the church was situated on the Polar Axis. What next?

The realisation that this scene depicted a Bear leading the hunt immediately pointed to the inescapable conclusion that this was no earthly hunt, but one taking place in the skies. Suddenly, this all made perfect sense, since it had always baffled me why, when so much planning and artistry had been lavished upon this font, the hunting scene was not portrayed with the animals' feet firmly placed on the ground. The whole scene is sculpted in a curious manner that suggests they are moving forwards in an upwards trajectory. Since there is plenty of room to show it otherwise, this is obviously a deliberate decision by the artist. Now it was clear why this should be the case. The hunt was not taking place on Earth at all, but in the sky. These images did not depict an earthly hunt, but one moving through the heavens. It represented constellations on their endless journey around the Pole.

We know about the Bear, but who could the hunter be? The answer to this was first suggested to me by David Elkington, a specialist in ancient star-lore, on a visit to Lostwithiel Church some years ago. When he pointed it out at the time, I had found it difficult to accept, but now I looked at it again with different eyes. There could surely only be one answer — the most brilliant of all the constellations in the night sky — *Orion the Hunter!* This is the star group that looks most like a man, with his arms outstretched, that rises in the winter skies like a giant emerging from the earthly horizon. Because of his sheer brilliance he has been venerated in every civilisation as a mighty and triumphant star lord of the skies, bringing light into the darkness. His appearance also heralds several adjacent constellations of great splendour to which he is often linked.

Orion is depicted in the Egyptian Denderah Zodiac as the figure of a man coming forth and pointing to the three bright stars that form his body; *Rigel, Bellatrix and Betelgeuse*. In Biblical texts he is referred to as the great hero or giant. In the classical world he is usually shown holding a club in his right hand and bearing a Lion's pelt in his left, or as a warrior with his sword. Here, once we have recognised the distinctive shape of the constellation and compared it with the pose of the figure before us it is possible to see that he is depicted in a similar manner as the classical version, but this time as a mounted knight blowing his horn (instead of a club), and with a hawk on his wrist (instead of a lion's pelt) as he rises up from the Earth towards the royal Lions on the next panel. The sheer brilliance of this symbolism is stunning, and is obviously rooted in a culture where hunting has always been one of the prime motive forces of human existence, from the earliest times of bear hunting (from where the Arthurian myth first originated) to the medieval age when hunts were conducted on horseback. Here is a striking image that combines the two, encapsulating the whole panorama of human experience from the earliest days to medieval times.

There are other astronomical considerations to take into account here. Orion occupies a unique position in the heavens during the Winter

Solstice, and at this time appears at his most upright exactly at midnight. Because of this, the constellation was the ancient world's prime meridian marker signifying the Winter Solstice, coinciding with the rebirth of the Sun. Could this explain why the hawk, as a solar symbol, is so prominent on his wrist?

For both the Hunter and the Bear to appear together must, in these terms, leave no doubt that the Normans were deeply immersed in ancient star-lore, and that they recognised that the topography of Arthurian sites was directly related to the patterns in the heavens.

The revelation that this font is encoded with such extraordinary symbolism inevitably leads us to wonder why these images are here, and what they might mean, beyond indicating the richness of learning in early medieval times. The Hunter, Orion, the original 'Rider in the Sky' is the leader of a Hunt that has been going on ever since the dawn of human civilisation. Before the age of mounted horsemen he was pictured as a giant figure striding across the night sky—later he adopted the fashion of the times and became a *rider* instead of a *strider*. The shape of his body, with outstretched arms, is faithfully shown in this remarkable image on the font, but there are other features as well that marry the figure with his giant astral counterpart in the sky.

Orion the Hunter

One is his sword, which is angled in just the right way to reflect the most easily recognisable feature of the constellation—Orion's Belt, with its three brilliant stars, *Alnilam, Alnitak* and *Mintaka*. In Arabic, these were called *Mezan AL-Haqq,* which means 'The Balance of Justice and Truth', a perfect metaphor indeed for a sword that in this case appears 'balanced' instead of in the more usual vertical position. These are the three bright stars that are seen to rise every winter's evening in Britain, weather per-mitting, and act as pointers to one of the brightest stars in the heavens that appears over the eastern horizon some time later, Sirius the Dog Star. Three stars also dangle from his belt, often called *Orion's Sword,* and the brightest, at the sword's tip, is the famous Orion Nebula, a stellar nursery where new stars are born and thrown into space—because of this, this particular star formation is sometimes called *Orion's Phallus.* Here on the font, this star pattern seems to be represented by the Hunter's right leg. Can there be any doubt that here we have, on a thirteenth century Norman font, a representation of Orion the Hunter, guided by the Great Bear, on his nightly quest across the heavens in pursuit of his eternal quarry? But what might this quarry be?

All across Europe and even further afield, especially in the Celtic, Saxon and Viking traditions, occurs the spectral phenomena known as the Wild Hunt. It is led, according to the religious and cultural backround of each area, by King Arthur, Herne the Hunter, the Saxon Woden, or, in areas of Viking influence, Odin. In the Celtic era the Hunt was led by Gwyn ap Nudd, the original British god who ruled these islands before the coming of the Saxons and Normans. He was Lord of the Underworld and the realm of Faery because every spring he was seen to disappear below the horizon and enter the realms beneath the Earth. Yet every autumn he rose again, reaching his apogee at the Midwinter Solstice, endowing him with a life of sacrifice and renewal, concepts ingrained in pre-Christian religion and incorporated into the new belief system.

The remarkable similarity between the Hunter on Lostwithiel font and the classic image of Orion. Allowing for different artistic interpretations, they are almost identical, the reason being both reflect the shape of the constellation of Orion the Hunter. The hilt of the sword can just be seen, protruding from beneath the Hunter's left elbow. This angle is exactly the same as the three bright stars of Orion's Belt, which point to Sirius, the Dog Star. The Hunter leads the Wild Hunt in the heavens and is guided by the Great Bear, hence these images are set not on the Earth, but at an upwards angle indicating their passage through the night skies.

Another common property of Herne, Odin and Woden is that they were all hung in a tree in order to gain supernatural knowledge (we know little of Gwyn in this respect, since, being one of the most ancient of them all, only fragments of folk memories persist). This was the World Tree or the Tree of Life that joined Heaven and Earth, and was a central feature of a shamanistic tradition leading back to prehistoric times. The location of this font thus becomes even more extraordinary in that it symbolises the Polar Axis itself as well as its cosmic significance, through the Hunter and the Capricorn image, with the Winter Solstice. This was the time when carnivals, with their wild character, wit and inventiveness, were held, a remnant of the old midwinter festivities associated with the Wild Hunt. In antiquity these celebrations were attended by revellers who often wore animal masks, later transforming into mumming plays and masked processions. It is a matter of lasting regret to many that these days such survivals have been virtually eradicated by bureaucratic regulations which have brought to an end many thousands of years of local communities continuing their ancient customs. These once high points of the annual seasonal cycle stemmed from ancient cosmology, since all these ancient gods of whichever guise are said to charge across the night sky led by ghostly hounds who howl in an unearthly fashion, especially on stormy, windswept nights. What are they hunting? Human souls.

The Hunter or God, the Lord of the Animals, is chasing his own destiny in the stars, gathering our souls as he goes. As a giant effigy of mankind he encapsulates each and every one of us and therefore represents the whole evolution and ultimate destiny of the race. All these old gods, Gwyn, Herne, Odin and Woden, were lumped together by the medieval Church to become the Devil in his various guises in an attempt to stamp out pagan beliefs. The Wild Hunt, or the gathering of souls that will leave earthly life for a new one amongst the stars, became an ideal vehicle for Church re-interpretation, which made sure that such a belief system assumed a far more fearsome and terrible character in order to guide the unwary into the protective comfort of the nearest priest.

Consequently the Wild Hunt was said to signify imminent death as it collected the souls of unbaptised children waiting for judgement day (an ironic idea, considering here we have the Wild Hunt on a font!), and hence it was said to strike fear into the heart of any that might speak of the Hunter on his nightly round. It thus became one of the most powerful tools of the medieval Church to terrify its flock with stories of sudden and imminent catastrophe, and served to alienate humanity from their true and most meaningful inheritance—the star lore of their ancestors. But before the Christian propaganda machine cranked itself up into a frenzy of fear, the Wild Hunt had a truly religious and heartfelt purpose; to guard and guide souls into the Otherworld. This was taken over by the Church in the guise of St Michael, the Christian psychopomp, and Archangel Gabriel, hence one of the names of the spectral hounds leading the Hunt was the *Gabriel Hounds or Gabriel Ratchets.*

In the Christian tradition the horn blown by the Hunter which announces the arrival of the Hunt signifies the day of the last judgement when all our deeds and actions are called to account, but in the esoteric system it also announces the arrival of some great event (just like the Archangel Gabriel in the biblical story of the annunciation). It is said that it takes a great champion to blow the horn and summon the power to initiate the Hunt. Once blown, the forces are awoken and nothing can return them to sleep except the completion, in success or failure, of the Hunt, which represents the questing journey of the Knights of the Round Table to gain mastery over all the aspects of their inner nature. In this respect, the Hunter is also the Keeper of the Gateways and the Guardian of the Underworld, the earthly realms. Capricorn is also known in astrology as the 'Keeper of the Gateway' as it is the sign that presides over the rebirth of the Sun at the Winter Solstice.

In *The Secret Tradition in Arthurian Legend,* Gareth Knight notes that the horn also symbolises the veil between the earthly plane and the Otherworld or Underworld, the invisible spiritual realm that co-exists alongside the everyday as if in another dimension. To him, *'The blowing of a horn is a particularly potent means to signal entry into the inner planes'.* Thus the horn is an instrument of communication between the inner worlds announcing coming events (such as the transformation that occurs at death). It has a dual function because of its androgynous shape and it is also a magical tool of polarity and balance of the male and female powers. The blowing of a magical horn is also said to be the sound that will rouse King Arthur from his deep sleep.

Another of the ancient guises of the Horn is as a drinking vessel — undoubtedly one of the earliest forms of the Holy Grail, or the endlessly-renewing cup of the Cornucopia. In the earlier Celtic tradition this was known as the Cauldron of Rebirth and Regeneration, through which all spiritual warriors must pass to be renewed to eternal life. What better place to find such eloquent symbolism as this, on a font that is really nothing less than the physical embodiment of a Grail, where human souls are initiated into their own quest for wisdom, knowledge and experience?

Cornwall symbolised as 'The Land of the Horn' with the royal crown. This stained glass window is from St Neot Church on Bodmin Moor, and refers to a very ancient tradition derived from the fact that Horn and Corn are from the same Celtic root word. Both signify fertility and abundance as well as a magical instrument used by the Lord of the Wild Hunt.

The Norse God Odin in his role as Lord of the Underworld, attended by guardian dogs and ravens, both creatures of the otherworldly realms.

11

MERLIN'S MENAGERIE

he Norman kings and their followers, including those notable Cornish families who returned to their homeland to reclaim their old territories and mythology, were, as we have discovered, essentially pagan. Yet it is clear that they were also followers of early Christianity—especially the form of it now known as Celtic Christianity, which flourished from around 400 until at least the twelfth century, judging by the available evidence. Vestiges of these beliefs continued for many hundreds of years after, but these seven centuries, especially those immediately after the Romans left Britain, are often called the *Age of the Saints*, when Cornwall played a pivotal role in the Celtic world, ideally set between Brittany, Normandy, Wales and Ireland.

This blending of Druidism and Celtic Christianity is understandable given that cultural history at that time was on the cusp of the two belief systems where primeval patterns, echoing down from prehistory, were being gradually transformed and adapted for a new era that considered itself at the cutting edge of modernism. This was probably why these apparently different religious attitudes were not at odds with each other as they later were, when Roman Christianity became a political force. During the advent of the Roman Church the assimilation of the old ways into the new was brought about by the tried and tested expediency of absorbing the old god-heroes and their festivals, such as Easter and Christmas, into the religious reformation. This process was to take many centuries, for old beliefs, especially when they are rooted firmly in the landscape, are not easy to dislodge. Some still remain to this day.

William I's son Rufus seems to exemplify the Normans' beliefs as followers of the 'old religion', for he did everything in his power to erode the new form of Christianity, plundering monasteries and openly ridiculing their claim that they represented the 'one true faith'. And although modern sceptics often tend to dismiss the ideas put forward by the Historian and Egyptologist Margaret Murray in *The Divine King in England*, she presents many examples supporting the idea that they thought of themselves as pagan god-kings. From a lifetime studying the concept of kingship in Europe and Egypt, she recognised that the driving force behind royalty was more than the lust for power, wealth and influence, and concluded that even so-called 'pagan' practices such as the ritual sacrifice of the king continued well into supposedly 'Christian' times. History is not just about the brutality and politics of battles in the field, but an encounter with one's personal destiny.

The Normans' veneration of the old gods was deeply linked in their minds to concepts of destiny and service, and this helps to explain why so much of the Druidic tradition was incorporated into the religious revivals of the twelfth and thirteenth centuries. Arthurian mythology became the main vehicle for this, since it encoded powerful symbolism from deepest antiquity that could be woven into a complex tapestry of stories and tales which audiences were already subconciously familiar with, elaborated and added to by the wandering bards and troubadours, the popular entertainers and news reporters of their day. In this way the old stories were updated for the emerging chivalric and heroic age of Crusader Knights, and a variety of authors were commissioned to retell them in a more modern guise.

Rufus was famously shot with an arrow whilst on a stag hunt in 1100 (the stag being a symbol of the old god Herne or Cerne) at the time of Lughnasad when the Harvest Corn-King was thought to die, sacrificing himself so that he may be born again. If this was indeed a ritual murder and willing sacrifice as Murray suggests, it certainly seems to have had the desired outcome, for it led to a smooth transition and the coronation of Henry I, who carried on the work of his forebears by initiating an era of elaborate pageantry and courtly kingship steeped in a mix of Arthurian, pagan and esoteric tradition.

Consequently the background of many of the mysteries we are investigating here should be seen through the lens of a system of beliefs that blended ancient myths with the rituals and obligations of kingship. This was based on a cosmological view of life, for all earthly life is ultimately determined by the cycles marked out in the heavens and the movement of the Sun, Moon and stars.

Relics from this era, such as the Lostwithiel font and the many other sculptural masterpieces that have miraculously survived the vicissitudes of time, often lie unrecognised for what they really are, in the dark interiors of little-visited country churches, seen as mere quaint artefacts decorated with imagery that may seem primitive or incomprehensible to us today. Yet some of these, like the magnificent font in Bodmin Church (a relic from the old Priory) believed to date from 1100, the same year that Rufus died, are of great significance, exhibiting wonderful 'mythological beasts' with the Tree of Life as a central feature.

There are many other similarly decorated fonts in the surrounding area (although on a smaller scale), that are infused with meaning when one understands they are like snapshots into the minds and beliefs of those who made them, frozen in time. Fonts in particular, usually the oldest stone within any ancient church, are real treasures of the past, repositories of a wisdom that is derived not from primitive superstition as some would have us believe, but mythic cosmology of very ancient character. These artefacts, amongst the finest works of art from the early medieval period, have stories to tell even beyond the generations who have been baptised in them. Baptism itself is a ritual of extreme antiquity where the naming ceremony of a new-born baby was accompanied by the sprinkling of the child with holy water. The Templars adopted this rite, and were especially devoted to the figure of John the Baptist. Thus the most important rite of Christianity was derived from the pre-Christian worship of sacred springs and Holy Wells, which honoured the female power of the Earth.

The massive and intricately-carved font from Bodmin Priory, dating from around 1100. Two dogs guard the base of a stylised Tree of Life whilst interlaced dragons coil around its top. In ancient stellar mythology the Dog guards the entrance to the Underworld or earthly planes, and the constellation of the Dragon circles around the topmost point of the heavens.

The Lord of the Otherworld, as we have seen, is variously called Gwyn, Herne, Cerne, Woden, Odin or King Arthur. They are all said to sound horns as they cross the threshold between the physical and spiritual worlds (the Anglo-Saxon word for *horn* is *hurn*—and this is the likely origin of *Herne*, which is pronounced the same). They all guide souls and travellers into the realms of otherworldly regions. The rising of the star-god Orion in the night skies of autumn and winter is particularly associated with these old deities, and often presages a period of storms and wild weather (hence the Wild Hunt) as well as the time of Hallowe'en when the spirits of the dead are said to be close to the world of the living, and the Winter Solstice, both times when the gates between the worlds are ajar.

There are, though, two ways of entering the Otherworld or Underworld, the secret abode of the Earth Goddess. One is through the transformation occurring at death, and the other is to achieve it through mystical means often involving ritual training and preparation, a shamanistic rite of passage since the earliest times. Right at the beginning of this quest we found that the legend of the birth of King Arthur was physically echoed by the image of a Great Bear drawn in the landscape where his birth is said to have taken place. We came to the conclusion that it represents both the cosmic and earthly Mother Goddess. We have also discovered giant Lions that are supremely connected with the concepts of kingship and the early history of Cornwall—the *Land of the Horn*, whose other ancient name was *Lyonesse*. Now we enter a different phase of the quest, and one that has the power to become intensely personal. For as we open the doors of perception to what this menagerie of mythic animals might mean, we begin to sense that there must exist a very profound reason. Might they exist so we can actually experience and understand them, as if they are aspects of our own nature? Is it possible that as we travel through the outer landscape we are somehow reading a map that can lead to that elusive Otherworld, as we simultaneously journey through the inner landscape of the spirit?

Totemism is probably the most ancient of all beliefs, derived from the direct observation of Nature. Bear worship one of the oldest examples, and, as we have explored at the beginning of this book, one of the most enduring, taking into consideration its mythical dimension. The reasons for this are many, not least the Bear's human-like characteristics, sharpness of intelligence and empathy with the landscape. It is entirely natural that tribal people would have associated themselves with particular animals such as the Bear because of their physical prowess and supposedly supernatural powers—this is something that has occurred all over the world since humanity first walked the Earth.

Tribes would claim descent from some primal animal mother or father, whose spirit would magically protect and imbue them with its own special powers. These ancestral spirits, often invoked in complex rituals involving masquerading as the beast itself and allowing one's spirit to become one with the animal's personality, did not die out when people became more civilised. Celtic societies always felt their ancestors were close at hand, just beyond the veil that separated them from the regions where the spirits dwelt. As the tribal ways declined, these animal totems that had guarded their spiritual and earthly welfare for many centuries were not abandoned, but became their guiding forces in a different way. The totemic beasts of prehistory evolved into a more formalised system where ancient families adopted their images (and sometimes their names) and included them on their shields as they went into battle under their protective influence.

These heraldic shields were eventually to become badges and Coats of Arms that told the story of the ancestors, with the presiding spirit of the totemic creature still in evidence. Even though the animals themselves may have long since vanished from the landscape their spirits still roamed the imagination, guiding and guarding the ancestral line. Intermarriage and the changing fortunes of families through the centuries may have created a tangled skein of such affiliations, but it was still considered a matter of honour to pay allegiance to one's totem animal by exhibiting it on a Coat of Arms as if pictorially tracing the genealogy back as far as possible.

But the beginnings of this way of thinking stem from humanity's experience of the natural environment, and here we enter an altogether more ancient, eldritch world, as far removed from the medieval mind as we today are from that time. This is the time when Celtic Saints wandered through a wild landscape teeming with fish, birds and beasts of all kinds, with great forests full of ancient trees that whispered of Nature untamed. These were adherents of the old religions—nature mystics who, like the Druids spoken of by Caesar, immersed themselves in the study of the stars, the rhythms of the universe, the mysteries of Nature and the evolution of the human soul. These were more than the popular image of early saints, intent on converting heathens (i.e. those who lived on the *heath*) to the true religion, an artifice contrived by the early Church to absorb their power over the hearts and minds of vast swathes of the land.

In the minds of those who lived in the Celtic world, gods, mortals and otherworldly beings and animals inhabited a realm where there were no fixed boundaries, and the living and the spirits of their ancestors could communicate freely. The land was a reflection of the otherworldly dimensions that interpenetrated it, and certain places acted as gateways where one could slip from one to the other with ease. Thus the mysterious occupants of other dimensions could, at any time, materialise into physical form. But the great difference between then and now was *time*, for it did not exist as we understand it today. Breton storytellers, for instance, are known to have begun their tales with 'once upon a time there was no time...'

So when we come across the popular image of Celtic Saints nowadays, we should recognise that the Church adopted them in just the same way as they did, for instance, Francis of Assisi, who was a virulent critic of the Church of his day, denouncing the Pope and his henchmen, yet as soon as his body was cold he was welcomed into the pantheon of Catholic sainthood to become one of their most popular figures. This inspirational man spent his whole life arguing that the Church had become too corrupt and bureaucratic, that it had lost its way. The true religion, he maintained, was the worship of Nature, the flowers, trees, birds and beasts, which, if approached with love in your heart, would never harm you, but instead share their innocence, experience and wisdom. God was a theophany, communicating to us through Creation. Honour Brother Sun and Sister Moon, urged Francis, a latter-day Druid who constantly challenged the might of the Roman Church yet ended up becoming one of its greatest assets.

Celtic regions such as Cornwall are still heavily populated with the memories of these saints, with many villages named after them, and major routes like the Saint's Way between the North and South coasts must once have been alive with them and their followers. Preserved in these names and the folklore connected with them are genuine elements of an essential truth that recalls a holy man or woman who once lived there and became a focus for the spiritual aspirations of those living in the surrounding countryside. Almost without exception, they were drawn to settle near a Holy Well, not simply for practical considerations, but because they were places of numinous power. Even today, after many have been filled in, piped away or lost forever, the county still has hundreds of these sacred springs, which can link us directly to the subtle sphere of the mind that perceives the spiritual dimensions. Sitting quietly there, far away from the bustle of the madding crowd, can be a humbling and transformational experience, as one relaxes into a state of natural meditation that gives access to the hidden realms of Nature. It is no accident that they are renowned as places of healing, perceptive visions of the past, present and future, and energetic focal points where psychic and spiritual experiences of all kinds occur. Dowsers find that at such places there are strong concentrations of earth energy that form a spiral leading down into the Earth—the 'dragon' or 'serpent' in the well spoken of by the old legends.

As we continue our quest, perhaps we can open our minds to the possibilities and potential of personal transformation as we reconnect not only with that underlying creative power behind all things, but with those who, in the distant past, also recognised it. They may have interpreted what they found in terms of the natural world of their time, and the world is certainly a very different place today, but we remain human, and can still evoke our inner nature to guide us and start to befriend our own inner beasts.

The Taming of the Bear

Deep in the north Cornish countryside, not far from Tintagel and in one of the most fertile parishes in Cornwall, lies the sylvan hamlet of St Kew, with its old church and pub close by a trickling stream. It was once an important monastery and a sacred place in Celtic times as we can tell from its collection of ancient crosses. Nearby are two prehistoric earthworks or 'forts' that are linked to the Arthurian legend. One is the Iron Age Tregear Rounds, or 'Castle Dameliock', thought to be the *Dimilioc* mentioned by Geoffrey of Monmouth, where Gorlois, the Duke of Cornwall, was killed in the sequence of events that led to Arthur's birth. This connection appears to be more than hearsay, for *Dimilihoc* is recorded in the Domesday Book of 1087, and has always been thought of in Cornish tradition as the site of Gorlois' death. The other site is *Castle Killibury* or Kelly Rounds, which the Arthurian scholar Geoffrey Ashe believes was *Celliwic*, or King Arthur's Court, mentioned frequently as his Cornish abode in the earliest accounts. He notes 'A letter written by St Dunstan in the tenth century mentions a Cornish estate which he spells 'Caellwic' and it is likely to have been in this area'.

It seems off the beaten track today, but the church at St Kew is dedicated to St James, a memory of the place as a stopping-off point for those embarking on pilgrimages to Santiago de Compostela in northern Spain, one of the main pilgrim centres of medieval times. Reputedly founded by St James the Apostle (although some say he was James the brother of Jesus), it is likely that Santiago was important before Christian times, for *Compostela* means *Field of Stars*, and implies that long before the Cathedral was built and it became sanctioned as an official pilgrimage centre it was connected with pre-Christian star-lore.

Probably the first thing you see on entering the church is a rough stone lying on the floor, with curious inscriptions highlighted in white chalk. This is St Kew's Ogham Stone, carved with an early form of Druidic script consisting of a series of lines arranged around its leading edge, along with a Latin version of the same inscription. It is thought to have marked an early monk's grave in the sixth or seventh century.

The next thing you might come across is a magnificent set of recently-restored stained-glass windows in the North East Chapel. These are very rare and quite outstanding, dating from about 1490. They are of international significance, partly because of their extreme age but also because they miraculously survived the time of the Reformation intact. They depict the last seven days of Christ's life, with two of them having direct links with Cornish miracle plays. At the top are two Coat of Arms belonging to the local families who originally paid for the windows' creation. One depicts a black bear. A similar fragment of glass showing a bear on a shield, although much faded and worn by time, can be seen in the Lady Chapel opposite.

But if you happen to stand at the high altar you will catch sight of something that, for those following this quest, will leap out at you. It is a beautiful stained-glass depiction of St Kew herself. Made in 1911 in memory of the Reverend Thomas Every's sixty years as vicar here, it shows the saint with a bear at her feet. Beneath this is a bear on a shield. This is a reference to the legend of St Kew, who is said to have tamed, of all animals, *a Bear*.

According to the *Life of St Samson*, one of the few remaining accounts of a Celtic saint's life written within memory of his lifetime, the place was, in the sixth century, called *Lan Docco*, or the monastery of Docco, who had come from South Wales and founded an important religious settlement. This mention is significant, for it gives the place the unique distinction of being the first recorded place in Cornwall that can be identified with certainty. Samson had just landed for the first time in Cornwall and was met by the 'High Priest' of the monastery, called Junavius, whose name, according to the chronicler, meant *Light* (this is a Latin form of the Celtic *Gwyn*, which means *bright* or *shining one*).

St Kew with her bear

Samson was, curiously enough, met with a polite refusal to accommodate him, and subsequently left to discover a group of pagans in the region of Tricurius (identified as the Hundred of Trigg, i.e. somewhere in North Cornwall or the Bodmin Moor area) worshipping a stone idol on the top of a hill. Through the miraculous healing of a dead man, he converted them to Christianity, and with his own hands carved a cross on their great stone (this is interesting in that it gives a contemporary account from these early days of how megaliths were converted into 'Celtic' Christian crosses, thus emphasising their cultural continuity).

St Kew is said to have been Docco's sister, who had also arrived at the monastery asking to join, but this time Docco made an unusual request. He told her that she could not be admitted until he saw a wild bear obey her. At this, she must have searched the forest for a suitable subject and tamed it, for on returning to Docco, who was suitably impressed, she was allowed to stay.

The details of this old tale are very sketchy, and some sources say that she tamed a *boar* instead of a *bear*. Yet it seems obvious that the Reverend Every, after his sixty years as vicar, must have been aware of the different versions of the legend and come to the conclusion that St Kew's association was definitely with a bear. Why the confusion? It was something that had intrigued me for some time, for Geoffrey of Monmouth referred to King Arthur as the *Boar of Cornwall*, and yet I could see that his original title was more likely to have been the *Bear of Cornwall*. Then I realised that in medieval times the two had become virtually synonymous. In local dialects the two words can and do sound practically the same. In addition bears had become virtually extinct in Britain at that time, and so references such as this were transferred to another creature popular in Celtic myth and folklore—the boar. The bear hunts of earlier times that were conducted at midwinter were now replaced by boar hunting, which took place at the same time of the year, and so the two hunts corresponded in everyday and mythical terms.

The discovery of St Kew and her bear, just a few miles from Tintagel, thus adds two new factors to our story. On the one hand it shows that the Boar and Bear were interchangeable and that Arthur was probably originally known as the *Bear of Cornwall*, and on the other, here we have a local legend concerning a Celtic saint who had to tame a bear before she was allowed to join a 'monastery', or perhaps it would be more accurate, considering these events are said to have taken place in the fifth century long before the accepted Christian period in Cornwall, to call it a Druid College. Was this why Samson was not allowed in? Because he followed a different form of religion from the Celtic Church which was far more Druidic than his own?

Have we here a folk memory of how those wishing to study the Mysteries in this area of Cornwall had to undergo some form of initiation by discovering or 'taming' the Great Bear in the landscape? Were they required to make a pilgrimage to the significant sites connected with the Bear's body, meditating in the midst of natural splendours such as St Nectan's Glen to bring them close to Nature before they could be accepted as a genuine seer and mystic? Of course the story of St Kew might be literally true, and she did indeed tame a wild bear. But we have to consider the possibility here that the Great Bear of Tintagel was some sort of spiritual test or initiation that must be undergone before the candidate could proceed with their further development, much as a shaman might have to contact the spirits of the land before he or she can gain their spiritual power.

Into the Otherworld

St Kew is only a mile or so from the village of St Tudy, where there is, in the fine old fifteenth century church, another impressive example of a rare 'coped' stone Viking memorial, heavily carved from Cornish granite in the same style as the one at Lanivet, which we may recall is decorated with two mythical beasts. This unique artefact was discovered in the churchyard in 1873, and Arthur Langdon, in *Old Cornish Crosses*, points out that the distinctive foliated scrollwork is also very similar to that at Cardinham, Lanhydrock and Waterpit Down between Tintagel and Boscastle, all places we have so far had reason to investigate.

St Tudy is said to have been proposed as the first Bishop of Cornwaille in Brittany, and is a popular figure there to this day, being the patron saint of numerous towns and villages as well as two large islands off the coast (although some authorities suggest she was a female saint, the natural daughter of King Edgar by Lady Wolfchild). The church is of great interest to those of an antiquarian frame of mind. Its ancient and very worn Viking memorial stone, because of its fine carving, must have been made for a local king or chieftain. Edward Trelawney, the brother of Jonathan (about whom *The Song of the Western Men* was written by R. S. Hawker), was incumbent here in the early eighteenth century, as well as, in about 1650, the wonderfully named *Obadiah Ghossip*. Captain William Bligh, of *Mutiny on the Bounty* fame also frequented the place, being born at the Bligh family's nearby manor house at Tinten. Among the exceptional splayed tombs is one carved in high relief with various shields, including that of the Denzells, one of whom, John, was said to have descended from the family of Henry VIII, having 'the unique distinction to claim descent from King Arthur and the right to remain covered or wear their hats in the presence of the sovereign'.

The area around St Kew and St Tudy was the next to engage my attention, for I felt there must be some further discovery to be made under the circumstances, especially as I had been intrigued for many years by the strange, otherworldly sound of the two nearby villages of *Helland* and *Blisland*, situated almost next door to each other and so tantalisingly named. Blisland had always been a favourite place, with its impressive church (with numerous Green Men), its village green (the only one in Cornwall) and excellent old pub, one of the best for miles. In many ways it did seem like *Bliss-land*.

Helland, on the other hand, was little more than a scattering of farms and houses, along with a rather neglected church to which I had never gained entry. Appropriate, perhaps, for a place called *Hell*-land, we may think. But the word *Hell* is one that has been much abused. In Christian terms it means a place of damnation and torture, where miserable sinners are tormented for all eternity. But that was not its original meaning. In pre-Christian times Hell referred to the Underworld, a place of initiation within the body of the Earth. The hellfire and brimstone was much further down towards the centre of the planet, where its molten magma boiled and seethed, for hell is also related to the Greek *Helios*, Cornish *Heul* and Welsh *Hoel*, all meaning *Sun*.

Intrigued by these associations, I returned to my (relatively) innocent hobby of map-scrying, and spent some time gazing at an old one-inch-to-the-mile map in the hope that something would reveal itself. I concentrated and relaxed alternately in an effort to shake off any preconceptions that may have been lurking at the edge of my consciousness, and may have influenced me. But I needn't have bothered too much, for what eventually did transpire could not have been further from my mind.

I first noticed that the two roads leading from Helland and Blisland, as they came together at the village of St Mabyn, looked a bit like some sort of snout that appeared tethered to the church. I then saw that this head that appeared to be materialising in front of me had a large ear that was so distinctive in its shape that it looked just like that belonging to a pig! I traced its outline and saw that Blisland seemed to be located directly above its back. At this stage I was convinced I was contriving all this by my own innate desire to find something, anything. But a pig? Surely not.

Studying the map carefully I saw that the lower part of the 'body' coincided with a very unusual road formation around the hamlet of Helland. It looked to me just like a pig's trotter. The coincidences were piling up. But if I were to accept this porcine shape I could see that this pig's body was not at all as I would have expected, for it was far too lean. Whoever heard of a thin pig? And, besides that, its rear end seemed to become impossibly indistinct, vanishing into the wild uplands of Bodmin Moor. To be frank, I did not want to acknowledge that a pig could be a part of this quest. A Bear, yes, because of its Arthurian associations. Lions, certainly, for their royal symbolism. But a pig? Was this turning into some sort of mythological Cornish farmyard?

The Little Pig

The figure, it struck me, was not as well-drawn as the others, and must this time be simply down to chance. For months I tried to ignore it, and pursued my researches elsewhere. I revisited it again and again, and there was no doubt that the 'trotter' and the 'ear' especially seemed to call out as being unusual features. And then there was Helland, located right on the pig's front leg, with Blisland above his back, and it began to make a modicum of mythic sense. His eye seemed to be marked by a place called *Longstone*, where the stump of a once-impressive megalith now stands, there was the ancient manor of *Helligan* near the centre of the figure (said by the Cornish historian Hals to mean 'holy' or 'sacred') and on his shoulder was *Merry Meeting*, indicating an old gathering place for fairs and celebrations. A faded copy of an *Old Cornwall* magazine also informed me that in 1939 an ancient stone cross that looked as though it had been cut from an even older standing stone was found in the hedge at the base of the pig's ear. What really puzzled me, if any of this was true, was the rather emaciated body. Then I realised it may not be a pig after all, but a piglet! For young pigs and weaners are indeed very lithe and long-bodied until they are fattened.

I also began to understand that pigs, in pre-Christian times, were one of the most sacred animals of all, holding a prime position within Celtic lore. In fact the pig was probably the most significant of the pre-Christian totem animals. In the old Welsh tales the pig actually comes from the Underworld, stolen by a hero from the King of the Dead, as re-counted in the story of *Math, Son of Mathnowy*. An animal that comes from the Otherworld sees and hears things in other dimensions, and, according to the stories, the spirits of the ancestors can speak through them.

Many of these Celtic saints had strong associations with them due to these supernatural and divinatory powers, and because they were especially associated with the Underworld. At Sancreed in West Cornwall, for instance, the Saint experienced a vivid dream that he should follow a pig to found his oratory, and was led to a Holy Well that remains one of the most ancient and evocative places in the county. King Bladud of Bath was similarly led to discover the famous healing springs that give the city its name by pigs. There are many examples throughout Celtic

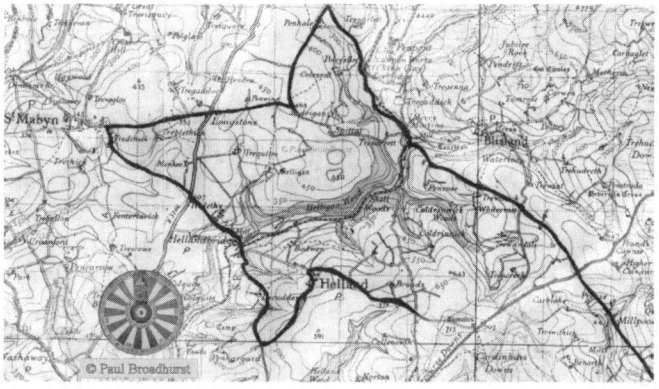

The 'Little Pig' of Helland and Blisland, with its snout tethered to St Mabyn Church. In Celtic mythology, the pig is a creature of the otherworldly realms.

legend. The pig, despite our modern sensibilities and the rather comi-cal aspects of its nature, was in previous times one of the most sacred of beasts. And there was always the possibility, I supposed, that this particu-lar youngster was a Boar!

As soon as I began to understand the possible significance of this symbol it seemed, yet again, that this was not just my fevered imagi-nation working overtime. The Pig, I now recognised, was actually a totemic symbol of the Underworld *par excellence*. I visited the interest-ing, but heavily restored fifteenth century church at St Mabyn, to which the piglet appears tethered by a rope, and found the place, like nearby St Kew, infested not with pigs, but bears! Inside, the stained-glass Coat of Arms of the Prideaux family had three bears, and that of the Barratt family of Tregarne no less than eight! The Godolphin Coat of Arms had three as well. What other treasures might there have been before the vicar ripped out all the old monuments and pews in 1818?

The St Mabyn Bear looking towards Tintagel

But most interesting of all were a number of finely-sculpted figures on the church tower (the tallest for many miles), among them a dog, a horse, a ram, a dragon and a winged cat-like figure, topped by four angels. There was no pig. But there was a Bear! It had a large muzzled head, and was positioned on the north-western corner so that it faces due North.

All this was now beginning to stack up in a way that could not be ignored. One might perhaps regard the legend of St Kew and her Bear as a casual curiosity, but here was a Bear that was looking northwards *directly to Tintagel*.

St Mabyn, I realised (said to have been one of the daughters of King Brychan of Wales) could be a Christianisation of *Mabon*—the 'Child of Light', a sort of Celtic Apollo, after whom the *Mabinogion* is named. This is one of the earliest collections of Celtic literature we possess, for although it was committed to writing decades after Geoffrey of Mon-mouth, it is drawn from the old Celtic oral tradition, and concerns what was the universal Mystery Tradition of ancient Britain. In this pervading myth, Mabon, the primeval ancestor of the British race, was taken from his mother Modron before he was 'scarcely three nights old'. As we have seen previously, Modron was the Mother Goddess who is likely to have given her name to the two churches dedicated to St Materiana at Boscastle and Tintagel, in the body of the Great Bear. In one of the stories, *Culhwch and*

Olwen, Arthur and his men go in search of Mabon, liberating him from his imprisonment so that he can go on a quest to discover the treasures of the Otherworld.

Another theme in the Mabinogion is that of animal totems, and one of the great keys to the discovery and release of Mabon is through an initiation involving the descent by King Arthur and his followers into the Otherworld with the help of totemic animals, each representing a certain power. One of the stories, *Pwyll, Prince of Dyfed*, begins with a hunt as a prelude to entering *Annwn*, the Otherworld, echoing the Wild Hunt. He also presents his foster-father Pendaran Dyfed with a swine that comes from Annwn.

The Mabinogion, since its first translation into English from Welsh manuscripts in 1849, has often puzzled mythologists and scholars because of its strange characterisations and powerful mythic motifs. There is no question it exemplifies the great Mystery Wisdom of ancient Britain, with its mythological themes and archetypal characters from the old oral traditions. The stories—or what remain of them—are a mixture of folk legend, fiction, myth and history, and hence can often appear obscure and somewhat impenetrable to the casual reader. Yet as Caitlin Matthews points out in *Mabon and the Mysteries of Britain*, this treasure trove of tales represents themes that are of immense significance, and have since become integral to our understanding of the old British mythology, with such themes as the Cauldron of Cerridwen (the earliest known form of the Holy Grail), Arthur Pendragon's quest to enter the Otherworld or Annwn, where he discovers the symbols of sovereignty or the Goddess of the Land, and the release of the 'wondrous child' Mabon, from imprisonment. These are all derived from Druidic lore, and therefore represent the oldest known native British traditions.

In the Welsh *Triads*, which, along with the Mabinogion, are similarly drawn from the old oral tradition, the original name of Britain was *Clas Merdin*, or *Merlin's Precinct*. Later, after settlement it became known as the *Island of Honey*. In the Mabinogion we also come across the figure of Merlin as the archetypal shamanic priest, who commands the stags of the forest, and, as R.J.Stewart notes in *The Mystic Life of Merlin*, this link with horns gives Merlin not only power over the natural world, but makes him the Lord of the Animals and the Wild Hunt. Stewart also points out that there are strong connections between Merlin and Mabon, both of whom were taken from their mothers at an early age and are linked to animal totems who assist them in their quest. He concludes they are both drawn from the same archaic Mystery Tradition.

As early as the fourth century St Augustine forbade 'that most filthy habit of dressing up as a horse or stag' in an attempt to stamp out the old animal-worshipping religion. Did he have much success in Cornwall? Judging by the continued existence even today of the old pagan traditions in the form of Padstow's Beltane Obby Oss celebrations it appears he did not succeed. It seems that these old ways continued far closer to the present time than we may imagine, judging by the existence of the evidence we have found so far concealed in Christian churches. Does the spirit of Merlin, Lord of the Animals, still hover over Cornwall? The legends would suggest he is at least as important as King Arthur in this respect, if not even more so, since he was the one who created the circumstances of Arthur's birth at Tintagel.

Tapping into the very earliest mythology of Britain, these stories in the Mabinogion, fragmented though they are, are somehow here clearly set in the Cornish landscape, with its sacred character and giant figures reflecting various stages of initiation. Might this represent a shamanic journey writ large, a quest to release that 'wondrous child', Mabon, from imprisonment within, so we too can find the treasures that lie concealed in the otherworldly landscape?

All of these ideas flooding out from the landscape were quite overwhelming, and I became convinced this image of a giant piglet was indeed a reality, despite the fact that it did not seem as well-drawn as the other animals in this bewildering bestiary. But that, I came to realise, was probably because of the steepness of the valleys and the undulating nature of the land itself. The sacred animal of the Underworld and the unexpected entrance of Mabon and Merlin into the picture seemed very extraordinary indeed. It is interesting that in one of the earliest of all collections of writings, *The Black Book of Carmarthen*, named after the legendary place of Merlin's birth and thought to have originated in the sixth century, Merlin actually has a long discourse with a *'little pig'*, where the animal appears as a totem of prophecy.

In this the pig, Merlin's familiar and companion in the wilderness, becomes his confidant, with the wizard telling him about his anguish at past and future events, which are all too vivid to his spiritual perception. Even the present is bleak, laments Merlin, but his shamanistic powers also reveal a future time when all the colour has vanished from the once-vibrant land. Just one verse from this lengthy conversation, translated by the Celtic and Arthurian scholar John Matthews and published in his *Merlin Through the Ages*, gives the flavour of his disillusionment:

Listen, little pig,
It's no use my hearing the scream of the gulls.
My hair is thin, my covering likewise.
The vales are my barn— Short on corn.
My summer harvest Brings little relief.
Once my passion was boundless;

Now I predict, Before the world ends,
Shameless women, Passionless men!

In this, one of the oldest references to Merlin drawn from the bardic literature of the Celts, he becomes a wild man of the woods, inspired by prophetic visions. Half-mad, 'Merlin the Wild' is the earliest of all the sorcerer's characterisations, long before he became the enchanter of Arthurian legend, and owes much to the shamanistic legacy of prehistory. Here he is a young man driven insane by his past sufferings, as well as tortured visions of the future.

Around 1134 Geoffrey of Monmouth rewrote these fragments of the old British lore that had been written down by monks such as Nennius in the ninth century. Geoffrey's *Vita Merlini* was included in *The History of the Kings of Britain*, which included Arthur's birth at Tintagel. This revamped early material struck a powerful chord in the Anglo-Norman psyche, conjuring up the untamed powers of Nature; a 'Green Man' living wild amongst the elements, with 'snow to my knees, ice in my beard'. These original poems that inspired Geoffrey are redolent of the old Celtic magic, as we can sense from the *Little Pig*, even if they were judiciously tidied up for a new audience.

Of course there must be a tailpiece to this story of the Little Pig in the landscape, and it is one that links to the previous chapter in an unlikely way. Appropriately, the tail of this piglet appears to be growing from Cardinham, in particular the site of Trezance, where the Celtic Saint Meubred had his Holy Well, whose waters now tumble out from between the roots of a great tree into ancient stone troughs. The figure also appears to manifest from the site of Old Cardinham Castle, the now deserted abode of the Cardinham family.

And where is our Little Pig looking? Directly towards a bridge over the River Allen (formerly the *Camalan*) called *Dinham's Bridge*. Beyond this his gaze is firmly fixed on *Castle Killibury*, the most likely site of King Arthur's stronghold of *Celliwic*, according to many historians. *Celli* means forest or grove (not much evidence of this today) and *wic* means way. Although the earthworks have been largely destroyed the site dominates the area between the Allen Valley and St Mabyn, and the old road leading to it bisects the site, entering at the old gateway and passing through to the other side. Is this the *wic* or *way* through the old fort that was once surrounded by a *Celli* or *grove*? When we put all the evidence together can we come to any other conclusion than that this is almost certainly the long-lost site of King Arthur's Cornish capital of Celliwic?

It is significant that the Mabinogion, set as it is in Wales, nevertheless frequently has King Arthur returning to his court at Celliwic *in Cornwall*, noted as one of the 'Three Tribal Thrones of the Island of Britain'. One might have expected patriotism to have placed Arthur's chief stronghold in Wales, but it is repeatedly stated as in Cornwall. The circular ramparts are very similar to those of Castle Dore, that other legendary Arthurian location, the one-time Court of King Mark. Besides commanding the area around the Allen Valley, it was in easy distance of the old seagoing trade routes across to Wales. Another Welsh tale recounts how the evil Mordred raided Celliwic and 'consumed all', leaving not so much as would 'feed a fly', dragging Queen Guinevere violently from her chair. This episode was the beginning of the end, and set King Arthur and Mordred against each other, leading inevitably to the Battle of Camlann.

The atmosphere of Castle Killibury today is perfectly in keeping with this story of desolation and abandonment, with decaying farmyard buildings built into the remains of the old earthworks and rusting machinery dissolving back into the elements from which they are made, a picture of sad neglect. But the last time I was there, something in the air made me catch my breath. It was the distinctive whiff of pigs...

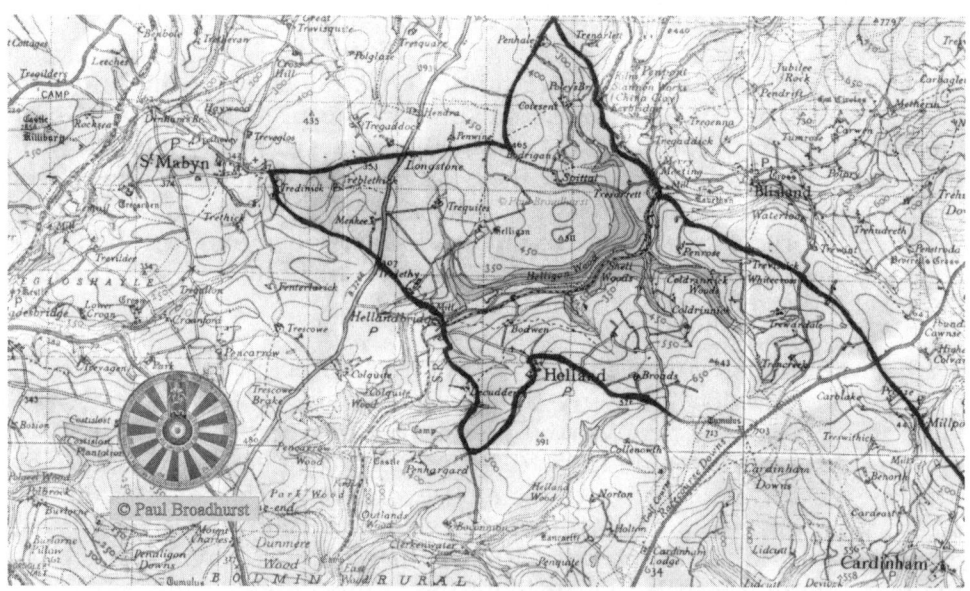

The 'Little Pig' of St Mabyn, looking directly towards the earthworks of Castle Killibury. This site is very likely the location of King Arthur's Celliwic mentioned in the Mabinogion.

12

THE CALL OF THE WOLF

As we have come to expect during this quest, the discovery of giant figures within the landscape, with all the imaginative leaps of faith that are required until confirmed by other evidence, is accompanied by a far more rigorous and scientific dimension, that of demonstrable North-South alignments. These invisible lines on the landscape are physically marked by monuments from various ages, and we have taken considerable care to present our findings in a way that can be verified by anyone who wishes to take the time.

In this way, the two different sides of the mind—the one that recognises symbols and what we might call the magical mode of perception, and the more rational one that is concerned with logic, numbers and measurement, are perfectly married to create a balanced approach to the mysteries of the landscape, with both the 'right-hand' and 'left-hand' brain working together.

So far the figures we have found have all been positioned on the Polar Axis, or Tree of Life, exemplified by the Great Bear and guarded by two Lions at its foot. Our 'Little Pig' too is located on this axis, which runs through the village of Blisland and the Pig's back, as if all these mythical beasts are tethered not only to the Earth, but the central point of the heavens as well. Can such a Polar Axis be fixed in the landscape by a single line? It is a question that perplexed us, and was now to be answered. Whoever surveyed this system obviously strove for an amazing level of accuracy, that much is clear from the results so far. But if you are surveying the surface of the planet a single alignment can never do justice to the diverse nature of the landscape through which it passes, due to many factors including the unique qualities of each part of the countryside, which must also be taken into account, such as its steep valleys, rocky tors, rivers and other natural features.

We are the first to admit that what we have found so far in the Cornish landscape appears extraordinary, almost unbelievable. Yet there it is. We leave it to the reader and other researchers to check our results and come to their own conclusions. But we have always been aware that what is being revealed here is necessarily only a part of a much larger, multi-layered and complex system that we may never fully understand.

That, however, does not stop us being drawn irrevocably into this strange web of intrigue involving the stars, the Earth beneath our feet, and the works of a group of mysterious people whose expertise in myth-making, star-lore and the practical sciences of surveying and building monuments of earth and stone was truly amazing. The scope of their vision still seems to us quite bewildering.

Every new discovery brings fresh ideas and concepts to grapple with. So far, we have found that this system was apparently laid down in extreme antiquity — certainly as far back as the 'Age of the Megaliths' — during the Bronze Age or Neolithic, a time lost to us yet whose works still remain even after many thousands of years. As stones cannot be accurately dated to determine when they were first set up, we will probably never be able to know precisely. But an equally fascinating aspect to all this is to discover that within the historical period, certainly from the coming of the Normans and the subsequent history of the Cornish, Welsh and Breton families who populated the land, there is ample evidence to show that they knew of these matters and continued to develop the system as if it were some form of personal legacy, an inheritance they were charged to maintain. If we had any qualms about this, what we were about to discover next should leave the reader in no doubt that this was the case.

The 'tail' of our Little Pig, indistinct though it may appear, seems to be growing from the two most important sites at Cardinham, set in the undulating valleys of the western flanks of Bodmin Moor. These are Trezance, the holy place of the Celtic St Meubred, believed to be the one-time home of the Cardinham family, and Old Cardinham Castle, which they built. Both of these are aligned North-South, and we also noticed that the 'Arthur Stones' as we had christened them — the white quartz stone row at Boscastle that was set into the hillside to point to the place where the constellation of the Great Bear comes closest to the Earth — was also located on the same longitude. Were they meaningfully connected? Drawing a straight line between them was eventually to reveal a possible solution to an enigma that had baffled us, and generations of previous antiquarians and researchers, for a very long time.

The line led across the western side of Bodmin Moor known as *King Arthur's Downs*, and ran along the central axis of the unique Neolithic monument called *King Arthur's Hall*. This is a rectangular structure lined with upright stones (many of which have collapsed over the last 5000 or so years) and surrounded by an earth embankment. Although it has been noted by previous observers that it is aligned North-South, no-one has ever come up with any ideas as to its function. Its location was carefully chosen, for it is in a very remote and somewhat boggy area, with extensive views of the Cornish 'sacred mountains' of Roughtor and the slightly less tumescent Brown Willy. As far as we can ascertain, it is unique, amongst only one or two other examples of rectangular Neolithic monuments known in Europe. Even more interesting is that it appears purposefully designed to contain a pool of water, likely fed by an underground spring, and today filled with rushes and water weeds. A previous seventeenth century visitor, John Norden, described it as a *'square plot about 60 ft long and 35 ft broad situated in a plain mountain wrought some 3 ft in the ground'.* It was *'set around with flat stones, and holds water.'*

A rectangular, stone-lined pool in the middle of nowhere, with the name King Arthur attached to it? What would a dark-age chieftain be doing at such a place? Was it King Arthur's swimming pool, a place to unwind after the latest wearisome battle?

Fortunately we have by now realised that the illustrious king stands for more than an historical character of dubious provenance, and that the name refers to an entire cosmology reflected on the Earth. This is why it belongs to King Arthur, for, like all those other countless monuments from the so-called 'Stone Age', thought by many to have been built by people who were primitive, bog-stomping savages who could barely enunciate 'Ug!', this artefact is nothing less than an astronomical observatory and a scientific instrument of considerable sophistication.

We realised this after discovering it was positioned astride the North-South axis that was marked at its northern extremity by the 'Arthur Stones' and the site of Old Cardinham Castle further south. After spending some hours there producing, to our knowledge, the first survey that had ever been undertaken with a theodolite, Robin showed that it was constructed according to the same Pythagorean geometry as that employed in the building of the original 'station stone' rectangle of bluestones at Stonehenge (see Robin's results on page 338). As it was angled towards the North with its raised earthen banks to create a level horizon, it would have made the perfect place to observe and measure the stars of the circumpolar constellations, including the Great Bear. We realised that if it was cleared of reeds and full of water this would have created an exceptional refinement to this star observatory, as one of the techniques for the precision measuring of stars, especially if one wishes to accurately determine True North by their transit across the meridian, is to set upright poles in a pool of water and work with the reflections by literally bringing the stars down to Earth.

It is probably easy to imagine our excitement at perhaps finally solving the mystery of King Arthur's Hall, a monument that had kept its arcane secrets for what may have been many thousands of years. We had only been led to it by the discovery of the 'Arthur Stones' which are not recorded on maps, and the Cardinham family's choice of site for the building of their castle. As far as we can tell, this latter site was virgin territory (although it too has never been excavated), so we must assume that the Cardinhams deliberately chose to position their abode on this axis before they moved to Restormel, which is similarly aligned on the parallel North-South axis of the Great Bear.

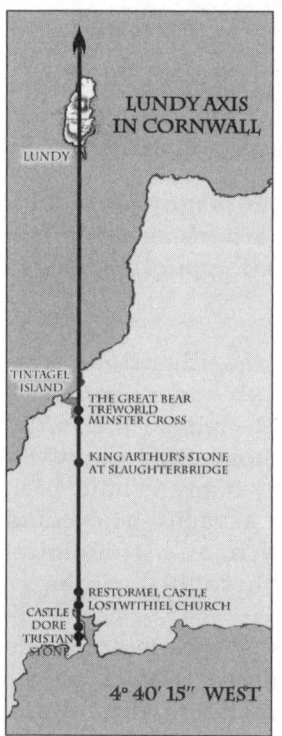

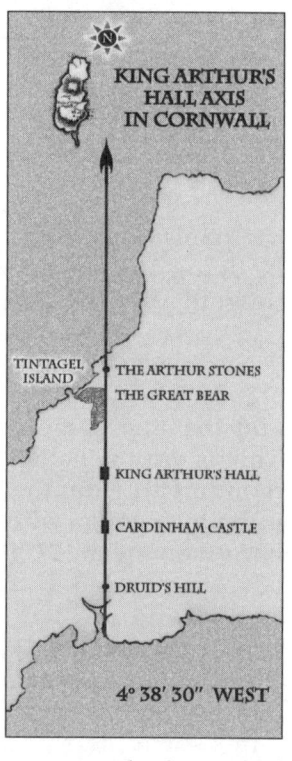

It seemed to us that this preoccupation with Polar Axes, with all that entailed, was not so much a preoccupation as an overwhelming obsession!

Here we had two Polar Axes running parallel to each other just over a mile apart, and both marked by highly significant sites. This created what was in effect a 'corridor of power'. Did these form the trunk of our 'Tree of Life'? Or were there more examples, waiting to be found?

The truth is that, as detailed in Robin's chapters towards the end of this book, this is not merely a Cornish phenomenon but one that extends into Wales and beyond, providing much food for thought about all those Welsh saints who came to Cornwall, the extant Arthurian legends, and the ancient connections between the two lands. It is our contention from these results that such North-South axes probably exist wherever ancient cultures decided to focus their attention, and that these areas are likely to be the ones that are mythologically potent. How could this highly distinctive feature of the megalithic and medieval cultures have been missed by archaeologists and researchers? It must be because very few have ever realised the real importance of True North and its mythic dimension, and consequently no-one has before related the sites to each other.

However, another Neolithic stone row was to herald an altogether equally intriguing discovery. It began, as all the others, by casually perusing a map, spurred on by a strange feeling that there was 'something in the air'. This time it came quickly, as if whatever it may be was keen to unleash itself. *It was the head of a giant Dog, imprinted onto the landscape around St Columb Major.*

Excited at the possibility of a new addition to the menagerie, we all duly set off to explore the area, and stopped off at the stone row known as the *Nine Maidens* on the edge of St Breock Downs between Wadebridge and St Columb. We had been there a number of times before and noticed that a ditch alongside the stones had caused some of the remaining ones to lean drunkenly, and that a causeway across the rather waterlogged field contained other large stones. The row pointed towards the north-eastern horizon, and, just beyond the hedge but out of sight, was the stump of a standing stone variously known as *The Magi Stone, The Old Man* or *The Fiddler*. This had once been seven feet high and surrounded by a small circle of stones, but been deliberately broken up around 1900 by Victorian evangelists. The row was clearly aligned to this stone but no-one had found out exactly why. Earlier enthusiasts for megalithic alignments such as Norman Lockyer and Alexander Thom had visited it, and Thom judged it to align to the star Deneb in the circumpolar constellation of Cygnus the Swan in around 2000 BC. Thom was unfortunately limited by the supposed date of construction supplied by archaeologists; if he had realised such megaliths were much earlier he may have come to different conclusions than he eventually did. Robin took some readings, and I noticed that if a ruler was placed along the stones as marked on the map, it led straight to St Columb Church. In the opposite direction it pointed right at Tintagel.

Robin, with the aid of his computer program, was to later confirm this, refining the result to conclude that it actually pointed to the churchyard of St Materiana's on the cliff overlooking the Island, where the unusual 'sighting stone' is located. John Norden, in *A Topographical and Historical Description of Cornwall* of 1650, described the stone row as 'nine great stones set upright in the wylde and vast downs' and included a sketch that showed an avenue or double row. Although probably inaccurate, there is no reason for him to draw something that did not exist, and so we might conclude that some of the stones have been resited, whilst others (whose remains may lie in the causeway) were removed in field clearance. But why leave them at all unless they were objects of special veneration by the local people?

The name of The Magi Stone, the oldest recorded version, is suggested by Robin Payne in *The Romance of the Stones* to have been so-called because it could have indicated a star, just as the three Magi of the Nativity followed theirs to the birthplace of Jesus. In this case though, the Magi led to the birthplace of Arthur! (I later discovered that the three stars of Orion's Belt which point to Sirius are also sometimes known as the *Three Magi*).

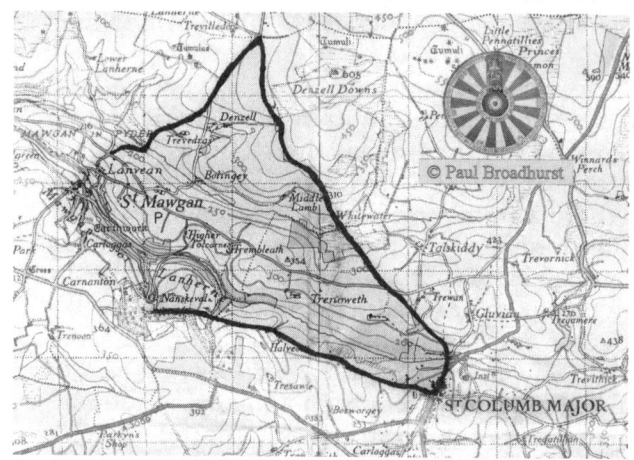

The Great Dog of the St Columb Area, when examined on the map, was quite impressive, with a lean and hungry look, wrinkled fur at the back of his neck and an alert-looking ear, poised as if listening out for something. His eye seemed to be located at Whitewater Farm (more eye-watering connections here), with his muzzle firmly placed on St Columb Church, and the River Menalthyl forming his throat. Just where the underside of his neck would have joined the body (had there been one — the construction of St Mawgan airfield has obliterated anything that might once have been there) was a curious and distinctive oval meadow with a small copse of trees at its centre, looking like some gigantic medallion hanging around the Dog's neck. And another notable aspect was that this figure was the first so far to be looking towards the East instead of West.

The outline led past Carnanton Woods to run along one of the most beautiful of all the Cornish scenic valleys, the timeless Vale of Lanherne that leads along a wooded path following the river towards Mawgan Porth and the sea. Firmly planted on the back of the Dog's neck was St Mawgan Church in the centre of the old village. After the 'Little Pig' which was perhaps not as simplistically figured, this particular hound appeared to be very satisfying, artistically speaking. Once seen, it cannot be forgotten.

As we drove into St Columb Major we could sense the sad air of undeserved neglect that hovered around the place. Undeserved, because the town was once amongst the most vibrant in Cornwall, and still exhibits much graceful architecture along its narrow streets. Even a few years ago, it boasted a fine array of shops selling just about everything. Now it seemed to be clinging on by its fingertips in the midst of declining business, in part due to the supermarket mentality that has ruined so much of Cornwall, along with the unavailability of free or cheap parking.

St Columb, though, was once an important market town on one of the main roads to the West, as revealed by its architectural styles, from late medieval to Venetian and Victorian Gothic. Barclays Bank in particular is eye-catching, with its ornate red brick façade and distinctive spire, along with a number of other buildings mainly designed by William White who succeeded in making the town so distinctive. Local resident Anthony Holloway explained that St Columb was at one time destined to become Cornwall's county town and the site of its only cathedral, until it was pipped at the post at the last minute by Truro during the time of Bishop Benson at the beginning of the twentieth century. As in so many places the thriving market has gone, and with it the prosperity, for the town was never built for the age of the car and vehicles are forever reversing and scraping each other in the narrow main street.

Nevertheless, St Columb has enjoyed a memorable past, with its imposing church and impressive rectory, known locally as the Bishop's Palace. Historically, it retains elements of its one-time influence to this day, and is famous as one of the few places left in Cornwall that still celebrates the old pagan tradition of Hurling—a cross between a wild lawless rugby match (played with a cricket ball!) and a frenzied rough and ready rite of spring. Every Shrove Tuesday, a silver ball (said to represent the Sun, or *Heul* in Cornish) is thrown aloft outside the Church gates and then two teams, one from the 'town' and one from the 'country' fight for possession. It is not necessarily a pretty sight, and can be dangerous for both participants and onlookers.

The businesses and residents of the town take the wise precaution of boarding and shuttering their windows against this heroic revelry, thought to be one of the most ancient of Cornish games. Some say it has connections with the beating of the bounds, and some that it comes from a primitive religious ritual. Whatever the truth (and it may be a combination of both) there is a sustained scrummage throughout the town until the ball reaches one of the two goals, situated a mile away from the town centre. The ball may lodge in a gutter or on a roof, or be thrown to women watching from open windows, so one can imagine the mayhem that might ensue. But the silver ball brings good luck and vitality to whoever touches it, and the winner is ceremonially carried back to the square where he proclaims victory and adjourns to a hostelry where 'silver beer' is made by immersing the ball in a jug of ale.

St Columb has always been known for the sturdiness and strength of its men, who invariably seem keen to engage in a general dog-fight. It is said that the Town Charter was awarded some six centuries ago by King Edward III after the resolute fighting of St Columb men at the Battle of Halidon Hill whilst fighting the Scots under their leader Sir John Arundell. No wonder, then, that the town on Hurling Day resembles a war zone preparing for invasion or riot.

A dog looks across to a lion on a bench end in St Columb Church. In the landscape, the Bodmin Lion is staring towards the Great Dog of St Columb.

Right on the tip of our Great Dog's nose is St Columb Church, one of the most important in Cornwall. It towers over the town from its raised oval tumulus or mound, and it is easy to see why this place was considered as a possible cathedral site. Its open tower has been built to allow a right of way through it, and contains a large megalithic-looking slab alongside another that looks like a worn crusader-type memorial. On entering the church, we immediately noticed the collection of ancient bench ends, made in around 1510. There were once at least a hundred, but today only 38 remain. Yet these old carvings, as I have found on many occasions, have preserved symbolism that had once been integral to local beliefs. Here was a *Veronica* or *Mandylion*, the image of Christ's face on a piece of cloth, that, like the Turin Shroud, was a source of marvel during late medieval times and especially venerated by the Templars. The Agnus Dei, or Lamb of God, another of their most popular symbols was in evidence too. There were also a number of mythical beasts which were of particular interest, including Swans, a dancing bear and a Lion facing a Dog. This last was an unusual combination, I thought, particularly since I had noticed that on the map our giant Dog was looking straight at the Bodmin Lion.

After a long chat with the vicar, who was very hospitable, we noticed that in the South Transept or Jesus Chantry (although it had been restored in the nineteenth century and could not rival the age of the bench ends) was a line of Coats of Arms. Among them was, according to the Church Guide 'The first arms of King Arthur' showing three crowns, and 'The later coat of King Arthur quartered with Uther Pendragon, King of Britain, his father, and incorporating the Vision he had at Glastonbury'.

The most interesting and historic part of the Church was the South Chapel, and this was where we first came across a family that was to become very important to our quest. These were the Arundells of Lanherne, who owned St Columb as part of their manorial lands. Either side of the altar, hidden under carpet, were two magnificent memorials—the so-called Arundell Brasses—for this had been their own special place of worship and had long been known as the *Arundell Chapel*. The Arundells had been, for some 500 years, one of the chief families of Cornwall, and in 1427 Sir John Arundell had established a Chantry of Our Lady at St Columb with a college of five priests, which had continued until 1701 when the building had burnt down.

In 1676 the Church had been violently changed forever when some youths set fire to a supply of gunpowder kept there for defence. They themselves were killed, the stained glass windows were blown out and several monuments including that of Sir John Arundell were destroyed. However, one of the brasses shows a later Sir John with his two wives and their children surrounded by armorial bearings in the form of six swallows (the name Arundell is said to be a pun on the French word *hirondelle*, meaning swallow). They were devout Catholics, and this particular John had been subject to a fine of £240 every year (a considerable sum in those days) for failing to attend service in the Church of England. Why should such an ancient Cornish family be such loyal followers of the Roman Church? Thereby hangs an interesting tale that gives much insight into those times, which we will presently explore.

The memorials also record other family members, including an earlier Sir John who was knighted by Charles I for his support. From the thirteenth century through to the eighteenth the Arundell family had been the benefactors of the church, the most valuable benefice in Cornwall. Consequently the building, throughout its various restorations, was largely the result of their patronage. The list of Rectors begins in 1257 with Richard de Lanherne and the family was responsible for a succession of rectors, although many of them were 'absent' due to other responsibilities. For half a millennium, the Arundells *were* St Columb, almost like a royal family.

So who were they and where did they spring from? Did they know anything of the giant Dog in the landscape, and the fact that their residence at Lanherne, adjacent to St Mawgan Church and now a convent, was also directly implicated in this mystery? What was the meaning of this Great Dog? Some of these questions were about to be answered as we followed the trail of the Arundell family to their old residence, the beautiful village of St Mawgan-in-Pydar, thought by many to be the most picturesque in Cornwall.

Because of the Arundells St Mawgan and St Columb have always had historic as well as geographic associations stretching back to the thirteenth century, and it almost feels as if you are stepping through time when approaching the village of St Mawgan, certainly one of the most charming in Cornwall. It has had a great influence on history, producing warriors, admirals, churchmen, conspirators, High Sheriffs and Members of Parliament. It is also of great interest in our current quest.

Raised on its tree-ringed ancient mound near a medieval bridge, the old church is indeed one of the most atmospheric in the county. Its fine old Gothic lantern cross standing above the entrance is probably in the same position as it has been since being first set up. This cross is highly unusual in that it depicts the image of what appears to be a king and a queen. According to artists and observers who saw it before it became so weathered, a serpent could be distinguished that looked as though it was kissing the king's face (this can still be discerned, even though the centuries have taken their toll). We arrived as the clock struck three and opened the creaking oak door to be greeted by a fustian darkness and very strong atmosphere. The old bench ends had thankfully been preserved from restoration and as we examined them Robin noticed a memorial plaque on the wall, with a knight's helmet on which was proudly mounted... *a dog!*

At that very moment, Gabriele also called out. She had come across an illuminated family tree of the Arundell family on display in a glass case. Here was another heraldic crest, this time with a silver dog with a black five-pointed star on its throat. We were, we have to admit, rather taken aback. We had come to St Mawgan hunting for a dog, and had already found two within minutes, one with a star displayed in just the area that corresponded with the curious 'medallion' hanging around the giant Dog's head.

One of the Arundell memorial brasses in St Mawgan Church, which lies within the head of the Great Dog.

Further exploration revealed another fine collection of memorial brasses from the Arundell family. One, in the darkest corner of all, and quite difficult to make out, had a dog on the crest with a pentagram star. It looked, we thought, rather like the Egyptian jackal-headed god Anubis. Gabriele dove into her bag and produced a pencil and a piece of paper with which she immediately made an impromptu brass rubbing.

Intrigued by this revelation that so closely echoed the shape of the Dog's head in the landscape, we repaired to the nearby Falcon Inn for a welcome *hair of the dog*. It was, after all, appropriately situated on the nape of the great Dog's neck.

On returning home we set about researching the Arundell family whose crest of a dog had given us plenty to ponder on. They had indeed been one of the richest and most influential of Cornish families, living at Lanherne opposite the church long before it had become a religious house. Although genealogy can create a tangled web and not all authorities agree, a picture began to emerge that had considerable implications for our researches.

The Arundells were said to have been 'at home', in the quaint ter-
minology of genealogists, when William the Conqueror came. It appeared
that the first real record of the family was in about 1260 when Sir Ralph
Arundell was Sheriff of Cornwall. It was probably he (or, according to
some authorities, Sir Renfrey; the actual records are hazy regarding this)
who married the heiress of a certain Simon Pincerna, who lived at a place
called *Trembleth* or *Trembleath* in St Ervan, a mile or so directly above the
Dog's head. Pincerna had been an influential character, having been cup-
bearer to King Henry II. Whilst some sources say that this just meant he
was a butler to the King, a little more research revealed that this position
had a more powerful aspect as well, for in antiquity the cup-bearer was
an officer of high rank in royal courts, and because of the constant fear of
plots and intrigues, whoever held the position was required to be above
reproach in guarding against poison in the king's cup. This confidential
relationship with the king gave the bearer a position of great influence,
and there are a number of Biblical and Egyptian references which show
that at those times the power of the cup-bearer was often only surpassed
by the king himself. And might we be forgiven for thinking that in the
Arthurian revivalist atmosphere of the Royal Court of the time, it may also
have had a symbolic resonance with the concept of the grail-bearer?

Of Simon Pincerna we know virtually nothing else, except that his
family may have come from the Liskeard area before settling at Trembleath, whilst Sir Ralph is said to have moved to Cornwall from Yewton
Arundell in Devon. His family were similarly very influential, and besides
Sir Ralph being Sheriff of Cornwall, Roger Arundell was, in the previous
century, Marshal of England. When Ralph (or Renfrey) married the heiress
of Simon Pincerna they lived at her family home at Trembleath (now
Trembleath Barton). And here was an unexpected surprise. For *Trembleath*
means *Wolf's Town*. It is derived from the Cornish word for wolf, *blythe*.
This is where the Arundell crest had originated. It was not a dog at all,
but a Wolf!

On reflection it had been an easy mistake to make, for dogs are,
after all, only domesticated wolves. And the lean-and-hungry look of the
landscape figure did perhaps look more like a
Wolf than a Dog. Close inspection of the map
revealed yet another place called *Trembleath*
or Wolf's Town right at the very centre of the
giant figure, just above where its jowl was
beautifully sculpted by the wooded valley of
the river.

So here were two Wolf's Towns—one,
the original abode of the Arundells and another meaningfully positioned within the
head of the Great Wolf itself. Surely none of
this could be a coincidence, and it seemed

The crest of the Arundells
- A wolf passant argent

even more remarkable that the Arundells had adopted as their crest the
actual image of a Wolf. Consequently it looked as though they must have
known about this giant effigy for it to become their chosen family symbol.
They were soon to leave Trembleath and buy Lanherne, positioned on the
back of the Wolf, where they were to live as virtual petty kings of Cornwall for almost 500 years.

Presently we will examine this great family in some detail, but as
we began to ponder the mythical significance of such a giant figure in
relation to the other effigies that had been so far discovered, it became
clear that it held great symbolic importance. For according to nearly every
ancient tradition, the dog, wolf or jackal was known to be the Guardian of
the Underworld.

*Entrants for St Columb Carnival in 1911 pose for the town photographer. They seem to have
a strong liking for masquerading as both Bears and Lions!*

13

GUARDIANS OF THE SECRET LAND

he best-known dog-headed guardian of the Underworld is Anubis, who appears in innumerable Egyptian tomb-paintings where he is often shown supervising the weighing of the hearts of the recently departed. In the Papyrus of Ani in the British Museum the jackal-headed god is depicted alongside the scribe Thoth, the God of Magic, to judge the deeds of the deceased so they may enter the realm of the Afterlife. The Egyptian pantheon may seem a far cry from the lush meadows, soaring cliffs and wild seas of Cornwall, yet it is of interest to us here because it is one of the few accessible religions where animal-headed gods and goddesses were the most notable feature. There were others but they have never achieved the popular attention that Egypt has, mainly due to its great longevity. The royal dynasties of the Nile lasted for many thousands of years, and were contemporaneous with much of the Neolithic and Bronze Ages in Europe, thus perhaps giving an insight into that time.

Here, then, is a useful place to begin a brief exploration of the meaning of our Great Dog or Wolf. And we should not be too surprised at any correspondences that may occur, for the classical authors such as Diodorus Siculus and Herodotus give a number of accounts of the maritime skills of the Phoenicians (who, according to many historians were the sea-going trading arm of the Egyptian 'empire'). The Phoenician connections with Cornwall are well-known because of these accounts, which describe how they came to seek tin, one of the most valuable commodities of the ancient world. Without it there would have been no bronze, for Cornwall was the prime source of tin at that time, making it one of the great centres of mercantile activity in the ancient world.

According to these authors the Phoenicians established colonies and secret trade routes to and from the Westcountry, which the Greeks did their best to discover (and eventually did). Tin, as in the later days of the Templars who were in many ways a medieval version of the Phoenicians, made both exceedingly rich and influential. Many of the curious-sounding Cornish place names may derive from those early times, for they are highly unusual, with a great preponderance of the letter z, (*Perranzabuloe, Tredrizzick, Zennor etc...*) which does not derive from the Brythonic Celtic languages and lends a exotic charm to the village names of Cornwall.

These connections with North Africa and the Middle East continued for thousands of years, and Jewish merchants carried on the trade developed by the Phoenicians, with places such as Marazion (Market Jew), adjacent to St Michael's Mount, the deep-water harbour of Falmouth and the Camel Estuary once busy places for the export of tin. Such long-standing traditions were readily incorporated into local folklore, and even in the nineteenth century miners used to declare that 'Joseph was in the tin trade', alluding to Joseph of Arimathea's reputation as a metal merchant. Persistent legends throughout the West of Britain also claim he brought the young Jesus with him when the country was under Druidic influence. Some say he came to study in their colleges during his 'lost years', and that after his death Joseph returned with the Holy Grail to live in Glastonbury.

Archaeological evidence is scant, although Egyptian artefacts have occasionally been discovered in the Westcountry, including faience beads found amongst grave goods. There may be more, for Sir Flinders Petrie records in his diary that he discovered a cache of such beads and artefacts, including scarabs, in a barrow on Dartmoor, which have since mysteriously disappeared. Other sporadic finds may exist in museum collections often misclassified because they do not fit in with the prevailing viewpoint, but there are some other notable examples that may show eastern origins, or at least strong influence.

Two of these are believed by some archaeologists to be of Mycenaean origin; the famous Bronze-Age gold cup found at Rillaton on Bodmin Moor and a bronze dagger from a barrow at Pelynt. The 'Cretan' labyrinth at Rocky Valley is also probably from this period and suggests common links. Tin ingots from Phoenician times have been dredged up in Falmouth Harbour, and beautifully-crafted gold torques have been found at St Juliot's near Boscastle (very close to the 'Arthur Stones') as well as golden lunulae at Harlyn Bay near Padstow, which could indicate Celtic connections with the Middle East where gold was more common. There is also the horde of Mediterranean pottery from Tintagel Island, showing that such links were more common than we may realise even into the Dark Ages. And although it has become fashionable amongst some academics to casually dismiss accounts such as those of Diodorus, where he details how the smelted tin was taken to an island called *Ictis* to be loaded onto waiting ships, this surely displays a certain hubris on their part, for these classical authors would never have invented such stories. Why should they? Their contemporaries would have laughed them out of the library!

The point here is that there was far more trade and commerce, in philosophy and religion as well as metals and pottery, between North Africa, the Mediterranean and the Westcountry than is generally realised today, although Victorian scholars, more familiar with classical works, accepted these accounts for what they were. The Egyptian empire extended throughout the Phoenician territories and right across North Africa, with Jerusalem itself becoming an Egyptian outpost. When the crusaders went to the Holy Land they were in effect re-establishing an association between Britain and the Arabic world that continued for many centuries. The idea that before Roman Christianity became the state religion, most of the world, and especially the Westcountry, was an essentially tribal place where people lived in virtual isolation is simply not true. There has never been any justification for such a view given the known trading links recorded in the classical accounts, the geographical nature of the place with its wealth of natural harbours, the richness of its minerals, the seagoing expertise of its people and all the other evidence of connections between West and East.

However as we have noted, the trade was not just in commodities, but in ideas and philosophies as well. Cornwall in particular has always been a melting-pot of different religions, showing a remarkable tolerance towards various attitudes and beliefs. So while we cannot infer too much about these connections with the ancient cultures of Egypt and the Mediterranean, we should nevertheless take account of this background and understand that the county was not a remote and inaccessible place inhabited by the odd Druid and a few mud-encrusted people living wild on the open moors, but a vibrant cultural centre of international commerce and philosophy.

There are many reasons behind the idea of totem animal deities representing certain mystical aspects of existence, but one of the most important is that they symbolise archetypal forces that are omnipresent throughout Creation. In Egypt the jackal became the guardian of the Underworld partly because it commonly prowled around graveyards and thus became a symbolic watcher at the threshold between the living and the dead. The indigenous Britons too, like people everywhere, would have noticed such associations and naturally assigned to the wild dog or wolf the role of a psychopomp, or guide of souls.

In the transition period between the Egyptian and Christian religions images from the two were often combined, and statues of St Michael, the Christian Archangel who guides souls, have been found with a dog or jackal's head signifying their common attributes. As Anubis weighs the hearts of the departed against a feather, so St Michael is also shown holding a balance, often along with the sword of justice, to judge whether they are worthy of being allowed to enter the Kingdom of Heaven. Cornwall has always had a special relationship with St Michael, who was the county's original patron saint long before the arrival of St Petroc or St Piran.

Strangely, before Anubis was adopted across the whole of Egypt he was only one of many such gods, and the earliest was not black at all but depicted as a *white wolf*. In the pre-dynastic Nile Delta at the beginnings of the Egyptian state, this god was known as *Wepwawet* or *Upuat*, meaning the *Opener of the Ways*, a mystical role that remained with Anubis when the black jackal god became more popular and was incorporated into the state pantheon as the son of Osiris and Nepthys, both deities of the Underworld. The place where this story began was not therefore originally connected with the jackal, and was known as Wepwawet, Lycopolis or *Wolf City*.

This apparent preoccupation with death in ancient Egypt is, though, not quite as it might appear. We have to remember that the great bulk of our information is drawn from tombs and so it naturally appears to us today that they were obsessed by the process of transition into the Afterlife, when kings were believed to live eternally amongst the stars. But Egypt was a civilisation steeped in magic, where the gods and goddesses ordered even the tiniest details of everyday life and the sense of ritual and religious observance was paramount. This was undoubtedly true of the religions of the West as well. In Egypt the miracles of creation were continuously honoured and blessed, as we know from the great number of papyri expounding wonderment and thanks for everything from the rising Sun to the fertile growth provided by the beneficent Nile. In this respect, concerning the more magical side of the civilisation, Anubis guarded over those who entered the inner realms, when their consciousness was outside the body in sleep or mystic travelling through the regions beyond the physical world. In this role he was the great protector and guide, ensuring that no harm came to those on their magical journeys.

Where did these beliefs originate? Like nearly all ancient religions, in the observation of the starry firmament. In the stellar religion of Egypt, Anubis was the constellation of Canis Major, the Great Dog, whose brightest star, Sirius, was for them the most important of all. In Persian star lore, this constellation was depicted as a wolf. In classical Greek mythology *Cerberus* was the dog that guarded the entrance to Hades which Hercules dragged to Earth and then released.

By coincidence, only a few weeks before the discovery of the Great Wolf on whose outline is positioned St Columb and St Mawgan Churches which had been the religious focus of the Arundells, (who, like the early Egyptians, had adopted a wolf as their totem), a curious thing occurred. At least it seemed so in retrospect. We happened to meet, at Glastonbury, the author of one of the most well-known books ever written on the subject. He and I were both giving talks at the *Megalithomania* conference, and had sat next to each other in the audience. Robert Temple had, in the 1970s, astonished the world with his book *The Sirius Mystery*, for its implications were profound. In it, he recounted how the Dogon tribe of Mali in West Africa were in possession of highly detailed astronomical information about the star Sirius, (or rather, the two binary stars, Sirius A and Sirius B). Some of this knowledge had only recently been discovered using sophisticated state-of-the-art equipment, showing that Sirius B was a 'dark star' which orbited its brighter cousin every 50 years, facts apparently known to the Dogon and used in their art. This knowledge, he found, was also encoded in Mesopotamian, Egyptian and Greek myth.

That a remote African tribe could know about the hidden properties of this particular star had led Robert Temple to look deeply into the Mesopotamian and Egyptian religions, for in Egypt, Sirius, or Sothis, the brightest star of all, located at the mouth of the Great Dog constellation, was the central focus for Egypt's mythology. To them, Sirius equated with Isis, the greatest goddess of their pantheon, who united with Osiris (Orion) to create the hawk-headed Sun God Horus. This seminal event was recreated every year at the heliacal rising of Sirius, when the star rose just before the Sun at the Summer Solstice to herald of the inundation of the Nile and the promise of renewed fertility. The Sothic Calendar was thus the most important cycle of earthly life, and many temples were aligned to this cosmic event, constructed in such a way to allow a shaft of light from the rising star to shine along the darkened axis of the temple, illuminating a statue of the god or goddess in the inner sanctum, or 'holy of holies'.

Back in Cornwall, as I picked up the copy of *The Sirius Mystery* that Gabriele had bought in Glastonbury, I mused on the synchronicities involved. Not only had Gabriele and myself later spent a very enjoyable evening with Robert and his wife Olivia, but he had, in a sudden flourish of literary outpouring, spontaneously written a long and witty poem for us on the endpaper of the book. As I thumbed through it to research the mysteries of Sirius I realised it was, coincidentally, the 20th of June, the eve of the Summer Solstice, the pivotal point in the Egyptian sacred calendar and the foundation of their entire religious system. It was a quirky bit of synchronicity.

At this time and at the latitude of Egypt, Sirius reappeared above the horizon after spending 70 days 'under' the Earth in the *Duat* or Underworld. During this period Anubis, the constellation of the Dog, was believed to embalm the star Sirius, hence throughout Egyptian history human mummies were subject to the same time period of preparation mimicking this stellar event. Then Sirius was reborn just before sunrise. The place on the horizon where the star rose was indicated by the three brightest stars in Orion's belt, which always act as pointers to the Dog Star. The next forty days were known as the *Dog Days*—the hottest part of the summer—when it seemed that the heat of the star combined with the Sun and melted the ice and snow deep within the African subcontinent, causing the inundation of the Nile. At this time the Egyptians performed Mystery Plays for the public, whilst initiates, deep in the sanctuary of the temples, were involved in secret rites that must have celebrated this renewal and regeneration of life.

The Egyptians (and the Dogon tribe) were not the only cultures to venerate Sirius as the great marker of celestial cycles, and in Greek mythology the constellation of Canis Major was said to be the dog set by

Jupiter to guard Europa. Another version says that it represented the hound of Actaeon, who was transformed into a stag whilst out hunting after he spied the Goddess Diana naked in the woods. The Arabian astronomer Al Biruni called it *Al Kalb al Jabbar*, or the Dog of the Giant. The brightness of Sirius is recalled in many words derived from the Latin *Canis*, or Dog, including *candle, candescence, and candid*, all drawn from the same root *'to shine'*. In Celtic and Viking traditions it was one of the dogs of Orion which became one of the spectral hounds that led the Wild Hunt, when the starry hunter god rose, because of the different latitude, in the autumn and winter.

The remarkable correspondence between The Great Dog of St Columb and the star constellation of Canis Major.

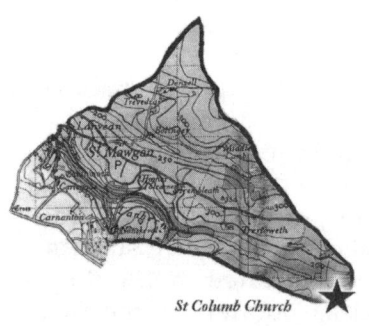

St Columb Church

How extraordinary, then, that in the constellation of the Great Dog the star Sirius is placed on the mouth of the Dog, exactly the same position as St Columb Church on our landscape figure. This correspondence seems highly significant. Is the site of the church an earthly manifestation of Sirius, with its location designed to be somehow influenced by its starry counterpart? If so, could this help to explain the meaning of the Nine Maidens stone row and the Magi Stone, which directly links the church (Sirius) with Tintagel (under the watchful gaze of the Great Bear)? Could it also be behind the fact that St Columb Church had very nearly become Cornwall's only cathedral? I was beginning to suspect that these giant effigies and their associated sites may represent some sort of ancient symbolic star-map laid out on the land, with Orion the Hunter, who, according to the first century author Manilius in his *Astronomica* 'leads the constellations as they speed over the full circuit of the heavens' as some sort of presiding deity. Along with the constellation of the Dog, Canis Major, both these star groups appeared to be central figures in this unfolding mystery.

The Great Arundells

Richard Carew, the Elizabethan Squire of Antony in south-east Cornwall, observed of the Arundell family that *'The country people call them the Great Arundells, and the greatest stroke, for love, living and respect, in the country heretofore they bare'*. Their position at the hub of Cornish life for almost five centuries had an immeasurable effect upon Cornwall, and it is possible to travel almost anywhere in the county and come across, in the local church, the memorial of an Arundell who had married into the local families or was the product of such a liaison. Carew also noted that the

Cornish gentry in particular were themselves like one large family, with everyone related to one another in a manner quite unusual elsewhere. As he put it *'all Cornish gentlemen are cousins'*. Cornwall's geographic position cannot really explain these constant intermarriages, since Cornishmen were particularly well-travelled and intimately connected in royal circles which often necessitated their frequent attendance at court.

Their interests were much broader than the confines of the county, as we might expect from a line with such royal links. The Domesday Book records that Roger de Arundell held no less than twenty-eight lordships in Somerset, and within the next hundred years several of his descendants had established themselves in Cornwall, with Sir Renfrey marrying the heiress of Trembleath or Wolf's Town and thus becoming 'guardians' of the Great Wolf in the landscape. They then moved to Lanherne on the nape of the giant animal's neck, which was to become their base for many generations, by the expedience of marrying another heiress.

Such was their enterprise they soon acquired vast tracts of land, until in Elizabethan times they held at least twelve seats in the county. As the one-time St Mawgan church organist and author of *The Vale of Lanherne*, Charles Lee observed, *'their appetite for heiresses was insatiable'* and they found that marrying into these old Cornish families was a sure route to becoming the most influential family the county had ever seen. This petty kingship extended even further over the whole hundred of Penwith, which was exempt from the authority of Crown or Duchy in day-to-day affairs. Altogether, at one time or another, various members of the family owned up to eighty manors in Cornwall alone. They also had great swathes of land throughout the rest of the Westcountry. The history of this one family alone reads like the legendary exploits of a collection of characters from some long-lost Arthurian romance.

A whole succession of Sir Johns followed the move to Lanherne, who were often noted for the lavishness of their hospitality and fashion. John Arundell I was vice-admiral of Cornwall and the first of the family to become a member of Parliament. One known as 'John the Magnificent' became an admiral in the navy of Richard II and went down with his ship in 1379, the chronicler Holinshed noting that he *'lost not only his life, but all his furniture and apparel for his body, which was very sumptuous, so that it was thought to surmount the apparel of any king; for he had two and fiftie new sutes of apparel of clothe of gold and tissew, as was reported, all of which together with his horse and geldings, amounting to the valew of ten thousand marks was lost in the see'*.

Sir John Arundell II, who was knighted in the 1460s and was the grandson of John I, whilst living at his coastal manor at Ebbingford near Bude, is said to have moved to a farmhouse at Trerice near Newquay to avoid fulfilling a curious prophecy. A shepherd who he had convicted told him that *'when upon the yellow sand, thou shall die by human hand'*.

However, in 1471 Sir John, then Sheriff of Cornwall, was ordered to take St Michael's Mount from the Earl of Oxford who had appropriated it, and it was during this that he was killed on the sands of Marazion beach, thus fulfilling the prophecy. Trerice was thereafter to become an important seat of a different branch of the family, and is today a magnificent Elizabethan manor house owned by the National Trust. Members of Parliament for the parish in which Trerice stands have been even more influential than the Arundells, and included Walter Raleigh and Sir Arthur Wellesley, Duke of Wellington. Like Francis Drake at Tintagel, this might make us wonder why they should choose these particular seats.

Another Sir John served the navy of Henry V with 1100 men under his command, and his grandson fought as a general in France for Henry VI. Sir John II's grandson, known as 'Jack of Tilbury' was Esquire to the Body of Henry VIII, a trusted position at Court and one of the King's most loyal supporters, helping to quell rebellions and overseeing preparations for the visit of the Holy Roman Emperor in 1518. After he wrote to the King about the danger of invasion from Spanish and French ships, two new castles, at Pendennis and St Mawes, were built to protect the county and he was later made vice-admiral of the western seas under Edward VI. Humphrey Arundell led the Cornish Prayerbook Rebellion in 1549, and massed an army at Bodmin before marching on Exeter. He was later taken prisoner and hanged for his beliefs. Sir Thomas Arundell was brother-in-

law to Queen Catherine Howard, and founder of another branch of the family who established themselves at Wardour Castle in Dorset. He too was involved in a conspiracy, this time against the Dudleys, and consequently lost his head in 1552. The last Arundell to leave their old seat at Lanherne to go to war was Squire John who fought for King Charles I at Boconnoc in 1644. He was a youth at the time but was knighted by the King for his service and became the last of the great Lords of Lanherne, dying in 1701.

But what of their religious faith? The Lanherne branch certainly held strong beliefs, and were renowned as staunch Roman Catholics, which sits rather uneasily with what is known about Cornwall during those centuries as a land clinging on to its old attitudes (although the Trerice branch, in accordance with their loyalty to the Crown, adopted more Protestant sympathies). The Lanherne Arundells lavished large amounts of money on St Mawgan, where they built a Lady Chapel, created the fine Arundell Chapel at St Columb, gave money to enshrine the head of St Piran to protect it from thieves who might make off with the relic, and helped rebuild Bodmin Church.

Jack of Tilbury, or Sir John Arundell II.

Much light is thrown on the mystery of why they were such loyal supporters of Catholicism when we take account of the singular situation in Cornwall. The Roman Church, which was in effect an alien force imposed on the country, could never hope to fully subjugate the people to its ways, so steeped were they in their traditions, many of which were rooted in prehistory. The English clergy who had supplanted the old Cornish bishops of the ninth and tenth centuries must have known that they could not impose their will through force, or all the ancient families with their strongly independent Norman and Cornish ancestry would rise up as one. The answer was to come to a compromise where the people could carry on with their own beliefs as long as they accepted certain changes along, of course, with the authority of the Church. The spirit of compromise, that time-honoured way of avoiding conflict, thus brought about a situation where the old ways could continue under the 'protection' of the Church fathers.

Cornwall has always been a special case. In Henry II's Charter to Truro, his subjects are referred to as 'in Anglia et in Cornubia', continuing the theme of his predecessors in recognising that Cornwall and England were separate countries. This attitude of 'live and let live' seems to have persisted for many centuries, and so it is no great surprise to find families like the Arundells loyal to a Church that allowed them to continue to practise their faith as they saw fit without excessive interference.

All that, however, was due to change when the English service was introduced in 1549 in an effort to standardise Church services and bring the Cornish into the fold once and for all. Up until that time services had been read in Latin and Cornish, but now many could not understand a single word of this alien foreign language, and there were no copies of the Bible in Cornish. Their widespread anger at this assault on their traditions turned into outright revolt as the government of the boy king Edward VI determined to replace the Mass with a new Protestant service in English.

Like the Cornish, the rest of the country had become used to the traditional rituals of Catholicism despite the fact that a decade earlier Henry VIII had broken with the papacy. As well as proclaiming himself the head of the English Church, Henry had maintained many ancient customs (*Green Men*, for instance, decked with flowers and foliage, danced in front of his wedding processions) for the Tudors themselves, being of Welsh lineage, were great protectors of the old British way of life.

His son Edward was sickly when he inherited the realm, so political power fell to Edward Seymour, the Duke of Somerset. Being a Protestant radical he was determined to replace the now 'traditional' Catholic liturgy with a simplified version in English. This amounted to the virtual destruction of a whole way of life, where the customary round of Masses, processions, saint's days and pilgrimages were to be ruthlessly uprooted, and the region's churches despoiled, with their ancient treasures stolen or destroyed. The Cornish were naturally outraged.

The new Book of Common Prayer was to be legally enforced in every parish on Whit Sunday 1549. Three days before this, the Cornish rebels led by Humphrey Arundell sent a petition to London demanding a return to the old ways. They secured St Michael's Mount and then began their march toward the River Tamar, where they captured Sir Richard Grenville at Trematon Castle and threw him into Launceston Gaol. They forced the capitulation of Plymouth and swarmed through Tavistock and Crediton until they reached the village of Sampford Courtenay, where the parish priest had, after initially obeying the new law, succumbed to pressure to revert to the original Mass. After one local yeoman, William Hellyons, was hacked to death with billhooks in the fray that followed, the Devon men made common cause with the Cornish, and laid siege to Exeter. Up to 10,000 rebels were camped outside the city walls, and attempts were made to tunnel under them, with continual demands for the reversal of the religious changes.

After some weeks Humphrey Arundell, rather unwisely as it turned out, decided to do battle with the Royal Army, and in a series of confrontations was eventually beaten back to Sampford Courtenay, where 600 rebels were to die in one day. Retribution was swift, with Arundell and his compatriots hanged, drawn and quartered in London and across the two counties those who opposed the changes were brutally executed, thus bringing to an end the era of Cornish independence, and soon, the Cornish language which had set it apart from the English mainland.

This foray into the history of the subjugation of the Cornish is important not only because it gives an insight into the strength of beliefs of the Arundells, but the atmosphere in which Cornish culture had previously thrived. The Arundells had always been fierce protectors of the old ways when these were safeguarded by their affiliation with the Roman Church, and this helps explain why they were so vociferous in their beliefs. They were trying to defend the old customs against what today we might call central control or 'modernisation', a process that still continues unabated to this day.

When the Arundells were in their prime, life seems to have been delightfully vibrant and colourful. Carew, the son-in-law of John Arundell IV, records how Lanherne was a place of constant comings and goings, where they 'gave kind entertainment to strangers'. They were famous across the region for their hospitality, and *a gentleman and his wife will ride to make merry with his next neighbour, and after a day or twain, those two couples go to a third; in which progress they increase like snowballs, till through their burdensome weight they break again'.*

Lanherne itself, whilst in no way ostentatious, is a fine building dating in parts from 1580, and has spent most of its life reverberating to the sounds of everyday bustle and the clatter of horses' hooves. If we think country life may have been dull in those days we only have to consider the 'open house' hospitality and seasonal celebrations that governed the rhythms of life. The Arundells were enthusiastic supporters of the old Cornish way of life, and one of the first recorded mentions of Morris Dancing in Cornwall was at Lanherne Manor in 1467 (St Columb's *Green Book*, or the Parish Records, notes that in 1585 goods were purchased for the dancers including '*v coates for dancers, a Fryer's coate, 24 dansing bells, a Streamer of Red Moccado and locram, six yards of white wollon clothe*). The Arundells found no clash between the traditional 'pagan' attitudes of the countryfolk of their day and yet were highly religious, with several of their number entering the Church. The first recorded Rector of St Columb was Richard de Lanherne, and St Mawgan also boasted two others among its early incumbents. One was educated at the monk's college at St Columb and in 1496 first became Bishop of Lichfield and then, in 1502, Exeter, exhibiting all the qualities of a true Renaissance man, being very fond of sacred music and a considerable scholar noted for his hospitality and kindness to the poor. Benedict de Arundelle, Rector of St Mawgan, left to become Provost of Glasney College, later a renowned Cornish seat of learning.

Today Lanherne still retains a poignant, if faded, atmosphere of those centuries of being at the forefront of Cornish life. It was given to a community of Carmelite nuns by the eighth Baron Arundell of Wardour after it had fallen into a ruinous state and they had been driven out of their own country. An underground passage leads to walled gardens, and somewhere in the house is said to be a secret chamber or priest's hole. The moody atmosphere of the rear of the building, which used to connect directly with the church, is enhanced by its rather neglected state, as well as the tall gates and walls, said to have been built after a 'shocking' incident took place. This was during a visit by a local family, when a '*sturdy young ruffian of five-and-twenty rushed across the room, and seizing the youngest and prettiest of the sisters round the waist, gave her a loud smacking kiss*'.

The offender was expelled from the neighbourhood for his outrageous behaviour, but from that time the place became cut off from the excesses of the outside world, with some windows being blocked up and a high wall built. Victorian visitors used to be welcome to visit the chapel, but unruly behaviour by some resulted in the house becoming even more remote from everyday life. Vestiges of its one-time grandeur remain though, and one of the finest decorated crosses in Cornwall stands outside the building, brought here from Gwinear, some miles away. This consists of a curious blend of the Christian and Pagan, with an image of intertwined snakes culminating in the head of a serpent pointing downwards, a Viking design known as a *Jellinge Beast* (this represents the life force in the Earth, a subject explored in detail in a previous work, *The Green Man and the Dragon*). The sculptor also incorporated a figure of Christ on the cross, dressed in a tunic and with a halo, and signed himself *Runhol* at the foot of the shaft. Elsewhere at Lanherne, the water pipes and hoppers are also a potent reminder of the good old days, for they are very ornate and emblazoned with scallop shells (a symbol of pilgrimage), lions and the old crest of the Arundells—the wolf.

What of the mythological background of the two churches so favoured by this immensely influential yet traditionalist family? Charles Henderson, in his *Cornish Church Guide* notes that 'there was doubtless a Celtic monastery at Lanherne' so it is interesting that it has returned to being a religious house, courtesy of the Arundells who were so deeply involved in the old Cornish ways. The dedication to St Mawgan, one of a family of hereditary Irish bards who is unlikely to have ever visited the parish, is however not very old, and the earliest records all speak of Lanherne and not St Mawgan.

And what of St Columb? She is said to have been a Celtic Saint— Columba the Virgin—who originated in Ireland. Her legend says she was pursued by a heathen tyrant who wished her to marry his son, but she declined and was decapitated for her stubbornness in refusing. But the word *Columb* is derived from *Columba*, the Latin for *Dove* (Irish *Colom*) and there is no mention of such a heavenly bird in the myth, although in the ancient world *dove* was a well-known name for a priestess. Yet the existence in the immediate area of St Columb Major, St Columb Minor and St Columb Porth seems to indicate something more than the tale appears to suggest.

There may however be an alternative explanation in that the name could be derived from someone far more well-known, and that is the St Columba who founded the Christian monastery on the Holy Isle of Iona. This was under the rule of St Bennet (we have already come across this name at Lanivet, for it is a contraction of *Benedict*). Columba may in fact be named after the holy island itself, for in the *Life of St Columba*, written 70 years after his death, the Abbot of Iona, Adamnan, notes that the Hebrew for dove is *Jonah*, pronounced *Iona*. Fiona McCloud, in *The Divine Adventure*, believed that this was where his name originated, from the island itself. She notes one old island poet referring to Iona as being called the Isle of the Druids before the *'cry of the sacred wolf was heard'*.

Why the cry of the sacred wolf? Because Columba's original name was, amazingly, *Crimthann*, meaning... *wolf!* It can surely be no accident that the saint renowned for reforming Druidism who famously said

'Jesus is my Druid' was originally himself called Wolf, and this Cornish parish, in which a Great Wolf figures, is known by the same name.

Could it be that Columba actually visited this area and left his name attached to this place? The idea is not so far-fetched as we might think, for North Cornwall was ideally situated on the main pilgrimage routes and there was much traffic between Ireland, Cornwall, Scotland and the North, as well as Wales and Brittany. It is an historical oddity, for instance, that the relics of St Cuthbert, on their way to Durham, were brought ashore at Holywell Bay near Newquay after a shipwreck, where his bones were said to have conferred miraculous properties to the Holy Well within a sea cave that gives the bay its name.

The great number of Celtic saints from Ireland (including Cornwall's patron St Petroc) that left their mark on the county, is, well, legendary! Did Columba, or Crimthann the Wolf, come ashore at what was later to become Saint Columb Porth and spend time at the Druid College or Celtic Monastery at Lanherne? The eponymous St Columba, if we accept this possibility, was also a prince, being of the Irish High King's family, and was consequently deeply immersed in the Druid traditions of royalty. And strangely, the legend of St Petroc, whose great monastery was located at nearby Padstow before being transferred to Bodmin, says that he left a *tame wolf* guarding his sheepskin mantle when he left Cornwall for Brittany.

It is no surprise that such historical facts may become inextricably tangled down the centuries due to changing fashions, and, it has to be said, the process whereby stories become utterly confused in the minds of country folk. This is a well-observed phenomenon whereby after many centuries local people often end up believing an almost impenetrably garbled version of the truth, much as rumours might circulate in a village after the gossip-mongers have added their own exaggerations.

When we put all these factors together with what we know of the figure in the landscape and the 'reign' of the Arundells whose home was very likely to have been on the site of a Celtic Monastery, we can see a picture emerging that has a remarkable continuity. It is easy to draw the conclusion that the Arundell family (which included so many Sheriffs of Cornwall and other notable figures who tried to protect the county against the onslaught of remorseless change that signified the death of the old beliefs) were somehow the appointed, or self-appointed 'guardians' of this ancient heritage, hence the adoption of the Wolf as their heraldic symbol. The immediate area around St Columb and St Mawgan seems to have been a focus of pagan traditions. One contributor to *Old Cornwall*, the magazine of the Federation of Old Cornwall Societies, Frederick Pedlar, emphasised this when he wrote that *'in that part of Cornwall that lies between Gwinear and Saint Columb, pagan beliefs persisted as an organised cult longer than in the far west, and longer than in the region which lies east of the river Fal'*.

The Arthurian legends may also illuminate such a tradition, for the Arundells as protectors of this legacy must themselves have been immersed in the mood of the Arthurian revivalism of the times, and especially the legendary King's protective role over the land. Interestingly, in the *Mabinogion*, Sir Kay is one of the earliest knights mentioned, where his name is spelt *Kai*. This, it so happens, is the Cornish word for *dog*. Although he is said to have been brutish and uncouth in Malory's retelling of the Arthurian mythos, no doubt symbolising his primitive origins, he is a central figure in the story of Arthur. He tried to draw the sword from the stone instead of Arthur, yet was nevertheless fiercely loyal and brave. He was the possessor of mystical powers, and called one of the 'Three Enchanters of Britain'. One of his functions at the royal court was as *gatekeeper*, whose responsibility it was to test and challenge all who wished to proceed. In this he performs the same role of the Dweller of the Threshold, just like Anubis, Cerberus, or even perhaps King Arthur's dog Cabal, who all guard the entrance to the Otherworld.

But the figure of Sir Kay appears to come from some earlier tribal tradition, and he is said to be able to go without sleep and live underwater. He is strongly linked to Nature and especially trees, able to grow as tall as one if he so wishes, and his limbs can impart warmth to his companions like a communal fire. A wound from his sword no physician might heal. He was also a slayer of giants. In Breton legend he became the Bishop of Glastonbury and tried to intercede between Arthur and Mordred during the rebellion that led to the fatal battle of Camlann. As the esoteric scholar Gareth Knight reveals in *The Secret Tradition in Arthurian Legend* such characters from the legends *'do however reflect original magical powers and inner plane attributes, which is a revealing demonstration of how old traditions pass from generation to generation and are capable of surviving passing fashions and being recoverable with the use of a little esoteric discernment'*. Sir Kay's father was Sir Ector (Hector being a heroic name in classical literature) who in some versions lived at Dunster Castle and was entrusted with fostering King Arthur when Merlin took him from Tintagel for education, training and initiation into the kingly arts.

In an unusual twist to the story of the Virgin Columba, in Arthurian legend there is the tale of Lanceor, an Irish knight with whom the Lady Colombe is so in love that she commits suicide over his dead body after he is killed. The place of these deaths is commemorated by King Mark of Cornwall, which later becomes the spot where Lancelot and Tristram confront each other.

Merlin himself has resonance with this mystery as well, for he represents the native British god of magic, learning and initiation into the Mysteries, equivalent to the Egyptian Thoth or Greek Hermes. It seems, then, a striking fact that the church of St Ervan, (made famous by John Betjeman's poem *Summoned by Bells*) just a short step away from the original Wolf's Town of Trembleath, is dedicated to *St Hermes*. Also of interest in this respect is that in *The Prophecies of Merlin*, his companion in the wildwood is a *wolf*.

Another possible link with Merlin reveals itself in the story of his conception and birth. The Norman chronicler Wace records that Merlin's mother was a virgin nun from Carmarthen, the daughter of the King of Demetia in Wales who had been impregnated by a 'daemon' or spirit. In those days the word *demon* had yet to come to signify an evil spirit, but referred to a lofty spiritual being and was often used to describe the Higher Soul or the Holy Guardian Angel. Intriguingly, the virgin St Columba is said to have come from the same area in Wales, anciently called Demetia, now part of Dyfed or Pembrokeshire, close to the region that the bluestones of the original Stonehenge came from. Merlin of course was credited by Geoffrey of Monmouth as building this national temple. Overlooking the landscape in which the Great Dog or Wolf's head is spread out below is a farm (now a golf course) coincidentally called *Merlin*.

All these links with Merlin, the creator of the original Round Table, from the Hermetic Saint of St Ervan to St Columba the Virgin being connected to the same place as Merlin's mother, could be fragments of a memory, however garbled, that was understood by the Arundells who became the guardians of this landscape. They performed this function for over almost 500 years, intermarrying with many other families of Cornish/Breton/Norman descent, many of whom had their origins in the Cornwall of prehistory, and appear to have jealously preserved the old mythology and legends of the ancient homeland.

What was the root of these myths and legends? From the evidence gleaned so far it appears to be some sort of spiritual quest involving totem animals and the power of the land itself. And as it seems likely that these shamanic beasts may have evolved into some early Arthurian characters (including that of Arthur the Bear) we have to ask the question; are we uncovering here one of the earliest versions of a mythological quest that later became known as the Quest for the Holy Grail? Both involve the initiate (or, in the early tales, Arthur and his companions) travelling into the Otherworld in search of spiritual enlightenment, symbolised by the sacred vessel of the ever-replenishing cauldron, the Celtic vessel that later became the Grail.

The Otherworld is a magical realm within the Earth which is the home of the elemental forces of Nature, the ancestral spirits and the collective wisdom of the old British culture. The families that guarded the Great Dog or the gatekeeper must, we may conclude, have been privy to this hidden knowledge, for it was nothing less than their mythic inheritance, imprinted onto the land in a way that could never be forgotten. Here the Grail Quest merges with the Wild Hunt, for they both seek to understand the purpose of human existence and its destiny as written in the stars.

There seems little doubt that the Arundells were the guardians of this knowledge. The Trerice branch of the family also adopted the Wolf crest of their ancestors, and as can be seen in their fine Elizabethan Manor, a variety of adaptations evolved. The overmantel in the Great Hall has two dog-like heads with rings in their mouths from which hang shield-like appendages with cornucopian bundles of fruit symbolising Nature's abundance. In their local church at St Newlyn East a memorial to Margaret, wife of John, Lord Arundell, who died in 1691, is flanked by dogs with flames issuing from their mouths and ears—a classic representation of the *Yell Hounds, Wish Hounds or Gabriel Ratchets* that lead the Wild Hunt, which are often said to have flaming red eyes as well. Further points of interest in this church, so closely linked with the family, include interesting animal carvings on the bench ends and an early font, with grinning cats (or primitive lions?) and dogs alongside a Tree of Life.

Margaret Arundell's memorial in St Newlyn East Church showing dogs with flames issuing from their mouths and ears, very like the Wish Hounds of the Wild Hunt.

Whilst researching the history of this remarkable family I had always accepted the received wisdom that their name was connected, through the medieval love of punning, to the French word *Hirondelle*, which gave rise to their shield emblazoned with swallows. But in an appendix at the back of *Hamlet's Mill* which concerns itself with polar myths and precession, I came across another possibility of an entirely different order. This involved the Norse *prose Edda*, where one of the heroes is called *Orendel* (variously spelt as *Erendel, Orewandel, Earendel* etc). One of the translators of this mythic series of tales notes that '*The story of Orwandel (the analogue of Orion the Hunter) must be gathered chiefly from the prose Edda. He was a huntsman, big enough and brave enough to cope with giants*'.

This concept of a great heroic hunter in the starry skies is found not just in Norse mythology but in Saxon beliefs too. The idea is reinforced in *Cynewulf's Christ* (that wolf name again, this time attached to the eighth century King of the West Saxons). They too had a strong tradition of totem animals, and objects with wolf decorations were unearthed in the Sutton Hoo excavations, thought to be a king's burial. These may have been talismans of the Saxon dynasty of the *Wuffingas*—the *'sons of the wolf'*:

Hail, Earendel, brightest of angels thou,
Sent unto men upon this middle-earth!
Thou art the true refulgence of the sun,
Radiant above the stars, and from thyself
Illuminest for ever all the tales of time.

As the authors of *Hamlet's Mill* point out, many scholars draw the conclusion that *Earendel* refers directly to Orion. Others say it means a 'beaming light or radiance', a brilliant star which they equate with the 'Morning Star' Venus, or the star Rigel, the bright star in the right foot of Orion. But de Santillana and von Dechend draw a different conclusion. They suggest that the name itself, with all its variations, is derived from *ör*, meaning arrow. They link this directly with Sirius, or the 'arrow star' as it was known in ancient cosmology. This, the oldest of all the names of the Dog Star, was, they conclude, because the three stars of Orion's belt have always been imagined as an arrow that points to Sirius. Their expert judgement is that *'Earendel, brightest of angels thou'* is therefore very likely to refer to Sirius itself.

In his scholarly studies of Norse and Saxon mythology, J.R.R. Tolkien, the creator of *The Hobbit* and *The Lord of the Rings*, was so inspired by the Anglo-Saxon hero Earendel that he transformed it into his own heroic figure in *The Silmarillion*. It appears to have deeply affected him and all his creative works, for he admitted that Cynewulf's poem cast a spell over him with its *'rapturous words from which ultimately sprang the whole of my mythology'*. Interesting, too, is that the earliest version of *The Lord of the Rings*, entitled *The Lost Road*, was set in Cornwall, where Tolkien spent many holidays familiarising himself with its landscape, people, culture and language.

Tolkien, an Oxford English Professor who translated Anglo-Saxon, Norse and Middle English manuscripts, immersed himself in these epic tales of former times to create the imaginative realm of Middle Earth with its eternal battle between good and evil. It seems remarkable that he drew his inspiration from the twin sources of the star-hero Earendel and the landscape of Cornwall. Like William Blake, he may have sensed a great mystery in the British landscape which crystallised into a parallel world with its own specific geography, history, languages, dialects and even alphabets. Like the Vikings and Celts, and the elves and faery folk of their traditions, he created dynasties with their own driving force to rescue the land from the malaise that threatened it, much like the Arthurian wasteland of legend. There seems no other conclusion to draw than that, for Tolkien, Cornwall was a gateway to Middle Earth.

Here is more illuminating evidence that we are dealing with ancient cosmology, for the very name of the Arundell family who guarded 'Sirius' in the landscape appears to be another name for either the Star-Lord Orion, or, as the authors of *Hamlet's Mill* conclude, Sirius itself!

Sirius is one of the prime stars for navigation due to its brightness and consequently this is the only star observed to set directly into the sea, the others becoming extinguished from view several degrees above the horizon. We are reminded how many of the Arundells were admirals and vice-admirals in the British Navy. The Norse/Norman/Viking mythology is here married to the Celtic traditions in a most profound manner. And just below the Great Wolf's mouth, where Sirius is located in the form of St Columb Church, is a place called *Walhalla*. This, it seems, must surely be a localised variation of the Nordic *Valhalla* — the legendary Great Hall where the souls of warriors gather in the Afterlife, just as their Celtic equivalents were regenerated by the Cauldron of Inspiration.

The Arundells, as the spiritual guardians of Cornwall and this area in particular, must have been aware of all these correspondences. They must have known that for centuries this place signified the entrance to an otherworldly realm where the Wild Hunt or Grail Quest was enacted in a highly symbolic and spiritually potent way that reflected certain star-patterns of the heavens which, like their earthly counterparts, were inhabited by archetypal beasts. And who leads the Wild Hunt? It is King Arthur, Gwyn ap Nudd or Herne. And where is the place the Arundells chose to live whilst guarding this Grail landscape? The site of the Celtic monastery (or Druid college) called Lanherne — which means *the Sacred Enclosure of Herne*.

Lanherne and St Mawgan Church in the nineteenth century. The home of the Arundells for many centuries, it is thought to have been built on the site of a Celtic monastery. Located in the head of the Great Wolf of St Columb both places have numerous examples of the heraldic crest of the Arundell family - a wolf.

14

THE HEARTLAND

he God's-eye view of these giant effigies on the land which may be glimpsed when studying a map reveals a consistency of themes far beyond that of merely the outlines of a series of great animals engraved by ancient roads and trackways. Taken together, the Bear, Lions, Pig and Wolf revealed so far all have potent mythological dimensions that, when we focus on them, reveal a pattern that is recognisable in terms of the earliest known beliefs of ancient Britain.

A further point of interest is that they all (except the *Little Lion* which appears to be leaping out directly at the observer) are positioned according to the cardinal directions. This rules out the possibility of random or accidental location, and implies deliberate intent. The Bear looks West, as does the Little Pig and the Great Lion. The Wolf, on the other hand, faces East on precisely the same line of latitude as the Lion, as if they are both staring each other straight in the eye. Both have their cardinal relationships with North as well, the Lion being situated on the Polar Axis guarded by the Bear, and, directly to the North of the Wolf is the area known as *Bear's Downs*.

To the West of this is an airfield, which, like that of St Mawgan below the Wolf's neck, has forever changed the landscape. Today, only the lonely church of St Eval stands there, surrounded by a stone hedge that, so local researchers believe, contains the remains of an old stone circle. The rest of the village to which the church once belonged was bulldozed during World War II to make way for the airfield, strategically located away from centres of population but close to mainland Europe. St Eval Church tower thus became an extremely welcome marker for pilots returning from overseas missions, many limping back from the continent in shattered aircraft. This church consequently became a powerful symbol of the homeland, and contains many memorials to those RAF personnel who lost their lives. Close to the perimeter of the airfield are *Higher Lanherne*, and, a little farther away, *Lower Lanherne*, both recalling the ancient significance of the place.

When we consider the symbolism of all this, it becomes apparent that the existence of the Great Wolf as Guardian of the Underworld has a deeply poignant aspect to it concerning the souls of these warriors, in

desperate defence of their homeland, that is echoed by the Valhalla of
Norse tradition. We are therefore obliged to acknowledge that although
these giant figures were apparently laid out in ancient times, they still
possess a living quality which can manifest when the national interest
comes to the fore, just as the legend of King Arthur informs us that he
will return when the country is in dire need. Behind the scenes, hidden
from our view, appears to be some sort of intelligent, sentient level of
consciousness in the land that still guards and guides human activity.
The word *animal*, and the concept of *animism* — the belief that everything
in Nature has a soul, both derive from the Latin *anima*, meaning life,
breath or spirit. Are we touching here some deep level of existence where
the Spirit of Nature pervades everything, including, unbeknown to us,
our own instincts? Why else should two such airfields be so intimately
connected with our Great Wolf unless it is completely in accordance with
some form of hidden natural law?

Another notable feature of these effigies is that they are set in
the landscape in a way that directs our attention to important ancient
settlements or prehistoric centres, often described as forts or castles. The
list so far is impressive in this respect, with the Bear looking at Tintagel
Island, King Arthur's birthplace, the Pig staring at Castle Killibury, most
likely the site of King Arthur's *Celliwic*, and the Great Lion watching the
Wolf. Positioned in between them is the village of Withiel.

Withiel seems to be the odd one out here, until we realise that it
was specifically chosen by one of the most influential religious men in
Cornish history as his abode, very like the Arundells' choice of Lanherne.
There are a number of other correspondences too, for Withiel Church,
situated on the Saint's Way, was also built on the site of an ancient manor.
Close by is another old manor, that of Trenance, which means *three swords*,
first recorded in 1087. The family 'de Trenance' married a Littleton and
moved to Lanhydrock (on the nose of the *Little Lion*), the oldest monastic
possession of Bodmin Priory. Thus the three sites of Withiel, Bodmin and
Lanhydrock are all strongly connected, and more than we may at first
realise. The family of Littleton Trenance sold Lanhydrock to Lord Robartes,
whose family lived there until it was passed to the National Trust. But a
half-share of the manor of Trenance (known as a *moiety* in medieval times)
was also owned by the Arundells of Lanherne.

There seems to be an almost invisible thread running through
the warp and weft of these Cornish families, which appears to confirm
our suspicion that they were privy to some type of knowledge that was
occulted from the history books. Close by the medieval church of Withiel,
which has a strangely otherworldly aura, is the Old Rectory, now Withiel
House. It was built around 1520 by Prior Vyvyan, the last Prior of St
Petroc's in Bodmin before it was dissolved by Henry VIII. He was not the
only famous historical character associated with the place even though
he was certainly the most influential in a religious sense. Withiel's most

famous son was Sir Bevill Grenville, born in 1596 at Brynn in the parish, who became the Royalist leader and won the Battle of Braddock Down near Lostwithiel, but was later killed in Somerset, famously with a letter from the King in his pocket.

Thomas Vyvyan was from an old Cornish family who believed they were descended from the Trevilians or Trevelyans, whose ancestor was reputedly the only survivor after the inundation of Lyonesse. The Prior's magnificent Tudor tomb memorial, one of the finest in south-western Britain, lies in Bodmin Church, having been removed from the ruins of the great Priory where it had been much damaged by falling timber and masonry. Elected Prior of Bodmin in 1508, he was also conse-crated Bishop of Megara in Greece, and was responsible for appointing new vicars, priors, rectors and deans to the churches and ecclesiastical colleges of Cornwall. When he had been Prior for 15 years he decided, for some reason that does not seem readily apparent, to rebuild Withiel Church and parsonage, both of which were in a ruinous state, and adopt Withiel as his residence. Almost 500 years later the church is very much as he left it, built in the then newly-fashionable Tudor Perpendicular style, together with an unusually large vestry.

That he was the King's man is evident from the tomb, made from polished Cornish Greenstone (and so finely worked that Leland, not long after the Prior's death, thought it was marble). The royal arms are conspicuously displayed on one panel, and some authorities conclude that the Prior was hoping that Bodmin would become Cornwall's Cathedral during the religious upheavals and re-ordering of the monasteries taking place at the time. There is much of interest on his tomb, including the traditional signs of the writers of the four gospels, along with their own 'totem' animals and signs; St Mark with the lion, St Luke with an ox, St John with an eagle and St Matthew with an angel. All are shown winged, and such a set of symbols, whilst quite common in manuscripts and on pulpits, are probably unique on a tomb. These attributions are generally accepted as deriving from the astrological signs of Leo, Taurus, Scorpio and Aquarius respectively, which form a great cross in the heavens.

Prior Vyvyan's Tomb in Bodmin Church, on the Crown of the Great Lion. He lived for many years at Withiel, which is situated mid-way between the Great Wolf of St Columb and the Bodmin Lion.

The recumbent effigy of Prior Vyvyan has an angel at each corner, and a panel on the south side of the tomb shows the family crest of three martins together with three bearded lion's heads. There seem to be a number of lions in evidence here, and we may be forgiven for wondering why Thomas Vyvyan, the most powerful religious figure in Cornwall at the time and the Prior of Bodmin (whose ancient monastic house lay on the crown of the Great Lion) decided to spend a large sum of money on restoring the church at Withiel and rebuilding its rectory as his principal abode. Could he have been aware of the giant animals in the landscape and wished to invoke their influence?

But to return to the Great Wolf of St Columb and St Mawgan, where might it be looking? We have already noted that it appears to be staring straight at the Bodmin Lion, and both seem to be looking at Withiel, set between the two. But if the Wolf drops his gaze a little, his line of sight leads to Cornwall's greatest hillfort, 850 feet in diameter and covering some 20 acres, known as Castle-an-Dinas.

This magnificent old fort is a scheduled monument of national importance, standing 700 feet above sea level with extensive views over a tract of Cornwall that was a centre of prehistoric settlement and trading activity. It occupies a strategic position overlooking the old trade routes through the county and has massive circular stone and earth banks with outer ditches. Archaeology has shown it was occupied between 400 BC and 150 AD, but two Bronze Age burial mounds also lie within the fort from around 2000-1500 BC, probably the graves of local kings or chieftains, demonstrating that the 'fort' may have been a ritual site long before it was used for defence.

Cornish legend speaks of Castle-an-Dinas as a seat of the Dark Age Dukes or petty kings of Cornwall from the fifth to the tenth centuries, but of special interest is its Arthurian associations. Its old name was *King Arthur's Hunting Lodge*, from where the King supposedly set out to pursue his quarry in the wilds of the surrounding area now known as Goss Moor. A stone at the foot of the hill was said to be imprinted with the hoof marks of Arthur's steed, and the nearby hamlet of Quoit has the remains of a megalithic dolmen called *The Devil's Coyte*, but once known as *King Arthur's Quoit*. Not far away is *Trewolvas*, which sounds like another *place of the wolf*, and on the opposite side of the hill, *Royalton*. Prominent across the moor is St Dennis Church with its unusual 'dartboard' field pattern, sometimes thought to have been the *Castle Damelioc* of Arthurian legend.

Here we have the place where, according to the local folklore, King Arthur set out on his hunt, and by now we may have a strong idea what he and his followers were hunting. They may not have been after the usual quarry at all, but an altogether different order of creatures possessing certain mystical powers, concealed within the landscape. From this lofty eyrie it is possible to see the mythic geography of the hunting grounds

The rocky plateau of Tintagel Island, with the castle ruins (top, centre) dwarfed by the grandeur of their dramatic location. Just below is the tiny roofless chapel of St Julitta which was in existence before the castle was built. At the bottom right of the plateau is the enigmatic rock-cut tunnel whose purpose remains unknown, but may have been connected with mystical initiation as an entrance to the Celtic 'Underworld'. The remains of many ancient buildings can be seen, and beneath the turf are hundreds more that give a clue to the Island's past as an important royal centre. This derives from very ancient times when it was linked with the constellation of the Great Bear or Arth Fawr (Arthur) in the old British language. The landscape effigy of the Great Bear of Tintagel is looking straight at the Island as if to draw attention to it as a place where the heavenly powers are reflected on Earth. As above, so below.

Church Bears and Sky Bears —*Top Left; chained Bear from a misericord in St David's Cathedral, Wales, which was, like Cornwall, a centre of the old British Mystery Tradition. The chain symbolises the circular motion of the Great Bear constellation which appears as if tethered to the Pole Star. Top right; stained-glass Bear from St Kew Church, once an important Celtic monastery just a few miles from the Great Bear of Tintagel. The legend of St Kew tells of the Saint 'taming' a Bear before she was allowed to join the monastery. Bottom left; a chained Bear looks towards the North—the Realm of the Bear—on the Elizabethan Colshull Chapel at Duloe Church, close to one of the most impressive Cornish stone circles. Sir John Colshull, the second richest man in Cornwall, married into the Arundell family, who, as revealed in* The Secret Land, *knew much of the true source of Arthurian legend. Bottom right; a muzzled Bear on the corner of St Mabyn Church tower, one of the tallest for miles. This Bear is looking straight at Tintagel, where, according to the famous legend, Arthur the Bear King was born.*

Above; the constellation of the Great Bear, from Urania's Mirror, *which can be seen hovering over Tintagel Island at certain times of the year before rearing up as if flying around the centre of the 'Round Table' of the stars.*

Merlin, here depicted in middle age, in one of the magnificent stained-glass windows in King Arthur's Great Halls in Tintagel. He is holding a scroll with the constellation of the Great Bear, for Merlin was originally a shamanic seer who made the Round Table of the stars and was instrumental in the birth of King Arthur.

A Viking King sits enthroned in a window at Crantock Church on the north Cornish coast. He is wearing a Bear pelt around his shoulders, much as a prehistoric shaman might have done, to invoke the strength and courage for which Bears are known. He also wears a helmet with a dragon crest linking him with the royal line of the Pendragon dynasty.

The Lord of the Wild Hunt, who has at various times since his prehistoric origins been known as Cerne, Herne, Odin, Wotan, King Arthur and the old British God of the Underworld, Gwyn ap Nudd. The artist who painted this watercolour appears to have well understood his ancient origins, for besides the stag's horns symbolising the Old Religion he blows his hunting horn to signal his entry into the inner planes of existence, and is attended by two dogs, guardians of the Underworld, and an owl, one of the totem creatures of Gwyn ap Nudd.

DRACO AND URSA MINOR.

PL. 1.

The constellation of Draco, the Dragon, which winds itself between the Great and Little Bear, Ursa Major and Minor. Its star Thuban was the Pole Star thousand of years ago before the current one, Polaris, in the tail of the Little Bear. This shifting of the centre of the heavenly 'Round Table' is remembered in the legend of Uther Pendragon who was the mythical 'father' of Arthur, the Bear King.

Camille Flammarion's visionary interpretation of a philosopher looking beyond the realms of the Starry Sphere to the celestial mechanisms of Time and Space beyond. The evidence in The Secret Land *shows that many of the great enigmas of history, including the reason behind the existence of many megalithic structures (which are often associated with King Arthur), as well as the origins of the Arthurian mythos itself, are derived from a deep understanding of cosmic cycles.*

Edward Burne-Jones' romantic painting of the wounded King Arthur after the Battle of Camlann. Otherwordly figures attend the scene, including one who carries a horn, symbol of death and rebirth. Ancient British tradition has always claimed that Arthur is not dead, but sleeping. Where does he lie? As discovered in this book, he lies slumbering in the land itself, as well as in our own collective memory, and may, as the old prophecy suggests, be ready to awaken.

The extraordinary sight of the Great Orion Nebula, photographed by the Hubble Space Telescope. The three bright stars of Orion's Belt can be seen, as well as his 'sword' or 'phallus' which hangs from it, the brightest middle star being a stellar nursery where new stars are continuously being born. Its reddish hue and the clouds of ionised gas that are created here make it visible to the naked eye. Attended by the constellations of Canis Major and Canis Minor, with Lepus the Hare at his feet, Orion the Hunter has been a primordial god of the heavens since the earliest times. He returns to the British skies in autumn and winter after a period in the 'Underworld', reappearing as a shimmering giant figure hunting the other constellations across the stellar sphere, the origin of The Wild Hunt of the old mythology, and an earlier version of the Grail Quest. Because of this he is strongly linked with Arthur the Bear King. In the Bible (Job 9:9) the Creator is referred to as 'the maker of the Bear and Orion', the two most important constellations of the night sky.

spread out all around — the setting for the quest to come. Ancient features still stand out and draw the gaze, even though the clay industry has obliterated the area to the South known as Hensbarrow Downs (*Oldbarrow* in Cornish), an area once teeming with ancient remains. Roche Rock, with the stark outline of its hermitage to St Michael built on top of a precipitous outcrop, can be seen against a backdrop of clay spoil, and the Neolithic settlement of Helman Tor (*Hel-maen*, or stone of the Sun) is visible, with Lostwithiel just beyond. Roughtor, which also has a ruined chapel to St Michael on its summit, can be seen too, as if guarding the land beyond wherein lies the Great Bear. St Columb Church is visible, along with, in the distance, St Mawgan surrounded by tall trees, and, in the East, beyond Withiel, Bodmin with its Great Lion.

This, then, is somewhere that is perfectly suited as a place to set out on a mythical Wild Hunt or Grail Quest, with the surrounding country concealing a bestiary of great animals hidden within the green valleys and high hills of the heart of Cornwall. In our imaginations we might picture those knights of Arthurian legend, and all their compatriots of former ages, preparing themselves for initiation into a mythical landscape of spiritual questing and self-discovery. As the Great Wolf, the guardian and guide of our journey into the mysterious realms of this otherworldly region, looks across at us before we set out on our pilgrimage and its awaiting adventures, we may even feel we have now become absorbed in this quest ourselves, partaking in a mystery long forgotten, but which is beginning to reveal itself once again.

The Heart of the Moor

The next giant figure was, like the others, entirely unexpected and also somewhat bewildering. Until, that is, I began to research its possible mythological relationship to the landscape and stellar correspondences. Then, what had seemed something of an impossible conundrum assumed proportions, quite literally, that were beyond anything I could have imagined at the time.

It manifested whilst studying the map of a region that had long fascinated me, and which, over the years, had beckoned me back again and again as if I was subconsciously drawn to explore it and immerse myself in its atmosphere. It lay in an area I had always considered as the Heart of the Moor, for its history could be traced from the Neolithic era down the ages in a way unlike many other parts of Cornwall. It had been a focus of prehistoric civilisations that had selected it as a great ritual centre surrounded by dense settlement and had later become a crucible for the birth of two major revolutions in human endeavour that changed it, and the entire world, forever.

This may at first seem a little melodramatic, but as we will learn, it is no underestimate of the area's role in history. But first to the discovery itself. The shape of the roads between Liskeard and the south-eastern edge of Bodmin Moor had drawn my gaze for years. There was something about them that called out, but I could not see what was there in front of my eyes, probably because it did not fit within any parameters I could imagine at the time.

But one day another giant creature began to crystallise in front of my eyes. Could it be real? Almost certainly not, was my first reaction. For why would the image of a gargantuan Hare be imprinted on this wild tract of land? I remembered I had felt this way about the other images too, and that by studying them in depth they had demonstrated their objective reality. But a Hare could surely have little or no relevance to a mythic tradition of apparently extreme antiquity that had, I suspected, been at the root of much of later Arthurian legend. I could not have been more mistaken.

This Giant Hare—which amazed me with its sheer size (approximately six miles from tip to tail), stretched from Liskeard in the South to encompass the northern slopes of Caradon Hill, where its nose was pointed upwards as if looking at the sky, and was, like the other figures, drawn with an exceptional clarity and simplicity. Its head was sculpted by Caradon Hill, with its great concentration of prehistoric barrows (and television masts visible across most of the county) and even its mouth was clearly sketched by a sharp bend in the road at Downgate (right next to an old pub, as if it were symbolically and continuously refreshing itself!) Just below this was the prehistoric settlement of Tokenbury Fort, an earthwork that, according to Philip Henwood in *Prehistoric East Cornwall*, is 'in a class of its own', with massive ramparts and two large monoliths framing the entrance.

The Hare's nose was formed by two of the crossroads at Upton Cross, and the back of its head followed another road that led through the village of Minions (past another pub, *The Cheesewring Inn*, said to be the highest in Cornwall). Beyond this, the road, which had once been an ancient trackway across the moorland, passed an old stone cross called Long Tom, a Christianised megalith leaning with age, and a notable marker in this landscape, which is notoriously prone to fog because of its altitude. It can descend at any time, when the rocky tors become largely invisible. When this happens the land assumes an especially timeless atmosphere, and to walk across the moors in the mist and see Long Tom standing there like an old man bent by time can give one quite a start.

Further along, the Hare's long ears appeared to be tucked down behind its body in the area of Higher Tremarcoombe, and its back,slightly rumpled, followed the moorland road past King Doniert's Stone, a broken monolith inscribed with a memorial to an eighth century Cornish

king who is thought to
have been drowned near
Redgate. On the tail of the
Hare (for it must surely be
a Hare rather than a rabbit,
which was only introduced
in medieval times) was Dobwalls, so-called because of
The Walls of Dobbe—the remains of an interesting site
with three prehistoric stone
circles, now sandwiched
between a modern housing
estate on the southern edge
of the village. These circles
(two of seven stones and
one of six) are probably the
smallest in the Westcountry,
and are unusual in other
ways too. Set in a dip they
seem unlike any others in
that visibility of the skies
would have been greatly im-
paired, the exact opposite of
the usual pre-requisite for
such monuments. Each circle
also has the rather alarming
intrusion, archaeologically

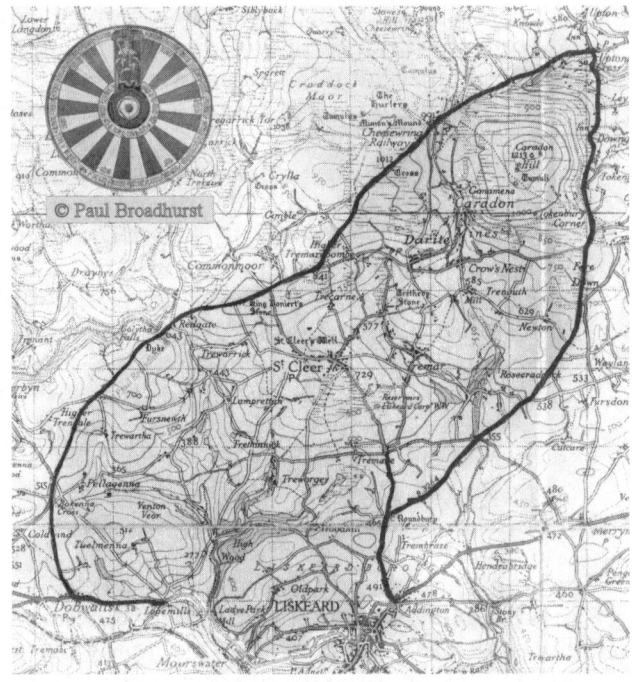

The effigy of a Giant Hare outlined by old roads across the eastern fringes
of Bodmin Moor, with ears tucked back into its body as it appears to gaze
skywards. Its head is formed by Caradon Hill, an important prehistoric
site, and the shape is also marked by a number of old crosses, stones and
enclosures. At its heart is the biggest megalithic structure in the county,
once known as King Arthur's Quoit.

speaking, of two cast-iron drain covers. Why they are there, and how such
an apparent act of vandalism was allowed, seems baffling. In the end I
surmised that each circle may be built directly over underground springs,
and that the drains were installed to carry the water away to prevent the
ground becoming boggy. If so, this makes the site even more intriguing,
since some have speculated that it may have been particularly associated
with lunar observations, and the Moon and underground water possess a
strong resonance.

This attribution of a lunar function to the stone circles was to be
an early clue to the likely meaning of this particular figure, whose mythological correspondences, soon to be explored, was to stamp it with a distinctive character within our terrestrial bestiary. Whilst it appeared to be
sitting on the main A38 road with the town of Liskeard where we might
expect its paws to be, this area was indistinct, probably due to roadbuild-
ing and urban development. Nevertheless, it was the most complete figure
yet, and consequently seemed to be of special significance. The front of the
Hare, where the leg joined the main body, was marked by another earthwork called Roundbury before passing near *Fursdon* to Tokenbury Corner
to join with the head.

This figure is certainly amongst the most striking yet, for it is not only virtually surrounded by prehistoric remains, but its body is crowded with notable sacred sites. To begin with, the head is outlined by the roads at the foot of Caradon Hill, which rises to 1,222 feet, the highest point of this entire range of hills. Positioned right at the centre of the head, this gives the impression of the land being sculpted by Nature to enhance the dominance of this giant creature. Overlooking the ancient route between south-east Cornwall and the Devon border, one can see from its summit deep into Dartmoor, as well as all along the coast from Dodman Point to the Tamar estuary. As Philip Henwood, who has lived in the area all his life, notes, although Caradon is studded with the largest collection of Bronze Age barrows on Bodmin Moor 'It is noticeable that no hut settlements have been found, either on the summit or the surrounding slopes'. He concludes '*It was a truly sacred hill, kept aside for ritual ceremony and burials... when walking on the top of Caradon one experiences the feeling of aloofness, as if walking on the roof of the world'*.

Sadly, this remarkable place has been largely wrecked by mining pits, spoil heaps and associated diggings, as well as piles of other rubble, some created by bombs dropped during World War II. The building of the masts has also left its ugly mark, with even more modern heaps of debris. Yet underneath all this rock clitter is a surprising depth of peaty soil, and in antiquity it must have been very lush and beautiful for such an altitude, especially as we know from pollen samples that the climate was considerably warmer. The concentration of cairns, barrows, earthworks and other remains in such a relatively small area certainly indicates the special character of the place in prehistory.

Right at the heart of this Great Hare is the most well-preserved Neolithic structure in Cornwall, whose image adorns the pages of many guidebooks. Believed to have been built around five-and-a-half thousand years ago, this dolmen, Trethevy Quoit (or *King Arthur's Quoit*, as it used to be known) presents a deeply impressive spectacle, raised up above the surrounding field on its earth-and-stone mound. Huge slabs of granite,

some obviously dressed and with one having an aperture cut through it, presumably to provide access, support a cyclopean rectangular capstone about ten by eight feet, and weighing almost eleven tons, which is angled alarmingly. In this case the laws of gravity seem to be suspended, for it is almost impossible to understand how it has not slid off during the millennia it has been standing. We might be inclined to think that perhaps some super-natural force keeps it in place. Cut through one corner of the capstone is a roughly rectangular hole, weathered by many centuries, that acts as a sort of lens when the Sun or Moon is overhead by creating a stream of light focussed on the small entrance forecourt.

King Doniert's stones at Redmoor

The purpose of the Quoit (described by Norden as 'a little howse raysed of mightie stones, standing in a little field') is not known, but it was evidently erected as some sort of ritual chamber with possible astronomical properties. Sir Norman Lockyer observed that because of the fact it had never been restored it was an ideal monument to survey; he found that the orientation of its entrance coincided with the direction of the November sunrise, and in the opposite direction the May sunset. He also found that King Doniert's Stone was exactly due West, marking the equinoctial sunsets. We are fortunate it has never been excavated, or this majestic structure might, like many others, today be just a jumble of stones. Some have speculated that it could have been a 'spirit house' like those from other cultures, inhabited by the deity that presides over this landscape. Many have wondered why it was built where it is, not on high ground where it could be seen to dominate the countryside but on a small hilltop which would in those days have been enclosed by forest. Could its position at the heart of our figure reflect the reason for its location? It is an intriguing thought, if we consider the place as a focus for the spiritual energies of this part of the land.

A short distance away from the Quoit is the moorland village of St Cleer, once a place of some religious prominence, said to have been founded by a Celtic Saint in the seventh century. The Norman church was rebuilt and enlarged towards the end of the thirteenth century when the patronage was granted to the Knights Hospitallers. Besides the church, impressive for a village this size, there is a fine reconstructed Gothic Holy Well chapel, now trapped in the middle of bungalow land. It was said to be a place of miraculous healing virtues as well as a 'bowsening pool' where lunatics were immersed in its waters in order to effect a cure.

Its proportions and elaborate design give a hint of St Cleer's impor-tance in previous ages. Lockyer found that 'from the holy well the crom-lech (Trethevy Quoit) marks the May sunrise'.

This cluster of sacred sites gathered in the head and heart areas of the Great Hare may strike us as meaningful under the circumstances. Within a couple of miles, and all located relative to it, we have a unique

St Cleer Holy Well

Bronze Age ritual site heavily populated with barrows, the most significant Neolithic dolmen in Cornwall, and one of the county's most elaborate
Holy Wells (although these days we are warned not to drink the water!)
As Holy Wells are amongst the oldest sacred sites of all, central to prehistoric people and every culture that followed down to Victorian times,
this trio of sites emphasises that the whole area was considered as some
type of sanctuary possessing a unique character. On a lighter note, there
are, situated on the back of the Hare's head, a farm appropriately called
Hopsland, and, on its furry haunches, *Fursnewth*.

    Just as significant, it seemed to me, was the fact that positioned
directly above the Crown of the Hare's Head was another of Cornwall's

greatest ritual sites, called
Stowes Hill (*Stowe* is a an
Anglo-Saxon word mean-
ing *sacred place*, similar to
the Celtic *lan*). Practically
everybody has heard of the
Cheesewring, or the *Devil's
Cheesewring* as it used to
be known, that great top-
heavy rock pile precariously
balanced at the edge of an
old quarry, known in Cornish
legend as a Druid idol whose

top stone revolves at sunrise. However, the hilltop on which it stands is of singular archaeological and historical importance, with a ritual enclosure overlooking the three stone circles of The Hurlers set in open moorland below. Slightly lower than Caradon Hill opposite, its massive stone ramparts can be clearly distinguished, even though large piles of loose stone lie strewn around the foundations.

The southern part of the plateau is clearly defined and once contained a number of extraordinary rock piles, of which the Cheesewring is the only surviving example. They were destroyed by quarrymen and stone-cutters who have ravaged the whole area for raw materials for gate-posts, cider presses and building stone. If we think the site impressive today, it is difficult to imagine how much more so it must have once been in Neolithic times when the hill was the most important centre of its type in south-east Cornwall. The hilltop was during this time a sacred ritual enclosure, held in such high regard that no remains of habitation have been found here, even though aerial photography has revealed a densely-packed village of hut circles in the ten acre compound on the northern slopes. The summit is ringed with natural rock platforms that give breath-taking panoramic views across Cornwall and Devon, with a sunken track-way enclosed by rocky outcrops and large standing stones that have led archaeologists to definitively date these structures to the Neolithic era.

The stone circles known as The Hurlers, everyone agrees, were also a very special ceremonial place, even though they have now been recon-structed after the intense mining and stonecutting activities of the eight-eenth and nineteenth centuries. Like many such monuments the Cornish word for the Sun, *Heul*, can be discerned in their name, and they were said by Christian propagandists to have been men playing the pagan game of hurling (like that still practised at St Columb) who were turned to stone for daring to enjoy themselves on a Sunday. No-one has ever come to any firm conclusion as to their precise use, although everybody appears to agree that they were set up to mark important Sun (and Moon) rises. Ex-cavations have revealed little except the original positions of many of the lost stones, which have since been replaced. However, Ralegh Radford, in the 1930s, uncovered a floor of quartz crystals in the middle circle, and Robin Payne suggests that 'such an array would have created a shimmer of ghostly blue-white iridescence in strong moonlight'. The three circles are oriented approximately SSW-NNE and were connected by a paved way linking them along their common axis, pointing towards a barrow emerg-ing from the furzy down.

The Rillaton 'Grail'

This is Rillaton Barrow, or *King Arthur's Grave*, the last remaining one of a group destroyed by miners and treasure-seekers. In 1837 it was broken into by miners who were said to have been looking for ballast or stone for mine building, but because of the enormous amounts of stone already lying everywhere it is more likely they were motivated by other considerations, especially as one local legend said it was the tomb of a king or chieftain and contained a boat of gold. Baring Gould, in his inimitable way, picked up on such legends and elaborated on them, recounting how a Druid used to sit on one of the rock piles near the Cheesewring and offer to slake the thirst of travellers by means of a magical vessel that could never be emptied. A passing hunter, following a wager with the Druid that he could drain the ever-replenishing cup, failed, and, in a fit of anger, rode off taking it with him. The Druid had his revenge though when the rider fell over a rocky precipice, killing himself and evidently being buried clutching the golden cup on the principle, we must suppose, that if he wanted it so badly, he should take it to the grave!

Whether this legend was current when the miners plundered the barrow is not clear, but what they found certainly confirmed that a golden vessel existed within it. When they opened it they found a largely intact skeleton which crumbled to dust on exposure to the air, with a bronze dagger and a remarkable Bronze Age gold cup. As is the nature of such things, stories soon started circulating and the relic gathered its own mythology. One story said that it was sold by the miners and then lost until recognised by a British Museum official who happened to be visiting Buckingham Palace, when, in the King's bathroom, he spied it being used as a shaving mug. However, other accounts from more reliable chroniclers exist, including one by Edward Smirke, Vice-Warden of the Stannaries, who was present at the excavation.

The Rillaton Cup

Now in the British Museum, the cup is finely worked in beaten gold, with concentric corrugations that echo the spiral designs of mazes and labyrinths, as well as the rippling effect of liquid. Being of gold, it is unlikely to have been for everyday use, and was probably reserved for ritual or magical purposes. The nearest equivalent vessel was excavated at Saint Adrien in Brittany, with which Cornwall had strong links in prehistory. It may have been made in Cornwall with Irish gold from the Wicklow mountains, but until it is analysed, which seems unlikely after all these years, we will never know. But the grail-like stories that have accumulated around the Rillaton Cup are typical of such a unique artefact, and even if some of them are invented or exaggerated, the fact is that the golden cup survives and is an extremely rare example of a vessel that, like the Holy Grail and its Celtic equivalent the Cauldron of Regeneration, possessed magical properties of an everlasting nature.

As we can see, the area immediately above the Hare's head is archaeologically one of the most interesting in Cornwall. It is also the site of one of the earliest-known open cast Bronze Age tin mines known, and

thus points to the place being at the forefront of the technological revolution of smelting tin and copper that gave rise to the Age of Bronze. Stowes
Hill was also to become, many thousands of years later, the site of the
beginning of another technological advance, the Age of the steam engine,
heralding the Industrial Revolution. Invented by Richard Trevithick and
developed in Cornwall, these engines were first tested in the mines and
adits that riddle the area, with the gaunt, gothic eyeless engine-houses
still standing as testimony to those days. It seems a far cry from the lonely
landscape of today, but the slopes of Stowes Hill once resounded to the
hellish sound of clanking metal and the bellowing of miners whilst the air
was thick with black smoke and belching red-hot fires, a scene of almost
Dante-esque proportions.

Stowes Hill, then, has been a remarkable focus of mankind's involvement with the land since the earliest days of human settlement. From
its beginnings as a ritual centre and sacred place it appears to have been
at the forefront of our relationship with the Earth for many thousands of
years. Once revered and of impressive beauty, where its inhabitants would
never have thought to dishonour an ancestral grave, it has stood by as
men have raped the rock and soil, smashing its bones and sucking dry its
mineral-rich blood. We may shrink at the idea that if the land really is sentient then we as a race have a lot to answer for, and have a huge challenge
ahead if we are ever to restore the country to even a shadow of its former
glory. There are other mysteries of the place that we will investigate soon,
but now it is time to explore the mythological dimension of the Great Hare
and see what we can learn of its ancient nature with regard to our quest.

Gazing at the Moon

When I finally accepted that this outline represented a Hare,
I realised that I had seen something like it before. It didn't take long to
discover that a hare, with its head thrown back as if looking at the sky,
was in fact a very ancient and almost universal image particularly associated with the Moon. So much so, that from India and China, Africa to the
Far East, and Egypt to the Celtic and European traditions, it was known as
a Moon-Gazing Hare.

This strikingly common tradition right across the globe reveals
that hare mythology was once deeply embedded in the folk religions of
almost every culture. Cave-paintings and fragments of Paleolithic and
Neolithic hare sculptures have been found, and ancient pottery, coins,
seals and hieroglyphs all speak of its potent magical powers to the people
of old, a symbol that is still very much a part of traditional paganism.
Many cultures considered that there was no Man in the Moon, but a hare
whose outlines can be imaginatively discerned especially when the Moon
is full. The death and rebirth of the Moon every month became a symbol
for the celestial hare that sacrificed itself—the very essence of the rhythms
of Nature and their continuous renewal.

In Egypt, Osiris was depicted with a hare's head during Nile sacrifices, whilst in China the hare became synonymous with the elixir of immortality which was made from sacred herbs, and a guardian of wild animals that comes from the North Pole as a harbinger of peace and prosperity. The Buddha was also, in his early career, saved by a hare, who sacrificed its life by throwing itself into a fire and was rewarded with a place on the Moon, thus becoming a symbol of resurrection. North American tribal myths speak of the Great Hare, the common ancestor of humanity, just like the Bear. In these, Michabo, the Great White Hare, invented picture-writing, ruled the weather and was the creator and protector of Earth and Heaven. He was also a mighty hunter who was identified with the Sun and its life-giving power.

In Anglo-Saxon mythology, Ostara the Hare represented the rising Sun, especially at springtime with all its associations of renewed life force, resurrection, potent sexuality and fertility (one doe can produce 42 young in a year). Easter is thus named after the Hare Goddess, as is the cardinal direction of East, where the Sun rises at the vernal equinox. The date of Easter is determined by both the Sun and Moon (the Sunday following the first full Moon after the spring equinox) and the sacred creature was believed to possess both male and female qualities (Pliny the Elder thought that the Hare was androgynous). The list of gods and goddesses associated with hares is extensive, including the Norse goddess of procreation Freya and the Celtic goddess Cerridwen, whose cauldron was an early version of the Grail.

In Ireland the hare is said to be the oldest sacred creature of all, and, on a personal note, one of my earliest and most vivid childhood memories, being raised in the wilds of County Tipperary, was being confronted by a huge hare that appeared vastly bigger than myself (and probably was), which stood motionless staring at me whilst its eyes felt as if they were peering right into my soul. It was a spine-tingling moment that only now comes into sharp focus.

Throughout the Celtic tradition it was believed that as well as being a creature of the Moon through its connections with fertility and the menstrual cycles that govern the gift of earthly life (the hormone *Oestrogen* is named after the Goddess *Oestre*), the hare was the favourite animal and familiar spirit of the Earth Goddess and a royal symbol of her sovereignty. As an attendant of the White Goddess the hare was the ultimate embodiment of death, redemption and resurrection and the cycle of love, fertility and growth. Every Easter the goddess was changed into a hare at the time of the full Moon, where it could be seen holding an egg — another symbol of burgeoning life. Its magical and protective powers were evident too in the defence of the Goddess herself, and Boudicca is said to have released a hare as an omen of victory before each battle, interpreting its movements as a form of divination.

In the Irish tales the warrior Oisin hunted a hare he had wounded which sought refuge in a bush that led to an underground hall. Within he found a beautiful maiden on a throne bleeding from the wound. Here the characteristics of the hare emerge as being those of a creature especially sacred to the Earth Goddess, which lives in the Underworld and is closely associated with the transmigration of the soul or the shape-shifting of the prehistoric shamanic tradition.

The hare's prodigious procreative appetite also meant that it became a symbol of love and sexual potency, and was, in classical times, the favourite creature of Venus, Aphrodite and Cupid. Its aphrodisiac properties were consequently much sought after. Its other attributes, being a creature that links the Underworld with the world above, endowed it with mystical powers of cunning, cleverness and a fondness for ritualistic displays, especially of wild dancing and mock fighting. Because of its animated antics during springtime when it leaps frantically about and appears to be 'boxing' it has always been associated with lunacy and madness, a tradition celebrated by Lewis Carroll's *Mad March Hare* (it was also, we may recall, the *White Rabbit* who led Alice into Wonderland). This epitomises a form of divine frenzy brought on by a heightened intoxication of spiritual energy that is concentrated in the Earth at this time.

Because the hare was such a powerful symbol of the old religions it became a prime propaganda tool of the Church, which, particularly because of the creature's licentious behaviour, it could not bring itself to tolerate. It thus became an animal of the devil, whose appearance signalled ill omen, and its dancing was likened to covens of witches engaged in ritualistic or orgiastic activity. Witches were frequently accused of shape-shifting into hares who sucked cows dry and caused all manner of mayhem. This does seem to have been founded on apparent cases of shape-shifting, for in 1662 the young Scottish witch Isobell Gowdie, during a trial lasting four days, freely admitted that a hare was one of the creatures into which she transformed herself. She is said to have delivered the following rhyme:

> I shall go into a hare
> With sorrow and sighing and mickle care
> And I shall go in the Devil's name
> Till I come home again.

If hares were wounded (as in the story of Oisin) the witch would be found the next day injured in the same place on her body. Like werewolves and other denizens of the Underworld, they could only be killed by a silver bullet or crucifix. This reversal of the hare's once sacred nature, into a creature of foreboding and bad luck, is still current today, and there is an extant Westcountry tradition that they must not be mentioned at sea for fear of terrible retribution. A Cornish superstition says that a young girl who dies of a broken heart after being abandoned by her

lover will be transformed into a hare so that she can pursue her faithless
love. Nevertheless, a dim memory of the hare's true power is preserved in
the folklore connected with the lucky rabbit's foot, which will protect its
owner from ill-wishing.

The secretive twilight and nocturnal activities of hares gave them
a powerful reputation as being creatures of initiation for those wishing
to enter the otherworldly realms, and they were especially associated in
the magical traditions with Thoth or Hermes, the classical gods of magic.
They were also the creatures of pagan woodland goddesses such as Diana
and Artemis, signifying their special allegiance to the feminine principle
in Nature.

But another of the many attributes of these magical animals was to
do with hunting, for, like the quest for true knowledge, hares lead their
hunters a merry chase, being astonishingly swift and quick-witted when
pursued, and notoriously difficult to catch because of their zig-zagging
coursing which bewilders and confuses the hounds. In this, they seem
perfectly suited to the Wild Hunt, for there is hardly a hunt wilder or
more unpredictable than that which chases the hare. Caesar observed
that the Gauls held the hare so sacred that to hunt it or eat its flesh was
forbidden, the only exception being at the old Celtic festival of Beltane
Eve. At any other time the penalty for flouting this taboo was to be struck
with cowardice.

Both the hunting and fertility aspects of hare-lore come together
in agricultural beliefs of former times, when the hare was believed to run
into the last sheaf of corn, where, like the corn-spirit John Barleycorn,
it must be killed to renew the land for the following year. 'Cutting' or
'killing' the hare was a ritual performed in many counties, when the
reapers would throw their sickles (symbols of the Moon) at the 'hare' or
last stand of corn.

In 664 at the Synod of Whitby the Roman bishops achieved one of
their greatest triumphs over the Celtic Church. Easter was subsumed into
the mainstream calendar and became a Christian celebration of the Crucifixion and Resurrection of Jesus Christ. What was originally a festival of
fertility became a symbol of the dying and rising god of the new era. Yet
the old ways were persistent—the Easter Hare or 'Bunny' is still a prime
symbol of this time of year, just as it has always been.

In summary, what does this Great Hare in the landscape stand for
in terms of our own quest? We have discovered that it is associated with
the Moon and the feminine principle, that it is the favourite creature of
mystical initiation through its connection with the otherworldly realms,
and that it therefore came, in the eyes of the Church, to symbolise everything to do with the old religion. In fact the hare became synonymous with
the persecuted pagan tradition to such a degree that the Roman writer

Tertullian, in the third century, observed that *'On us, as if we were hares, is the hunt focused'*.

The Tinners' Hares

A constant theme throughout this quest has been how the search for metals has characterised the history of Cornwall from its beginnings in the early Bronze Age up to the Industrial Revolution. This has greatly influenced much of the Westcountry's development and folklore, and we have spent some time looking at the role played by the Templars in all this, as the prime metal merchants of their day and the economic engine behind much of Devon and Cornwall's medieval prosperity. There may even be remnants of Nordic influence at the Great Hare, just as we found at the place called *Walhalla* close to the Wolf. Here, virtually on the Hare's breast is *Wayland* — and in Norse tradition Wayland the Smith is the god who forges metals from the Earth. On the Franks Casket he is depicted holding a cup or grail-like vessel that he has presumably just made.

Engraving of 1717 by the German Benedictine monk and alchemist Basil Valentine, showing the Hunt of Venus or dogs chasing the 'Tinners Hares'. The symbol is linked in alchemical texts with the metal Tin.

Whilst examining the exquisitely-painted roof bosses at the Templar church of Widecombe in the middle of Dartmoor (known as the *Cathedral of the Moor*), another centre of the metal mining and smelting industry in medieval times, we noticed one in particular that 'leapt' out. We may recall that these bosses are notable for, amongst other things, their representation of Perceval, the Arthurian Grail-seeker, as a Green Man, indicating that the true Grail is a vessel of inspiration to do with the Mysteries of Nature. But the other image that drew our attention was that of three hares chasing each other round and round, and drawn in such a way that whilst they appear to have two ears each, they in fact only have three between them. This is, like hare lore itself, a well-known image in certain places, including the Far East, but is particularly associated with the Westcountry. Known as the *Tinner's Hares* or *Tinner's Rabbits*, this symbol is said to be the emblem of the medieval Tinners (i.e. the Templars, who controlled the tin trade) which has a number of different levels of symbolism. At its most prosaic it may be that hares and rabbits, like miners, spend a great deal of their lives underground.

The alternative name for this symbol is the *'Hunt of Venus'*, which is probably a sexual allusion to do with the classical Goddess of Love and the fertility of hares (there is more to this than meets the eye - see appendix III). Most authorities appear to agree, though, that the three hares in a circle symbolise the 'Trinity' of the phases of the Moon, which represent the new, full and waning lunar cycles. The earliest reference to the symbol at Widecombe is from 1856 and this, besides making the point that the three hares is the sign of the Tinners, states that it also has an alchemical connection. In fact archaeologist and historian Tom Greeves suggests it may actually have been an alchemical sign for Tin itself.

It is perhaps not something we may consider particularly relevant these days, but the finding and smelting of metals in pre-industrial ages was thought of as a powerfully magical activity to do with working with the earthly elements, the raw materials of Nature, and refining them through various processes of sublimation and transformation. A common misconception is that alchemy is purely to do with changing 'base' metals such as lead into 'gold', thereby bringing great riches. However, these golden riches are of another order entirely in the true tradition of alchemy. They are a metaphor for the mystical transformation of our own 'base' natures into the 'gold' of spiritual enlightenment. The Templars, so immersed in magical tradition, understood this, and so the symbol they adopted here had hidden within it other levels of meaning.

One of these may be that in the production of bronze, tin is alloyed with copper. One of the sources for copper (traditionally the metal of Venus, the Goddess of Love) in antiquity was Cyprus (the two words derive from the same root). This island is said to have been the birthplace of Venus or Aphrodite, and both the Phoenicians and the Templars traded there. The fact that Westcountry tin and Cypriot copper were the essential raw materials for the production of bronze in the ancient world may be of relevance here, as the symbol of the Tinner's Hares or the Hunt of Venus appears to possess these various multilayered correspondences. We should thus not ignore that the lore of alchemy, which was freely practised during medieval times by Abbots and high-ranking churchmen as well as magicians and philosophers like John Dee, Newton and Paracelsus to mention a few, was an allusion to the transmutation of the human spirit; that is, a spiritual process that ran parallel to that of the actual refinement and transformation of metals.

Examples of the Tinner's Hares occur at a number of Devon churches besides Widecombe, including Sampford Courtenay, the site of the Prayerbook Rebellion massacre, which may lead us to conclude it may have had a special role with respect to the Templars (two examples of Tinner's Hares are to be seen, along with numerous Green Men and a Green Dragon, symbolising the life force within Nature). Yet so far only one has been found in Cornwall, at the Elizabethan Manor of Cotehele.

It is surely more than a 'coincidence' that this symbol of the hares is echoed closely by our own Great Hare, located in an area that was so important at the beginning of the Bronze Age and the period of great wealth during the medieval era and the start of the Industrial Revolution. The question that beckons here is why did the Tinners adopt the image of the hare as their emblem unless it signified some very ancient tradition that predated their own? The hare has always been linked to the Moon, and in the case of the Tinner's Hares, which relate to its three phases and the circular motion of the Moon, particularly so. It is one of the most significant totem animals of the old indigenous religion of ancient Britain.

Where is this Great Hare looking? Its head is angled so that it is gazing directly at the Moon at what is known as the Major Standstill Moonrise (sometimes called the *Lunstice*, as opposed to the *Solstice*). This marks the extreme northerly position of moonrise in relation to the Earth, and, like the Solstice, had deep significance in the ancient world as the point at which the Moon's cycle is reborn. The Great Hare of Bodmin Moor, then, we may speculate, could well be the original sacred creature behind the idea of the Tinner's Hares, since it is the guardian of the landscape in which both the Bronze Age and the great wealth of medieval times began. How or why it is found in places so far afield as China and India is baffling. Were the Tinner's Hares endlessly chasing each other once drawn from some antique tradition? Or was it introduced by travellers? The Knights Templar are believed to have traded with both China and India. We have no way of knowing, but here the Great Hare is, like the other totem animals, positioned within the landscape according to its cosmological function, as a truly Moon-Gazing Hare, looking towards the north-east.

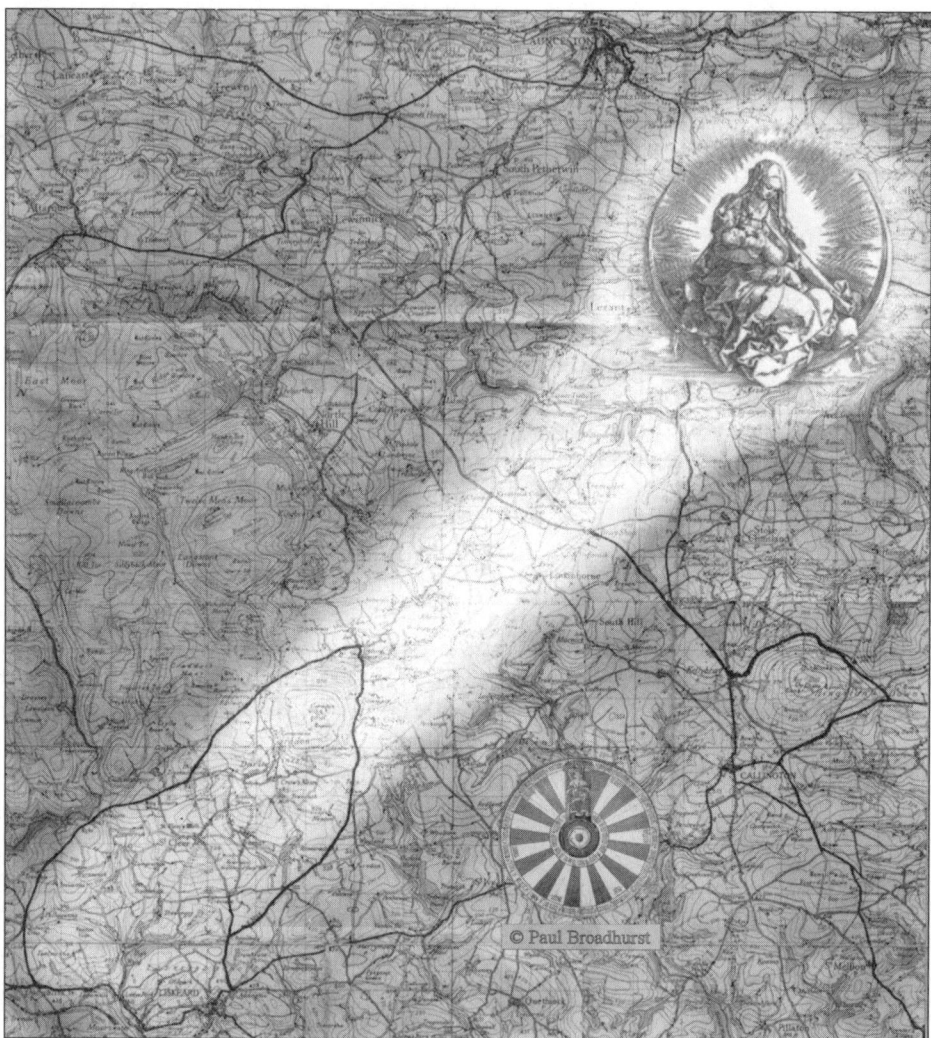

The Moon-gazing Great Hare of Bodmin Moor. Its head and body is directed towards the precise angle of the most northerly position of the Moon's cycle, the Major Standstill Moonrise. This axis includes a number of sites connected with the Divine Feminine principle of which the Hare is an ancient symbol, including a once-famous Holy Well and chapel and the site of an early medieval chapel of St Mary Magdalene. The Hare is located in an area rich in prehistoric sites, with Stowes Hill ritual complex, The Cheesewring and the Hurlers all to the North of its head on Caradon Hill.

15

GODDESS OF THE UNDERWORLD

he significance of the Hare as a totem creature of the Moon and the subterranean depths of the Earth, so closely linked to the Underworld of mythic tradition, is, as we have seen, one of the most ancient and universal survivals of what was originally a prehistoric shamanistic belief system. As totem animals go, it cannot boast the strength of a Lion or Bear or the ferocity of a Wolf, but its other legendary characteristics, of being able to see in the dark and being born and sleeping with its eyes open make it a creature of the night and the liminal regions of human consciousness. In this it connects us not only with the Earth but with the sky and the female powers of the Moon in a way that none of the other giant animals so far discovered can equal.

As a symbol for the Divine Feminine principle in Nature it represents the prehistoric era in a singular way. Historians and archaeologists believe that in the earliest times society was almost certainly matriarchal, and that the magical instincts and powers of womankind exceeded that of their male peers. This long-standing pattern of beliefs was still in evidence in Celtic times, when Druidic priestesses maintained a parity with Druid priests, and even warriorship, like that of Boudicca, was not solely a male preserve.

The decline of female power within the last few thousand years, the rise of aggressive warmongering and the distinctly male attributes of materialism and empire building have all brought about a crisis in human affairs that now threatens our continued existence. How very different, then, are the contrasting female traits of nurturing, mystical insight and the gift of bearing life itself to those destructive powers and technologies that currently rule the world. The Earth Goddess, the very land itself, must be inwardly crying out to be revered and honoured as it was in past times, with rituals designed to bring harmony between humanity and the cosmic rhythms that govern the planet's changing ages.

No wonder then that the Hare, a symbol of the old religion, has in the past been demonised and become, under the auspices of the male-dominated controlling influence of the Church, associated with the Devil and all his works. The Mysteries of the female powers have always challenged and threatened the status quo, and yet this antagonism has only ever driven them underground. All this helps to explain why the Hare has been a favourite familiar animal to witches, who have always claimed to follow the old religion of the Earth and Moon, the female side of Nature, as distinct from the solar, more dominating aspects of the male psyche. The witch burnings of the late medieval period show how fearful the Church had become of women's power and how desperate they were to destroy it at any cost.

We are in a position now to return to another of the many enigmas that have arisen during this quest—that of the Divine Feminine and its place in this scheme. We began with the discovery of the Great Bear and saw how it was the cosmic symbol and totem animal of Mother Earth, whose sons, the followers of Arthur the Bear King, in some long-distant time perhaps analogous to the Dreamtime of Aboriginal cultures, believed the world was originally created by sacred animals and sought to reclaim their mystical inheritance of harmony and order.

Having discovered the Great Mother in this dreaming landscape, we then found two Lions, one of great age and dignity, and one with a more youthful demeanour that symbolise our relationship to the Earth in the sense that it is our own 'royal' natures we quest. The Wolf is a signpost which way to go; we must embark on our own Grail Quest to recognise the beasts in our own being and thus conquer our lower instincts by realising that although they are part of our essential nature, they can indeed be tamed and transformed for the better.

The Pig is a lesson in humility. It does not seek to dominate or control, but to become aware of its own existence by entering the Underworld of the earthly soul of Nature. When we do this, we come close to the revelation that it is the feminine power of the Hare, in the guise of the Moon, which governs earthly life on all its different levels. Our hunt is thus a great lesson in human nature, for the hunter must know and understand his quarry otherwise he will return empty-handed.

In relation to this Great Hare, then, is it possible to discover some vestiges of this understanding, as we have already done by noticing that certain old Cornish families connected with the Norman/Celtic stream of tradition appear to be recipients of this wisdom? Is there a hidden theme running through these 'guardians of the land'? So far we have come across a considerable weight of circumstantial evidence suggesting that the Bottreaux, Arundell and Cardinham families all appeared to know and understand something of this, and that the fashionable myth of their day, *i.e.* the Arthurian legends, were a vehicle for encoding much of this knowledge. Perhaps if we scratch at the surface of this faded manuscript that is the Cornish landscape, more messages will come within our purview. If this is the case, then we should at least be able to find some references to the female power of Nature as embodied in the symbol of the Hare.

I first began following this train of thought by speculating that, if the Great Hare was oriented towards the Major Standstill Moonrise just as the Great Bear and the Lions appear to be the presiding totemic creatures of the Polar Axis, then this direction may indicate certain places that will help throw some light on the mystery. I imagined a corridor or Moon Axis projecting from the body of the Hare, as well as a North Polar Axis, since this latter concept seemed to be such a noticeable feature of some of the other figures. An exploration of this area North of the Hare's head was to lead to some interesting places that seemed to be related to the mystery. I started by noticing that, besides the ritual centre of Stowes Hill that we have already briefly looked at, just to the North of the Hare's head is the Darley Oak, an ancient hollow tree reputed to be up to a thousand years old. Whilst this may just be chance, we should at least note that this is the oldest surviving oak in Cornwall, and a living symbol of the old Druidic religion (the name Druid is believed to mean *wise man of the oak*). Exactly how old it is we cannot tell; some specimens live to a very great age indeed. Its position here seems curious considering its proximity to the primal symbol of the Hare. Although it is 'only' a thousand years old, this would take its date back to the Norman era and I had also noticed that the nearby village of Caradon Town once belonged to the Knights Hospitallers.

The land on which the Oak stands was owned continuously from the twelfth to the early twentieth century by the Dingle family, whose ancestors were contemporaries of the Black Prince. The tree is said to be the first in the area to bud, and was revered long before the present farmhouse

was built in 1733. Anyone passing through the hollow trunk and walking around it will, according to local belief, have their wishes granted, and it also possesses healing powers. Its acorns (which used to be profuse, but are no more) were once collected as charms to bring fertility and ensure good health during pregnancy, properties very much in keeping with the characteristics of our Hare.

Then, whilst exploring the church at Lewannick, one of the most interesting in the area, with its inscribed Ogham stones and also directly due North of the Hare's head, I noticed a number of artefacts that seemed apposite. Firstly there was an extremely rare cresset-stone or lamp, a sort of font-shaped stone with seven bowl-like hollows for oil and floating wicks, which reminded me of the Seven Stars of the Great Bear. Cresset-stones such as this

The Darley Oak, said to be at least a thousand years old.

have a long tradition behind them as lamps where perpetual flames were kept burning. This was linked to the ritual of the Easter fire, when all hearths were extinguished to symbolise the sacrifice of Jesus Christ, and then a new flame was kindled to represent resurrection. This fire would then be carried throughout the neighbourhood, spreading its light as it went, and new fires lit in the homes of the district by the sacred flame. It was common Christian practice to create this first spark from flint and stone, exactly in the way that prehistoric peoples created fire. The Druids are reputed to have used crystals with which to focus the Sun's rays and so make the new fire directly from beams of sunlight (these later evolved into the *monstrum* or crystal-embedded crucifix; see *The Ancient Secret* by Flavia Anderson for a comprehensive account of this). Creating fire from the Sun is, in fact, not as difficult as it sounds, even in springtime, for a properly focussed clear crystal can generate a surprising amount of heat. This connection with death and resurrection at Easter, the time of the Hare Goddess and the symbolic creation of sacred fire as the Sun's power increases, all seemed to reflect ancient patterns of belief that could be directly linked to Hare mythology.

At Lewannick Church another treasure can be found. It is a fine granite font, which is incised with maze patterns, pentagrams and other symbolic designs, making it one of the most impressive examples of its kind in Cornwall. Mazes, labyrinths and the pentagram or five-pointed star are all very much connected with the old religion, with mazes particularly symbolic of the Underworld regions, yet the font, a Norman creation, shows that this was nevertheless incorporated into the Christian era. The Pentagram is a symbol of Venus and is especially appropriate here, above the Head of the Great Hare, so closely linked with the 'Planet of Love'.

The church, raised on its Celtic *lan* or sacred enclosure in the middle of the small village possesses a considerable collection of unusual works of art. A painting behind the altar has a group of lilies, long associated with the Divine Feminine. Some appear to be wilting, as if to perhaps signify a lack of sustenance. But most remarkable in the context of our quest are the oldest carvings of all, from the local Polyphant stone. They are so worn as to be barely discernible in some cases, but one can just make out the features of animals disporting themselves in a very lively manner. Located beneath the stone seats of the porch is a series of creatures that are engaged in hunting a Hare!

Now yet again, we might think nothing particularly unusual about this, for hare-hunting must have been a common enough occupation in the past. Yet to my knowledge this is the only such hunting scene in a Cornish Church (except for the font at Lostwithiel, to which we will soon return), and its location, due North of the Great Hare, seems very apt indeed. Weathered and worn though these carvings are, this only confirms their considerable antiquity, and it is still possible to experience the vivacity of the original designs, which, I later learned, are mentioned by Baring Gould in his Victorian collection of Cornish curiosities *A Book of Cornwall*.

These discoveries at Lewannick alerted me to the possibility that the preoccupation with North we have noticed before, especially with regard to the Great Bear and the Lions, looks as though it applies to the Hare as well. The church appeared to be crowded with clues to this (one wonders what else may have once been there, for the building, including its fine collection of ancient bench ends, was gutted by fire in 1890). But between here and the Hare's head was the church at North Hill. Why North Hill? What is it North of? The only obvious explanation is that it is North of Caradon Hill, the centre of the Hare's head. As if to emphasise this idea in a way we could not ignore, hovering right above the head is the hamlet of *Kingbeare*, or, as it is spelt on old maps, *Kingbear*. King Bear, precisely North of our Hare? It stretches credulity to its limit to imagine this could be yet another coincidence.

Following this northerly axis further up, we come to Egloskerry Church, which we may recall was under the control of the Bottreaux family, and notable for its two unusual Norman carvings—a magnificent early Agnus Dei (symbol of the Templars and Hospitallers) and, over the North Door, the only carving of a Dragon to be found on a Cornish church. It is so designed that it corresponds with the sign for infinity—a figure of eight lying on its side, with the Dragon biting its own tail (this too is an alchemical symbol known as an *Ouroborous*). This may exist to point to the fact that some sort of northerly axis passes through the place, for the Dragon surely stands for the circumpolar constellation of *Draco*, which twines its body between Ursa Minor, the Little Bear and its Pole Star and Ursa Major, the Great Bear, and implies a sense of timelessness to do with this area of the sky. Standing in front of this blocked-up North Door you can see the tower of another church, that of North Petherwin, rising up a few miles away. This was once of considerable importance, as one can judge by the massive columns of the Norman arcade which appear far too large for such an isolated country church.

The Egloskerry Dragon

The phenomenon of North Doors in churches is of considerable interest to us here. Anyone who visits old churches will be aware that they are almost invariably blocked up. The official explanation always refers to the fact that they were originally built so that the Devil could escape through them, especially when a new-born child was being baptised, hence their common name of the *Devil's Doorway*. However, on examination this is patently absurd, even by the strange internal logic of these supernatural beings. What would the Devil be doing in the church anyway? It is noticeable that in some very ancient churches that preserve their original layout the North Door is the main entrance, often with a porch, that has always been used by parishioners and processions. A good example of this is at Stowe near Hartland in North Devon, where the North Porch looks out across the churchyard valley, and even has a room over it that is reputed to have once contained an altar.

So why were North Doors such an important original feature of old churches, and why are most of them now blocked up? A reasonable conclusion must be that in antiquity North was the direction one entered the sacred building, echoing the tradition that human souls were believed to come to Earth via the North Pole. In fact in many places where the door was left unblocked it was frequently opened to allow departing spirits to pass through during funerals. This idea must have been deeply ingrained in popular religion. But then the medieval Church discovered what was probably its greatest weapon of all time — the Devil! Every symbol or salient feature of the old religion consequently became attributed to his evil powers, notably anything whatever to do with cosmology and our place amongst the stars. So the Dragon, *Draco*, who coils around the Pole, became the most potent image employed because it stood for the time before Christianity, when the star Thuban in Draco marked the Pole. Bears too were demonised and became objects of popular ridicule and systematic torture, and even the lowly Hare, such a powerful symbol of the Moon magic of former times, became an omen of impending ill fortune. The old stones, those celestial markers of the heavenly rhythms, were often destroyed by zealous evangelists, or if this could not be achieved due to their continued importance to the local populace, the Devil's name was attached to them along with the dire threat of retribution if anyone should dare to frequent them.

In a final last desperate attempt to stamp out 'paganism' or the traditional belief system of those who, like the people of the Westcountry, still stubbornly clung to the old ways, an edict was pronounced that in future, North Doors were to be bricked up (so that the Devil could not enter) and South was to be the only way in and out. Of course the irony probably escaped those responsible for this law, for now parishioners would have to walk in a northerly direction to enter the church, and thus the Polar Axis was still in evidence, but at least one could make the Devil a talking point and object of derision, as people imagined him banging, red-faced, on the blocked-up doorway trying to get in.

Axis of the Moon

The Great Hare, then, seems to be a central feature amongst our totem landscape creatures, with a polar corridor as well as another in the direction of its line of sight towards the Major Standstill Moonrise (this is related to the lunar nodal axis, once called the Dragon's Head and Tail because ancient astronomers thought that during solar or lunar eclipses the Sun or Moon were swallowed by a Cosmic dragon). I soon began to realise that this Moon Axis had, gathered around it, a collection of other sacred places that once honoured the Divine Feminine, and a fascinating series of sites and their associated histories began to materialise. Firstly, there was Trefrize, the site of a once-important chapel and Holy Well (its memory preserved in the neighbouring farm of *Halwell*). This used to be called *Trefry's* or *Treffry's* because it was once an elaborate chapel-house owned by Lord Treffry, from an ancient Cornish family who were married, baptised and buried there. This chapel stood next to the renowned Holy Well, but in 1891 it was already in a dilapidated state, its masonry held together by the roots of an old tree.

Curiously, about twenty years ago whilst researching *Secret Shrines*, a book specifically about Holy Wells, I received a phone call from George Bishop who lived in a cottage near to the site of the Holy Well. He had made some interesting discoveries about the place while digging in his garden, unearthing a massive stone trough that looked as though it had been a place for visitors to the healing well to bathe in. Other shaped and carved stones were found in the hedges and the importance of the site was becoming increasingly apparent (even though the waters from the spring were now contained within a rectangular box made of concrete blocks).

This was a poignant reminder of how these natural treasures of the landscape, once so central to people's lives and traditions, were now little more than a convenient source of water, which may as well be full of chlorine and chemicals for all the reverence it attracted. Once it had been a mystical entrance to the Underworld, its magical waters impregnated with spiritual powers, located in relation to invisible geomantic figures in the land and the cycle of the Moon, and now it was the epitome of ugliness. The old name of the well was, according to George's researches, *All Hallows' Well*, and he had turned up another interesting fact; records showed that in 1332 there had been a manor house on this spot belonging to Sir Reginald Bottreaux.

Further on from this, along the same Moon Axis, was Trecarrell. This is one of the best-preserved medieval farmhouses in the county, with, uniquely in Cornwall, a private chapel to Mary Magdalene. Although not open to the public, it is one of the great architectural gems of the county. Trecarrell is so called after Sir Henry Trecarrell (although some historians say there is no record of him ever having been knighted), who was one of the area's greatest benefactors. He was responsible for renovating nearby Lezant Church (incidentally with a striking Green Man in the porch), and he was, according to local tradition, the victim of a truly tragic set of circumstances. He had intended to build the finest mansion Cornwall had ever seen at this spot, made from elaborately-carved Cornish granite. But in around 1511 his only son, whilst still an infant, drowned in his bath after a moment's inattention by his nursemaid. It is said that within a week Lady Trecarrell too was dead from a broken heart.

The preparations for the manor house were immediately halted, and a bereft Sir Henry decided to divert his attention to works of a more godly nature. The finely-carved stone was transported to nearby Launceston, the ancient Cornish capital, and here, over a period of the next thirteen years, the church of Mary Magdalene was rebuilt using the stone originally intended for his own chapel and house, transforming it into a place embellished by the most intricate designs of the granite-sculptor's art (not an easy task considering its hardness). It is a striking sight, set at the foot of the steep conical mound crowned by its Norman castle. The array of designs incorporated into its fabric are quite extraordinary, including what appears to be the Tree of Life and the repeated design of a feather (from Egyptian times connected with goddess worship, especially that of Maat, goddess of truth and justice). At the eastern end is a reclining figure of the Magdalene with her grail-like vessel of sacred oil, set in a landscape of trees. This figure has become part of local folklore, for if you can lodge a stone on her back, good luck will come your way.

Mary Magdalene reclines on the heavily-sculpted exterior of Launceston Church. Around the building runs a Latin quotation in prominent lettering (seen here at the bottom of the photograph) that is found at other sites connected with the Knights Templar.

Most remarkable of all about this heavily-encrusted building and its carvings is a series of shields running around it engraved with foot-high letters, that announce in Latin *'Hail Mary, full of Grace! The Lord be with thee! The Bridegroom loves the Bride. Mary hath chosen the best part. Oh, how terrible and fearful is this place! Truly this is no other than the house of God and the gate of heaven'.*

The last two sentences of this biblical quotation are from the story of Jacob in Genesis 28.17 where he uses a stone as a pillow and dreams of a ladder reaching between Earth and Heaven, with many angels ascending and descending. This has a resonance with the idea of the Tree of Life down which souls come to Earth and return at the end of their lives, and also refers to the notion that certain stones have spiritual powers. The other lines are, so many Templar historians think, a direct reference to the belief that Mary Magdalene and Jesus were married, a fact that was expunged from history by the Church who wished to portray him as a celibate priest (and to permanently remove the idea that the Magdalene may also have been a priestess herself, and therefore a symbol of female power). The further implications are that there were children from this union who went on to generate certain royal dynasties, including, some authors claim, the Merovingians, Plantagenets and even the royal family of today.

As far as our exploration of the Hare's Moon Axis is concerned, all this seems very significant, since this finely-carved exterior, so replete with symbolism and carved from granite as if designed to last forever, was originally intended for the site at Trecarrell. So, within a mile or so of each other we find a chapel and Holy Well dedicated to St Mary at Trefrize, once owned by the Lords Treffry and Bottreaux, as well as another chapel to Mary Magdalene at Henry Trecarrell's old house (where, incidentally, King Charles II was later to stay during the Civil War). Launceston, the Norman capital, had a chapel to the Magdalene as well, first recorded in the thirteenth century (now the magnificently-carved church), and we cannot ignore the fact that both these latter sites are the only ones in Cornwall dedicated to her. It seems evident that this could well be due to vestiges of ancient goddess-worship that is perfectly in keeping with the fact that the Great Hare, symbol of the Earth Goddess, is looking straight at all these three sites.

Launceston, the administrative capital for over 700 years, was chosen by the first Norman Earl of Cornwall, Brian de Bretagne, as his stronghold because it was the gateway to Cornwall, guarding the crucial crossing over the River Tamar. It had previously been a Saxon fortification, but by 1086 Count Robert de Mortain had acquired Brian's Cornish possessions, being the half-brother of William the Conqueror and consequently, it is said, more trustworthy. He was the greatest landowner in England after the King (owning at least 793 manors) and obtained the dramatically-steep mound (the core of an extinct volcano) from the Bishop of Exeter, implying that it may once have had a sacred function. The Cornish historian T. G. F. Dexter believed it was formerly a centre of Druidic ritual, because its ancient name, *Dunheved*, derived, according to him, from *Dun-hafod*, the *Mound of the Solstice*. The later name Launceston comes from *Lansteffan*, the sacred place of St Stephen, a monastic foundation gathered on the hill opposite, and the site of a royal Saxon mint.

Count Robert followed in a long line of overlords when he took it as his Cornish capital, which, it is said, was founded in the year 900 by Eadulphus, brother of the Saxon Earl of Cornwall. Some sources indicate that Viking influence may have been in evidence as well, for a certain Othomarus, who was of Danish extraction, was hereditary Constable of the Castle up to the Conquest, hinting there may have been a castle here long before the Normans. Later, Earl Reginald tried to establish Launceston as the ecclesiastical as well as administrative centre of Cornwall by making what was to become the Church of Mary Magdalene the Cathedral church, but he did not succeed. Later, in the thirteenth century, Earl Richard, the richest man in Europe and the builder of Tintagel Castle, granted the Town Charter and seemed to have a certain affection for the place, bringing his third wife here on honeymoon.

An interesting relic from these times is the Feudal Dues ceremony, said to date back to the time of Robert de Mortain and enacted whenever the King or Earl came to Cornwall. This was revived during the twentieth century when a number of monarchs, and later, Charles, Duke of Cornwall, visited Launceston. As a quaint survival of these bygone times there are within this ritual a number of peculiar references to matters of ancient historical and symbolic significance. Records from the time of King John show that the landowner of one manor presented 'one cloak of grey serge on the coming of the Lord King into Cornwall' as he crossed the Tamar at Polson Bridge. In 1921 the revival of this medieval custom of receiving the Duke of Cornwall invoked these ancient rituals once more when the Prince of Wales (later King Edward VIII) came to Launceston. This included reading out a collection of things given in exchange for rent for the various towns and manors in the county, and included, amongst other arcane objects 'a pair of gilded spurs, a brace of greyhounds, a salmon spear, 300 puffins from the Isles of Scilly, and... *a hare!*' This inclusion of a single Hare as a symbol of the Goddess seems very meaningful under the circumstances.

Given all these correspondences, might we be correct in thinking that the ancient symbol of the Hare as a creature of the White Goddess, the Moon and the Earth Goddess may have evolved during the Christian era into a veneration for the female principle in the guise of Mary Magdalene, who in other regions of Templar influence is particularly associated with initiation into the hidden Mysteries? She is often depicted within a cave, representing the Underworld, and has long been the most prominent focus for the idea that the female power is equal to the male. If the marriage between Jesus and the Magdalene did indeed take place, then it perfectly symbolises the alchemical fusion between the male and female principles within Nature, as stated in the motto on Launceston Church *'The Bridegroom loves the Bride'*. The name *Bride* actually comes from one of the old Celtic names for the Earth Goddess, whose sacred centre in Ireland was at Kildare, where a perpetual fire was kept burning.

It is worth dwelling further on the possible mystical meaning of this passage, so prominently displayed in a manner that defies the weathering of centuries. *'Hail Mary, full of Grace, the Lord be with thee'* could allude directly to the Divine Feminine and its union with the male. But what about *'Oh, how terrible and fearful is this place'*? In the original Latin, *terrabilis* does not mean terrible as it is used in English, but rather venerable or inspiring awe. *Terra* is also the word for *Earth*, as in *terra firma*, which gives it a different inflection altogether, indicating the power in the land. Curiously, Sir Thomas Malory's *Le Morte d'Arthur*, which begins with Arthur's birth at Tintagel and thus firmly locates the story in Cornwall, also mentions Castle *Terrabil* as the place where Gorlois, Duke of Cornwall, seeks refuge. It is besieged by Uther Pendragon whilst Gorlois' wife Ygerne is shut up in the island stronghold of Tintagel. Throughout medieval times Launceston was commonly known as *Castle Terrible*, and certain romantic sources also say it was connected with Sir Lancelot, which is spelt *Launcelot* in various versions. As for *fearful*, we might perhaps expect any initiation into the Underworld to present the candidate with challenging situations. In this context it is interesting that the castle sits directly on a plug of volcanic rock, which is by its very nature connected to the depths of the Earth. Dowsers have noted how energy is transmitted to the surface via such geological features, and Launceston Castle in particular is, because of this, a sort of power-house of earth energy.

'*Truly this is no other than the house of God and the gate of heaven*' seems self-evident in that it states that the site possesses certain spiritual qualities particular to its location. It is significant that this motto occurs at a number of other famous Templar sites in Europe, including the Church of Mary Magdalene at Rennes-le-Chateau, and also over the entrance to the prehistoric cave-church at Monte Sant'Angelo in Italy. Both these places are suffused with mystical power and noted as centres of Templarism. Might we say the same about Launceston and Cornwall as well? It is interesting that Cornwall is known for its affiliation to Freemasonry, said to have evolved from Templarism. Tintagel has, for instance, one of the few women's Masonic lodges in Britain, Cornish churchyards are full of headstones exhibiting Masonic emblems, and even the traditional Cornish motto *One and All* is almost exactly the same as that well-known saying employed by Freemasons, *All for One and One for All*.

Launceston has connections as well with the Arundells, although of the bloodthirsty variety in this case. In 1549 Sir Humphrey Arundell marched through the town before laying siege to Exeter. Eventually defeated, he and his remaining men retreated to Launceston to make a last stand. After fighting in the narrow streets of the town he was wounded and captured, and executed the following year at Tyburn. Another matter of interest concerns the Catholic priest Cuthbert Mayne who, during the reign of Elizabeth I was arrested whilst being sheltered by one of Cornwall's richest men, Francis Tregian. Mayne, who had been ministering to the recusants in Cornwall, was tried, found guilty and dragged to Launceston Square where he was hanged, drawn and quartered in front of a baying mob. Every year his memory is honoured by a pilgrimage through the town, where part of his head is carried on a glass-domed flower bedecked bier accompanied by a procession. For the rest of the time, Cuthbert Mayne's sacred relic is kept at *Lanherne*, the Arundells' old house.

Of interest as well is that Lawhitton Church, along with Lezant, Henry Trecarrell's local place of worship, was originally part of a 'peculiar' deanery long before Launceston came into prominence. Charles Henderson, the church historian, states that in around 830 this was given to the Saxon Bishop of Sherborne so that he could carry out his campaign to rid Cornwall of its Celtic Church. Both Lawhitton and Lezant are positioned on the Hare's Moon Axis, and this whole area may thus have been a centre of the old religion which the Saxons, as agents of the Church of

Rome, sought to stamp out. Later, in 909, Eadulph, the Saxon Bishop of Crediton, had been likewise granted Lawhitton 'so that from thence he might every year visit the Cornish race to extirpate their errors', as Arthur Venning quotes in *The Book of Launceston*.

Star lore of the Hare

Before moving on to what must be our final discoveries in this quest we must look at the stellar implications of the Hare, for, like the other symbolic creatures, it possesses many different levels of meaning. For this, we must follow the old trackway across the moorland back to Stowes Hill, but first let us return to that repository of so much hidden knowledge, the Lostwithiel font. To begin with we may remember that opposite the weird gargoyle head that I have argued may represent Baphomet is another image, altogether more pleasing to the eye. We have already commented on how this Green Man with its bishop's mitre looks very youthful, but there may be more to this than is at first apparent. Gabriele was studying this and observed that its features seemed far more feminine than male. As we looked at it more closely, it seemed we may have previously jumped to the wrong conclusion. This, we felt, was no Green Man but a Green Woman! It surely represented the fertile spirit of the female side of Nature, the power of the Earth Goddess to make things grow. In fact it now appeared to be a Flower Goddess, with blossoms issuing from her head and mouth. Or was it an unambiguous statement that harked back to the Celtic tradition of female bishops and woman priests?

This whole question of the worship of the Divine Feminine was, after all, a central feature of Arthurian tradition, with its courtly chivalry and honouring of women. This was, in effect, an updated version of the old matriarchal religions of pre-Christian times, and was certainly one of the great themes of the Plantagenet era and the Angevin dynasty, epitomised by the famous Queen of Henry III, Eleanor of Aquitaine.

Just as pertinent to our investigation is another rather perplexing panel with an image that looks as though it has been carefully defaced, but from its shape appears to have been a lizard-like creature, possibly a salamander. One explanation for this image might be that in medieval alchemy the salamander represented the element of Fire, in the sense of purification through intense heat. Salamanders were believed to be produced by fire, and that it was impossible for fire to exist without them. They were the elemental creatures that created sparks from flint, steel or

matches. Leonardo da Vinci noted that they 'ate' fire. Could this salamander be a Tinners' symbol like the Hare?

We are in the fortunate position here of being able to categorically affirm this to be the case. In star lore Orion is directly linked with the Hare, for at his feet is the constellation of *Lepus the Hare*. With a group of about twenty individual stars this asterism of the Hare completes the mythological Hunt that takes place in the night skies, along with Orion, The Lion of *Leo*, the Dog of *Canis Major* and the Great Bear, *Ursa Major*. In this Hunt, Canis Major, Orion's hound, is seen chasing Lepus, ready to bite its tail, *almost exactly as shown on the font*. This amazing artefact, with its encrypted designs which are carefully contrived to be a sort of 'Rosetta Stone' of Templar beliefs is here yet again shown to be in effect a star-map of the heavens, and its mythic reflection on Earth.

As synchronicity would have it, whilst pondering all this, I happened to glance at a copy of *The Western Morning News* (of December 19th 2007), the regional daily paper for the Westcountry which had previously triggered a number of lines of investigation. I flipped the pages and a headline jumped out: *'Ancient stone circle is aligned to the stars'*. The subheading explained *'moorland monument tracks Orion's Belt to determine date of solstice'*. I immediately recognised the accompanying photograph — it was of The Hurlers, the three stone circles above the Hare's head.

The story ran *'scientists say they may have discovered what could be one of the few ancient monuments on earth aligned with the constellation Orion — in the Cornish countryside. Researchers now believe The Hurlers on Bodmin Moor, Cornwall, were built to mirror the stars in Orion's Belt as well as aligned to the constellation to indicate the exact date of midwinter.'*

A dog biting a Giant Hare on Lostwithiel font. This is stellar symbolism for the constellation of Lepus the Hare, found at the foot of Orion with Canis Major, the Dog, chasing the Hare. Yet again, the images on the font show an amazing preoccupation with stellar mythology.

Brian Sheen, a retired research chemist and astronomer at the Roseland Observatory near St Austell had found what he believed to be a remarkable correlation between the three stone circles and Orion: *'Just once a year, at midnight on the winter solstice, their north-south orientation aligns exactly with Orion's position—due south in the night sky'*. He went on to explain that using a computer program he could match the exact moment when the megalithic monument replicated the angle of the stars of Orion's Belt, and this was at the Solstice, marking the rebirth of the Sun and the beginning of an entire new annual cycle.

It is probably easy to imagine my reaction to this idea, for at the time I was one of the very few who knew about the Great Hare, which in stellar lore is positioned at the feet of Orion. What Brian Sheen was suggesting seemed to fit perfectly with the discovery of the Hare in the landscape and the idea that what was happening on the ground was a reflection of the heavenly constellations above.

The reaction from others quoted in the newspaper, was not, though, quite as positive. Many dismissed the idea as ridiculous. Why should people from three or four thousand years ago go to the trouble of building stone circles to mimic stars in the sky? But the suggestion that The Hurlers represented the brightest stars in Orion and the fact that they were built in perfect correspondence to the earthly Lepus, the Hare, struck me as quite profound.

Gabriele and I had also noticed other points of interest during our visits in the immediate area of The Hurlers. A short distance away are two tall outlying standing stones known as *The Pipers* which mark the parish boundary. The unusual squareness of their shape, which suggests they were originally cut at some time in the distant past, gives them a different appearance to the more rough and ready megaliths that are more commonly seen. This had led some to question whether they are prehistoric at all, while others suggested they may be a sort of 'grand entrance' or megalithic portal to the hallowed area containing The Hurlers.

On one visit, however, we noticed how they appeared to perfectly frame the great rocky sanctuary of Stowes Hill and The Cheesewring, and also that they were aligned to create a visual North-South axis leading to the sacred centre. As if to emphasise this, I also spotted a large triangular 'pointer' stone just to the right of The Cheesewring that had not registered before. Set very close to the edge of the quarry

The megalithic 'pointer stone' just a few yards from the Cheesewring, a perfect sighting stone for the circumpolar constellations.

that disfigured the hill, I think I had probably dismissed it previously as something to do with the workings there. But now it assumed an impressive prominence as though it was an important original feature on the summit of the plateau. We climbed up to examine it and realised straight away it was, as suspected, a massive megalith sunk in the earth in such a way as to angle it towards the sky. Perhaps this was why no-one had apparently noticed it before, assuming it was just a naturally-occurring feature. After all, we tend to expect such megaliths to be upright as a matter of course. When the eye is trained to see vertical stones, is it easy to ignore ones that lean in such a wild and rocky landscape.

But it seemed to me that this was deliberately placed at the very edge of the sacred enclosure, just a few yards from the great rock-pile of the Cheesewring, I leant with my back against it, got out the compass and realised it was perfectly set to align to True North and observe the sky in this region. This stone, it seemed, was a previously unsuspected 'observatory' for tracking the circumpolar constellations, set on a North-South axis running through Stowes Hill, and designed with comfort in mind! One could spend hours here, and because of its angle and the smooth surface of the stone, be extremely content to gaze at the starry firmament all night if need be.

A later expedition with Robin confirmed our initial findings. On a wild and wintry day, with the sort of wind and rain that can only be truly appreciated by practised masochists who have spent years exploring Bodmin Moor, we visited The Pipers, and, after taking GPS readings found that they were set to frame the Pole Star as it culminated over the southern end of Stowes Hill (unfortunately it is impossible to know what was once there since it has been eaten away by the gaping chasm of the quarry). Clambering up the rocky slopes to the pointer stone, slipping and sliding as we went, gave us a taste of the true atmosphere of the place, with rocks and strange shapes looming out of the mizzle like spectral Druids. When we finally arrived at the summit, frozen and dripping with rain stinging our eyes, GPS readings here also confirmed the intuition that this great triangular stone had been consciously set to observe the Northern sky.

On a slightly less atmospheric day I returned to view it in a clearer light and saw that the axis created by the pointer stone led the eye, when standing at the northern edge of the summit, to Bearah Tor, with Twelve Men's Moor beyond. Noting that here again was a Bear name due North of a Neolithic ritual site, I blinked and caught my breath. Focussing my eyes on the Tor to the North I got quite a shock. To the naked eye the rocky outline silhouetted against the horizon looked to me just like a giant Bear on all fours.

Taking a wider view of the landscape, it looks as though this North-South axis or corridor may extend further to the South, taking in The Hurlers and Trethevy Quoit, eventually leaving Cornwall at St George's Island just off the coast near Looe. This was once an especially sacred place and has the legend attached to it that Jesus visited here as a child accompanied by his tin merchant uncle Joseph of Arimathea. In medieval times it was owned by Glastonbury Abbey and in the 1930s Croft-Andrew excavated the remains of a Celtic chapel on the summit. Another chapel on the mainland opposite was called *Lamanna*, and was evidently built so that Michaelmas pilgrims did not have to risk drowning in the treacherous waters in order to reach their goal, something that was all too common at those times. Before it became St George's Island it was dedicated to the Archangel Michael, who, in esoteric tradition, rules the South and thus presides over the Polar Axis.

We cannot leave this area, so replete with mysteries concealed within its deceptively chaotic landscape, without mentioning another curious facet of its long and remarkable past. Just below The Cheesewring is a rough cave-like structure built of stones, its roof a great leaning capstone with a geometric figure carved into the top. In fact eagle eyed observers may note a number of such rocks in the vicinity with triangles, squares and rectangles incised on them. At the entrance to this 'cave' is another stone carved with the initials *D.G.* and the date *1735*.

This is all that remains to remind us of the extraordinary life of Daniel Gumb, a humble stone-cutter who was born in a simple cottage nearby and once worked on the high moor. He was one of a long line of eccentrics whose genius did not really fit with the attitudes of the day. A lonely, unsocial boy, from an early age he was fascinated by mathematics and especially Euclidian geometry. His voracious appetite for knowledge could not be satisfied by the village school, and so he soon took to wandering the moors with his books, mallet and chisel. Vanishing for days at a time, when asked where he had been, he would reply 'Where John the Baptist slept' or 'at Roche, in the hermit's bed', according to that other great eccentric R.S.Hawker in *Footprints of Former Men in Far Cornwall*.

But Daniel's overriding ambition was to understand the planets and stars. He lived at a time when great discoveries were being made (another local Cornish lad from a humble background was John Couch Adams from Laneast, a mathematical genius who through his calculations first discovered the planet Neptune). Daniel, so Hawker, who saw his notebooks and spoke to local people, tells us, would frequent the craggy summits of the moor to spend all night there 'learning the customs of the stars' and 'finding out by the planets things to come'. William Cookworthy, the discoverer of China Clay, and inadvertently the destroyer of the ancient landscape around St Austell, took him under his wing and allowed him access to books and scientific instruments, including an orrery to further his understanding of planetary motions. Surrounded by the rocks of his ancestors he must have sensed some spiritual dimension to the land, and the poverty-stricken stonecutter who had become obsessed with studying the wandering stars eventually married a local girl, making a cave for them to live in close to his favourite place, The Cheesewring. His stone-cutting skills fashioned a well-appointed abode and they apparently lived a long life there much as his prehistoric ancestors had, having a brood of children who were brought up amongst the stones and ancient habitations of the moor. We may consider such a life excessively harsh, but Daniel died 'an old man full of days' and became one of the great legendary figures of the area.

The remains of his home (dismantled by quarrymen and roughly re-erected where it now stands) is an enduring testimony to that timeless spirit of the land which can deeply affect those of a sensitive and enquiring disposition. From what we know so far, we can greatly sympathise with someone like Daniel Gumb, surely a reincarnation of those old stargazers of remote antiquity who sensed the unity in Creation, and who, like those masters of old, dedicated his life to trying to understand its mysteries.

The roof of Daniel Gumb's 'cave' below the Cheesewring, with its geometrical carving. The triangular 'pointer stone' can be seen to the right of the rock-pile.

16

LORD OF THE HUNT

he element of surprise in the course of our quest has been an
ongoing feature which is, we must assume, an essential characteristic of any initiation into these Mysteries concealed in the
landscape. Each symbolic figure has a special meaning and purpose in
this scheme which connects the powers of Nature with our own inner
landscape and links these earthly dimensions with the wider cosmos
and the realms of time, space and the stars.

It was surprising to discover a Bear until we realised it stood
for the centre of the revolving universe and hence the concept of
heavenly order reflected on Earth. The Lions are also totally unexpected
as we would not normally associate them directly with the British
landscape; however they represent an archetypal and universal principle
that embodies spiritual courage and our own potential royal nature. The
Lion is also one of the oldest symbolic totems of Albion, the mythical
name of ancient Britain.

After the discovery of the lordly animals of the Bear and Lions,
the Little Pig is the next on our list and again seems quite bewildering
until we recognise that it represents humility and another deep aspect
of human nature, the Underworld or Annwn of Celtic legend, the territory in which our quest, the Hunt, takes place. The Dog or Wolf is our
guard and guide in this between-the-worlds region, and stands by our
side to offer protection and companionship as perhaps our best friend,
who leads the Hunt and is fiercely loyal.

The unexpected appearance of a Giant Hare in this cosmic bestiary is also challenging for us, but as the presiding female power of the
Moon, Venus and the cycles of earthly fertility it is now understood to
be a true creature of the White Goddess. It is an animal whose powers refer to that part of our own being which responds to the secret rhythms of
the universe and the forces that bind everything together to create life.

Each giant figure appears to be challenging any preconceptions
we may hold, and seems to be asking, like Perceval in the Grail myth,
'Whom does the Grail serve?' According to the myth this question has the
potential to reclaim our forgotten inheritance and restore the wasteland

to its former glory of abundance, harmony and creativity. In the story, Perceval initially neglects to ask this question, which is, as the legend implies, probably the most significant factor in enabling the great restoration and our reconnection with the Spirit of the Earth. All these aspects of our own beings in the underworld of the human psyche have their important roles in leading us onwards, as we hunt them through the inner landscape of our own souls. There is an ever-deepening realisation that these animals and the powers they stand for are totems and talismans of human existence as a whole, without which life on Earth would be impossible.

Can we reclaim the wasteland by asking the right question? And what could the next, and for us in this current quest, final, shamanic being be? Which animal powers would speak of the culmination of this Wild Hunt through the tangled undergrowth of our own history, the history of the human race itself? Whatever we might guess, it must surely bring us to some sort of conclusion at the final sprint that allows us to capture the quarry we seek—that of self knowledge.

This knowledge, the true record of our time on Earth, is written in the land, and we must learn the language used by our ancestors before we can understand it. Language is deeply rooted in the land, and we should hear the messages encoded in the shape and structure of the landscape, punctuated so dramatically by the enigmatic monuments and sacred sites built by those who understood its sentient qualities. These places are often linked to death, yet the death we speak of here is not the mere cessation of life but, as the Druids and early Christians believed, the demise of that part of us which is cast off when we rise above our lower nature. Then we assume our rightful place in the world, not as vanquishers of our fellow creatures but as co-creators or co-creatures recognising our common destiny.

The purpose of the geomantic mysteries of the land and its mounds and monuments is not that of death as we usually understand it, but the cycle of life. They were not built and sculpted into the Earth as funereal structures but instruments of the highest human aspirations. Can we see through eyes that penetrate both the twilight of the Underworld and the Upperworld of the stars to glimpse a reality where everything is connected? The megaliths and holy places of antiquity were not created to focus our attention on death any more than churches were built to guard graveyards. They represent the alchemical refining of the human spirit and the transformation that comes with the realisation of our true place in the scheme of things. These places are not tombs, but wombs.

The Arthurian legends encode many aspects of this ancient wisdom, and even though they have accumulated much that seems obscure, they preserve many fragments of genuine truth that shine and reflect the light, for we are like archaeologists who glimpse the glitter of gold in the dark earth. Here and there fragments beckon and make us wonder what they might mean? Strange characters and situations occur as a matter of course. In Malory's version of the Arthurian tales, a compilation of genuinely ancient material with imaginative flourishes designed to captivate the audience of the day, there is, for instance, one such obscure character called Bruin le Noire (literally the *Black Bear*) who achieves distinction by rescuing Queen Guinevere from a lion and is consequently ennobled by King Arthur, who makes him a Knight of the Round Table. This strikes a chord with our own findings, as if a dim memory has somehow been preserved. Queen Guinevere is the Goddess of the Land, the White Goddess, as her name, in its various forms, which includes the word *Guin*, *Gwen* or *Gwyn*, meaning white, shining or bright, indicates.

Queen Guinevere's father was King Leodegrance (*the Great Lion*) of Cameliard, the Lion-King of Lyonesse who was one of Uther Pendragon's most trusted lieutenants. It was he who was given the original Round Table by Merlin; the most important part of her dowry at her wedding to King Arthur. The Round Table, the starry vault of the heavens, which stands for cosmic order and harmony, cycles reflected in the earthly patterns below, is thus the gift of the King of Cornwall's daughter, the luminous Guinevere. The table was made by Merlin, the great seer, astronomer and shamanic priest, but according to the legends he was not the originator. Merlin himself was taught the secrets of this magical artefact by an even more obscure character called Blaise. Is it just coincidence that a few miles from the Lion of Bodmin (with its royal and dignified air personified by the Leodegrance of legend) and the Lion of Lostwithiel (in this case more like the youthful ebullience of adolescence—perhaps representing the current phase of human evolution) is a place called *St Blazey* (originally spelt *St Blaise*). Is it just another accident of fate that this St Blaise is, amongst other things, the patron saint of wild animals?

The Polar Myth and the geomantic obsession with True North is quite literally central to this Round Table whose pivotal point is watched over by the Great Bear, and we can begin to see how the story of Arthur's birth at Tintagel is an ancestral memory of the changing ages of humanity's occupation of the planet. The legend of Uther Pendragon shape-shifting so that he conceives King Arthur on Tintagel Island, when stripped of its later accretions, is surely a reference to the gradual shifting of the Pole Star at the centre of the Round Table, which may have first been observed by astronomer priests who used the Island as a polar observatory. Around 2500 BC the apparent centre of the universe was located in Draco, the constellation of the Dragon, marked by Thuban or *Alpha Draconis*, its main star, which due to the cosmology of earthly precession slowly changed and transformed into the Bear. So Arthur the Bear King who rules the Round Table is born of the Pendragon—the Dragon's Head who presided over the age when these legends were first formulated. Arthurian mythology is in many ways the story of the changing ages of the evolution of the Earth, and humanity's role in it.

The Questing Beast

Another of the many curious characters that inhabit the other-worldly realm of Arthurian myth is a Saracen knight called Sir Palomides. Although he comes from the East he is baptised into the Christian faith at the commencement of the Grail Quest (this seems to refer to the cross-fertilisation between East and West through trade and philosophical exchange, especially between Cornwall and the Middle East exemplified by the Phoenician links, and later the Knights Templar). Palomides is also on a quest of his own in parallel to the Grail Quest. In this he seeks a marvellous and unattainable creature known as the Questing Beast. We may suspect that these ideas hint at connections between an archaic shamanic tradition, the knightly excursions of the crusades and the common motif of a quest to discover the true vessel of spiritual power. These were all, it appears, mingled together to form a bond of brotherhood between East and West, one of the prime motivations behind the establishment of the Templars. They brought this idea literally 'down to earth' by rebuilding churches and cathedrals with Eastern architectural innovations like the Gothic arch, a symbolic bridge between Heaven and Earth.

This Questing Beast is so strange that it appears to come from a different world altogether, a place of the unconscious regions of the soul. It is said to be a strange hybrid with the head of a serpent, the body of a leopard, the hind quarters of a lion and the feet of a stag. This sounds similar to many weird beasts that adorn the pages of medieval alchemists' works, which often combine different animal characteristics into a composite form. The allegories may seem arcane to us today because we are much less well-versed in the meaning of symbols and especially the correspondences and puns employed in those times.

King Arthur too finds himself engaged in this weird hunt. After a prophetic dream where monsters burn the land and kill its people, defeating the King and destroying the Round Table, he rides off into the wildwood and hunts a white hart in order to forget his nightmare (the White *Hart*, according to Merlin, signifies the beginning of marvellous adventures concerning the *Heart*, of which *Hart* is a pun, symbolising purity). Outpaced by his quarry, his horse falls dead and as he sits in the forest he suddenly sees the Questing Beast, this unearthly animal whose body gives rise to the sound of a pack of baying hounds, just like the Wild Hunt. Merlin explains that the Beast exists only to be quested and lead its pursuer into the Underworld. It is followed by King Pellinore, whose special destiny is to forever pursue it. This King represents a more ancient time long before that of King Arthur and is reminiscent of an era before the attitudes and ideals of the later Quest for the Holy Grail. It is also King Pellinore's destiny to become a stalwart member of the Round Table when it is later founded, as he is absorbed into the new form of this primeval challenge.

A fresh horse is brought for Arthur but Pellinore seizes it and doggedly refuses to give up pursuing the Questing Beast so that Arthur can chase it instead. In this respect, as Gareth Knight notes in *The Secret Tradition in Arthurian Legend*, he seems to represent a power rooted in the past who refuses to accept changing times. Sir Palomides, the Saracen knight who also quests the Beast, longs to be accepted as a true knight, but this can only take place when he is baptised into the Christian faith, when the Quest for the Holy Grail commences. Up until that time he is a freebooting adventurer, but with the onset of the Grail Quest and the Fellowship of the Round Table he dedicates himself wholeheartedly to the new task.

Are these stories memories of an earlier 'Round Table' that involved hunting mysterious otherworldly beasts before they were replaced by the Grail Quest? Did the nature of this quest radically alter with the onset of Christianity, when it transformed into the hunt for a mystical vessel promising spiritual vision?

Later, as Arthur fights the old King Pellinore in order to avenge a young squire, he is saved only by the intervention of Merlin, who casts a spell on Pellinore causing him to fall into a deep sleep. Was the power of the old King too much even for the changing times? Does Pellinore, who quested the Beasts before Arthur, still sleep in the wildwood of our collective imagination? As Pellinore falls into his slumber, Merlin says that he is not an evil person, but merely the strongest at the present time. From his bloodline will spring two great figures of the future, the mighty Lamorak and Perceval himself, who eventually achieves the Holy Grail to become the great hero of Medieval Romances. Here we are confronted by a strong and recognisable link to the pre-Grail way of the Questing Beast and the eventual triumph of the Grail Knight in achieving his true goal, all cloaked in the mystic allegories of old Celtic magic.

We have ourselves quested a variety of beasts. There are undoubtedly others yet to be revealed, but after ten years since the discovery of the Great Bear I thought it right to communicate these findings to those who may wish to embark on the quest themselves. As you continue your journey I have little doubt other discoveries will surface to widen our understanding and the true meaning behind the mysteries. These things will be unveiled in due course to those who embark with the sincerity and humility demanded of the true Grail Seeker. For now, though, it is time to move on to our final discovery and see what we might learn from it.

It began, as with the others, with the feeling that something was in the air—or in the Earth, to be more precise. I was looking for another totem beast, but could fathom nothing. That was probably because I allowed myself the luxury of such a dangerous preconception. As is so often the case, when the conscious mind is exhausted by its limitations it tends to shut down and then another level of reality emerges. Even so, it came as something of a shock; certainly it was the last thing I had anticipated. In this case it really did come in a flash while studying the map of one of my favourite areas that included Lostwithiel and the course of the River Fowey towards the sea.

Two figures, with characteristic pronounced noses, hold the Wheel of Life (Hallstatt Museum, Austria).

This was no beast, but the unmistakable head of a Giant. Growing out of the country to the east of the course of the Fowey was a gigantic head. He—for its features were distinctly male—was staring directly due East, towards the rising Sun at the spring equinox, and his most prominent feature was a large and well-formed nose of the type commonly depicted in Celtic art. I had seen faces very like this on a recent visit with Gabriele to the Museum at Hallstatt in Austria, where a sophisticated culture had flourished during the so-called Iron Age. At first I dismissed this possible effigy as a series of accidental shapes created by the curiously twisting nature of the Cornish lanes. But on recognising its similarity to Celtic artwork I began to look more closely at the figure with reference to old names in and around it, and especially the placement of significant features.

Positioned right beneath his nostrils on the crest of a hill was a huge circular hillfort or prehistoric earthwork known as Bury Down, looking as if he were about to inhale it. Or perhaps he was more interested in the breathtaking views—to the North Bodmin Moor, including Brown Willy and Caradon Hill, the head of the Hare, and in the East the high hills of Dartmoor. The western vista is of Hensbarrow Downs, and the South the sparkling sea, with Dodman Point projecting out into the ocean. But the next most notable thing about this giant's head was truly astonishing. Protruding from his forehead where we would expect his 'third eye' to be was what appeared at first to be a fashionable 'quiff' of hair, but on closer examination was clearly a prominent single oddly-shaped *horn*. As we were studying the map one day it was pointed out by Trish Osborne that this horn-shaped appendage, studded with a group of prehistoric barrows, looked strikingly similar to the weird protuberance on the goatish head on Lostwithiel font just a few miles away.

One of the other things to jump out from the map was that his chin and part of the lower jaw appeared to be delineated by parts of a long serpentine prehistoric earthwork called the *Giant's Hedge*. More like the *Giant's Edge*, I commented, attempting a bad theatrical Cornish accent. Groans all round. When we looked at the figure with fresh eyes we realised he was a truly proud and handsome-looking fellow, and he somehow

evoked a playful and mischievous response. In jocular mood
we noticed the top of his horn
was marked by the two villages of Middle Taphouse and
East Taphouse. As *tap-house*
in Cornwall means ale-house
or pub, I wondered what the
identity of this lordly-looking
giant might be. Was he, like
Bacchus, Dionysus and other
horned deities of the forests
and wild places, a god of intoxication?

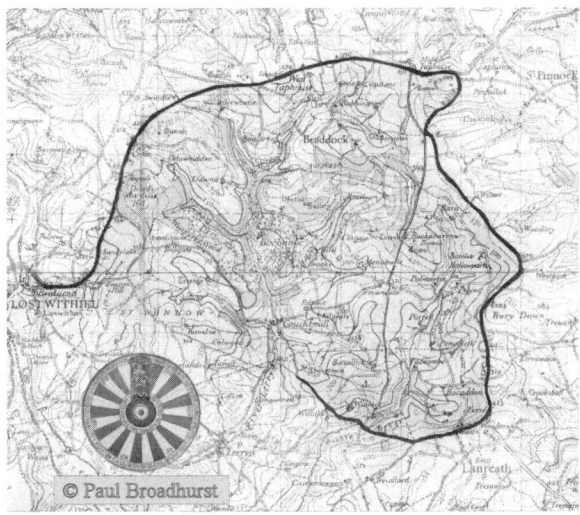

© Paul Broadhurst

*A Giant in the landscape to the east of Lostwithiel, with a pronounced
nose similar to the style of Celtic art and a 'horn' on his forehead.
Does he represent the old primal God of Britain?*

Peering at the trusty
old one-inch to the mile map
(which, if you can get them, are
the best for such work; modern
maps such as the Land-ranger
series in this case cut the head in half), other tell-tale names and features
began to emerge. I noticed that just below where we might expect his eye
to be was Buckabarrow Downs, with a number of tumuli. *Buckabarrow—
the barrow of Buck?*

Buck (Cornish *Bucca*) in this context is very significant, for it is the
name given to a he-goat, another direct link with the Lostwithiel font. But
the word is also used to describe the male of a number of other animals,
including the Deer, and perhaps even more meaningful to us—*the Hare*.
It also means, figuratively speaking, a dashing young fellow, very like
the image confronting us. Its associations with virility are particularly
apparent when the adjective *buckish* is used, for it means lascivious,
and is in perfect keeping with the character of our horny friend. These
attributions blend together in the old English figure of Puck, described
by Shakespeare as '*that shrewd and knavish sprite*'. Although in those times
he was reduced to a mischievous hobgoblin who could shape-shift at will,
in his original form he was a lordly deity who was half-faery and half-
human (just like Merlin, who was born of a human mother and a daemon
or spiritual being).

Rudyard Kipling, an initiate into the mysteries of Freemasonry
and other esoteric disciplines, recognised the original power of Puck in
his novel *Puck of Pook's Hill*, where he saw the old god as a giant who
was sleeping in the hills, watching the centuries come and go, very like
the idea of King Arthur, who waits to be recalled from his own slumber.
In this he appears to have been tapping into a tradition of immense
antiquity concerning the spiritual power of the landscape seen as an actual
god-like entity.

Medieval woodcut of Puck, Robin Goodfellow or the the Horned God of ancient Britain, in a circle of dancing figures.

Brewer's *Dictionary of Phrase and Fable* says of Bucca; *'A goblin of the wind, once supposed by Cornish people to foretell shipwrecks. The name is also that of a sprite fabled to live in the tin mines'*. The connection between the Cornish Bucca and mining, or the tunnels of the Underworld, is of interest here. In recent times Bucca has also become a central figure in the revived pagan celebrations of Golowan in West Cornwall, where he is associated with a horse's head that leads the procession. Whilst all these variations might be expected of such an ancient denizen of folklore, it seems as though Bucca was once a particularly important figure, who, as with so many others, became stripped of his original power and was changed into a faery or sprite.

Another name for Puck was *Robin Goodfellow*, and a tract of 1638 shows how this native spirit of the British Isles was commonly conceived in the seventeenth century, for it depicts him as a horned figure with goat's feet dancing in a ring of witches. The folklorist Christina Hole, in *English Folk Heroes*, observes 'The fairy known as Robin Goodfellow was closely associated with the Devil, and probably started life not as a fairy, but as one of the many forms taken by the Horned God of witchcraft'. Already, this Giant is seen to be endowed with many of the attributes we might expect of such a figure in relation to our other discoveries. His horn, which represents the organ of spiritual perception and consequently his ability to move between the earthly and invisible planes of existence, is directed towards the Hare, whilst if we see the main A390 road between Liskeard and Lostwithiel as his flowing long hair, it leads to the old crossing-point of the River Fowey and the tail end of the Little Lion. This is where the goat's-head gargoyle with its own horn-like appendage is located in St Bartholemew's Church. We can only conclude that this extraordinary image has a meaningful correspondence to the Giant in the landscape. In this case the coincidences seem to be too close to imply anything other than deliberate design.

Robin Goodfellow was the favourite deity of the followers of the 'Old Religion' and witch covens throughout Britain used to, and still do, summon him to their rites. Margaret Murray believed that he may have been the original god-like figure behind the folklore hero Robin Hood, who, like Goodfellow, dressed in green and lived in the wildwood. She suggests that 'Robin with the Hood' may have referred to the Grand Masters of the witch-cult (which was not exclusively female, despite a common misconception) as well as the mystical brotherhood of the Templars, who also wore hoods during their rites. As Christina Hole notes with reference to the Robin Hood legend where he becomes an outlaw who robs the rich to give to the poor (an understandable characteristic of any old god which the establishment tries to undermine by calling him the *Devil*); *'If, in fact, there was such an individual in the Middle Ages he may have been only the best known amongst many who bore a nickname perhaps originally associated with the Horned God, or with fairies, and later transferred to those who also haunted the forests, though for other reasons and in a different manner'.*

Could our Lord of the Faeries be the Horned God of the Templars and the primal deity of the Old Religion as practised by witches? It certainly looks more than likely. Right on the back of his head is *Fairy Cross*, exactly due North of *Druid's Hill*. This, as its name suggests, is one of the old ritual sites of the area, and, as with the Lostwithiel font, I had been here before, many years ago, while following the St Michael Line through Cornwall. In *The Sun and the Serpent* I described it as:

'a secret, magical place... a wooded area in the private Boconnoc Estate. In the midst of thick rhododendrons and ancient trees was an enchanted glade, where there stood a twenty-foot high granite cross on its huge plinth. Eight tracks radiated out into the surrounding woodland in what could only be a ceremonial arrangement. This particular spot had been remembered since remote times as a Druidic ritual centre, and later as the site of confrontation in the Civil War.' Inscribed on the cross are the words *'On this hill, once the site of Druid idolatry and in later times the scene of civil bloodshed, this ancient symbol of the holy religion of the redeemer is erected in greater acknowledgement of the blessings of a pure faith and of a peaceful country'.*

At this stage I found myself wondering whether the features of the Giant's head might correspond in any way to the parts of the human brain—after all, this great shamanic being with his ability to transcend the planes of existence must surely have well-developed spiritual organs which allowed him to perceive the Otherworld. I couldn't help noticing there appeared to be no feature which corresponded to his eye. Was there once an eye that did not now appear on the map, something which had not survived the passing of the centuries? Or was this omission deliberate? Shakespeare may have written that 'the eye is the window of the soul' but if your third eye is as well-developed as this Giant then maybe normal sight becomes eclipsed or unnecessary. As if to compensate for this lack of ordinary vision I noticed that located just behind his horn in the area of the forehead where the Pineal Gland would be was a place called *Penventon*—in Cornish the *Head of the Spring*. It is now a farm but had once been the site

Druid's Hill Cross

of a monastery. Druid's Hill was located where the primary visual cortex of the brain is to be found, at the very back of the Giant's head.

The Boconnoc Estate, today about 20 acres in extent and the home to a deer herd of about a hundred strong, occupies the centre of the Giant's head and has had a long and impressive history. The name is said to derive from 'Connoc's Dwelling' but I was intrigued by the unusual sound of the word, especially as the syllable Oc or Og (C and G being cognate in the old British language) meant Giant. Og or Gog was the great pre-Christian god of the British Isles, a solar deity who gave his name to the Ogham language of the Druids. In Scotland the rebirth of the Sun God at midwinter, Hogmanay, is named after him, and in Irish tradition he is known as Ogma Sunface, depicted with long flowing hair (like our landscape Giant) representing the Sun's rays. He was the God of poetry, speech and eloquence. To the Gauls he was Ogmios, a Celtic Hercules dressed in a lion-skin with a club in his hand. This is also one of the classic representations of the constellation of Orion. Could our Giant be the Hunter God himself writ large, corresponding to the image on the Lostwithiel font that has already been shown to reflect the pattern of stars forming the stellar Giant?

Geoffrey of Monmouth called Stonehenge The Giant's Dance as if it is connected with the idea of a nightly hunt, or dance, in the skies. Considering that Merlin is reputed to have made Stonehenge and was also responsible for the Round Table (after being initiated by Blaise) might we be tempted to speculate that Merlin, as the shamanic wild man of the woods and Lord of the Animals, just like Herne and Robin Goodfellow, may be a memory of how all these God-like figures of folklore are descended from an original horned God of ancient Britain?

The first recorded mention of Boconnoc was in 1086, when it was owned by Robert de Mortain. Early in the fourteenth century it became the property of the Carminow family, who were, like the other families we have noted, well-connected with royalty. Sir Oliver Carminow married a daughter of Joan Holland (known as The Fair Maid of Kent) who was a grand-daughter of Edward I. She took as her second husband the Black Prince, for whom the Duchy of Cornwall was created. The connections go on and on. Margaret Carminow married Sir Hugh Courtenay, and his grandson William, Earl of Devon, married Katherine, daughter of Edward IV. Their son Henry, a claimant to the English throne, became Marquis of Exeter in 1525. He was beheaded for conspiracy and his estates confiscated, being granted to John Russell, First Earl of Bedford. In 1579 the Russell family sold Boconnoc to Sir William Mohun, the last Earl of Devon. With the death of Charles, 4th Baron Mohun who was killed in a duel, the estate was sold to Thomas Pitt, the late Governor of Madras for £54,000. He raised the money by selling the famous Pitt Diamond which was later set in the crown worn by Louis XV at his coronation. It finally ended up set into the hilt of Napoleon's sword.

His son, Robert, had two notable male heirs, Thomas and William. William Pitt was to become Prime Minister of England, whilst Thomas' son, another Thomas, was responsible for additions to the house and many of the drives around the Estate (whose layout suggests a preoccupation with landscape geometry, as we will presently find). He also pioneered the Cornish china clay industry around St Austell that was to become the source of much wealth, just like the tin trade of medieval times. In 1784— and here is a point of particular interest—he was created Lord Camelford. Camelford, as we know, lies at the foot of the Great Bear, and Boconnoc, where Thomas Pitt lived, is right at the centre of the Giant's head. Would we be rash to entertain the idea that these families who had such a great impact on the life of Cornwall and Britain as a whole knew something about these mysteries and wished to create a tangible link between the Lord of the Hunt and his oldest totem animal, the Great Bear? Or is it the case that the land does indeed have a power that can transmit itself to those who inhabit certain spots, inspiring them with the courage and intelligence of the Hunter, which manifests according to the times in which they find themselves?

The Second World War saw Boconnoc occupied by American troops, with much of the grounds used as an ammunition dump for the coming invasion of Europe. We have noted before how these giant effigies appear to have attracted to themselves functions associated with the defence of the Realm, in empathy with their mythical natures. Here we have yet another example, but there is an even more interesting episode in Boconnoc's history that seems significant.

During the Civil War Boconnoc was the scene of two battles (besides the skirmish on Druid's Hill), the first of which was in 1643 when the Parliamentary forces marched into Royalist Cornwall. The Cornish commanders were Bevill Grenville (who was born near Withiel between the Bodmin Lion and the St Columb Wolf) and Ralph Hopton. Camping at Boconnoc they are said to have met the opposing army near Braddock Church, just below the Giant's horn, and the victory was a remarkable day in Cornish history. As Grenville wrote enthusiastically to his wife at Stowe on the north coast that very day;

> My dear love
>
> It hath pleased God to give us a happy victory this present Thursday being the 19th of January for which pray with me in giving God (thanks). We advanced yesterday from Bodmin to find the enemy, which we heard was abroad...We were not above three miles from Bodmin...But night coming we could march no further than Boconnoc Park where (upon my Lord Mohun's kind motion) we quartered all our army that night by good fires under the hedge. By next morning (being this day) we marched forth at about noon, came into full view of the enemy's whole army, upon a fair heath between Boconnoc and Braddock Church. They were in horse much stronger than we, But in foot we were superior I think.'

After engaging for about two hours Grenville and Hopton decided to resolve the matter quickly by marching towards the Roundheads, and after solemn prayers;

'I led my part away, who followed me with so good courage, both down the one hill and up the other, that it struck terror in them...But their courage so failed them as they stood not our first charge of foot but fled in great disorder and we chased them divers miles. Many were not slain because of their quick disordering, but we have taken about six hundred prisoners...And without rest we marched to Liskeard and took it without delay...And so hope we are now again in the way to settle the country in peace...All our Cornish grandees were present at the battle...and we lost not a man. So I rest. Yours ever, Bevill Grenville.

This outstanding victory, according to Grenville's account, took place in the 'frontal lobe' of the Giant's head, just below Braddock Church. The following year another battle took place at Boconnoc. Lord Robartes of Lanhydrock had spread a rumour that the Cornish were ready to surrender and the Parliamentary army marched west. Unbeknown to them the King with an army numbering 16,000 was following. He made his headquarters at Boconnoc and pushed the Roundheads into Lostwithiel and Fowey, and they finally surrendered at Castle Dore, the prehistoric fort famous as the Court of King Mark in the Arthurian tales. King Charles gave thanks in a service at Boconnoc Church, for the surrender of the Parliamentary forces had proved a shattering blow to Cromwell and Fairfax and another glorious victory for the Cornish. But as history relates, despite the Cornish victories it was not to last, and the King was eventually deposed in favour of Cromwell's new regime aimed at creating a puritanical and godless society.

But it is of interest that these battles which symbolically stood for the ideals of Cornish independence and their loyalty to the Crown were both masterminded from Boconnoc. The site of the Battle of Braddock Down described by Grenville has recently been questioned by some historians who say that there is evidence that it may have actually taken place in a triangle of land between Middle and East Taphouse and Calamazog Cross (that *Og* name again)—that is, right in the middle of the Giant's horn.

It is worth emphasising that these battles, if other national circumstances had been different, may have been instrumental in preserving the unbroken line of British royalty, thus saving the country from Cromwell's joyless tyranny which effectively destroyed so much of the old way of life. During this time many innocent pastimes like Maypole dancing and other celebrations that linked people to the land and the annual cycle of fertility were ruthlessly suppressed, and this ushered in a time of grey and colourless repression until the restoration of Charles II, who attempted to bring back the vibrancy of the old ways. But the puritanical mindset was by then established to become an unwelcome part of the nation's psyche even to this day, with bureaucracy's humourless regulations bearing down on the sense of community that once so characterised British life.

When we look at the proud and confident demeanour of our Giant he seems to exemplify those former times; and so this small area around Boconnoc seems poignantly, almost supernaturally, to have been a symbolically potent place to make a last stand for the traditional freedoms and independence of the Cornish, especially since Druid's Hill and the Giant's horn feature so strongly. The question of whether this military activity came about by accident or design is tantalising. Did circumstances conspire behind the scenes or was there a certain level of conscious participation? If the latter, then we might expect some evidence—however sparse—that there lived in the minds of local people, and especially the aristocratic families, a memory of what made this area so special. Are there any vestiges of such beliefs in a mythological Giant to be found in the vicinity?

The long linear earthwork known as the Giant's (or the Devil's) Hedge that runs through some particularly evocative countryside from Lerryn to Looe certainly seems to fit the bill to begin with. This prodigious work of prehistoric engineering is unique in Cornwall and its purpose obscure, but its existence, and the large number of barrows that lie around it, suggests that it must have been built to protect a very special tract of land. It also protects our Giant, for its great ditches (many of which have been ploughed up and virtually disappeared) almost entirely insulate the Giant's head from the country to the south. There is the unmistakable impression that the Giant's Hedge is there to separate this inland area as if it were some sort of sanctuary, bounded in the west by the wooded creeks of the Fowey and in the east by the West Looe river. Before the rivers silted up the place must have been even better protected.

Boconnoc Park, with its twenty-two miles of drives, is also a sanctuary, for technically the public are not allowed there without written permission. To visit the parish church which stands just above the manor house is something of a challenge, for the right-of-way to it is only granted to those living within the parish. Others have no legal right to use the church path, there are no provisions for parking, and in winter like so many others, it is locked. However, this secret abode of our Giant whose church perhaps marks the 'corpus callosum'—the bridge between the left and the right-hand hemispheres of the brain—is open during the summer, and, braving the possibility of being confronted by blunderbuss-waving eagle-eyed park-keepers, I eventually managed to gain access, looking, but not really expecting to find, evidence of a Giant.

The 'Giant' of Boconnoc Church, with his strange 'horn' similar to The Giant in the landscape, who may be an ancient Lord of Time.

Inside the largely fifteenth century building with its unusual octagonal belltower and Minstrel Gallery all was peaceful, its atmosphere of remoteness from the outside world enhancing the idea of this being a place set apart. As my eyes slowly grew accustomed to the twilight, I noticed a strange carving set into the wall high up in the Nave. Not for the first time during this quest, I caught my breath. It depicted what was without question a Giant. He was standing over the bed of what looked like a sick child; an hourglass was in the act of falling, and behind him stood a skeletal figure which must, I thought, represent death. The deathly scenario was completed by the fact that the Giant was wielding a scythe.

Even more amazing to me was that the Giant, strong and muscular, had a most curious hairstyle! Protruding from the top of his forehead was a pronounced quiff that looked very like the horn of the great Giant in the landscape. The church guide suggested this figure may be the Christian giant St Christopher, but I had other thoughts. In a niche close by, a separate figure of a woman in prayer may be the child's mother.

What are we to make of this? The last thing I had expected was an actual sculpture of a Giant, who was obviously closely associated with death. This was not the Saturnine 'Old Father Time' as we know him, for he is bearded and semi-naked, which, along with his 'horn' gave him the appearance and charisma of a warrior-god. This was a watershed moment, for I now suspected the likely identity of our Giant. He could certainly be said to represent a number of horned figures from traditional folklore, including Puck, Robin Goodfellow, Herne or even Pan, along with others that, as we have seen, may have all originated from a single god of extreme antiquity. He could just as well be Saturn or Chronos, the God of Time, echoing the goat-headed image on the Lostwithiel font, for Capricorn the Goat is ruled by Saturn. But here, it seemed, was clear evidence that local beliefs had preserved the memory of some giant deity associated particularly with death. And the only figure which perfectly fulfilled this role was the old pre-Christian god of the Celts, Gwyn ap Nudd. He had been the original Lord of the Underworld and psychopomp who guided the souls of the dead long before the Christian Archangel Michael had adopted his role. Was this eye-catching sculpture an actual representation of Gwyn conducting the soul of a dying child to the afterlife? Was the Giant in the landscape, with his horn-like extension, actually an image of the old original primal god of prehistoric Britain?

I later discovered that in Braddock Church, just below the horn, there was another similar image, of, so it is said, 'Old Father Time' (where did this idea originally spring from, we may wonder?) Intent on examining this carving and others that were referred to as of 'very unusual Celtic-type folk art' I set off for Braddock (Cornish *Bradoc*—emphasising the *oc* component). The wind howled around the isolated church and a mountain of leaves were piled up against the door. Not only was it locked and deserted, it had the atmosphere of a set from a Gothic Horror film. Attempts to track down the key led nowhere. It was to take half-a-dozen visits before I eventually gained entry by sheer luck, spotting the gardener from the Old Rectory next door, the first sign of life I had seen there.

The faceless figure of 'Old Father Time' carrying a head under his arm.

As the key turned in the lock and I let myself in, the atmosphere was very different to that outside— the place seemed to buzz with a static that sent a shiver up my spine. My eyes immediately fell on two heavily carved panels, the remains of the original rood screen, and I saw that one showed a human head emerging from a writhing mass of foliage. The other panel sported a number of other interesting images, including that of a boar playing bagpipes in a tree!

The quality of these dark, highly-polished oak carvings was exceptional, but nearby, built into the front pews, were others, including the one I had particularly come to see. Here was the 'Old Father Time' figure, which appeared to have been deliberately defaced. He was holding the traditional scythe, but with his other arm was carrying a *head*. Why his own features had been hacked away we can only guess. Yet here was another carving which, like that at Boconnoc Church, was associated with death and the afterlife.

At the western end of the building was a finely-carved Norman font with a head at each corner, with striking and unusually large carvings of the Tree of Life. Opposite, hidden behind a trestle table, was another carved panel with a very curious set of carvings indeed. It consisted of figures in seventeenth century costume in a number of poses together with a collection of Celtic-looking beasts including dragons and serpents. One woman was holding the tail of a serpent while another couple appeared seated around a Tree of Life, with one pointing towards it and the other holding its foliage. Another figure was blowing a curly horn while a dragon-like creature issued from his cloak. This very lively and archaic set of carvings was highly unusual, not only in its imagery but the style of carving, which seemed to hark back to a world where mythological ideas held sway. Another panel had a strange figure that was being stared at intently by two rather comic looking characters. Then I noticed another, half-obscured by some later timberwork; the panel had obviously been cut down. What was depicted here was even more intriguing than the other images. A couple were sitting either side of a table on which rested a human head. This would have been curious enough, but by its size in relation to the figures themselves it was clearly not human at all. It was the head of a Giant!

When I had begun to look for possible evidence of giants in the area around Boconnoc it had seemed highly unlikely that any vestiges of earlier beliefs would remain. How wrong I was. Two churches within a mile of each other, and both significantly located with reference to our landscape effigy, had carvings of giants. It seemed likely that the unusual panel with its motifs of people gathered around a Tree of Life, a figure blowing a horn, and now a couple apparently in the act of 'worshipping' a giant's head, did indeed point to a strong local belief in the existence of some mythical giant connected with the area.

In particular, the figures with the scythes seemed appropriate (and very rare in Cornish churches as well). They may be described as 'Old Father Time', but under the circumstances could it be that this epithet may itself derive from a former spiritual guardian of the Celtic regions who ensures the safe passage of souls into the Afterworld—the god-giant who rules that very place; Gwyn ap Nudd?

The Celtic Otherworld and its guardian Gwyn (who was, according to some stories, appointed by King Arthur himself) were not just for the dead, however. This region that exists alongside the mundane world can be entered by those who know how to cross its threshold. As John Matthews writes; *'The Underworld is not a dark and sinister place, but a world within the world we know, lit by stars in the earth, and filled with a multitude of wonders.'*

Seventeenth-century carved wooden panel from Bradoc Church, with two figures apparently 'worshipping' a Giant Head on a table or altar. This is just one of a series of remarkable images on the panel, which, as can be seen, has had its top sawn off.

17

STAR-GOD OF PARADISE

he early thirteenth century *High History of the Holy Grail* (author unknown) is one of the earliest sources of the Grail Quest and, like the other Arthurian legends, contains a number of ideas pertinent to our own discoveries. In one episode the Grail Knights are out hunting a Great Lion. They also quest Giants and a fiery Dragon in the mysterious Kingdom of Logres, the *Lost Land*. The Holy Grail itself, we are told, was in existence when the Copper Bull was worshipped, probably a reference to the great Age of the Megaliths when Taurus was the predominant sign. Is this when the Cornish landscape temple was originally created? Could it be one of the 'Mighty Labours of Britain' mentioned in the *High History?*

Six hundred years after the *High History* the Welsh scholar Iolo Morganwg (the bardic *nom-de-plume* of Edward Williams), a charlatan to some and inspired historian to others, claimed to have translated a medieval manuscript recording that Gwyn, son of Nudd was one of the 'three renowned astronomers of the Isle of Britain... such was their knowledge of the stars, their natures and qualities, that they could prognosticate whatever was wished to be known until the day of doom'.

Whether we can rely on Morganwg's researches is something that will always be the subject of fervent debate, for it often seems that historians are paid to disagree with each other as a basic requisite. Perhaps we should ask ourselves why he should have claimed such a pedigree for Gwyn if there did not already exist some long-standing tradition that Gwyn, like the Druids and their precursors, the megalith-builders whose works demonstrate unequivocally an overwhelming obsession with the stars, was a master astronomer. From what we know about the megaliths (and the churches that now often occupy the sites on which they once stood) it seems likely that each location was carefully selected to reflect celestial patterns, and that the movements of Sun, Moon and stars were encoded into the positioning of the stones which were set up to record these cycles. Gwyn, then, was a god of many parts, who inherited, amongst other things, the star-lore of former ages as well as a deep understanding of the rhythms of time. Is this why he may have been an early precursor of 'Old Father Time' who knows the number of our earthly days and ushers our souls into the Otherworld when that time arrives?

Morganwg was not the only one to note that Gwyn was an accomplished astronomer; one of the greatest mythologists of recent times, Robert Graves, also refers to this tradition from the Welsh Triads. In *The White Goddess* he calls Gwyn 'One of the three happy astrologers' of ancient Britain. Translations and opinions may differ, but Gwyn's reputation and expertise in understanding the movements of the cosmos does not seem in doubt.

Gwyn's home was in Annwn, and his father Nudd (alias *Ludd, Lyr, Nodens* and *Nuada*) was said to have had a school of astrologers who, like the priests that officiated at King Arthur's coronation, prophesied the future. Consequently Gwyn became a High Initiate of the star-lore of ancient Britain and the Land of Nudd, or Nod, as it is remembered in fairy tales, the realm of the star-world. Nudd was especially associated with the Milky Way, and so he was a river god too, as earthly rivers were considered reflections of the greater one in the sky. As the name *Gwyn* means white, signifying brightness and clarity, it perfectly describes the glimmering stars which illuminate the night sky, as well as the Sun which dispels the darkness at dawn. Is this why our Giant is looking to the East? Or is he watching the changing ages of the Earth as each different astrological sign rises in the East at the Spring Equinox, marking the precessional epochs? Either way, he is a God of Light, locked in a continuous battle with the forces of Darkness, for every day has its night, every year its winter and every age its dark period. This is the very nature of earthly existence, the world of polarity.

These Welsh legends are the main source of the early material that tells of Gwyn ap Nudd, just as they preserve other elements of Arthurian lore, both being a memory of the last remaining fragments of the old British traditions. There is no doubt that the Cornish were also the inheritors and keepers of this mythology, but this can never be proven since the old books that may have kept these beliefs alive were destroyed by Saxons who took over the Celtic Christian monasteries, the repositories of the Druid knowledge. They brought their own religious ideas and were in effect agents of the Church of Rome, whose political aspirations for Britain resulted in a suppression of its native beliefs, as they sought to eradicate the ancient Wisdom Tradition that threatened its authority.

But if the astrologers of ancient Britain (when astrology and astronomy were one and the same) could really foretell what was to come in ages far distant by studying the precessional movements of the Earth in relation to the stars, how could they ensure the survival of such knowledge in the face of changing, even apocalyptic, times? Books, it is evident, can be easily destroyed by those who wish to deny other philosophies. Besides, the Druids themselves were known to never write anything down in case it fell into the wrong hands; they developed extraordinary memories (there are accounts of some reciting poems word for word that lasted up to nine days) and encrypted much of their Mystery Wisdom into monuments where only those who were already cognisant with their purpose could apply it. The other major method of encoding this information was the use of mythology, which can be adapted from age to age to suit the language of the time. It was this that gave rise to the early Arthurian material resurrected by the Normans.

By far the best way to transmit this depth of understanding is inevitably through the use of the landscape (especially when it is populated by mythic heroes) which is essentially unchanging and forever locked into the movements of the heavenly bodies. In asking the ultimate question why anyone should go to such extraordinary lengths to arrange and sculpt the land in such a way as has been outlined in this book, we can perhaps here see a possible answer. It seems as though the astronomer priests of ancient Britain encoded their knowledge in a way that could withstand the depredations of time as well as the destructive hand of man. This is the only method which might endure the rise and fall of many cultures, each of which tends to destroy the achievements of the one that went before. Was this the motivation behind our Wild Hunt in the Cornish countryside, imbued with stellar lore and the myths of their Gods, Goddesses and animal powers?

If so, how did they do it? It seems such a mammoth task, involving many different disciplines including precision surveying and land engineering as well as others of a more artistic nature, where the living spirit of the land is an important factor. This involves understanding hydrology, geography and the secret life of Nature, besides some mechanism with which to ensure the designs are correctly proportioned and in the right relation to each other. If it appears an impossible dream to create such a Temple where the Earth becomes a reflection of the heavenly powers, we only have to consider the achievements of those who built the massive and sophisticated astronomical monuments of Stonehenge and Avebury. Thousands of years later, the creation of a network of Gothic cathedrals was to rival these works for their architectural and astronomical expertise. No-one knows where the resources to fund this came from—it is one of the great enigmas of history—but it demonstrates that the scale of such a vast undertaking is indeed possible if the motives are considered sufficiently important.

Stellar lore, passed down through many generations who lived their lives under the stars and knew each constellation intimately, must have been a powerful force which once bound people together whatever their cultural background. Such a project as this might seem an incredible, unbelievably demanding task to undertake. And yet I hope it is clear by now that such a task was indeed undertaken—certainly here in Cornwall and in other places too that were deemed to possess certain spiritual qualities, including the areas around Glastonbury and Wiltshire, where other massive and virtually indestructible monuments were built within the living landscape.

Another question that arises is how could astronomer priests (for want of a better description) possibly be able to view such figures to ensure they were as finely-drawn as they appear? This is a natural but highly perplexing question. Were their surveying techniques so advanced that they could literally project such images onto the land from plans?

Or did they employ what what we would call more magical methods? At the core of shamanic and other mystical systems is the act of projecting the shaman's consciousness outside the body, thus releasing it from the prison of the everyday senses. In many traditions this takes place, after due ritual and awareness-enhancing techniques, along a central axis that acts as a microcosm of the cosmic Polar Axis.

Native American Indians consider their tepees as a circular arrangement that mimics the cosmos, with the fire centrally placed and a hole at the very top symbolising the crown of the World Axis, and it is likely that the traditional British roundhouses were viewed in much the same way. For many tribal peoples this axis is the hub around which shamanic practices revolve, enabling the magician to travel up into the sky. These days we might call such a technique *astral travelling*. But it remains an interesting speculation that these priests, so well versed in the nature of the spirit, may have actually viewed their creations from above, just as we now look at a map.

A further possibility we might consider is the use of psychoactive plants which are likewise known to be an integral part of shamanic traditions worldwide. Some of these also have the effect of releasing the consciousness from the body, especially when used during controlled ritual. There are many such examples in the Westcountry, and witches still gather herbs and plants from the hedgerows to make preparations exactly for this reason.

During excavations in Tintagel churchyard to uncover the 'Dark Age' royal tombs in the 1980s one thing in particular struck archaeologists, for they came across large quantities of burnt seeds surrounding the graves. When they were sent for analysis they were confirmed as Henbane, which used to grow wild on the cliffs until a hundred or so years ago. Since this is one of the principal ingredients of the 'Flying Ointment' used by witches we may draw our own conclusions. Were the people of those times inhaling the smoke from the seeds to access spiritual realms and communicate with the spirits of the departed? Could they have used this substance in the same way as that claimed by witches, that is, to *fly*? An intriguing tailpiece to these excavations is that after the graves were filled in, an unusual plant was found growing in the corner of the churchyard, which had not been seen in the area for over a century. It was Henbane.

The Shining One

To return to Gwyn and his god-like wisdom, that invaluable source-book for such researches, Spurrell's *English-Welsh Dictionary*, contains a clutch of related words that give an insight into his true character. The word *gwyn* is listed as meaning *white, fair, blessed* or *holy*, with *gwynnem* or *gwyneman* signifying *diamond* or *brilliant*. *Gwyndwm* means lay land, or land never ploughed, a clear reference to Nature in its virgin state. *Gwynfa* is the modern Welsh word for *paradise*, emphasising that Annwn, or the Otherworld, is not just a place of departed souls but a paradisial or heavenly realm. *Gwynt* means *wind, breath* or *smell* (reminding us perhaps of the prehistoric hill-fort of Bury Down just below the Giant's nose). *Gwntillio* means '*to ventilate*' or '*to winnow*', and, curiously, our Giant is to be found in the parish of... *St Winnow*. Robert Graves observes that many place names in Britain that begin with the prefix *Win* are derived from *Gwyn* (the initial letter having disappeared as is still common in modern Welsh), such as the Arthurian site of Winchester, where the famous medieval Round Table, repainted during the Tudor period, hangs in the Great Hall. Geoffrey of Monmouth relates that Uther Pendragon was crowned at Winchester, a great royal centre in his day where Arthur was believed to have held court.

In the story of *Culhwch and Olwen* from the Mabinogion, Gwyn is locked in an eternal battle with Gwythyr ap Greidawl, for they both seek the hand of Creiddylad, the Spring Maiden. This is one of the most an-cient themes of the British Mysteries, where the Summer and Winter Kings fight for the hand of the Goddess of the Land. This runs right through later traditions such as the story of Tristan and Iseult and is also incor-porated into Arthurian romance where Queen Guinevere is abducted from King Arthur's court by Melwas, King of the Summer Country. In this version Arthur represents the Midwinter King, for he is crowned at the Winter Solstice. Gwyn's opponent Greidawl is also known as *Victor the Scorcher* in keeping with his characteristic summer heat.

This timeless battle that is fought every year bears a striking resem-blance to the images depicted on the tower of Lanlivery Church, where the head of the old king is shown rolling on the floor whilst two crowned men triumphantly hold aloft the head of the new king, the essence of the Be-heading Game in *Sir Gawain and the Green Knight*. We may wonder whether that story does not retain elements of some previous aspects of Gwyn's characteristics and the Battle between Summer and Winter, for Gwyn and Gawain are remarkably similar names. This, along with all the other sup-porting evidence emphasises that the early Arthurian material incorpo-rates much of the Celtic and prehistoric traditions at its core.

Shakespeare used this theme in *King Lear* (Lyr, Ludd or Nudd) and was drawing on a story of immemorial antiquity which his audience would have been familiar with even in Elizabethan times. In his version

Creiddylad the Queen of the Earth was renamed Cordelia. The mingling and overlaying of these stories can be discerned everywhere. In the battle between Gwyn and Greidawl, it is Arthur himself, called upon to judge who will be victor, who rules that they should fight every May Day (Mayday is the time of the Faery Queen or the Goddess of the land) even though neither one shall win her until the Day of Judgement. Until that day comes, she is protected by her father Nudd or Ludd, who in earlier times was known as Nuada of the Silver Hand, a maimed king who has lost his sovereignty.

The Starry Crown, from a stained glass window in Tintagel Church.

Graves points out that in the Triads, Arianrhod is the mother of the heroic twins Gwengwyngwyn and Gwanat. As he writes; '*Gwengwyngwyn is merely 'the Thrice-white-one' or Gwyn's name three times repeated.*' Gwyn's duty was to conduct souls to the Castle of Arianrhod. Arianrhod, the mother of Gwyn, means 'Silver Wheel' and refers to the circling stars around the central pole. Her abode, or 'Spiral Castle' is said to be the constellation known as the Corona Borealis, the Northern Crown or *Caer Arianrhod*. Here the celestial crown signifies heavenly as well as earthly sovereignty and Graves concludes that Arianrhod is but one aspect of the Goddess Cerridwen, the *White Goddess* herself, whose grail-like cauldron of rebirth is the reason for King Arthur's quest into Annwn. Here are links between the North Pole, Kingship, and the descent into the Underworld, all themes that recur throughout our own quest, and which look as though they come from a primal tradition where Gwyn, born of Arianrhod, is a central figure, with Arianrhod portrayed as both Birth-Goddess and the Goddess of Initiation who turns the Wheel of Heaven.

Two animals especially are connected with Gwyn. One is his faithful dog, Dormarth, who is described in *The Black Book of Carmarthen*, the oldest reference to Gwyn extant, as

'Handsome my dog, and round-bodied,
And truly the best of dogs...
red-nosed, ground-grazing,
on him we perceived the speed
Of thy wanderings on Cloud Mount'

This sounds very like our Giant's fellow companion and guardian of the Underworld, the Great Dog of the Arundells, who accompanies those who embark on the spiritual quest. The description 'ground-grazing'

certainly sounds as though this is no
ordinary hound, but one that exists
in the 'round-bodied' Earth. In the
Glastonbury Zodiac one of the most
easily-recognisable of the giant figures
is the *Girt Dog of Langport*, whose nose
is formed of the red earth of Burrow
Mump and whose tail falls on the
village of *Wagg*. Here we have another
giant hound sculpted by old roads and
marked by significant places. But we
note that the Dog's name, *Dormarth*,
contains the word *arth*, the Brythonic
word for bear, and so it looks as
though our Underworld guide serves
not only Gwyn, but Arthur too.

The owl of St Veep. Is it a memory of one of
Gwyn ap Nudd's totem creatures?

The other creature that is
strongly linked to Gwyn in the Triads
is the owl, his very own magic totem
bird, universally associated with wisdom, as well as a symbol of Blodeu-
wedd the Flower Maiden. In Culhwch's search for Olwen (the daughter of
a giant) one of the knights seeks the advice of the Owl of Cwm Cawlwyd,
which was regarded as one of the oldest and wisest animals in existence.
Interestingly there is a superbly carved oak roof boss of an owl placed
directly over the entrance to St Veep Church, just to the south of our Giant,
which because of its prominent position gives the impression of an ancient
talisman of protective power. Could it be yet another memory of Gwyn's
presence here?

Another church that is close by our landscape Giant and has
some striking correspondences is the exquisitely-situated church of St
Winnow on the banks of the River Fowey. Although difficult to get to by
road these days, it was once on the main shipping route to Lostwithiel,
and so was a very significant site, with an ancient manor house next door.
In 1086 it was the property of Osberne, Bishop of Exeter. The legend of
St Winnow is of great interest to us here. We have already noted that
Gwntillio means in modern Welsh *to winnow*. This describes the practice
of throwing threshed corn into the air so that the chaff is blown away
by the wind and the corn can be used in breadmaking and brewing. It is
also a universal metaphor for the purification of the human soul, whose
outer husk is associated with the lower nature which is cast aside as the
inner spiritual seed is released. Winnowing is thus strongly connected to
the breath, for in the form of wind it is the breath of Mother Earth. It is
the breath that gives life, and so in Greek, *anima* (soul) and *animos*, (wind)
are closely related concepts.

This is especially appropriate for a place called St Winnow. But the metaphor runs deeper when we consider the legend. Winnow (or *Winnoc*, as it is spelt in Cornish, thus combining *Gwyn* and *oc*, meaning literally the *White Giant*) was said to be an early Celtic saint who set up a *lan* or sacred enclosure here in the seventh century. According to the story, when he became too old to run the monastery he was banished to the kitchen to grind flour (he is shown in a stained-glass window in the church carrying his handmill). As the supply of flour diminished his fellow brethren complained, and it was discovered that Winnoc was neglecting his kitchen duties in favour of prayer. The Lord declared that his prayers were far more important than grinding flour, and consequently sent an angel to do it, so releasing the pious saint to continue his devotions.

Anyone who has read *Hamlet's Mill*, the seminal book dedicated to the study of polar mythology, will recognise the legend of St Winnow as a familiar mythic theme. The Mill in the title of the book refers to the centre of the universe that grinds away through the ages, whose gradual shift causes precession and the changing astrological epochs of the heavenly Zodiac. St Winnow's legend is obviously part of this widespread mythology. But if Gwyn was born of Arianrhod as the Welsh Triads say, then he too is associated with the symbolic mill that provides the motive force of the cosmos. Here we have yet another example of how the stories of Gwyn may have been transformed down the ages, and in this case were apparently adopted by the early Church who, unable to banish them altogether, made them their own.

Another intriguing fact about the church at St Winnow is that St Dunstan, the Abbot of Glastonbury, is said to have spent time here. Considering the fact that this remote church is a long way from Somerset this seems an unlikely tradition—unless it is a dim memory of very ancient connections between the two places. And this makes a lot of sense when we realise that the earliest legend associated with Glastonbury Tor is of Gwyn ap Nudd, the Lord of the Faeries and God of Paradise, as its original deity. In the sixteenth century *Life of St Collen* we are told that the hermit saint was living on the Tor when he overheard two men talking about Gwyn, and the saint, evidently a somewhat dour and joyless character, remonstrated with them. Gwyn, he said, was a

St Winnow Church on the banks of the River Fowey. Its legend connects it with Glastonbury and the realm of Gwyn ap Nudd, Lord of the Celtic Otherworld.

devil. They in turn told him to mind his language, for it would not do to offend the Lord of the Tor.

Soon a denizen of the faery realms arrived at Collen's hermitage inviting him to meet with Gwyn, but the irascible saint declined. After a succession of other visits he was warned yet again not to treat Gwyn with contempt, and eventually climbed the sacred hill to suddenly find himself within a shimmering otherworldly castle. Inside, Gwyn was sitting on a throne of gold, attended by beautiful damsels, musicians and an array of faery folk, all making merry. This was all too much for the curmudgeonly saint, who refused to eat the faery food and accused Gwyn of ruling over a hellish place cunningly disguised as Paradise. With a sprinkling of holy water, the whole scene disappeared and the saint was suddenly alone on the windswept Tor, having banished Gwyn for ever, or so the Church would have us believe.

Such childlike propaganda probably had the desired effect in its day, and even when the Arthurian scholar Geoffrey Ashe (who lives at the foot of the Tor) discovered this manuscript he encountered opposition from those who said it was too recent to be credible. But since that time it has become accepted as a genuine Glastonbury legend, which, like the Welsh Triads, were written down long after the oral tradition had been current. As he comments; *'What is virtually certain is that it supplies a glimpse of truly ancient beliefs about the Tor being a hollow hill, a point of contact with a pre-Christian Underworld.'* In the context of our own quest, the Glastonbury connections are easy to understand if there was a popular belief that Gwyn, and his successor King Arthur, both presided over this Underworld Initiation and that at both places giant figures were set into the landscape; a zodiac at Glastonbury and in Cornwall, an earlier version more concerned with circumpolar and other prominent constellations connected with the Wild Hunt.

What other churches around the head of our Giant may retain a memory of Gwyn's presiding influence? St Pinnock Church, plain though it is, is located right in front of his horn and at least preserves *Oc* in its name, reminding us that along with *Boconnoc*, *Bradoc* and *Winoc*, this group of old sacred sites were dedicated to a pre-Christian Giant long before they had churches built on them. The oldest artefact in this church is an early Norman font with a primitive gargoyle sporting pendulous ears that looks as if it comes from another age altogether; the rest of the building has been stripped out by its 'restorers'.

Just below where the Giant's Hedge intersects his chin is Lanreath, a place that has a number of further clues. Even if it did not, it would be well worth visiting for it retains its old charm and gives a poignant reminder of what Cornish villages were like until quite recently. The seventeenth century Court House, the one-time home of the prominent Grylls family, is a fine and unprettified example of a genuine old Tudor Manor,

and close by is a similarly atmospheric old Inn. I couldn't help noticing the sign swinging in the wind—it shows a Punch-like figure with a large nose, much like our Giant, and I speculated that this Mr Punch might just be a dim and distant vestige of the effigy in the landscape (*The Devil's Punchbowl* is quite a common name in Britain associated with landscape features—I wondered if in this case it could refer to the great earthwork of Bury Down). Inside, high up above a corner of the bar, is another curious example of this image; a small carved head with a Punch-like nose that must have looked down on many centuries of mirth and merriment. The wood-panelled room now used as a restaurant has a small doorway leading to a 'secret' tunnel that runs under the road to the church opposite.

Lanreath Church admirably demonstrates what we have lost due to the evangelistic zeal of Victorian restorers, who ripped memorials from the walls, broke them up and cast them aside whilst indulging their pyromaniac natures by burning old pews and carvings which preserved local history, mythology and folklore in a way that only ancient artefacts can. The atmosphere within the building has a sort of effervescence that is missing in so many churches today, but it reminds us how all these old churches were once transformers and generators of spiritual power. The magnificent Grail-like Norman font is finely carved with lively zig-zag designs that exemplify this energy, and still retains patches of its original colouring.

We are so used today to experiencing many churches as rather sterile places with bland, plastered walls and plain furniture. We are liable to forget that in medieval and pre-Victorian times they were glowing with vibrant colour. The walls were decorated with murals or lively designs, the stained-glass windows filtered dancing sunlight, the ceilings were painted with starry skies and brightly-coloured roof bosses, and the whole experience would have been more like entering a richly-decorated palace; a real celebration of the senses. It is a source of great regret that these places are so little visited these days, and are often left locked due to lack of interest (except from thieves who would no doubt steal the altars and fonts for garden ornaments if they could). It is a tragic comment on our godless society that these once sacred places often now only attract vandals. I have even come across neo-pagans who would not go near a church because of its religious associations. Apparently they are unaware that they are built on former pagan sites and are often full of pagan symbolism.

Yet these places are repositories of irreplaceable history and can reconnect us with our ancestors and the land in a way that nothing else can. Instead, they have frequently become burdensome responsibilities for local people. Maybe the churches should be sold to their communities for a small symbolic sum, or leased for a peppercorn rent, and then, stripped of any cloying religious doctrines, they could once again become the heart of every town and village, open to all and resounding to the sounds of music, children and laughter just as they did in earlier times.

Lanreath church has a wealth of notable works of art, including one of the finest memorials in the Westcountry, to Charles Gryles (or *Grylls*) and his wife, dated 1623. Carved in wood and painted to imitate stonework, it is very elaborate, with touching statues of the couple at prayer above their eight children. Sir John Gryles had been knighted by King Charles I at Liskeard in 1644 for his loyalty to the Royalist cause, and no less than four members of his family had been rectors of the church. They were not the only prestigious local family — Anne Boleyn, the wife of Henry VIII, was from the Bullers, another distinguished line who had bought the Court House from the Gryles in 1718. The church is full of treasures, and the Norman altar stone is a rare surviving example of a time when they were more portable, this one superbly carved with geometrical patterns and a curious spiral design. The sixteenth century rood screen has thirteen paintings of biblical figures and saints, some with their 'totem' animals. These were originally gilded and painted in vibrant colours and once numbered forty, but at some time in the past, probably after the Civil War, most were scrubbed away. Amongst the images, which include an unusual moustache-less Christ, a pregnant Virgin Mary and Elizabeth (mother of John the Baptist) is one of St Ursula (named after *Ursa*, the bear). There is no bear shown, but surprisingly, behind the screen is a veritable menagerie of them!

The choir stalls, made from original seventeenth century pews, are literally teeming with rampant bears rearing up on the hatchments, or Coats of Arms, of the Grylls-Bere families. This might strike us as a little surprising considering our interests, but there is more. Whilst it may appear natural that the Bere or Beare family had as their totem animal the Bear, it came as something of a shock to recall that there is a place called *Tregrylls* (in Cornish, *the dwelling-place of the Grylls*), located right in the middle of the Great Bear, just outside the village of Boscastle.

Grylls-Bere Coat of Arms in Lanreath Church

Here was a most unlikely connection between the Great Bear, where this quest began, and the landscape in which our Giant figures. The Grylls family had been very influential in Cornish life for centuries, and it had been in 1610 that Sir John Grylls married Grace Beare, coheiress of William Beare of nearby Lewharne. However, this connection with Boscastle and the Great Bear was not to be the only one. An even more striking 'coincidence' was yet to come. This, like the Grylls-Beare link, was to take us right back to the beginning of our quest, for this area, and in particular the ancient manor of Botelet within the Parish of Lanreath, was the haunt of another family we have become more familiar with. These were the likely builders of Tintagel Castle, the Bottreaux.

William de Bottreaux, Ist Lord of Boscastle, had actually been born at the ancient Manor of Botelet (looking across to *Buckabarrow Downs*, on the Giant's nose). When he died in 1391 his widow, dowager Lady Bottreaux (formerly Elizabeth Daubeny) continued to live, not at Botelet, but at the now-vanished manor of.... *St Winnow*. At this time it was the property of Edmund Lacy, Bishop of Exeter, and it was to remain the home of the family until the death of William, 3rd Lord Bottreaux in 1462. He was succeeded by his daughter Margaret (widow of Lord Hungerford) before the house was sold to the Loure or Lower family, which was to include three Sheriffs of Cornwall. In 1609 Sir William Lower, Knight of St Winnow and Treventy in Carmarthenshire, became MP for Bodmin and, later, Lostwithiel.

Intriguingly, Jane Lower had married George Carminow of Polmawgan, St Winnow, who died in 1599. In 1390 the Carminows had been involved in a lawsuit; they claimed that the heraldic crest of their ancestors had been in existence since the time of King Arthur, and even that they were descended from him. In the judgement, well-known to those who peruse the abstruse annals of Cornish genealogy, they famously won. Both George and Jane, who died in 1609, the same year that Sir William became MP for Bodmin, are buried at Lanhydrock Church, on the snout of the Lostwithiel Lion.

Of all the amazing discoveries during this quest, finding that the Bottreaux family had been so intimately connected with both the Great Bear and the Giant was probably the most surprising. It was certainly the most unexpected. And yet here at Lanreath was a church teeming with bears, a link between one of the area's most notable families the Grylls, who had given their name to a place within the Great Bear, and the Bottreaux family who had given their name to Boscastle, or Bottreaux Castle, as it was formerly known. Both these families had lived at the Crown of the Bear's Polar Axis or the Tree of Life and also near its base, in the area of the landscape Giant. How could we ever have learnt of all these connections if it were not for these Cornish churches which preserve in their fabric the unwritten history of the land?

But the Bear/Giant connection was not the only one to come to my attention. A few miles from St Winnow Church is the tiny remote chapel of St Nectan's, unmarked on most maps and generally only stumbled across by inquisitive tourists exploring the area. Much changed from what must once have been a quaint and picturesque medieval chapel, its position is nevertheless enchanting, and it is intriguingly situated right at the back of the Giant's Head.

St Nectan's Chapel in the head of the Boconnoc Giant. Does its dedication derive from the old British god of prehistory?

St Nectan, so we are informed by the guidebook, was 'one of the most important figures in the ancient Kingdom of Dumnonia'. Reputed, like so many other Cornish saints, to have been the offspring of King Brychan of Wales (after whom Breconshire is named) his legend says he was beheaded in the seventh century by robbers. Anyone who studies these ubiquitous legends concerning saints 'losing their heads' soon realises that they are mythic allegories concerning gaining higher consciousness, when the spiritual organs within the head become the focus of perception, and the body is 'left behind'. That is the reason why so many of these legendary figures are said to have 'picked up their head' and continued to live thereafter (much like the *Green Giant* in the medieval story of Sir Gawain).

St Nectan's original chapel is known to date from at least 1281, although it is likely there was an early building on the site long before this. It was an important daughter church of St Winnow. The Civil War battles that appear to have been concentrated within the Head of the Giant also greatly affected the chapel, and in August 1644 much damage was caused, with the tower battered down and the bells removed. One of the pinnacles from the tower remains at the old steps. The final indignity for this ancient building was when it was restored in 1825 and 1864, which resulted in it being enlarged, according to the guidebook 'in a cheap and ugly style'.

At this stage, a small voice may be reminding us that we have come across St Nectan before. This saint is the same as the Nectan who gave his name to one of the most powerfully-evocative sites in this quest, that of St Nectan's Kieve and Waterfall—the roaring 'throat' of the Great Bear of Tintagel. St Nectan is reputed to have prophesied from his death-bed that one day the old true religion would return to these islands. All this is intriguing enough, but who was St Nectan? Yuri Leitch, in the only book ever devoted solely to Gwyn ap Nudd, called simply *Gwyn*, suggests a direct link between the two. Gwyn's father Nudd (pronounced *Neath* in the Brythonic language) is, he points out, *Nathanus* in Latin, rendered into Cornish as *Nectan*, the old River God and Master Astronomer who passed his knowledge onto his son Gwyn. The existence of an ancient chapel dedicated to him within the Head of our Giant is thus of more than passing interest.

Gwyn and the White Goddess

Wherever one travels in the area of this Giant effigy, a notable landmark is ever-present in the landscape. It is a massive Egyptian-style Obelisk similar to the one located right at the centre of the head of the Bodmin Lion. Situated at the heart of the Boconnoc Estate, a long, straight, imposing tree-lined avenue leads to it, and the first time I travelled along it I experienced that tingling of the spine that so often indicates magic is afoot. Such obelisks always seem, like the one at Bodmin, to be built in geomantically significant places. The origins of obelisks are obscure, but they guard the entrances to Egyptian Temples and are believed to be (amongst other things) sighting instruments for stellar transits, the topmost point or pyramidion giving a fixed point against which to observe the passage of stars. I didn't know if this might be the case here, but I did suspect the long avenue leading to it might be of interest. Initial checks with a compass did not, however, point to the 'usual suspects'—alignments associated with the Summer or Winter Solstices, or the old 'quarter days'. Yet the feeling it was important was insistent. There was only one thing to do; ask Robin to survey it with his trusty theodolite.

So one bright sunny day, the next time Robin and Trish visited us from Wales, we drove to Boconnoc and set up his equipment to take the necessary readings. There was nothing immediately apparent in its orientation, but Robin said he would have to do what he calls 'office work' to calculate any other possibilities when he returned home. A week later I got an excited phone call. 'You'll never guess' said Robin. 'It is aligned at 41 degrees 51 minutes directly to the Major Standstill Moonrise (the most northerly position of the Moon's cycle). This was as unexpected as it was intriguing. 'And,' he continued, 'If you project the avenue of the Obelisk it points exactly to Stowes Hill.'

The Boconnoc Obelisk avenue, aligned perfectly towards the Major Standstill Moonrise over Stowes Hill.

Stowes Hill is where the Cheesewring stands, and the centre of the Neolithic ritual complex that dominates the area above the Great Hare. As we had already found, the Moon-Gazing Hare is looking in the direction of the Major Standstill Moonrise. Given the fact that a number of sites in that area are connected with the Divine Feminine (including the only Cornish chapel dedicated to Mary Magdalene), this news was of great interest. The alignment of the Obelisk avenue, when projected across the high ground at the top of the Giant's Horn (seemingly marked by a barrow, although the woodland of the Estate rules out any intervisibility) ran parallel to the Hare's Moon Axis, right along the back of its body. Also exactly on this axis was the 'crossed swords' symbol that gave the site of the Civil War battle of 1643.

Perhaps most striking of all was that in the opposite direction this Moon Axis led straight to St Winnow Church. This revealed that the alignment had three notable sites all in exact relationship to each other, and each from very different eras. Stowes Hill was a Neolithic sanctuary, St Winnow Church was a Celtic monastery, and the Obelisk and its avenue had been built in the late eighteenth century. The conclusion to be drawn from this can only mean that these heavenly patterns laid out on the landscape must have been understood in all these different ages, a geomantic legacy from the earliest times.

This was something of a revelation. This is the first time we had come across such a major axis associated with the Moon. Over the years various examples of such long-distance alignments had come to our attention, but always linked to the Sun and its position at important times in the annual cycle (the most famous being the countrywide St Michael Line which corresponds to the Mayday sunrise). The geometrical arrangement between St Winnow's Church, the Obelisk (positioned in the middle of the Giant's frontal lobe), the ritual area of Stowes Hill, the Magdalene Chapel at Trecarrell and the other sites was of singular importance. The Major Standstill Moonrise Axis, clearly laid out and marked by the tall Obelisk, which reminded me of an antenna or aerial that might pick up the influence of the Moon, seemed pregnant with possibilities. It implied that one of the most important elements in this Giant effigy was the female lunar power. It seemed as if the power of the Moon is being channelled into the very centre of the Giant's brain. If this is the case, then our Giant exhibited an extraordinary balance between the Male and Female principles—he was looking due East to the Spring Equinox sunrise whilst he was receiving, through the top of his Horn, and along the avenue to the Obelisk positioned in his head, the power of the Moon at the time when the Moon is at its most northerly point in sky.

This God-Giant appeared to be essentially hermaphrodite, where the cosmic powers of the Male and Female were harmoniously balanced. As such, he represents the ultimate goal of many spiritual disciplines, including the object of medieval alchemy—to blend the opposing forces within one's own being to achieve a perfect synthesis of the two. This is a remarkable concept. It is tantalising to find that we here have proof positive that whoever had built the Obelisk and laid out the avenue had known something of this mystery. In fact I was tempted to go further, and conclude that the knowledge of these cosmic powers and the movements of the heavenly bodies, although laid down in megalithic times, had been transmitted across thousands of years at least until the eighteenth century, when the Obelisk was built. This confirmed that certain families had been the custodians of this knowledge and understood its real significance.

The Obelisk had been erected in 1771 by Thomas Pitt, Ist Lord of Camelford (on the 'paw' of the Great Bear) on the supposed site of the Battle of Braddock Down. It commemorates Sir Richard Lyttelton, his wife's uncle and benefactor. Its inscription states *'In gratitude and affection to the memory of Sir Richard Lyttelton and to perpetuate that peculiar character of benevolence which rendered him the delight of his own age and worthy of veneration of posterity MDCCLXXI'*. Whether these families were perpetuating this knowledge consciously did not now seem in any doubt; the old carvings in Bradoc Church showed that apparently even in the seventeenth century there was a strong local tradition of worshipping a giant head. Here, it seemed, was proof of such an assertion: the owners of Boconnoc, the Pitts, who had given Britain one of its greatest political leaders, had gone to considerable effort and expense to construct a physical axis that fulfilled no apparent practical function, yet, as we have discovered, was deeply concerned with geometry and the movements of the Moon.

This marriage of the Male and Female, the Solar and Lunar, or the polar opposites from which earthly life is created, must have had a deep and powerful significance. As the guardian of this land of initiation, our Giant, Gwyn, faces East in the direction of St German's, the site of a Saxon Cathedral and Bishop's Palace. This had been the earliest cathedral site in Cornwall before being replaced by, at first, Crediton, and then Exeter, both in Devon, as Cornwall was absorbed into the English system. It had been granted to Conan, who was appointed the first Saxon Bishop by Athelstan in 926. Before that it had been a Celtic Christian monastery, when the Cornish Church was independent of outside influence and preserved the old traditions which had come down from Druidic times.

Alchemical engraving of the marriage of Sun and Moon, the harmony of male and female powers.

The Celtic foundation is thought to have taken place in 429 when St Germanus first settled at this spot on the banks of the river. The site of the Bishop's Palace is now occupied by Port Eliot, the residence of the Eliot family for almost five hundred years, and, remarkably, in the basement with its massively thick walls are the remains of some very rare glazed floor tiles from the third and fourth centuries. That such artefacts still exist is fortunate, for it shows that a building of great importance occupied this site from a very early date indeed. The earliest written reference to Port Eliot is in a ninth century liturgical fragment from the Bodleian Library, which calls it *Ecclesia Lanledensia*. But John Michell, that indefatigable scholar of things arcane, just before he left this earthly plane to study the universe from a different perspective, had once mentioned to me that Port Eliot (where he often stayed as a guest of Lord and Lady Eliot), had in the earliest times been called *Lan-y-Neath* (the sacred place of Nudd). He had no way of knowing that I was on the trail of Gwyn, in fact neither had I at that time, but unfortunately he was himself to enter the real Land of Nod before we had a chance to discuss his researches, so we will probably never know exactly where he got his insights from.

But the evidence suggests that the oldest, pre-Christian associations of Port Eliot, or Port Priory as it was called for the many centuries when it was a thriving monastic port, was as the spiritual gateway of the land to the West. Did St German's once guard the river crossing into the land ruled by Gwyn, the leader of the Wild Hunt, long before King Arthur became the mythic hero of a new age? Some years ago a curious artefact was dug up in the grounds of St Germans—it was the sculpted head of a horned god, a Pan-like figure. Could it be a vestige of the Nature worship that lingered on long after Churchianity had established itself in the region? Did an undercurrent of Druidism and Celtic Christianity still survive in these hinterlands of Cornwall? On the opposite side of the St German's river is a place called on old maps *Earth*, almost as if travellers bound for the land of Gwyn ap Nudd were leaving the ordinary world for a different realm altogether.

Within the house of Port Eliot itself, and the adjacent great Priory Church, are further clues to this mystery. Over the fireplace in the drawing room of the house (formerly the monk's refectory) is, amongst one of the finest collections of portraits by Sir Joshua Reynolds in the country, a portrait of William Pitt. Prime Minister before he was twenty-five, his family lived at the Boconnoc Estate and his brother Thomas, Ist Lord Camelford, had built the Obelisk and laid out the avenue.

Head of a Horned God or Pan-like figure reputed to have been found at St German's Priory.

Their sister had married Edward James Eliot, oldest son of John, Ist Earl of St German's, thus linking both dynasties as well as two of the most important locations in early Cornish history.

The oldest wooden carving in St German's Priory - a misericord depicting a hunter on his way home accompanied by hounds.

In the Priory Church next door is something else that may surprise us. The oldest artefact in the building is an ancient oak misericord—the only surviving fragment of the monk's seating within the choir. By a happy coincidence it has been preserved when everything else has been lost to the depredations of time. It depicts a lively scene of a hunter striding home carrying his quarry, amongst a pack of hounds, two of which appear to be leaping and biting the creature he has successfully pursued and caught. The liveliness of the carving is typical of such an early piece, and it has gathered around it some local folklore that links it with a knightly Lord called Dando, who is said to have drowned in the river whilst out hunting. This Knight was from Sheviock, a few miles away from St Germans, and close to Antony, the seat of the Carew family. Did Richard Carew, who wrote *The Survey of Cornwall* and was a boy when John Eliot bought the house which had once been the Bishop's Palace know something of this? He was certainly immersed in the history and genealogy of old Cornish families, and may have dropped hints here and there, although he would surely have been bound by loyalty not to give away too many clues.

We are used to the way that old traditions have other layers of meaning grafted on to them over the centuries. But under the circumstances we may wonder at the coincidence that we came to St Germans looking for any evidence of the Lord of the Wild Hunt, and here is an archaic carving that is just too close to ignore. It may indeed commemorate a knight who drowned, although there is nothing to suggest water in its design. It could equally well be an actual representation of Gwyn himself, whose influence, remembered into monastic times, was perpetuated in this old, worn and worm-eaten carving. In fact there are similarities to the Orion figure on Lostwithiel font, and the two jumping dogs are also reminiscent of the hound shown there. Examination of the creature he is carrying did not reveal conclusively what it might be, such is the style of carving and the centuries of wear and tear, but its size in relation to the leaping dogs suggested to me that it could be a *Hare*.

This fragment from the Priory's past has captured the imagination of others too. In the Round Room within Port Eliot, the walls are covered with a huge mesmerising mural by one of the greatest artists of recent times, the late Robert Lenkiewicz, which is full of riddles, arcane meaning and symbolism. Prominent amongst the many portraits of people he had come to know on his frequent visits to Port Eliot over the twenty years he worked on the mural (which remains unfinished) is a painting of this carving with a ghostly figure in a shroud leaning against it. What was going on in the mind of Lenkiewicz when he painted it we cannot tell, although the subject of death was certainly one of his great interests. But he seems to have made a connection between the carving of the Hunter and the idea of a deathly guide of departing souls, just like Gwyn himself. I was stunned, as well, to see, peering out from the many portraits, all of which have the incredible intensity for which Lenkiewicz was known, the aquiline features of John Michell, who had only left this earthly realm a few short days before. Everything seemed quite magically apposite and suffused with meaning, and I stood there for some time in silent reverie, wondering at the strange synchronicities that seemed to be beckoning from some otherworldly dimension.

Who was St Germanus? *The Oxford Dictionary of Saints* gives two possibilities; Germanus of Auxerre (378-448) and Germanus of Man (410-475). The first of the two was a Gallic-Roman governor of the borders of Armorica, or Brittany. He was sent to Britain twice to counter the Pelagian heresy which was widespread throughout the land and was fundamentally opposed to the concept of original sin. He is also said to have led British troops in battle against Picts and Saxons and won, apparently without bloodshed, by urging them to shout *Hallelujah* at the enemy! Miracles attended him and he became famous for his sanctity, with widespread feasts and dedications throughout Britain.

But confusion reigns. The second candidate is Germanus of Man, who has churches in Wales and Cornwall dedicated to him, which are *'sometimes wrongly attributed to Germanus of Auxerre'*. Baring Gould has him born in Brittany in the early fifth century and then travelling to Ireland to stay with St Patrick. Later, in Wales, he lived at the monasteries of Brioc and Illtud (Llantwit Major) before leaving to meet Patrick again on his journey to Britain. At this time he is said to have *'engaged in a magic contest with Gwrtheryn'* before becoming bishop of Man. In the Mabinogion, Gwyn and Gwythyr are the two rivals for the affections of Creudyladd, described as 'the most splendid maiden in the Three Islands of the Mighty'. *Gwythyr* and *Gwrtheryn* are so close as to make us wonder whether St German's 'magic contest' is not a reference to the saint taking over the role of Gwyn, the original guardian of the place. Might the legends of Gwyn and the Celtic saint have become intertwined down the centuries to such an extent that they were both remembered as being involved in a mythic battle, as recorded in the Mabinogion?

One other point of interest occurred to me when I looked at the map. Further to the East of our Giant's head, beyond St German's and across the River Tamar which marks the Devon/Cornwall border, is Plymouth Hoe. This is the spot where Geoffrey of Monmouth claimed Brutus, the legendary founder of Britain, came when the land was 'inhabited by giants'. His general, Corineus, was said to have killed the last Cornish Giant here by hurling him off a cliff, a legend commemorated by the two chalk-cut giant effigies called Gogmagog described by Carew; *'Upon the Haw at Plymouth there is cut into the ground the portraiture of two men, the one bigger, the one lesser, with clubbes in their handes... it is renewed by order of the Townsmen when cause requireth...'.* It looks as though Gogmagog may be a contraction of *Gog and Magog*, the two mythical giants of British legend, and Geoffrey's account of the founding of the country a half-forgotten memory of how Plymouth was the last outpost of England before entering Cornwall, the Land of Initiation dedicated to Gwyn ap Nudd. Could these Giants originally have represented Gwyn and Gwythyr—the two primordial gods of ancient Britain, forever locked in their battle between Light and Dark, which was, according to the legend, presided over by King Arthur?

Adam and Eve in the Garden of Eden. The Tree symbolises the Polar Axis, around which coils the serpent, or the circumpolar constellation of Draco, the Dragon.

18

THE TREE OF KNOWLEDGE

e find the place called 'Paradise'—the actual site of a Cistercian monastery—on the Crown of the Great Bear at Boscastle. Before the Pole Star became centred in the tail of the Little Bear it was located in Draco, the Dragon, hence the Pendragon myth that gave rise to the Age of Arthur, the Bear King. In Christian terms, this axis was symbolised by the Tree of Knowledge of Good and Evil in the Garden of Eden, with the serpent or dragon coiled around it, the very beginnings of life on Earth as recounted in mythic terms in the *Book of Genesis*. It is interesting to note that the Eden Project, which has become such a worldwide symbol of human aspirations to empathise with Nature, is found near the base of this Polar Axis on the land. Paradise at the top; Eden at the base. The continuity of this paradisial theme even into modern times suggests that there are forces within Nature that are still active in the human subconcious, even if they operate on a subliminal level.

What must this landscape have really been like in former times? One of the great attractions of this particular Grail Quest is to find ourselves lost in an otherworldly dream where it is still easy, when exploring these areas, to sense an awe-inspiring wonderment in the woodland, meadows, moors and cliffs of this Cornish Garden of Eden. Certain places appear to be especially potent with spiritual force, where we can step from one world to another. The truth is that paradise is all around us, yet we cannot see it.

The Templars were said by Wolfram von Eschenbach to be the keepers of the Holy Grail, and this landscape Temple (in which there is a Templar Church called *Temple* close to its centre) was protected by certain old Cornish and Norman families who were the guardians of the secret. The Arthurian romances, as we have found, were not mere fairy tales but contained genuine lore from very ancient times, and their central feature is a brotherhood of Knights, Seekers of Truth. Wolfram claimed that the 'Paradise Garden' and 'The Grail' were one and the same; *'the crown of blessing, the fullness of the earth's delight, and its joys I right well may liken to the glories of heaven's height.'* Paradise, in the earliest recorded English meaning, simply means *Heaven*, the Druidic *Gwynvyd*, and so this earthly Temple is merely a reflection of the heavenly one that revolves endlessly in the skies above.

The traditionally deep connections between Tintagel and Glastonbury, one the birthplace of Arthur and the other his place of burial, may well derive from the memory that both places were associated with landscape Temples that employed stellar symbolism. Of the Somerset Zodiac and the Cornish Star-Temple the latter appears to be the oldest, due to its obvious shamanic origins. Since sympathetic magic is probably the oldest form of shamanism, the belief that everything is interconnected and all things in creation share a special invisible link that bonds them together, is the root of all attempts to synchronise the Underworld with its own starry genesis. If the creation of this bestiary is a result of the heavenly powers manifesting on Earth, then it would surely have created a mystical enchantment throughout the land, a paradise on Earth.

In this story of the Earth's dreaming we have encountered many reasons for celebration of this unique landscape. It reminds us that our destiny lies in the stars as well as that it is our role to recognise that we, the Earth and its creatures are all indissolubly linked. That others before us knew of these secrets seems clear, even if the memories have faded over the great distance that separates us from those times. Clues are everywhere. This stage of the current quest can be marked in no more appropriate way than by once more referring to the legends which encode fragments of this knowledge. One, in the medieval *Perceval le Gallois*, is of special interest. In this, King Arthur is said to boast to Sir Gawain of the magnificence of his Round Table, yet Queen Guinevere says she knows of one 'immeasurably finer', although she will not tell where it is. On hearing this, Arthur vows never to sleep two nights in one place until he sees it for himself. He sets out on his quest and ultimately finds himself, where else, but in *Cornwall*. Can this reference be anything other than yet another clue that the original Round Table was located in Cornwall?

As our journey draws ineluctably to its close we find that we have been travelling through a landscape whose central focus has been the Polar Axis, guarded by the Great Bear and, at its base two Lions, symbols of earthly sovereignty. Along our way we have encountered a number of strange and magical beasts, each with its place in the depths of the human psyche. Our guardian Giant emphasises that this menagerie was designed and created for the benefit of humankind, and the final revelation, that as a symbolic representative of ourselves he is endowed with the feminine powers of the Moon as well as the masculine force of the Sun, inevitably reveals a powerful message for our times. Of course it is not quite as clear-cut as we may wish, for the Sun has its female side in the same way that we speak of the Man in the Moon, for both male and female powers have within them the essence of its own opposite, as shown in the Chinese symbol of the Tao.

This message is one we cannot afford to ignore; it is to do with the separation that occurred deep in the Earth's past when man and woman were divided, reconciling us to what has become a war within our own selves. This war has been going on for millennia, and has manifested outwardly in a culture of tyranny and aggression that could even destroy the Earth itself. The medieval alchemist sought to bring these opposites back into balance, creating a synthesis of polarity that restored the paradise of Eden as it was before The Fall. This, it would seem, is an important aspect of the message from the land which we have uncovered; acknowledge the multi-faceted dimensions of our humanity and strive to re-create that harmony between the Sun, Moon, and the heavenly balance of the Cosmos. Our forgetfulness has caused a dis-ease peculiar to humanity; a lack of respect for each other, our fellow creatures and the planet, Mother Earth, on which we live.

Is this why, in Arthurian mythology, the era of the Round Table comes so dramatically but inevitably to an end? Is the battle between King Arthur and Mordred the eternal fight between the twin forces of Light and Dark within human nature, where the balance is disrupted and humanity enters an age of turmoil, with one killed but the other destined one day to return? In later versions of the stories, does the betrayal of Guinevere and Lancelot also symbolise the disruption caused by the shift in the balance that makes the Round Table turn on its central pivot, just as in the story of Adam and Eve? Eve bites the apple and offers it to Adam, and King Arthur is ferried away to Avalon, the Isle of Apples, for this fruit has always symbolised the Sun, the returning Light, whose god in the Greek myths was Apollo, the Apple-God. It was Diodorus Siculus, in the third century BC, who recounted the legend of Hyperborea whose 'inhabitants venerate Apollo more than any other god,' and many scholars believe that Britain was this fabled land, since its description as 'an island opposite the coast of Celtic Gaul' perfectly fits Diodorus' account. The Tree in the Garden of the Hesperides, guarded by a dragon and laden with starry fruit is an enduring myth which, in various forms, pervades every culture. In this particular mythic landscape the area around Slaughterbridge was called, in the Domesday Book, *Guerdevalen*, which could refer to this Tree of Life, the Celtic Avalon, the otherworldly axis which the souls of warriors, like that of Arthur, ascend.

There can be no doubt that the Biblical myth of the Garden of Eden refers to the Polar Axis—the Tree of Life with the dragon or serpent at its crown. This Tree of Knowledge is a metaphor for the changing ages of the Earth during which humanity learns according to the influence of each zodiacal influence. This has been the core of mystical teaching of the ages; that the moving centre of our universe determines the astrological influence in which we live. For each twelve-fold division of the zodiac whose changing influence is brought about by the gradual polar shift represents an opportunity for us to acknowledge an aspect of our own selves that may have previously been largely unexplored. As the authors of *Hamlet's Mill* note, *'Precession took on an overpowering significance. It became the vast impenetrable pattern of fate itself, with one world-age succeeding another, as the invisible pointer of the equinox slid along the signs, each age bringing with it the rise and downfall of astral configurations and rulerships, with their earthly consequences'.*

There are various symbols that capture the essence of this understanding, but the most prominent in this quest has been that of the Tree of Life, whose crown gradually traces a circle in the heavens. It can be seen most significantly on ancient fonts (often with the dragon or serpent and other 'mythological' beasts we now recognise as having symbolic meaning). They are where the newly-incarnated soul that has travelled along the Axis of the Tree is ritually immersed in the spiritual energies of the Earth by being baptised and symbolically 'earthed'. According to the old beliefs we will go back along this Tree when we leave the earthly plane. This is one of the reasons so many churchyards traditionally have ancient trees in them, so that we can be buried in their roots and begin our journey back to the stars. Some of them, many thousands of years old, have been there longer than history can recall, and Yew trees in particular are reminders of the evergreen nature of the human soul. These ideas long predate the Christian era, and, as John Michell observes in *The Centre of the World*; '*The Tree of Life, the Irminsul of Nordic mythology, was the chief symbol of the pagan religion, as is the cross of Christianity.*'

And what of Adam and Eve and the forbidden fruit of Earthly Delights? As we might have now come to expect, the story of the separation of the male and female psyches is echoed in our own paradisial landscape, right at the foot of the Tree presided over by the Great Bear. Arrayed along the banks of the River Fowey are a collection of ancient sites that are indissolubly connected with one of the world's most tragic love stories, that of Tristan and Iseult. And, even more interestingly, this legend appears more than pure fable, for amongst the various versions is one in particular, a poem by the thirteenth century chronicler Béroul, whose story tallies remarkably with the history of these sites. Others set the drama largely at Tintagel. This suggests it must surely be more than another coincidence. It is interesting here to look briefly at this famous tale of how two lovers were ensnared in their own story of passion, power and politics. It may read like a fast-paced action tale that would be ideal for a modern film or novel, yet it was perfectly tailored to suit a medieval audience. It reminds us that a good story with powerful characters set in a real landscape, as long as it has archetypal elements driving it, has a truly timeless appeal.

A LOVE STORY

Long ago, when King Mark ruled Cornwall, Rivalen, the King of Lyonesse came to his aid when he was besieged by his enemies; in return Mark offered Rivalen his sister Blanchefleur. Their wedding took place at Tintagel Minster. When Rivalen's old rival Duke Morgan attacked Lyonesse they set sail to protect their land, and Blanchefleur was heavy with child. As she waited for his return from battle news came that Rivalen been killed and

Blanchefleur, utterly distraught at her loss, brought forth a son who she called Tristan, whose name means 'child of sadness'. But Blanchefleur lost all will to live; her broken heart killed her. Tristan grew up to become a skilled hunter, warrior and bard, whose singing and harp-playing became famous throughout the realm. After many foreign adventures he was seized by Viking pirates and cast adrift in a small boat which happened to come ashore on the north coast of Cornwall. After stumbling across a band of hunters pursuing a magnificent white stag he came to Tintagel, where the King was enchanted by the singing and harp playing of this wandering bard. They became firm friends and Tristan a favourite of the court before Mark eventually found out that he was really his nephew. But his joy at discovering Tristan was his sister's son was tempered by the fact that Tintagel was about to receive an annual visit from the ruthless Morholt, the brother of the Queen of Ireland, who each year demanded 300 young Cornish slaves and 300 pounds of precious metals to ensure the safety of the kingdom.

None of those present at Mark's Court were courageous enough to intervene against Morholt except Tristan, who, as the King's nephew was of noble birth and so entitled to challenge him on equal terms. He swore to rid Cornwall once and for all of the Irish predator. The battle was to take place on the Isle of St Sampson (a now-vanished island that was referred to in a document of 1301 as situated opposite St Winnow Church), but as Morholt moored his boat Tristan let his drift free, saying only one vessel would be needed after the battle, for only one would leave alive. As the Irish lined the bank at St Winnow, with King Mark's men on the opposite bank below Lantyan, the two joined in battle. After a desperate fight that went on for many hours, Tristan landed the fatal blow, and a splinter from his sword lodged in Morholt's head. The dying Irishman was taken back to his own country where he was miraculously healed by the Irish Queen who removed the splinter and treated his wound.

When Tristan returned triumphantly to Tintagel all his wounds were healed except one caused by the treacherous Morholt's poisoned spear, and, in agony with no hope of cure, he set sail in a boat without sail or oars that would carry him where it may. He drifted to the Irish coast where his mournful harp playing and haunting voice were soon heard by the King. Taking pity, he sent his daughter, the fair Iseult, known for her healing powers, to treat him with certain magic herbs which were eventually, along with her tender care, to restore him to full health. As he regained his strength he feared he would be recognised as Morholt's foe, for the name Tristan was hated throughout the land. He had little choice but to return to Cornwall before anyone realised who he was.

Overjoyed to see his nephew again, King Mark resolved to make Tristan his heir, but his Cornish barons disagreed, saying he should marry and beget a son to inherit his kingdom. Seeing two swallows with a shining golden-red hair in their beaks he took it as an omen and vowed only to marry the woman from whose head it had come. It fell to Tristan to find out who she was. He set off and eventually found himself yet again in Ireland, where a ferocious dragon had been laying the country waste, and the Irish King had promised the hand of his daughter Iseult to its vanquisher. Tristan tracked it to its lair, killing it and hacking off its tongue as a trophy, but its venom caused him to fall into a deadly faint.

Found by Iseult who failed to recognise that this was the ailing and ravaged minstrel of her previous encounter, he was again brought back to the castle and nursed back to health, whilst a scheming member of Morholt's Court claimed that it was really he who had killed the dragon. But one day Iseult saw that Tristan's sword had a nick out of it and recognised the shape as the same as that which had almost killed Morholt. She rushed at him in a fit of anger, but then realised that if he died she would have to marry the lying steward who had claimed the death of the dragon for himself. Tristan produced the dragon's tongue as evidence and, because of the King's promise, was offered Iseult's hand in marriage. However, knowing that the golden hair had come from her head, Tristan claimed her on King Mark's behalf as he had agreed. This, it seemed, was a great opportunity to make peace between the Irish and the Cornish for good. But the Irish Queen, who did not want her daughter to marry an unknown man and enter into a loveless union, prepared a love potion which, when drunk by Mark on their wedding night, would create an irresistible passion between them.

The voyage back to Cornwall in an open boat was hot and humid, and made Tristan thirsty. He asked for wine. Then Iseult's maid accidentally poured the potion into the goblet and it had immediate effect; the two gazed into each other's eyes and quickly became besotted. Before dawn came they had consummated their love. By the time they landed at Port Hern, the rocky landing place on Tintagel Island where King Mark was holding his summer court, there was no going back. On the King's wedding night Iseult was forced to arrange for her virgin maid to occupy his bed instead of her in case the King should find out the truth. The scheme worked well. They made love and then Iseult took her place by Mark's side. He fell madly in love, and was deeply grateful for Tristan bringing her.

Mark's court then moved to Lancien or Lantyan opposite St Winnow where he had a castle overlooking the River Fowey. For Tristan and Iseult it was to be a summer of love, of secret assignations whilst the King was hunting. When his courtiers became suspicious they told Mark and he discovered them together, flying into a fury and banishing Tristan to a nearby town. But they could not stay apart. The magic of the potion was too strong. Tristan would send messages to Iseult by breaking off twigs from an apple tree and floating them downstream to where she could see them from her window. They met in the orchard beneath the sun-dappled apple trees.

Their rendezvous was not to remain a secret, though. A dwarf called Frocin from Mark's court had once been the King's favourite and was jealous of Tristan. He betrayed their love-bower, and one night the King hid in the branches of a tall pine tree whose trunk was exceptionally straight and at whose base rose a spring forming a pool of crystal water. As the lovers approached they both saw the reflection of the King and pretended they were meeting to arrange Tristan's return to court. Such was their skill in feigning innocence that Mark believed utterly in their loyalty to him, and soon Tristan was sleeping on the floor of the King's chamber again as a trusted retainer.

But the lovers became reckless, even using the King's bed when he was hunting. The dwarf, determined to expose them to the King's wrath had, however, left flour on the floor between the beds to prove their betrayal, but the athletic Tristan leapt from one to the other without leaving any footprints as the dwarf had hoped. Nevertheless a trail of drops of blood from an old hunting wound stained the floor as he hurried back to his own bed on the King's return. This time Mark was overcome with great anger and, his love turned to hatred, condemned them both to death. Tristan was to be burnt on a great pyre on top of a nearby hill, and en route he and Mark's soldiers came to a hermit's chapel where a beacon warned seafarers of dangerous rocks. Tristan persuaded his captors to grant him time to confess his sins and pray for his soul. Inside, he leapt from a small window above the altar, escaping down the steep cliff and onto the beach.

Iseult too was condemned to be burnt, but a friend, Dinas of Dinan, managed to persuade the King to relent. Instead, to humiliate her, Iseult was handed over to a band of lepers. As they struggled through a marsh Tristan leapt from the undergrowth and grabbed her and they escaped to live as fugitives in the wild forest of Moresk. Life was full of hardships in the wildwood, but Tristan's skill as a hunter made sure they did not starve. Coming one day to a hermitage built onto a rocky crag in the middle of a moor, they learnt from the hermit, Ogrin, that Mark had offered a large reward for Tristan's head. But when he heard of the love potion he took pity on them and allowed them shelter before returning to their nomadic lifestyle. Spotted by a passing forester they were soon reported to the King at Lantyan, who accompanied the woodsman to their retreat. The lovers were asleep, with Tristan's sword between them. The King, overcome with emotion and touched by Iseult's beauty, exchanged rings with her and replaced Tristan's sword with his own. As Iseult dreamed of being in a great wood with two fighting lions he shielded her face from the strong sunlight by placing one of his riding gloves over a gap in the canopy of the trees.

A few days later the power of the potion expired, and the lovers were overwhelmed by feelings of guilt and treachery. They asked Ogrin to write to the King for forgiveness, and explain that Tristan had no choice but to rescue Iseult from the lepers. Tristan himself took the letter to Lantyan whereupon Mark agreed to Iseult's return in three days time, but that Tristan should leave Cornwall forever.

Meanwhile, Ogrin had left his hermitage and gone to St Michael's Mount where he bought a rare silk dress of royal purple for Iseult to wear on her reunion with Mark. As Tristan handed her over to the King he was distraught and rode away to the coast. The next day Iseult led a great procession to the church of St Sampson overlooking the river, where she presented her rich jewelled robe to the church, thereafter to be brought out every saint's feast day. This was followed by a great celebration.

But Tristan had not kept his bargain; he concealed himself in a forester's house and awaited news. It was just as well, for the barons at Mark's Court demanded that Iseult should undergo a public trial by ordeal to clear herself of all guilt. She agreed as long as it was held at Blancheland, at the King's hunting grounds on the high moor, and that King Arthur and his knights, including Gawain and Sir Kay were present as witnesses.

She sent a secret message to Tristan that he should again disguise himself as a leper and lie in wait. First King Arthur passed by, and then Mark. Three of the barons asked the way, and were directed towards the marsh where they sank in the quagmire. When Iseult arrived on her steed, dressed in fine robes and jewels, she dismounted and demanded that the grimy Tristan carry her across the muddy ford at Mal Pas, much to the amazement of onlookers.

The following day the trial began, with King Arthur and Mark presiding before a fine silk cloth on which lay all the holy relics from chapels and churches throughout Cornwall. Iseult swore a solemn oath, and said that no man had ever come between her thighs other than her husband King Mark—except, that was, the leper who had carried her across the ford.

Everyone was impressed by the Queen's oath, and, with the matter settled to the satisfaction of all present, Arthur left and Mark and Iseult returned to Lantyan. But the lovers were still to meet in secret, and, discovered yet again by their enemies at court, Tristan killed one of them by piercing the man's eye with an arrow. Realising the danger of his predicament, he knew he had to finally leave Cornwall, and so left for Wales, where he joined the Duke's court. Here, in return for killing a giant he was given a faery dog, around whose neck hung a magic bell that soothed his misery at being apart from Iseult. Thinking that it might do the same for her, he gave the faery dog to a Welsh harper who took it to Tintagel where it became the Queen's favourite, removing all anguish from her heart. But in the end, she preferred to suffer the loss of her love and threw the magic bell from the cliffs at Tintagel.

Meanwhile Tristan had sailed to Brittany for refuge. The Breton legends say he lived for some years at Carhaix, lonely and despondent, until he met a princess, mysteriously also called Iseult. This was Iseult of the White Hands; they married, but because of his love for the Cornish Iseult it was never consummated. After many battles and adventures he returned with a serious wound, and in despair sent his green jasper ring to Cornwall with a message for his true love to come and heal him as she had before. He ordered that if, when the ship returned, it had Iseult on board then it was to carry a white sail; if not, then it was to be black.

On hearing of Tristan's plight, Iseult immediately left Lantyan to sail for Brittany. At this, Iseult of the White Hands became uncontrollably jealous and, as the ship approached, she told Tristan it carried a black sail. Utterly distraught, Tristan lost all will to live and succumbed to the fatal wound.

As Iseult entered the town the bells were tolling Tristan's passing. When she heard he was dead her heart broke and she lay beside him, dying in his cold arms. Soon King Mark arrived seeking his wife, and finally heard of the love potion and understood everything that had taken place. With great spirit of generosity he forgave the two people he had most loved in the world, and their bodies were carried back to Cornwall where they were buried side by side. From their graves a hazel tree and a golden honeysuckle miraculously grew, which were cut down three times but grew back stronger than before. Eventually they were left to flourish naturally, entwining their leaves and flowers as a symbol of Tristan and Iseult's unquenchable love.

We may recognise many archetypal themes running through this tragic love story, but equally we may wonder why it takes place in this part of Cornwall? Knowing what we do from our study of the mythic landscape, how appropriate it appears that this tale should be so firmly anchored on the Polar Axis or Tree of Life. This Tree is implied by the repeated references to Tintagel, (in fact some versions place nearly all the action there), the appearance of King Arthur and the sites mentioned by name between Fowey and Lostwithiel, especially St Winnow, St Sampson's (where Mark and Iseult regularly worshipped) and Lantyan near Castle Dore. Kilmarth, nearby, is said to mean 'Mark's Grove', Ogrin's hermitage is said to have been Roche Rock near St Austell and Lancien or Lantyan was, as late as the fourteenth century, the manor house of a large estate stretching from St Germans to Lizard Point, almost certainly a vestige of the domain of a Cornish King. We have seen before how this axis was marked by large standing stones, like the elaborately carved Minster Cross or the more megalithic one at Slaughterbridge. Here at Castle Dore once stood another such marker, even better known, called the Tristan Stone.

It originally stood in a small enclosure next to the earthworks and has been moved many times, but is shown on a map of 1785 lying in a nearby field. Now it stands at the side of the road to Fowey a few miles away at Four Turnings, having been moved there when the roads were widened for modern traffic. It is inscribed DRUSTANUS HIC IACIT CUNOMORI FILIUS (Here lies Tristan, son of Cunomorus). As Joy Wilson, in *Cornwall, Land of Legend*, comments, this inscription can still be discerned when the afternoon sunlight strikes the stone. But the stone was once considerably taller, for weathering has caused a fragment to break off. When Leland saw it he described a third vertical line of lettering which read CUM DOMINA CLUSILLA (with the Lady Clusilla). Joy Wilson points out *'Now Clusilla is an Irish name and could be transposed into the rare Cornish name of Eselt. Both have the meaning of golden meadow flower and could refer to the golden-haired princess Iseult of Béroul's story...'*

Also to be seen on the reverse of the stone is a Tau cross carved in relief. This may be significant; Druidic lore regarded the T-shaped cross as a perennial symbol of eternity and sacred trees were cut into this shape, a fore-runner of the Christian cross. Did it once signify that it stood on the axis of the Tree of Life?

King Mark, or Cunomorus (meaning 'horse') is a well-documented High King of Dumnonia, and the Breton monk St Pol de Léon writes of him as a powerful king of the sixth century who, like Arthur, presided over a time of peace and prosperity, ruling a kingdom that spoke four different languages. Such historical veracity seems to indicate a blending of mythological and actual events, for it is known that during this period Irish incursions, and maybe even the taking of Cornish youths and maidens as mentioned in the story, were a feature of Dark-Age life.

Other, more fanciful references may recall very different memories. What of Iseult's dream of two lions in the wildwood, or Tristan's faery dog with a magic bell around its neck? The Great Dog of St Mawgan—a creature of the faery realms if ever there was one—is notable for the round shape drawn in the landscape that hangs below his neck like a medallion or perhaps, *a bell*. Here is a very curious correspondence indeed between the story (drawn from *The Romance of Tristan and Iseult* by J. Bédier and Hilaire Belloc) and an otherwise inexplicable feature of one of the giant effigies. And, according to the tale, this faery dog, which has the power to allow humans to transcend the emotions of loss and sadness, travels from Wales to North Cornwall to become the favourite animal of the Queen.

As ever with such legends, there are inner and outer meanings, depending on whether they are interpreted as fairy stories or initiatory tales of the human condition. These different levels of meaning create a complex web of mythology, fact and fiction. Yet underneath it all is a tale of man and woman separated, and of how their estrangement results in misunderstandings, and, ultimately, death. The King that is betrayed is, like so many other legends including that of the Arthurian mythos, wounded in his heart (the wounded Fisher King in the *Parzival* story is the cause of the wasteland, which may refer to this separation). But the cause of Tristan and Iseult's illicit passion is a result of a magic potion, similar to the apple of the Genesis story. In the Biblical myth, it causes knowledge of their separateness and a loss of innocence.

In terms of our own discoveries, this archetypal love story that appears to blend historical fact with a more ancient mythology has a strong resonance with Gywn ap Nudd, the Giant in the land, who seems to come from an earlier time before the male and female elements of the psyche were alienated from one another. The proximity of the Tristan and Iseult legend to our Giant is suggestive of a primal memory when human beings were more balanced in this respect, with the legend recalling in mythic terms a separation that occurred in remote times. And when we look at Gwyn's relationship to other ancient sites this seems to emphasise that once the power of the Divine Feminine was equal to that of its opposite.

The female power is represented by the Moon Axis, where, every 18.6 years the Major Standstill Moonrise would be seen to occur directly over Stowes Hill to the north-east, aligning with the avenue that now leads to the Obelisk, right in the centre of the Giant's head. This alignment is more than simply a local affair, though, for if extended south-westwards it passes through Tywardreath. Although only a church stands in the village today it was once the site of an influential monastery founded by the Cardinham family, whose buildings stretched right to the water's edge. In fact Leland reported that before the monastery was dissolved, it contained the actual tomb of Robert de Cardinham himself.

Continuing towards the position of the Major Standstill Moonrise, this axis passes through St Winnow Church (and maybe the site of the disappeared Isle of St Sampson where Tristan fought Morholt as if it were a mythic battle between the sensitive, music-loving bardic nature and the brutal, domineering warrior psyche) through the Obelisk, over Stowes Hill, through Trecarrell, the site of the chapel to Mary Magdalene, the Holy Well at Trefrize, and Lawhitton Church, the original Celtic foundation of the Launceston area, the ancient capital of Cornwall. This axis is consequently very much a Major one, passing through a host of significant sites connected with the female power of the Moon, virtually from the south coast to the present border at the River Tamar.

The male power is epitomised by the countrywide axis known as the St Michael Line, which is determined by the position of the rising Sun at Beltane or Mayday, on which both Glastonbury and Avebury are situated. This corridor of solar power passes through the top of our Giant's Head, and merges with the Moon Axis deep within his brain. The fact that Gwyn is associated with Glastonbury suggests that this alignment originally may have not been a St Michael Line. Although many sites along it are dedicated to the Christian Archangel of Light, this only occurred when the land was Christianised. Before that, other gods ruled these places. What their names were we cannot tell, except in the case of Glastonbury Tor, whose legend recalls that it was Gywn ap Nudd. It seems highly likely that Gwyn thus preceded St Michael as the primal guardian of the land, and that in Cornwall in particular he was regarded as the patron deity who was later supplanted by his Christian equivalent, in the guise of Archangel Michael.

The fact that these two major axes—one associated with the Sun and the other the Moon, meet one another in the Giant's head indicates that he is a god who has assimilated both cosmic powers within his own being. The solar and lunar energy thus creates a 'sacred marriage', taking place within. Gwyn becomes whole and therefore healed.

Yet according to the legend Gwyn has to do battle every Beltane with his opposite force Gwythyr, in order to try and win the hand of Creuddylad, the Goddess of the Land. Thus the forces of Sun and Moon are brought into balance on Earth, with a celestial marriage between the twin polarities in the world of duality. It is no accident that the Sun and Moon axes cross the ritual centre of Stowes Hill, for this dome-shaped upthrust was once the geomantic centre of the whole area. The Winter Solstice axis from Tintagel also runs across its plateau, and links the Arthurian tradition with the annual battle between Gwyn and Gwythyr. And who presides over this yearly contest that brings fertility back to the land? None other than King Arthur, the Bear King who eternally watches the Round Table guarding the Polar Tree of Life.

Stowes Hill may well have represented, many thousands of years ago, a true cosmic centre of the cycles of continuous creation, re-enacted every Winter Solstice, Mayday, Major Standstill Moonrise and other crucial times of the year. From its perfectly-angled stone on the edge of the plateau, observers would also at the time of the Winter Solstice have seen the constellation of the Great Bear being born from the land beyond Bearah Tor, just as at Tintagel, with the Seven Stars of the Bear as the motive force that keeps the whole system turning. It may thus have symbolised the sacred mountain, the hub around which the rhythms of life revolved, the bond between Heaven and Earth. As the esoteric writer Gerald Massey observed of such places 'The Mount of the Seven Stars... represented the birthplace of the initial motion and the beginning of time'.

19

ARTHUR'S DESCENT INTO THE OTHERWORLD

'It is thus clear enough that the whole Grail myth is founded in the central idea of the cauldron of inspiration of Annwn, the mystical plane, that this is, indeed, the hub from which all the spokes of the wheel radiate'

The Mysteries of Britain
Lewis Spence

The mysterious poem known as *The Spoils of Annwn* is the oldest account we have of Arthur as the leader of a group of warriors, or knights, engaged in an attempt to seek the cauldron, or Grail, in the otherworldly plane of Annwn. Here he is portrayed as the god of a mystical cult who must periodically make a journey through the Underworld. According to legend he was born at Tintagel, probably, as we have seen, on the Winter Solstice, when the Great Bear is seen rising above the Island just before the Sun is reborn. Druidical lore named this time of year *Arthan* (Arthur's Season), when he was engaged, like Gwyn, in fighting the powers of darkness. The Winter Solstice axis running from Tintagel across Stowes Hill to Plymouth Hoe marks this time and thus links the mythology of Arthur's birth with the land wherein he is said to be 'sleeping' and its eternal cycles of Light and Dark. Arthur, it appears, has absorbed many characteristics of his predecessors, and is in many ways a later version of Gwyn, for they are both gods who lead a Wild Hunt and are the spiritual protectors of Britain. They are also connected with St Michael, the Archangel who leads the heavenly warriors, as all three, at one time or another, have been the presiding deities of the Westcountry, and especially Cornwall.

Throughout the mystical traditions of both Western and Eastern religion and philosophy a central tenet has been for the initiate to enter the Underworld—often quite literally—by leaving the ordinary world behind to undergo a period within some dark place. Three days, as in the case of Jesus Christ, was common in the classical tradition, when the candidate for spiritual enlightenment withdrew and focussed the attention within, to emerge, or be resurrected, with new-found god-like powers of perception.

This is why in every land the native god or goddess is always remembered as having descended into the Otherworld in order to be regenerated. Celtic heroes entered Annwn in order to learn the secret mystery of death as part of their initiation into manhood and immortality. *The Spoils of Annwn* is recounted by the bard Taliesin, who, along with Merlin, represents the last vestiges of a very ancient Celtic tradition, according to Caitlin and John Matthews in *King Arthur's Raid on the Underworld*. As an initiate of the magic cauldron himself and keeper of the old knowledge *'His authoritative voice speaks of leaves in the wind: core traditions about the role of the underworld prisoner, the cosmography of the underworld itself and descent of heroes to fetch forth the hallowed treasure that can change all things'*.

In mythic terms this regeneration takes place on a deep level and was believed to extend beyond the consciousness of the individual. When performed at certain times of the year such a ritual was thought to have far-reaching effects, even extending to creating a regeneration within Nature itself. This is the esoteric truth behind the Easter miracle, where the god dies and three days later is resurrected, and with him the spirit within the natural world. In the Grail Tradition the Dove flies down from Heaven on Good Friday bringing Divine Power, and three days later a new cycle of life begins on Easter Monday, or *Moon-day*. The association of Easter with hares, rabbits and eggs is a reminder that in former ages this was a time when the feminine power of the Earth Goddess (symbolised by the Dove, which was also the name of female priestesses in the classical world) were at their highest, which probably explains why the initiate was required to enter a cave, crypt or other opening within Mother Earth's body to be 'reborn'. The concentration of energy inside a subterranean chamber has always been thought to enhance spiritual vision, hence the fact that many ancient temples or mystery centres had a suitably cave-like structure at their core. The Dolmens and megalithic chambers of prehistory were undoubtedly used for such purposes, being artificially-constructed caves located at powerful geomantic spots.

In the Christian tradition, which absorbed so much of its lore from those that went before, St Michael is frequently depicted holding the keys to the Underworld regions and many of the great cave sanctuaries of the ancient world are dedicated to him, like that at Monte Gargano in Italy, one of the most famous pilgrimage centres of antiquity. Hence St Michael became the Archangel of Initiation into the Mysteries. Christianity, though, often found it expedient to employ its favourite tool, *fear*, in its interpretation of these places. Many were no longer to be the entrances to the Underworld but to the infernal regions of Hell, to which sinners might be consigned for all eternity. This control over the earlier ways of achieving mystical consciousness gave the Church great power, yet it kept a thread of continuity in aligning St Michael with the Underworld traditions of earlier times.

Another way of entering the Underworld was by way of a maze or labyrinth, a psychological tool or mandala which had the power to take the conscious mind deep within. This pattern represents the inner pathways of earthly existence, its seven coils echoing the seven veils of the subtle planes of manifestation. The esoteric scholar Gerald Massey wrote that *'the first form of the mystical seven was seen to be figured in heaven, by the seven large stars of the Great Bear, the constellation assigned by the Egyptians to the Mother of Time and the seven elemental powers'*. The core of the design is the still centre around which these worlds revolve. Following the spiral path towards its centre leads to a symbolic death, and the journey outwards to a new life. This dance of life and renewal is associated in the classical tradition with Ariadne, whose thread allows the initiate to follow the path there and back safely, having faced and conquered the beast within.

In performing this ritual which was once widespread throughout the world the candidates were aligning themselves with the spiralling motion of the cosmos itself. Ariadne is the Arianrhod of the native British mythology, whose spiral castle continuously revolves around the Pole of the heavens. As we have seen, the seven coils are almost certainly a reference to the Seven Stars of the Great Bear, the guardians of the sacred centre. Using a maze or labyrinth is thus a true ritual, for it harmonises the terrestrial plane with the heavenly, consciously manifesting a cosmic pattern throughout earthly existence. To enter a labyrinth in full consciousness is to go deep within one's own being, to bring together the two hemispheres of the human brain and to return to the Pole which represents eternal life. The spiral paths of the revolving universe are thus brought down to Earth, and the Macrocosm becomes the Microcosm, the soul having undergone the same journey to and from the Pole that was believed to occur at death. The old British name for a labyrinth was a *Troy Town* (Welsh *Caerdroia*), and rustic turf mazes were once common in towns and villages. In modern Welsh *troi* still means *to revolve* as well as *to plough*—a reference to the Great Bear during a time when Hunters turned into Farmers.

The two labyrinth carvings at Tintagel that have proved so perplexing to historians appear in this light to be meaningfully placed to indicate the spiral pathways of the circumpolar constellations, located at the head of the Great Bear. By contemplating them and their meaning it is possible to understand their message—that this landscape is a reflection of the movements of the heavens, with the Polar Axis guarded by the Seven Stars of the Bear.

As we have discovered, this axis is merely part of a greater pattern that includes Lundy Island, the site of the Preseli bluestones and the location of Stonehenge. Lundy, which is often clearly visible from Tintagel and yet can also vanish as if it has disappeared into another dimension, is, like a ghost island, a place that must have appeared to the old mythmakers as the ultimate Otherworldly realm, a sacred isle of the dead situated perfectly on the axis that symbolises the return of the soul to its source. Although once briefly owned by the Knights Templar its true importance has been shrouded by the mists that so often shield it from sight, and yet from what we already know we can see it must have been of great mythic significance.

As this chapter was being prepared an article appeared in the archaeological magazine *Time and Mind* that concerned itself with exactly this line of investigation. Entitled *'There was a Holy Race of Men on Lundy': A Speculative Literature Search for the Otherworld Island* it was written by Robert Farrah who had been a lighthouse keeper on the Island for some five years up until 1992, perhaps the closest one can get these days to experiencing the spiritual rapport of the early hermits with elemental Nature. During his time he had become fascinated by hitherto unexplored aspects of Lundy and had published another paper, *The Megalithic Astronomy of Lundy*. This was researched with the help of Professor Gerald Hawkins, who had written the seminal work *Stonehenge Decoded* in which he convincingly showed that our 'national temple' was a sophisticated astronomical computer incorporating, amongst other things, solar and lunar movements.

Farrah's article explored the ancient names associated with Lundy, which seem to describe traditions belonging to the 'magical realm of the Otherworld'. In it he refers to the archaic traditions of the Celtic world which regarded islands as particularly sacred places, citing classical authors such as Plutarch (84 AD), who heard from Demetrios of Tarsus how he had visited Britain and concluded that 'many of the islands off Britain were inhabited and widely scattered, some of them being named after deities and demigods'. Lundy especially, he noted, was always described with 'extraordinary supernatural and mysterious associations'. The oldest name for this semi-fabulous Island, according to some authorities, was *Herculea*, and it is certainly the case that the second-century geographer and astronomer Ptolemy called Hartland Point, eleven miles away on the Devon coast, *Heraclis* on his famous map. This may be another clue to Lundy's past as an island associated with heroic gods such as Hercules during a time when classical traditions were the fashion.

The Arthurian scholar Geoffrey Ashe had already written that in the old British mythology 'The most important hill is the Tor at Glastonbury, the most important island is Lundy' thus emphasising a possible link between the two places and Glastonbury's most ancient deity Gwyn ap Nudd. In *Archaeology of Lundy — Sacred Island of Annwn*, Sharon Higgins notes that *'In mythology, islands feature as sacred places, or as entrances to the 'otherworld'. Lundy, in particular, holds an importance to the Welsh as Annwn, the realm of Gwyn ap Nudd and the place where departed souls go.'* No wonder, we may think, that one of the folk names for Lundy in Welsh was 'the fortress of the faeries'.

In *The Spoils of Annwn* Arthur and his followers sail in the ship Prydwen to seek a magic cauldron, but the perilous journey claims many of them and few return. In another poem, *The Thirteen Treasures of Britain*, those that do succeed in their quest return to the world with a collection of magical objects which include a wondrous drinking vessel called the *Horn of Bran*, a *Giant's Cauldron* which distinguishes the brave from the cowardly, and *The Mantle of Arthur in Cornwall*, a cloak of invisibility whereby the wearer could observe everything although he himself could never be seen. Since these old Welsh (British) poems are concerned with the Otherworldly realms, Lundy certainly seems to be one of the main contenders for the entrance into Annwn, partly because of its isolation and the fact that it can be seen from both Wales and Cornwall (and regularly disappears), but mainly, as we know from our researches, because it lies on the great main Polar Axis along which the souls of the dead were believed to travel. It is like a more remote version of Tintagel, unassailable and aloof, supernaturally protected by its soaring cliffs. As one historian put it 'Here is no entrance except for friends'.

Where were the souls returning to? To Annwn, also known as *Caer Sidi*, the Castle of the Sidhe or Faery Folk. Since Gwyn is the 'Lord of the Faeries' this realm, like Caer Arianrhod, the revolving castle of his mythical mother, appears to specifically refer to the Polar Axis and the prominent constellations that circle it. In *The White Goddess* Robert Graves also suggests that Lundy may have represented Caer Sidi as one of the 'island Elysiums'.

The Welsh Triads speak of the 'Three Exalted Prisoners of the Island of Britain', or Llyr, Mabon and Gwair. These fragmented records, however garbled, still appear to contain clues that the Island represented the heavenly axis, for as Farrah points out, Gwair was said to have been imprisoned in *Ynys Weir*, another old name for Lundy. Was the Island believed to be the abode of ancestral spirits and the old gods of ancient Britain? Was it here that the souls of the mighty heroes of the Celtic world were thought to reside? Are the remains of an early Christian community on the Island evidence of its one-time crucial significance in the old British tradition?

Some time after the discovery of the Great Bear of Tintagel but before I came to recognise its real significance, both Robin and myself had visited Lundy in 2002 in the company of his brother Richard, son Matthew (with classical guitar), Trish, and a motley collection of assorted megalithomaniacs and metrologists which included Ray Bowler, John Neal and John Michell. The circumstances of this visit were remarkable enough to recount, for at the time Robin Heath and John Michell were researching *The Measure of Albion*, and both were convinced that while Lundy was positioned on the Polar Axis and formed a right angle to the East-West axis to Stonehenge, they needed to demonstrate this through fieldwork. Robin thought it would be amusing as well as instructive to gather a group together to take part in the necessary measurements (he is always looking for volunteers to carry his heavy theodolite), and see if the precise point was marked in any way on the ground. After a call to the Tourist Office it appeared such a visit would be impossible. The Island was fully booked for the next year, such was its popularity.

Then, literally within minutes of the gloomy news, the phone rang. It was the Tourist Office again, saying they had at that very moment just received a cancellation for nine people—exactly the number of the group! It was as if the gods spoke, and their will was to be done. Accordingly, within a few weeks we all boarded the *MS Oldenburg* along with the necessary assorted paraphernalia for a sort of Druids' outing. Landing on Lundy after a boisterous sea crossing we all headed immediately up the mile-long steep incline to *The Marisco Tavern* for a celebratory libation to thank the old gods for making it all possible.

Most of us stayed in the Old Lighthouse, and we noticed that this modern place of Light had been built almost next to the original church of St Helen's on Beacon Hill, the highest point of the Island, whose ruins were still in evidence in the small walled graveyard. Extraordinarily, this ancient church had been robbed of much of its stone by an Ordnance Survey team in 1804 who used it to build a cairn, but was believed to be of great antiquity. Robin had already found that one of the old names for Lundy was *Ynys Elen*, meaning *Island of the Elbow*, or right angle, and that St Helen or Elen was connected in the old British legends with long straight roads and lines in the landscape. One morning I rose early and spent some time amongst the leaning stones, lost in a dream. Set against the rough wall of the churchyard were two prominent inscribed standing stones, one with the name *igerni* cut into it picked out by the slanting sunlight, thought by some to represent *Vortegerni* or *Vortigern*. Although this seems to have been a fairly common name during the Dark Ages, such a stone with the name of a king associated with the legend of Merlin seemed intriguing, to say the least.

The site of the old church struck me as powerfully evocative, with the sort of atmosphere that draws the imagination back to a remote era where legends were first formed in the crucible of time. The church-yard itself had developed on the site of a Celtic *lan* or raised curved mound which, quite astonishingly for its small area, harbours the remains of at least a hundred early cist graves. During 1969, Professor Charles Thomas along with a group of university students spent five weeks excavating part of the southern section, having noticed an alignment of upright gran-ite slabs protruding through the surface. These were unusually aligned North-South.

When they were exposed it was found that several of these stones were very large and formed part of a rectangular structure that showed signs of earlier occupation from the Romano-British period. Within this a cist grave (aligned East-West) had been built and the whole structure filled with loose stone. This created what Professor Thomas called a 'spe-cial grave' because of its elaborate nature, which had later been broken open and its contents removed. Nevertheless, further graves had been placed as close as possible to the original, a common practice associated with the burial place of a particularly saintly character.

Charles Thomas draws some very interesting conclusions from his exploration of Lundy. In *And Shall These Mute Stones Speak* he puts forward the idea that this saintly character was none other than... *St Nectan*. He suggests that the remains were exhumed from the Island and transported to Hartland on the mainland during a time when saintly relics were especially venerated, a process known as *translatio*. They may have rested for many centuries here until the dissolution, for Hartland's church at Stoke is known to have been a large monastic site dedicated to St Nectan and re-founded in the eleventh century by Gytha, the mother of Harold Godwinson who fought William at Hastings. It was at nearby Hartland Abbey that a *Life of St Nectan* was composed probably during the early thirteenth century, combining old stories of the saint with more recent accounts of miracles attributed to him.

Having studied old manuscripts which, like The Mabinogion were written down in early medieval times but derive from the Dark Ages, Thomas makes an even more interesting point, theorising that Lundy was the *Ynys Brychan* mentioned in these old accounts and that Brychan was an earlier name of St Nectan who was buried in the old churchyard. Brychan was originally the King of Brecon, a very famous character in Welsh and Cornish tradition, having produced at least 24 sons and daughters who all became early saints, travelling widely and leaving behind their names in dozens of locations throughout the Celtic lands.

Now it might seem that 24 progeny is stretching the imagination a bit too far, even for such a mighty king as Brychan. As we are dealing here with legendary history might we conclude that the illustrious Brychan could have been some form of god-king whose 'sons and daughters' were in fact followers of the old original religion of the British Isles; Druid-like savants who were absorbed into the early Celtic Christian Church? If so, then Charles Thomas' idea may not be far from the truth. Of course we may wonder why, if this theory is correct, did Brychan take the name Nectan later in his life when he moved to Lundy? Could it have been an allusion to the fact that *St Nectan, Nathan, Neath* or *Nudd* was directly connected with the Polar Axis and the concept of Caer Sidi? Was Brychan, one of the leading figures of Celtic Christianity, aware of some immemorial tradition in which the North-South axis was central to the beliefs of the time, interred in a stone structure deliberately aligned with it? Certainly, with the removal of his relics to the mainland the Cult of St Nectan flourished, leaving St Nectan's Kieve at Tintagel and St Nectan's Chapel near St Winnow, both linked to the Polar Axis of the Great Bear, as testimony to the continuing influence of the old British God.

The Druid's outing, a cross between *Nine go mad on Lundy* and *The Last of the Summer Wine*, was to produce further revelations, especially concerning the exact location of the central point of the Island marking the corner of the right angle to Stonehenge. After many long discussions in the Marisco Tavern with rulers, maps, calculators and the inspirational effects of copious quantities of *Lundy Light* beer, it was time to explore the centre of the Island on foot. On a sunny morning we set off following the central North-South axis that 'coincidentally' runs right along the Island's length. Where was the exact centre? No-one could know until we found it and measured its co-ordinates. As we looked around for some distinctive feature that may harbour a clue, we passed a reedy pool of water and then heard a loud exclamation. It was John Michell, who, in his old Etonian manner, exclaimed with the practised air of a lifelong antiquarian 'Look what we have here'.

We rushed over to the spot where he was stooping and saw he had found something quite extraordinary. It was an old tin box, concealed under a stone. Inside its rusted interior was a rubber stamp together with a book in which were written a collection of names. It was a sort of letterbox with its visitors' book and a stamp which proclaimed that here was the officially-recognised *Centre of the Island*. We laughed, acknowledging the wicked wit of the gods and of course added our own signatures to the book before ambling off, chortling as we went, to continue our quest to discover the true geometric centre of Lundy. Not far away we discovered a raised mound of earth which exactly fulfilled all the criteria — the instigators of the *Centre of the Island Club* had very nearly got it right! The theodolite was set up and readings taken which were to confirm that this place, which we called *The Tump*, marked the intersection of the Polar Axis and the Stonehenge alignment. It looked as if it had once been considerably larger before being worn away by perhaps thousands of years of wind and weather, and gave the impression that it may originally have been an artificially-constructed mound.

The result of these adventures on Lundy convinced both John and Robin that the geometry of these alignments was explicitly marked on the land. The implications were clear; the geometric perfection of these axes meant that at some time in the remote past an entire system of earthly and heavenly correspondences had been laid out across this part of Britain. This system locked together the concept of a central axis with the chosen location of Stonehenge. It also, as I found when later investigating the Great Bear of Tintagel, led directly to the bestiary of animals reflecting various constellations hidden in the Cornish landscape.

Was all this the work of an elite group of astronomer-priests whose skills greatly transcended mere star-gazing? Were these people the followers of a religion rooted in the natural world who knew that earthly life should be in perfect harmony with the movements of the heavenly bodies? Were they acolytes of the god that lies sleeping in the land, Gwyn, and his father the Star-Lord Nudd?

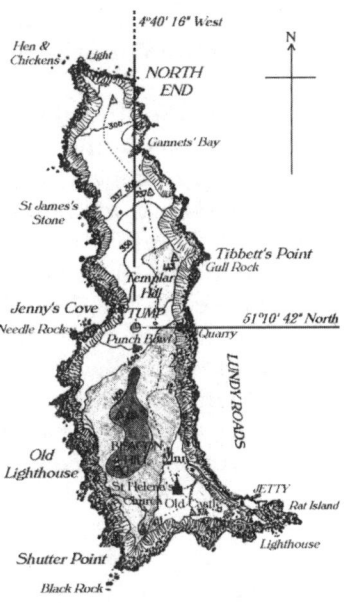

Lundy Island, which is aligned on the North-South Polar Axis. Directly due East of 'The Tump' is Stonehenge.

Giants in the Earth

The recorded history of Lundy is as curious as its ancient history is obscure. Because of its situation, isolated in the Severn Sea, it has for centuries been infested with pirates, privateers and all manner of those seeking sanctuary from the mainland. Even today it is one of the few places—a sort of private kingdom—free from all the petty regulations and official restrictions that make modern life so complicated. The Marisco Tavern has never been governed by licensing laws, and when the generator is switched off at midnight, there is no electricity to disturb the velvet tranquillity of the night skies. When the Island was auctioned at the turn of the nineteenth century (fetching the sum of £700) it was described as having *'never paid tax or tithe, acknowledged neither king or parliament, nor law civil or ecclesiastical, and that its proprietor was Pope and Emperor at once in his scanty domain'*. It was certainly a place apart from the ordinary world. Even when the Normans came it remained part of West Wales, and received no mention in the Domesday Book of 1086.

The oldest remains are the chapel of St Helen's and its ancient oratory, built on the site where St Nectan is thought to have been buried, and from which, on a clear day, it is possible to see deep into both Cornwall and Wales. In the distance, the Cornish Tors of Bodmin Moor are visible, and to the North the Preseli mountains. The fact that the Island itself is aligned North-South means it is perfectly suited to act as a sighting point to establish a Polar Axis—this would take no great expertise

since fires lit on the Preselis and in Cornwall could be aligned with the
minimum of organisation.

For instance, standing on the Cornish cliffs at the head of the Great
Bear one would be able to see a fire at Beacon Point on Lundy (or The
Tump at the centre of the Island) and, beyond it, perhaps another on Caldey Island, also on the axis, and, twinkling in the far distance, yet another
at the Preseli bluestone site. In our mind's eye perhaps we can imagine a
great line of fires stretching away North and South, perhaps flickering on
the sea in the distance, and leading deep into Wales and Cornwall. There
must surely have been a powerfully mystical dimension to such a display, since Gwyn and his father Nudd were themselves Gods of Light (the
necht in *Nectan* means 'pure, clean or white', just like *gwyn*). It is particularly interesting that a visitor to St Helen's Chapel in 1787 clearly states
that the entrance was from the North, as if this ancient chapel still retained
a memory of the Polar Axis.

Within the bounds of the chapel are five graves of members of the
Heaven family, who bought the Island in 1834 and (the wit of the gods at
work again) thus gave rise to Lundy being known for the next 83 years
as *The Kingdom of Heaven*. Such a coincidence that echoes its mythical
ancient character may make us suspect that occasionally the veils between
this world and the Otherworld do indeed vanish to reveal a great truth,
especially in a place such as this.

The cemetery, which has been in use for at least 1500 years, seems
to have been regarded as a special place in which to be buried, since at
least two other ancient stones have been found there besides the Vortigern and Tigernus monoliths, all of which are of great rarity. But there
is a further clue that Lundy may have had a reputation as a blessed Isle
of the Dead in keeping with its mythic function. In Holinshed's Elizabethan *Chronicles of England, Scotland and Ireland* of 1578 he tells of a race
of magic-working giants said to have come from Cornwall who were eventually buried near the Island's centre. Such legends are of course widespread, especially in Cornwall, where giants were said to have laid out
and created the massive megalithic structures, picking them up effort-
lessly and often hurling them about with abandon. The links between
the legendary giants and the siting of megaliths appear to have been an
integral part of folklore since prehistoric times.

In the middle of the nineteenth century whilst foundations were
being dug for a farmhouse in a field called *Bull's Paradise*, not far from
Beacon Point, an unusual discovery was made. A few inches beneath the
surface two large stone coffins were uncovered, each having a single block
of granite with sloping sides for a lid. The first was ten feet long and had
within it a cubic piece of fine granite as a pillow, carefully worked for the
head to rest in the hollow. Another stone rest was provided for the feet.
The other coffin was much the same, except without the pillow.

Fortunately William Hudson Heaven was present at this discovery, and so there is an apparently reliable witness to confirm these facts.
Each of the tombs contained a skeleton of unusual size. The first proved
to be eight feet two inches long, and was in a near-perfect condition, which
would have been thought incredible and probably widely disbelieved it
had not been for the presence of Mr Heaven. One of the workmen picked
up a shin bone and, placing it against his own leg, it reached more than
half way up his thigh from the foot. The lower jawbone fitted easily over
his own jaw, including his beard!

The other skeleton, believed to be that of a woman, measured at
just over seven feet, and within the same burial site were seven normal-
sized bodies and a pit containing a mass of bones of all sorts and sizes
jumbled together. Shards of pottery, beads of glass and the remains of ornaments of copper and bronze were also found, as well as a large quantity
of limpet shells. The skeletons were immediately re-interred and today
the site is unmarked, with nothing except a few of the beads preserved.
These are now in the Bristol museum and have been dated to the ninth
century, of possible Viking origin. Further excavations of the adjacent area
have been conducted during the twentieth century (including one by the
pioneer dowser Tom Lethbridge) and altogether the bodies of twenty-five
people, excluding the disarticulated bones, have been found.

The elaborate character of the two stone coffins and their gigantic contents will forever remain a mystery, but at the very least here is
concrete evidence for the existence of giants just as the legend recalls.
The fact that another cemetery close to that of St Helen's has been discovered leads us to consider whether there may yet be more such remains;
there are a number of stories of human bones being ploughed up in other parts of the Island. These Giants' Graves and the stones and ancient
tombs in the churchyard lend an intriguing air of mystery to Lundy, as
if it may well have been venerated as an especially sacred place in which
to be buried, in accordance with its role as an Otherworldly realm.

There are other interesting features on the Island (besides,
that is, the extraordinary collection of weirdly-shaped rock piles that
cling to the cliffs) which include the remnants of what earlier chroniclers
have thought to be the foundations of Round Towers, similar to those still
existing in Ireland. These are of finely-cut stone and it is entirely possible
that they were built by the Irish, for both Cornwall and Wales were ruled
by Irish kings at various times. The remains of one, near the centre of
the Island, is close to a rock outcrop that looks something like a Knight's
head looking towards the East, called *Knights Templar Rock*. This seems a
curious name, since according to the records although the Templars were
granted the Island (then called *Lundeia*) at the start of the reign of Henry
II, they never took possession of it. Lundy was throughout this time the
property of the de Marisco family who refused to relinquish ownership.
They were affiliated to the English and Irish branches of the Norman

Montmorencey family, and their tenure of this wild and independent place was to continue until the thirteenth century. Even then they kept a strong interest in Lundy, but luck, or royal favour, was to go against them. Their original castle, long since demolished, stood, it is believed, in *Bull's Paradise*, where the Giants' Graves were found.

Knights Templar Rock

The Kings of Lundy

Of course as ever, there is the unwritten history to take into account as well, and we can never know the intrigues and behind-the-scenes machinations that may have taken place on an island that is such an inaccessible and virtually impregnable fortress. That its position was critical for Vikings and other seafarers is apparent; Lundy is mentioned in the famous *Orkeyinga* Saga of 1148. The de Mariscos themselves were a highly influential family with strong Welsh connections, the 'kings' of Lundy who controlled the Bristol and St George's Channels. The first mention of their connection with the Island is in 1154. They were one of the great Norman families, so powerful that Henry VI of France referred to them as the leading family in Europe after the Bourbons.

The English branch probably descended from Geoffrey de Marisco who arrived with William the Conqueror. They may have had a strong claim to the English throne, since one of Henry I's many illegitimate children was known as William de Marisco. A very curious episode is recorded during the time of Henry III. The King, holding court at Woodstock, was confronted by a strange intruder who demanded the King resign and hand over the kingdom to him, because he 'bore the sign of royalty on his shoulder'. Later the same man, armed with a knife, broke into the royal bedchamber. He was overpowered and confessed to a plot to murder the King, implicating Sir William, the younger son of Geoffrey de Marisco, who was eventually arrested and hung, drawn and quartered.

All this intrigue suggests the de Mariscos felt they had some sort of genuine claim to the royal throne. Whilst they never achieved their ambitions they did succeed in establishing themselves as sovereign in their own independent kingdom of Lundy. Did they feel that somehow they were the guardians of an ancient tradition that linked Lundy with royalty, very like the Cardinham family of Restormel and Lostwithiel, further down the Polar Axis? This would help to explain why they aroused such powerful emotions and why they were implicated so often in royal affairs. It may also indicate why they were so successful in fulfilling important offices under the Crown despite having a reputation for being beyond the law. In many ways they parallel the Arundells of Cornwall. One was Admiral of the Fleet at the time of King John. Sir Geoffrey de Marisco was the Lord Justiciary of Ireland in the early thirteenth century, and Richard de Marisco was a noted Bishop of Durham. Sir Jordan de Marisco married the daughter of Hamelin Plantagenet, the natural son of Geoffrey of Anjou, Henry II's father.

During the time of the de Marisco family the skull and crossbones flag fluttered freely over Lundy (one of the insignia used by the Templars), and it was a notorious base for piratical raids and smuggling, the caves and underground passages ideal for stowing contraband of all sorts. It attracted all manner of outlaws and those seeking refuge from the authorities. It became a wild and lawless place and this was to continue for the next four hundred years. Even when it became part of Sir Richard Grenville's estate it continued to be a haven for pirates, with Queen Elizabeth unsuccessfully attempting to remove them. The Island, it seems, has always maintained a certain aloofness, as if it were above such mundane matters as ordinary law and order.

One of the Island's later owners was Sir Geoffrey Dinan, who may be related to the Dinan family which in Cornwall became the Cardinhams. He was Lord of Hartland and would have been well aware of the Cult of St Nectan since the account of Nectan's life, the *Inventio Sancti Nectani Martyris*, is said to have been written at Hartland Abbey.

King Edward II even sought the Island as a place of refuge when he was being hounded by his rebellious barons. But when he set sail from Chepstow a contrary wind and severe weather forced him to abandon his attempt and land in Wales. So instead of proclaiming himself Lord of Lundy, whose presiding spirit was St Nectan, he took up residence in Neath Abbey. *Neath*, of course, is another version of *Nectan*. His eventual murder—surely the most horrific in British history—remains a testament to those cruel and troubled times. He was held down on a table whilst his attackers thrust a red-hot iron into his intestines through a tin pipe, planning there would be no visible signs of death. Despite his terrible screams, the body was displayed to the public the following morning with the claim he had died suddenly in his sleep.

Yet Lundy at that time was apparently truly a 'Kingdom of Heaven'. The contemporary *Stow's Annals* described the Island as a paradisial place of plenty: '*abounding with pasture grounds and oates, very pleasant; it bringeth forth Conies (rabbits) verie plentifull; it hath pigeons and other fowles...also it ministereth to the inhabitants fresh springing waters flowing out of fountains... it aboundeth altogether with victualles, and is verie full of wines, oile, hony, corn, bragget, salt fish, flesh and sea or earth coales...*' If it was such a rich land in the mid-fourteenth century what was it like in antiquity? It is almost impossible to judge from its appearance today, after many centuries of agricultural degradation and quarrying, with almost every bit of ancient stone being recycled, often many times. The fertile soil of the Island has even largely disappeared due to fires lit to destroy bracken and gorse in the past. Yet there seems to have been something very magical about the Island that was beyond that of a mere refuge for outlaws and the Marisco family. As John Chanter writes in *Lundy Island*; a monograph of 1877 '*in reviewing the long list of noble owners or governors, and the grasping ambition of the Crown to seize it whenever opportunity offered, we are forcibly impressed with the importance that Lundy either possessed, or was deemed to possess, in those early days.*'

When the Island did eventually return to the Crown, Edward III at first gave it to Otho de Bodrigan in 1327. Later that same year it was granted to Philip Lord de Columbers and William de Botereux. We may have expected the Bottreaux family to show up here sooner or later. A few years on it became the property of William de Montacute, Earl of Salisbury. Many owners later it was passed through marriage to Sir Richard Grenville, Admiral of England and close compatriot of Drake and Raleigh (and the builder of the harbour pier at Boscastle, still one of the most distinctive features of the place). Raleigh became one of the trustees of the Grenville estate which included Lundy when Sir Richard set off on his voyage to the New World, and he also mentions Lundy in his memoirs as the place where his betrayer, Sir Lewis Stukely, spent his last days in insanity, to 'die a poor distracted beggar... having for a bag of money falsified his faith'. Sir Richard was also the father of Sir Bevill Grenville who was born, as we have discovered, in the parish of Withiel between the Great Wolf and the Bodmin Lion. These families who produced such great soldiers and sailors seem to be very much implicated in these mysteries. Did they, like the Arundells appear to have done, know something of these archaic traditions?

During the Civil War the Island was still a troublesome haven of buccaneers, and one account records how a band of Turkish pirates had taken about sixty men from a Cornish church, landing afterwards on Lundy. At one stage a Spanish Man-of-War took the Island and helped themselves to everything they could. At another time one of the ships from the Spanish Armada, scattered by a storm, was dashed to pieces on the rocks. It was probably one of the most adventurous and dangerous places in Britain. Ever since there have been tales of hidden treasure concealed in its caves or buried in the ground.

The Crown did eventually assert itself, and Lundy was fortified and held for Charles I, being one of the last places in Britain to surrender to Parliament. It was still the haunt of outrageous characters in the following centuries, as such a place could never be truly defended against the wild rovers of the high seas. In 1750 it was leased to the notorious Thomas Benson, MP for Barnstaple, who took over where the pirates left off, carrying on the long tradition of smuggling and transporting prisoners, even secretly populating the Island with them as labour for building and farming. His downfall came when he heavily insured the cargo of one of his ships, unloaded it onto the Island, hid it, and then set fire to the vessel. Benson was forced to flee to Portugal to avoid arrest. In 1794 there were twenty-three inhabitants and a number of forts together with the Old Lighthouse, and less than fifty years later the 'Kingdom of Heaven' arrived, ushering in a new age of stability and peace on the Island. In 1925 the naturalist Martin Coles Harman bought the Island and introduced many animals, as well as Lundy's own coinage, the *Puffin,* and its unique stamps. His son, Albion Harman, inherited it and on his death it was bought by the National Trust and then passed to the Landmark Trust, who maintain it to this day.

For an Island three miles long and half-a-mile wide this rocky outcrop in the Bristol Channel seems to have had an astonishing history. For most of its existence it seems to have been very much an independent kingdom, ruled by whoever happened to find themselves there, which, in the centuries after the coming of the Normans, were the de Mariscos, who invested themselves with sovereign power. But beyond its known history lies the fact that in deep antiquity it was an important part of a system of geomantic correspondences whose true purpose we can only guess at. Nature contrived to place it where it is, visible from both Wales and Cornwall, and also determined that its axis would align with True North. This Axis Mundi symbolised the most important cosmological function to our ancestors 'through which the eternal energies of creation poured continuously into time... the sign and the promise of life eternally renewed' as Anne Baring and Jules Cashford poetically describe.

Before any inundation of the Severn Sea (which is likely to have taken place in early prehistory), it may have been possible to walk across what is now the seabed and Lundy would have been a prominent flat-topped mountain at the mouth of the Severn estuary, its great plateau perfectly suited to observing the skies as well as the high ground to its North and South. What is most extraordinary of all is that having realised its unique natural properties, a high culture which has been virtually lost to history decided to construct around it a vast pattern of geometry encoding information that proves they understood the movements of the heavens in amazing detail. Their greatest achievement, which the whole world still marvels at, was the construction of Stonehenge, a monument designed to last until doomsday and remind us that there were once people who were motivated to create massive works of civil engineering so that their knowledge could never be lost.

It is no accident that Stonehenge lies exactly due East of Lundy, or that Glastonbury lies virtually on the same axis (the Tor, being a natural hill, could never be expected to conform to such precision geometry in this case). Likewise, the discovery of the Great Bear of Tintagel, together with its collection of giant figures relating to the stars that was engraved in the landscape for all time, seems especially appropriate for our age.

We have lost contact with the Earth and have become arrogant, forgetting that we are truly children of the stars. Did the sages of old know we would one day become so unaware of our true place in Creation that we would threaten the very planet on which we live? Did they leave virtually indestructible messages in the land so that we could recover the wisdom they knew? Were they so wise that they created a mythological system based on cosmology so that whatever wars and depredations the human race might undergo, the myths will adapt and survive and one day be seen for what they are? Many questions remain, and yet we might by now feel that we are at least discovering parts of this tantalising mystery laid out so long ago.

When the mystic Rudolf Steiner visited Cornwall in the 1920s he had a vision of Arthur and his Knights of the Round Table at Tintagel, and said that St Michael was the mystical power behind Arthur, and that the coming age would see them both return. Another visionary, Wellesley Tudor Pole, who founded the Chalice Well Gardens at the foot of Glastonbury Tor once ruled by Gwyn ap Nudd, also concluded that St Michael would preside over the next astrological epoch. If they are correct, and Arthur's sword is the same as that wielded by the Arch-angel Michael, standing for Light, Truth and Justice, we may yet hope to witness a renaissance of these vanished threads of old tradition.

Where should this re-awakening begin? In the very land itself, where these ancient gods slumber. The Earth, after a long, dark, age must now enter a new phase in its relationship with the human race. This will undoubtedly be challenging in many ways we cannot yet envisage.

Will we draw the sword from the stone, and with it the wisdom that lies in the rock and soil of the land? Will we descend into the Otherworld, and, like King Arthur and his followers, return with its golden treasures and the Grail of renewal, inspiration and abundance? It is now up to us to accept these challenges and restore our sense of belonging. Let us remember our place amongst the stars, respect the Earth's creatures, honour each other and those ancient ones whose feet once trod this green and pleasant land.

REX QUONDAM, REX FUTURIS

THE QUEST FOR THE PREHISTORIC ARTHUR

ROBIN HEATH

INTRODUCTION

My role in this book began quite simply. I began using surveying techniques to quantify Paul's researches and this type of evidence became astonishingly revealing. Techniques I had previously employed to investigate Neolithic and Bronze Age sites proved immediately adaptable to suit Paul's project. In the chapters that follow I give an analysis of the sites, the evidence from surveys, and the implications that follow on from this work.

The kind of evidence presented here demonstrates an enduring cultural preoccupation with the *location, alignment* and *form* of both natural and built monuments together with their relationship to each other within the landscape. The astronomical and geometrical techniques used by the megalith builders have been found to apply to sites and monuments throughout the so-called Celtic Church Period and even into the Medieval. More than this, these later cultures appear to have understood and were utilising the original prehistoric landscape patterns. The evidence for this is abundant and observed best through the identical patterns measured between sites and monuments from different cultural epochs. I have investigated this material as rigorously as possible and presented it in such a way that it may be understood by non-specialists.

The evidence presented here points to a single fact:

Large-scale accurate surveying of these islands was undertaken in prehistoric times and the original landscape patterns laid out during this enterprise were adapted by subsequent cultures.

This is a large claim, and it needs to be supported by solid and consistent evidence. In this book, the authors have attempted to demonstrate the following three axioms:

1. That the Arthurian mythos is inextricably bound up with these earlier technologies and their artefacts. Originally a polar mythology, the prehistoric landscape patterns were adapted to suit new purposes and eventually became embedded within the Arthurian legends as the culture changed.

2. That prehistoric people in Britain, whether indigenous or not, were engaged in astronomical and geometrical practices, with the associated development of metrological skills, in order to furnish an impressively accurate survey of many western parts of the British Isles, some examples of this endeavour suggesting that these skills were applied in order to provide practical maps.

3. That this technology survived many subsequent cultural overlays, up to and including the medieval period. The extent and nature of this time-line of cultural continuation, from the prehistoric to the medieval period is backed up by convincing evidence from many varied sources.

The scope of this project has taken the authors over a wide compass that has embraced most of south-western Britain, including Wales. To cover a wider area of these islands is beyond the energy and resources of just two people working with little additional support. The reader will be left in no doubt that there remains much more yet to be uncovered. Taking the matter further will require either a later work or other people keen to walk the landscape and recover what is clearly and abundantly waiting there to be revealed. However, for any future researchers in this field, a path has been found and fires have been lit to mark the way forward.

Robin Heath,
St Dogmaels, September 2009

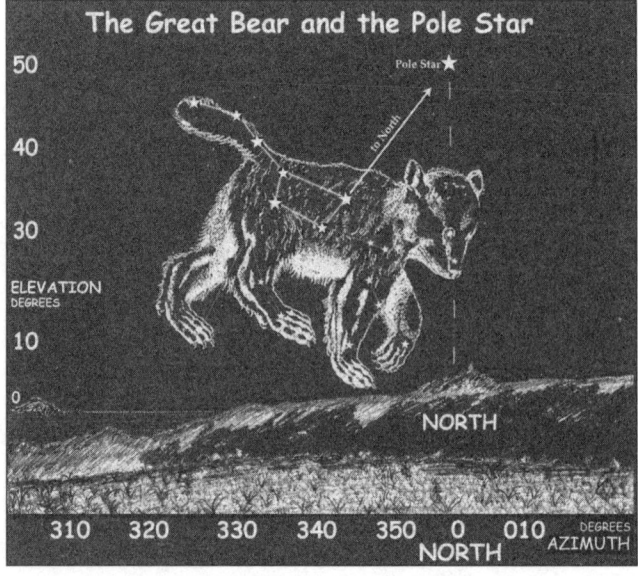

Figure 1.1. The Great Bear.
This constellation in the northern skies consists of seven large and equally bright stars that form the familiar 'plough' or 'wagon' shape, universally used to locate the Pole Star, and hence determine True North. All navigation and surveying depends on being able to determine True North. In Welsh, the Great Bear is known as Arth Fawr, linking Arthur, the Bear and North together (Arth is Bear, and Vawr is Great, the mutation from Mawr follows the rules of Welsh grammar). Wherever one happens to be located on the surface of the earth, other than at either the North or South Pole, looking to the South the stars appear to be rotating clockwise, while looking to the North they will appear to rotate anticlockwise.

1

THE BEAR IN THE LANDSCAPE

In an earlier age, when Cornwall was Cornwales, journeys between Wales and Cornwall would have been undertaken by boats sailing from the many historic small ports that fleck the coastline, such as Burry Port, St Clears, Boscastle, St Ives, Porlock, Bideford and Ilfracombe. Until the arrival of the railway, this had been the normal mode of travel between these two westernmost lands of the British Isles. The two countries are at one and the same time culturally and linguistically linked and geographically connected North and South of the dividing and dangerous tidal waters of the Bristol Channel. And between the two countries stands little Lundy Island, sometimes visible from either side and quite often not.

I live in Wales, Paul lives in Cornwall. By boat, traversing the Bristol Channel, our homes are just under 100 miles apart. Yet using today's transport system we must travel 300 miles in order to meet. In the process of making such a journey one must leave behind the wild landscapes of the west coast of Britain and plough deeply through the industrialised modern landscape of Avonmouth, Bristol, Cardiff and the one-time mining and steel centres of South Wales. The contrast could not be a starker reminder that times have changed.

It is only partly true that my contribution to this book came about because I live in Wales and Paul lives in Cornwall, that Wales is my home patch and I know the ancient landscape of Wales quite well. Mainly my involvement came about because I am an archaeoastronomer, that mouthful of a word for anyone who investigates the links between the locations and astronomical meaning of ancient sites and landscapes. Put more simply, archaeoastronomers reveal links between sky and landscape. This approach to understanding sites has been largely ignored by archaeologists, academic historians and amateur enthusiasts alike, and yet the reader will come to recognise it as an invaluable and vitally important component for investigating ancient history.

During previous visits to Cornwall, my partner Trish and I have invariably been involved with Paul in walking the landscape in some kind of ancient site assessment. The same has been true of Paul and his partner Gabriele's visits to Wales. Whether one terms such activities as questing or research depends on one's perspective, but it has frequently revealed complex landscape patterns that have demanded explanation, surveying with a good theodolite and subsequent long hours of 'office work' analysing the information gleaned during otherwise seemingly simple and certainly pleasant days out in the country.

In 2006, during one such visit to Cornwall, Paul drew my attention to a discovery he had made. That began my involvement in this book. He claimed to have found the outline of a huge bear etched into the landscape around Tintagel. Such an unlikely thing led me along a well trod path of initial disbelief which then led on to "show me!", "prove it!" and, finally, "let's get some objective evidence, then!" This knee-jerk response is adopted automatically, my having once been a research scientist. On another level belonging more to the right hand side of the brain, I also value all the 'other' evidence, the folklore and the legends, surrounding my work with the landscape. It would be hard for anyone not to acknowledge the historic and social importance of the Arthurian legends. Paul's antiquarian expertise and his deep understanding of Cornwall's past enabled him to present me with compelling mythic and genealogical material to back up his discovery. It suggested to him (and me) that it was well worth adding the input from astronomy and landscape surveying into the investigation. He had clearly done his homework. I became involved.

Appropriately, it was another Arthur, author and scientist Arthur C. Clarke, who announced to the modern world that any sufficiently advanced technology that is misunderstood by the current cultural order tends to become regarded as magic. Our scientific world has arrogantly pronounced that magic no longer exists, and therefore, in the sense which Clarke refers, any suggestion of 'magic' - evidence that may support an advanced technology from an earlier civilisation - is deliberately played down, derided or ignored altogether.

Nowhere is this statement more applicable than in the study of the siting and astronomical significance of megalithic sites. Because the modern world has yet to grasp the nature of prehistoric aspiration and thought, it has so far failed to understand its resultant technology, examples of which lie arrayed before us throughout many areas of the British Isles. These sites are presently labelled by those who are charged with defining what we think about such things as primitive or more dogmatically, non-existent of any larger pattern and certainly devoid of any geometrical or astronomical meaning. Or, as Clarke might have said, magic.

A few people clearly do recognise that there is a much bigger purpose behind the siting and function of ancient sites. Books on this subject sell in significant numbers. Millions visit the sites each year in the hope of experiencing this 'magic' and many of these people are evidently able to tap into it. Unfortunately, although often astonishingly able to intuit meanings and 'atmospheres' at sites, the majority of these people are ill-equipped to translate this 'magic' into modern terms that everyone can understand nor have they been adequately educated in order to perform the required analysis of geodetic and astronomical data in order to demonstrate the role these sites take on within the larger landscape.

People who have tried to integrate these aspects in the recent past have become branded with the title 'loony fringe'. I am officially placed in this category, as is Paul and as also were John Michell, Alexander Thom, Alfred Watkins, Guy Underwood and T C Lethbridge before us. Looking at the names on the list, we can wear this badge with pride!

To narrow down or bridge the culturally imposed chasm that separates objective and subjective experiences at sacred sites has been a major desire driving my work, and Paul's 'Bear in the landscape' seemed a worthy project upon which to cut my teeth further with this type of integrative approach. But where to begin? Exactly where within this sphere of activities may *The Bear* be placed? To answer this one first needs to make a small journey of understanding to the North Pole, to find out why finding True North has been so important to human development.

Finding True North *accurately* is the starting point in the defining of *location* and *direction* on the surface of the Earth. It always has done and always will do! In addition, it lays the *bear*ings - starts the process - of two techniques of paramount importance in human communication and trade - surveying and navigation. And it is here where we meet our first Bear.

The Bear Facts -
The Visual Astronomy of the Great Bear

There is scarcely an astronomy book ever printed where orientation of the heavens does not commence with identifying the Pole Star (Polaris) by first locating the Great Bear - the constellation of Ursa Major. The reason is simple enough - these stars are circumpolar - they never set - and are all about the same brightness, always present in the northern sky and always visible in a clear night sky. One of the first astronomy books I ever read, McCready's *A Beginner's Star-Book* (Putnam's, NY, 1912) begins chapter three, 'Learning to Observe' with the following quote from Tennyson's *The Ancient Sage*:

> 'Earth's dark forehead flings athwart the heavens
> Her shadow crown'd with stars - and yonder
> Out to Northwards - some that never set, but pass
> From sight and night to lose themselves in day'

This poetic way of describing the circumpolar stars paves the way for understanding more complex astronomical ideas such as Precession, Precessional 'Ages', the defining of the Cardinal Points, North, South, East and West, and hence opening up the sciences of navigation and surveying. The simple truth is that nothing could be more important in understanding *location* than locating and then understanding the physical reality of the Earth's polar axis, around which the whole planet turns and which *defines* True North. The familiar and normally astonishingly useful Ordnance Survey maps make it quite hard for the casual researcher to determine true North-South lines (or East-West lines), the superimposed blue grid squares being misaligned from the cardinal points due to distortions that result from trying to represent a curved and three dimensional planetary surface onto a flat, two dimensional sheet of paper.

The seven stars which form the constellation of the Great Bear are ever present in the northern skies, rotating anticlockwise, but they are not always visible. We cannot see them during the day because the effect of daylight on the atmosphere of the Earth renders all stars invisible. But at night, and looking to the North, the constellation of Ursa Major is both ever present and ever visible and those seven stars comprising the Great Bear appear, unusually, of about equal brightness and are thereby easily identified. Also known as the Plough, the Dipper, the Wagon or Arthur's Wain, presently the two stars furthest from the tail of the Great Bear lead the eye to the Pole Star and hence to the polar axis of the Earth, true North writ large in the sky (*see figure 1.1. page 292*).

Two important practical applications now become available:

Firstly, the line from the two stars near the Bear's shoulders presently points to the Pole Star when projected. This determines True North. An imaginary plumb bob dropped from the Pole Star onto the horizon would always appear to touch the Earth north of an observer of such an unfeasible event! Once one has determined North, the angular direction of any other object around the local horizon to the observer can be then found. The angle between the north point and this object, taken clockwise, is termed the *azimuth* or *bearing* of the object. Astronomers, navigators and surveyors alike have agreed that the azimuth of True North is taken as zero degrees. Thus East is azimuth 90 degrees, South 180 degrees, and West 270 degrees. These four angles define the Cardinal Points of the compass.

Secondly, the *latitude* for the location of the observer can be determined. The angle of elevation of the Pole Star varies only by a tiny amount when viewed from any given location within the northern hemisphere and it *always* matches closely the latitude of the location of the observer. Even this small variation can be accounted for. Thus the position of the Pole Star *defines* the latitude of the location of the observer.

In Britain, the angle of elevation of the Pole Star will therefore always measure between 50 degrees, the latitude of the south coast, and 60 degrees, the latitude of Orkney. This ten degree change in the angular location of the Pole Star in the northern skies is of course very noticeable, and would have been to those travelling up and down these islands in ancient times. The determination of latitude was comparatively easy, provided one knew how to locate the Pole Star, and knew that the Earth was a globe revolving around this point. Our history books omit to tell us that these things were known about, despite the evidence that ancient people had grasped the fact that the Earth is a globe and were clearly using the Pole Star to navigate around it.

In a book review in the *Journal of Archaeoastronomy* (Jan-Mar 1981, page 37) no less a sailor than Thor Heyerdahl makes these comments,

'A more exact indicator of direction than any modern compass is the steady rotation of the sun and stellar heaven which the ancient navigators knew by heart. Even those of us who are trained neither as navigators or astronomers but have spent many months at the tiller of open craft begin automatically to perceive the consistency of the revolving star paths, to observe the zenith constellations, and even to interpolate the position of the Pole Star from the handle of the "Great Dipper" when the star itself is hidden behind a cloud or [in the southern hemisphere] sunk below the horizon. By taking the latitude directly from the Polar Star with a simple wooden device, it was possible within a margin of 1 to 1 and a half degrees to plot the correct mark for the latitude during the crossing of the Atlantic with the reed ship Ra.'

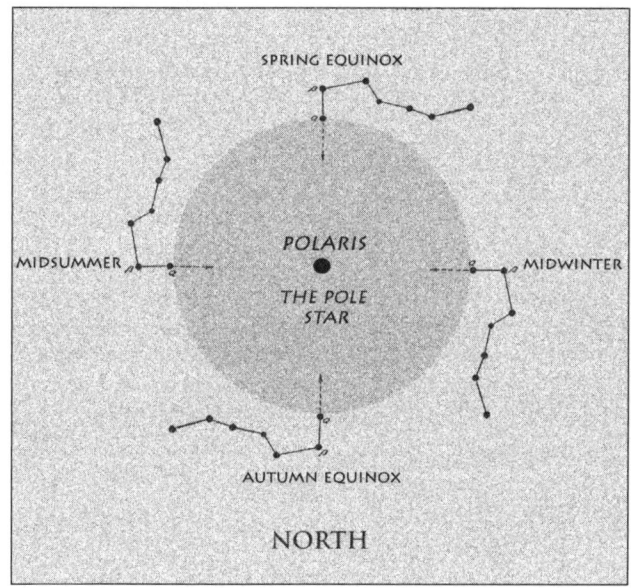

Figure 1.2.

A Bear for all Seasons.

The annual change in the position of the Great Bear around midnight, as seen from Britain and Western Europe. The midnight position at the four key solar dates - solstices and equinoxes - currently form a cross or swastika aligned to the calendar and which identifies the commencement of the four seasons at the summer and winter solstices and the spring and autumn equinoxes.

Coincidentally, but only in Britain and northwestern Europe, the position of the Great Bear in the middle of the night during the course of one year forms a cross, aligning with the cardinal points of the compass at the four key defining solar events of the year - summer and winter solstices and the two equinoxes, spring and autumn. This yearly cycle is synchronous with the solar or calendar cycle, being the time it takes for the Earth to complete one orbit around the Sun. This most fundamental constant of earth-time brings us the four seasons and a year of just over 365 days. Taking the solstice and equinox positions of the Bear together the resultant pattern resembles a swastika, that most ancient of sacred solar symbols, more recently and infamously usurped by the Nazi party during the era of the Third Reich (see Figure 1.2. above).

The Day, the Year and a Circumpolar Star Clock

If latitude may be relatively easily determined, the determination of longitude in the times before chronometers and global positioning systems demanded a thorough understanding of time cycles and sky-lore. It is known from extant texts that lunar eclipses were used as far back as Egyptian times to determine longitude. The position of the Moon in the sky at the start of a lunar eclipse was noted, as accurately as possible. Meanwhile, the commencement of the same eclipse was observed at another location on the Earth and a similar measurement taken. The difference in measured angles gave the difference in longitude angle between the two locations.

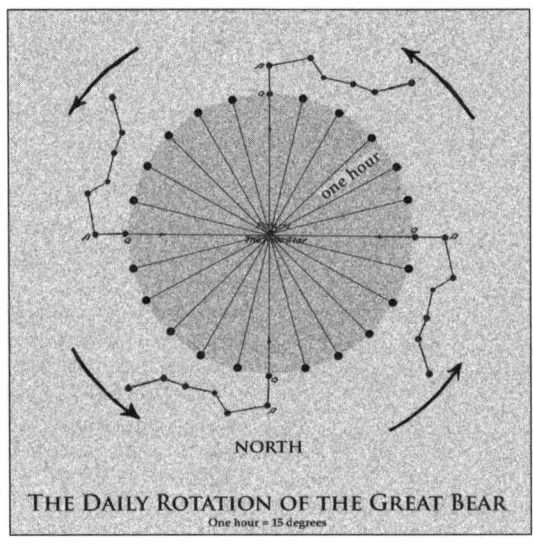

Figure 1.3.

The Daily Bear.

Every hour the stars of the Bear, along with all the other circumpolar constellations, rotate anticlockwise by 15 degrees, making it possible to record the passage of time at night or even longitude when travelling.

Lunar eclipses are not available very often in order to facilitate such a process, averaging about one eclipse per year, but from clay tablets and other sources there is widespread evidence that they could be predicted in advance to make the process described above a viable method for the determination of longitude. And there is no reason to suppose that the accuracy of these observations would be any worse than Heyerdahl's 'simple wooden device' for measuring angles, that is 1 to 1 and a half degrees, which translates across the surface of the Earth to a maximum error in longitude of about 70 miles. There is a second method. A long distance traveller measures at dawn or dusk the angular position of a chosen star within an easily identified constellation, and the daily change in its position - i.e. the daily change in longitude - then adds up to deliver an estimate of the longitude at the traveller's destination location.

The Great Bear makes one anticlockwise revolution around the pole daily, emulating the annual journey already described. Thus locating the Great Bear and then the Pole not only provides a ready indicator of the time of year, but also of the passage of time at night, and the constellation becomes the 'hour hand' of a rudimentary 24 hour clockface. This is illustrated opposite in Figure 1.3., where the black dots mark the change in position of the Bear every hour.

The angular separation between the dots is 15 degrees, and this converts the time difference (one hour) into degrees of longitude, making it possible to use the Great Bear (or any other circumpolar star or constellation) to determine, night on night, changes in longitude whilst travelling. These may not have been accurate, but they could have provided some guide over long distance sea voyages. To an ancient mariner, or a land-based traveller, the Pole Star and the circumpolar stars provided compass and GPS combined, and this must have been astonishingly useful and reassuring during long distance journeys, especially across open seas, prior to the use of magnetic compasses, nautical almanacs and, more recently, GPS devices.

We are most fortunate, more importantly sailors, navigators and surveyors are most fortunate, to live in an epoch where this crucial north-indicating point is filled by a sizeable bright star, our present Pole Star, Polaris, which marks the tip of the tail of the Small Bear (Ursa Minor). It makes navigation more simple if there's a Pole Star on the axis. In our Age, a Pole Star does lie at the Earth's polar axis, always north of the observer, but this has not always been the case.

Precession and Planetary Wobbles

As far back as the early Christian era, the present spatial arrangement between the Pole Star and the Great Bear shown in the diagram (*Figure 1.1. see page 292*) has displayed more or less the same pattern. However, if one could travel progressively further back in time, the present Pole Star would be seen to drift more and more 'off axis'. This is because the Earth's rotational axis undergoes a slow, constant wobble around the perpendicular to its orbit around the Sun. As a result, the position of the Earth's axis relative to the stars gradually, but inexorably, changes. The rotational pole, around which all the stars seem to rotate, moves around in a circle taking just under 26,000 years to complete a circuit. Astronomers call this the Precessional Cycle.

Around the time of Classical Greece, *Kochab*, another star in the Small Bear (Ursa Minor) was the Pole Star. Further back, a much better 'Pole Star' was provided by the star *Thuban*, in the constellation Draco (The Dragon) which was almost exactly at the Pole during the Neolithic period, centering around 2700 BC. This star remained useable as a Pole Star up to around 2000 BC, and was therefore the Pole Star during the Neolithic period and during the early Egyptian dynasties. During this epoch, the Bear would still have been the prime pointer to the Pole. Appearing even nearer the polar axis than it does now, a line from the bear's back legs (the gamma and delta stars of the constellation) would then have pointed directly to the Pole. Further back still, around 5000 BC the polar axis loosely coincided with *Edasich*, another star in the tail of Draco, but this star fell quite a few degrees away from True North, and would have noticeably rotated anticlockwise around the unmarked axis, like every other star in the polar firmament.

It is from this evolution in time of the position of a Pole Star from the constellation of the Dragon to that of the Great Bear that we glimpse something of the astronomical basis for the mythological birth of Arthur, known as *The Bear*, from his 'father', Uther Pen*dragon*. The story becomes more than a myth, it records an astronomical reality. Those periods when a new star ousted a previous star at the Pole were taken to portend great changes in human affairs on the Earth. Arthur as *The Bear* fulfils both myth and astronomical fact, and appears during the period when the Pole Star moved from the head or top of the Dragon (*Pendragon* in both Welsh and Cornish), to the tip of the tail of Ursa Minor, the Little Bear. Perhaps because the other stars in this diminuitive constellation are quite faint, a Greater Bear, with seven bright stars, was employed to reinforce not only the Bear myth but also to provide a practical aid to the traveller who needed to identify the Pole Star and hence determine True North.

Great Ages, Precession and the Bear Mythology

The precessional wobble of the Earth around its axis causes gradual but significant changes in what is seen in the sky. During an average lifetime, the stars and their constellations overtake the seasonal calendar by one degree, a complete rotation taking just under 26,000 years to complete. This is traditionally measured by observing which degree of the ecliptic (or Sun's apparent position within the twelve constellations near the equator) the Sun occupies at the Spring Equinox. When this constellation (or Sign of the Zodiac) changes there is a change in the World Age, so that, in the period of building the huge megalithic monuments and the Cult of the Bull in Crete, the Age of Taurus was in force, to be superceded by the Age of Aries, identified in Jewish history with Abraham and the Ram. In astrological lore it is identified with the Iron Age, the planet Mars, warfare and the metal iron being associated with the Sign Aries and planet Mars. Two millennia later the Christian era marked the beginning of the Age of Pisces, with the symbol of the fish, as the *vesica piscis*, and theme of healing, saviourship, sacrifice, confusion and duplicity. Due shortly at a planet near you this Age will be superceded by the Age of Aquarius. The completion of all twelve Ages marks the end of what is often referred to as the Great Year, but more correctly the Platonic Year.

Thus it is believed by astrologers and an increasingly enlightened number of historians that this periodic change in the World Age brings synchronous and momentous changes in human cultural priorities, the sky seen to actually change cultural priorities on the Earth. Because earlier cultures were more familiar with this type of reasoning, they each built on an archaic astrology, the twin sister of astronomy, based on observations taken over centuries and which eventually became medieval astrology.

The Enlightenment saw these two sisters, astronomy and astrology, prised apart, one taken into care within the modern scientific world, and the other cast out into the cold, and regarded as a worthless relic of a superstitious past.

However unlikely, astrology survived this process, and has recently been reconstituted, and its rich symbolic language focussed into a proto-science for understanding time cycles on the Earth. It is beginning to again command attention by those who study cycles of weather, economic activity and human social behaviour, although it is rarely referred to as astrology any more, and is often given a more scientifically acceptable name such as Cosmobiology, or Cycles Research.

Modern astrology is based on the twelve ecliptical Signs of the Zodiac and largely ignores the effects resulting from precession that drive the processes of the changes of the World Ages. Several respected researchers have recently brought this neglect to light in their lectures and published books. This alternative way of interpreting the heavens appears to be much more ancient than the astrology of the twelve Signs of the Zodiac.

Finally, it has been suggested within academic journals that much of the mythology of the Bear originated from prehistoric cultures living in northern or arctic latitudes. Perhaps it has been the case that circumpolar has become confused with observations taken near the actual Pole. It is easy, perhaps too easy, to draw such a conclusion. If researchers and scholars have indeed been correct in assuming that the Bear's disappearance below the horizon during the night time at certain months of the year may have signified to prehistoric cultures a hibernation period in a cave, or in the underworld, during those months, then this mythology could only have originated from lands far from the polar regions, south of the Mediterranean. It is no longer a circumpolar myth. Any cultural myth concerning the Bear 'hibernating within a cave' - disappearing below the horizon, cannot originate from what is seen in the sky in northerly latitudes, but only from those lands south of the Middle East.

Further South, on or near the Equator, the Pole Star is seen at night located just above the horizon, again stationary and again directly north of an observer. Here the constellation of Ursa Major will only be above the horizon during one half of any particular day/night period. No longer circumpolar, the Great Bear rises and sets like all the other constellations in the equatorial regions.

Move northwards to the latitude of Egypt and the Middle East, the so-called 'cradle of civilisation', and the constellation spends only a small proportion of the day/night period below the horizon, and therefore lost to view. It is only when the latitude increases to above 45 degrees, such as defined by the latitude of Bordeaux, Venice and Belgrade, that all seven bright stars comprising the Great Bear finally become circumpolar. Above this latitude and the Bear is never seen dipping below the horizon. Prior to the Christian era, these same seven stars remained circumpolar right down to the latitude of middle Egypt. It strains the hibernation theory to its credible limit when applied to the skies in say Canada where although the Great Bear is lowest in the sky during winter nights yet it never descends anywhere near the Earth yet alone beneath the horizon anytime during the year.

This brief astronomical journey into the importance of the Great Bear as the prime signpost to the Pole Star and to True North now leads us back to the legend of Arthur, and the idea that the name of our 'Once and Future King' may be synonymous with northness.

ESTABLISHING TRUE NORTH

Using compass, OS maps, Google Earth and GPS with this book: for those readers wishing to confirm the alignments in The Secret Land, it is important to understand the following:

1. The most commonly met pitfall is an assumption that the blue grid squares on an OS map align to the cardinal points of the compass. They do not. Confirming the veracity of North-South lines from Ordnance Survey maps requires that you refer to the latitude and longitude printed around the edge of the map, from which North-South and East-West lines may then accurately be drawn onto the map. Large scale maps emphasize this distortion to the level where most people think that Liverpool or Cardiff lie West of Edinburgh. They do not.

2. If you use Google Earth, the indicated latitude and longitude will be slightly different from those on an OS map, and you will need to convert from WGS84 (Google's) to OGB36 (OS). The website www.nearby.org.uk does this and will also convert a grid reference to lat/long. Google Earth is useful for indicating distances between sites although not always as accurately as do GPS readings taken on site.

3. There is no substitute for visiting the site. Landscape work must eventually move from mapwork to the landscape itself. Why? Because modern OS maps take liberties with where they mark the location of sites. Secondly, when at the site, a GPS reading will establish the latitude and longitude (and altitude above mean sea level) often to within 20 feet, which is far better than can be achieved easily from maps.

4. Determining direction. The magnetic compass is best regarded only as a very rough guide to estimate direction in this type of work. The geology of Wales and Cornwall varies the compass reading, sometimes even reversing it! Much better is to use a GPS. From the site walk a constant longitude (North-South line) or constant latitude (East-West line) marking the ends of this aligned trek after a few hundred paces.

A theodolite is the ultimate tool to determine angles, and was used throughout the book.

2

ARTHUR, ARTH FAWR
AND ALIGNED SITES

During my previous work with prehistoric monuments I had purposely made a point of avoiding any entanglement within the web of enchantment that surrounds the legend of King Arthur. I thought there to be no connection. Whether Arthur was the 'Once and Future King' or a mythologized Dark Age war-lord had also not concerned me in my work, research largely concerned with understanding the geometry and astronomy of prehistoric sites. Arthur began post-Roman, or so I had thought, together with an assumption that there was no connecting link between the megalithic period and the cultures of Roman Britain onwards.

Where Arthur was allegedly conceived, born, grew up, reigned, fought and died was therefore of no direct consequence to my work either. I have listened to and read authors on Arthur; some have placed him in Cornwall, others in Wales, while some insisted convincingly that he was essentially Scottish. I decided that I did not have to become immersed in this messy Arthurian business, nor commit to any particular *School of Arthur*. But all that was about to change.

This refusal to engage with one of Britain's most enduring legends was to prove a big mistake on my part. If the name Arthur could be shown to be a touchstone connection with an aspect of the siting or design of monuments from the prehistoric past then, forgive the pun, the entire landscape changes. So following Paul's request for assistance, I set off on a quest to investigate whether or not there existed any evidence to support this conjecture.

Significant prehistoric and medieval sites containing the name Arthur can be found littered all over the western half of the British Isles, and down into Brittany, but this proves nothing concerning Arthur's life neither does it connect to the source of any myth concerning his name. It simply confirms that the Arthur legend held a huge importance in ancient times. For instance, King Arthur's Quoit is without doubt the most commonly found name for a cromlech or dolmen in these lands. But when did this naming all begin? Was it a product of the Dark Ages, medieval or from a much older time, even from the prehistoric period?

Churches throughout the land are dedicated to St Michael, St Mary, and all of the apostles, yet despite the masonic symbolist and mystic Blake asking 'And did those feet in ancient times, walk upon England's mountains green?' almost no churches are directly dedicated to Jesus. Furthermore, it remains unproveable that the other once hugely important iconic religious characters, again largely mythologized, were ever of these lands, yet alone, as some have claimed, even visited here. The myriad of Arthur related site names over such a wide area suggests that the Arthur myth was deeply embedded into the cultural past of western Europe. And unlike the churches, the head man is everywhere, while his entourage, aside from Merlin, is hardly mentioned.

Living in Wales for over a quarter of a century I knew that the Welsh word for Bear is *Arth*, and that *Arth Fawr* is Great Bear. Twelve miles from my home lies the sleepy and somewhat forgotten parish of Llanfihangel ar Arth. The name refers to St Michael (the 'f' is a mutation from 'm' in Welsh), so that the Parish is literally named the parish of Archangel Michael on (or over) the Bear. 'Llanfihangel' churches are quite common in West and Mid Wales and several such churches are said to encircle and thereby retain the troublesome Dragon of Radnor Forest.

It seemed highly synchronous to now mention this parish to Paul, not only because he coauthored *The Sun and the Serpent* and *The Dance of the Dragon* with dowser Hamish Miller, perhaps the two best loved and certainly best known books about St Michael's geomantic manifestation, but also because Paul had just told me that he had discovered the outline of a huge Bear embedded in the landscape of North Cornwall. This Parish appeared to mysteriously connect both St Michael and Arthur, as Arth Fawr, a Great Bear, and neither of us had the first clue as to why this should be so.

We duly visited the Parish with its very ancient 12th century church but nothing was revealed. We asked at the pub and could find nothing. We drew a blank as to why this Parish had been so named. Just exactly what was the Great Bear that St Michael was apparently placed on or over? Yet asking this seemingly unanswerable question commenced a process that was to connect me back to some apparently unrelated research I had been undertaking for some months previous to learning of Paul's discovery.

If Arthur is synonymous with northness, and thereby linked with ancient astronomy, as has been proposed, might the name Arthur also be connected with North-South alignments laid down in Britain during ancient or even prehistoric times, when indigenous Britons spoke a similar language to modern Welsh and maybe understood that Arth Fawr was related to this process? Early work was to indicate with surprising conviction that this was indeed the case.

I had recently concluded work on what turned out to be a very accurate rectangle laid out along the cardinal points of the compass starting from Stonehenge. The rectangle's side lengths were in the ratio of 3 to 4, making their two diagonals each five of the same units. The rectangle was in effect two Pythagorean 3-4-5 triangles clamped together. At three of the four corners of this rectangle were very well known megalithic sites indeed. The opposite corner from Stonehenge was perhaps the best known site on Anglesey, Bryn Celli Ddu. The other two corners were provided by 'The Stonehenge of the North', Arbor Low, in Derbyshire, and Morte Point, near Woolacombe, that ridge of rock jutting out towards Lundy Island and which marks the tip of the North Devon coast. There are two ruinous burial chambers shown here on older maps.

The illustration (*Figure 2.1. below*) gives an idea of the accuracy and scale of this construction. If it be thought that this construction is fanciful, then checking the accuracy of the geometry shows it to be astonishingly solid (an original paper on this work is available at *www.skyandlandscape. com*). In addition, the metrology is entirely consistent with those units of length shown by other researchers to have been commonly used in the prehistoric world. It is also helpful to remember that Bryn Celli Ddu, until it was restored in the twentieth century, was also a ruinous burial chamber, like the two located near Morte Point.

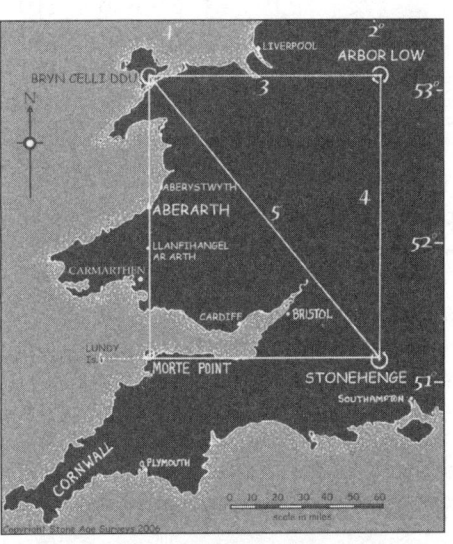

Figure 2.1. Geodetic connections between major prehistoric sites.

In 2006, it was discovered that Stonehenge, Bryn Celli Ddu and Arbor Low are accurately arranged as the corners of a Pythagorean 3-4-5 triangle, aligned to the Cardinal Points of the compass.

An East-West line joining the centre of Stonehenge to that of Lundy island cuts the North Devon coast at Morte Point, and provides the fourth 'corner' to complete a 3:4 rectangle. Morte Point accurately cuts the line to Lundy into the ratio 5:6

The North-South line from Morte Point to Bryn Celli Ddu is just under 140 miles in length and runs through many sites and towns in Wales that bear the words Arthur, Arth and even Merlin. Figure 2.2. and Table 2.1. list these towns, sites and monuments.

The evidence I was looking for now arrived thick and fast. The visit to the ancient church of Llanfihangel ar Arth may have revealed very little *per se*, but its location was to prove anything but meaningless once applied to the idea that Arthur may be connected with the Bear, and hence to northness. The geodetic rectangle cut the mid-Welsh coast a little north of the colourful town of Aberaeron, at the tiny hamlet of Aber*arth*, on the estuary of the River Arth. High above this village is a church, half hidden by a steep ridge. Now dedicated to Dewi Sant (St David), it is a perfect example of a large church on the summit of an impractically steep hill, to all intents and purposes entirely remote from any suitable size of congregation. It commands a magnificent view over Cardigan Bay. I took Paul to see it for good reason - Aberarth and this church lie accurately North of Llanfihangel ar Arth.

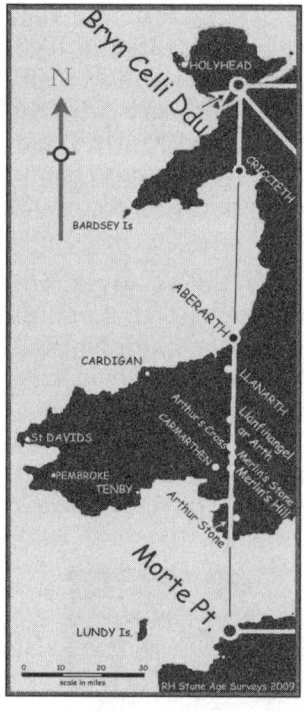

Figure 2.2. The North-South alignment that forms the left-hand side of the geodetic rectangle described in the text and illustrated in Figure 2.1. connecting Bryn Celli Ddu on Anglesey to Morte Point in North Devon. This alignment passes through or near a remarkable number of towns, monuments and other sites that contain Arthur, Arth and even Merlin in their name.

The sites which define the corners of this large rectangle are all archaeologically dated at over 5000 years old; they are assuredly prehistoric. That the left-hand boundary of the rectangle cuts through so many sites carrying the key word 'Arthur', or the root word 'Arth' in their names amply supported the 'Arthur as prehistoric' quest. Having placed my perspex ruler on the map and aligned it with Bryn Celli Ddu and Morte Point, I then read off the edge of my ruler the following sites to Paul - The Arthur Stone, Carmarthen, Merlin's Hill, Merlin's Stone, Arthur's Cross, Llanfihangel ar Arth, Llanarth, and Aberarth. The addition of two well known sites naming Merlin himself is a remarkable bonus in this exercise (*see Table 2.1. below*).

The names of these sites between Morte Point and Bryn Celli Ddu clearly support the suggestion that this prehistoric line was understood into the Dark Ages. And there is a later, post-Norman monastic link too. Aberarth was once a significant enough port to have received the stones used to construct one of mid-Wales' biggest Cistercian abbeys at Strata Florida, eight miles north of Tregaron. The alignment cuts the North Wales coast at the magnificently sited thirteenth century Castle built on a commanding mound at Criccieth (*longitude 4 deg 14 min*), overlooking the sea. No earlier archaeological occupation of the site has been identified - the Castle is apparently of medieval Welsh origin.

SITE	LATITUDE (N)	LONGITUDE (W)	ERROR (FROM MEAN)	
Bryn Celli Ddu	53° 12' 27"	4° 14' 05"	+ 7.5"	
Criccieth Castle	52° 54' 50"	4° 13' 50"	- 5.5"	
Aberarth	52° 14' 54"	4° 14' 07"	+ 9.5"	
Llandewi Ch., Aberarth	52° 14' 50"	4° 13' 52"	- 5.5"	Total length of alignment is 140 miles
Llanarth (Parish Town)	52° 11' 50"	4° 18' 24"	+ 4' 27"	
Llanfihangel ar Arth	52°02' 10"	4° 15' 00"	+ 1' 03"	Azimuth (bearing) of alignment from
Arthur's Cross	51° 54' 34"	4° 13' 38"	- 19.4"	Morte Point to Bryn Celli Ddu is 0 4' 20"
Merlin's Stone, Abergwili	51° 52' 16"	4° 14' 30"	+ 32.5"	
Merlin's Hill, Abergwili	51° 52' 14"	4° 14' 30"	+ 32.5"	The Mean longitude is 4 13' 57" (14 sites)
Aberarthne	51° 51' 40"	4° 08' 10"	- 5' 57"	Average second of longitude = 62 feet (19m)
CARMARTHEN (County Town)	51° 51' 37"	4° 18' 11"	+ 4' 14"	
Arthur Stone, Gower	51° 36' 43"	4° 11' 20"	- 2' 37"	
Burial Chamber, Morte Point	51° 10' 42"	4° 11' 30"	- 2' 27"	
Morte Point	51° 11' 20"	4° 14' 20"	+ 22.5"	

Table 2.1. 'Arthur' and 'Bear' related sites and their coordinates on the North-South alignment running from Morte Point, in Devon to Bryn Celli Ddu on Anglesey. Just under 140 miles in length, this is extremely close to being two degrees of latitude (one degree of latitude is 69.12 miles), and suggests that the builders of the rectangle could have understood and been able to measure latitude to a high accuracy.

Impressive though this may appear, this 3:4 rectangle was not the first example of a geodetic construction based on Stonehenge that had revealed itself. In 1988 I had noticed that the site of the famous bluestones in the Preseli region of West Wales, from where the bluestones were quarried and then taken to Stonehenge, was geometrically related to Stonehenge. The two sites formed opposite corners of a second accurate rectangle aligned to the cardinal points this time with side lengths in the ratio of 5 to 12, matching a similar, but much smaller example built into the main construction at Stonehenge and known as the station stone rectangle. And a third point was clearly highlighted. Lundy Island provided the third corner, and the required right angle, to define a Pythagorean 5-12-13 triangle (*see Figure 2.3. below*). The larger rectangle is 2,500 times larger than the smaller one contained within Stonehenge itself (40 by 96 Megalithic Yards of 2.72 feet).

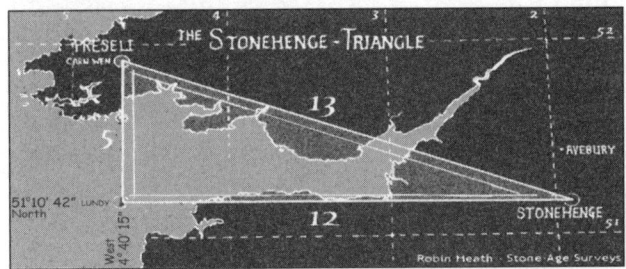

Figure 2.3. The geodetic link between Stonehenge and the Bluestone site, via a 5-12-13 Pythagorean triangle which locates the centre of Lundy island as the right angle. Might this be an explanation as to why the Bluestones were taken to Stonehenge, in order to define this shape on the landscape of Britain, prior to 3000 BC?

In prehistoric times important built sites and natural landscape features were located to suggest these massive geometrical forms. Each one is so accurately defined that geodetic techniques of surveying must have been employed in their siting. These same techniques have been required to recover the original designs! While there may be no actual line connecting the corners of these sites, we can be assured that the shape was intended and cannot be accidental. How can we be sure of this? Because both these constructions were precisely aligned to the Cardinal Points, each possessing long North-South and East-West alignments. So too the the 3:4 rectangle that cuts through the entire length of Wales and whose left hand side passes through a wholly unlikely number of sites named after Arthur, Bears and even Merlin!

Here are to be found the first two triangles in the Pythagorean set, laid down in a most impressive and accurate display of surveying skill, some two thousand years before Pythagoras was even born! The analysis on the Morte Point - Bryn Celli Ddu line was as good as I could have expected, and it fired my interest further, impelling me look for other connections between Arthur, the Bear and North-South alignments determined in prehistory. I recognised that something of real substance was emerging from the landscape, and it is this which still has the power to stir me to walk scores of miles a month across often difficult landscapes while carrying inordinately heavy surveying equipment.

The Bear hunt was on!

Figure 3.1. - Arthur and Northness.

The Moon culminating at its lowest elevation over Carningli, 'Angel Mountain', near Newport, Pembrokeshire. Viewed from Coetan Arthur, a large dolmen located on the northern side of the town, the Moon skims through the peak to the right and its entire disc then becomes visible as it transits South, before appearing to roll over Carningli Common. The dolmen is uniquely located as a place to detect and observe the major standstill and this event not obviously attracted some other visitors! Located directly North of the point on the Common where the 'lunar wheel' is most visible, the dolmen is also at the northern end of a much longer North-South alignment between Trefdraeth (Newport) and its 'twin-town' Tywardreath, in Cornwall. Both towns' names mean the same - 'Town on the beach'. [Author's photograph -13th June 2006; 2:05 am]

3

ARTHUR AND NORTHNESS

Within the loosely defined subject of 'Earth Mysteries' there have always been well meaning enthusiasts who have suspected and then attempted to confirm that our forebears were capable astronomers, surveyors and geometers. Most did not have the the required skill base to succeed in this venture, but some well-known public figures have made strong contributions to this subject.

In the eighteenth century the renowned antiquarian William Stukeley was first to report that the axis of Stonehenge was directed towards the midsummer solstice sunrise. In the early years of the twentieth century the one-time Astronomer Royal, Sir Norman Lockyer, discovered many examples of astronomical alignments at megalithic sites, including a midsummer sunrise alignment at Bryn Celli Ddu. More recently Alfred Watkins proposed a ley system of alignments connecting ancient sacred sites, outlined in his classic book *The Old Straight Track* (1925). In 1969, John Michell published his best selling *The View Over Atlantis*, building on Watkins' and others' work and truly founding the modern interest in what is now termed 'Earth Mysteries'.

It fell to a retired and somewhat retiring Oxford Professor of Engineering to provide the bulk of the hard evidence that our prehistoric forebears were capable astronomers and geometers. Alexander Thom possessed precisely the required background and skill mix to demonstrate scientifically that this statement was indeed true. Thom completely rewrote the rule-book for investigating the evidence for prehistoric astronomy, and became the acknowledged father of modern archaeoastronomy. In his obituary on Thom, archaeologist Richard Atkinson began, 'It is not often that a man can be said to have created, single-handed, a whole new academic discipline.' In his essay in the book *Records in Stone*, Anthony Aveni wrote 'Thom raised the engaging question; do the remains of ancient civilisations reflect a knowledge of astronomy by virtue of the way they are laid out on the landscape?'

Thom revealed important missing aspects in the history of human development. Without these excluded components the current model of British prehistory appears flat, two dimensional, diluted with ten parts of water. Prior to Thom, comparatively few important astronomical links had been made between megalithic monuments and their alignment to key solar sunrises and sets. There was almost no interest in relating these monuments to the cycles of the Moon, and nobody thought to ask the most basic of engineering questions: did the builders employ a standard unit of length and, if they did, what was it? Thom shifted the emphasis away from the florid rhetorical questions of antiquarians and mystics and replaced these with hard scientific technique. In this way Thom changed William Blake's question to 'How long were those feet in ancient times?'

Accepting Thom's findings carries enormous implications for the model of prehistoric Europe. The present model is completely mismatched to the evidence that Thom eventually supplied in over 250 notebooks, 500 survey plans, four seminal books and a prime-time television documentary. All of this material offers an alternative picture of prehistoric intent.

Thom's interest began in 1933 when he sailed a chartered yacht into the uncharted waters of archaeoastronomy. Thenceforth the whole subject was placed under the watchful care of an expert scientist/engineer. The tiller was in capable hands and Thom's new career began with a seemingly chance event, a moment of serendipity. Sailing late in the evening into East Loch Roag in the Isle of Lewis, Thom was lucky enough to see the Stones of Callanish 'like fingers silhouetted in front of the rising Full Moon'. After dinner he and his crew set off to look at the stones of perhaps Scotland's most famous megalithic monument. Thom noted that the main axis of the monument, a line of huge stones, was oriented along a North-South axis, and he asked himself an innocent question: how did the people who erected this cruciform monument manage to determine northness?

The answer is not immediately obvious. A fellow of the Royal Astronomical Society, Thom was a very able amateur astronomer and quickly realised that during the (then) proposed date of erection of the monument there would have been no Pole-Star to determine northness. Prior to drawing up his own survey plan of the monument, Thom pored over Admiral Somerville's old plan of Callanish, and pondered on how the builders of Callanish had laid the bearings for such an accurate North-South alignment.

Thom was to spend all his spare time for the next forty four years pondering, surveying hundreds of megalithic sites in the process. His plans are acknowledged as the best there are, and for many of the sites there simply were no plans, or only rough sketch plans. In his astronomical work astonishingly accurate solar and lunar alignments emerged, yet *the initial impetus that began archeoastronomy in modern times was Thom stumbling across an obvious North-South polar alignment on a bleak Scottish coastline.*

In my earlier research I had noted that the North-South axis through Lundy was found to pass through an astonishing number of other ancient sites, including many found on the little and not so little islands that rise out from the western sea-board of Britain, Lundy, Caldey, Cardigan Island, Bardsey Island (a little off-axis), Holy Island on Anglesey and the southwestern corner of the Isle of Man. Following this rather odd realisation and during a visit to see Paul while I was researching *Sun, Moon*

& *Stonehenge*, I had noted a most mysterious and seemingly bizarre fact - a North-South 'mirror' effect between certain town names in Cornwall which are 'reflected' in the landscape of West Wales. St Cleer near Liskeard is south of St Clears near Carmarthen, and Launceston (Llansteffan in Cornish) is south of Llansteffan, Carmarthenshire and is identically named, even to the spelling in the original Cornish language. Both towns hold impressive ruins of once-powerful Norman castles. Tywardreath near Fowey is due south of Trefdraeth (Newport) in Pembrokeshire and both names mean 'Town on the Beach'.

In case the reader thinks this is stretching coincidences too far, then a look at a map or the table 3.1. below will rapidly confirm that each of these identically named pairs of locations do lie at the ends of North-South lines. The accuracy of these alignments may surprise the reader sufficient to require a strong cup of tea!

Very strange! Not only are three pairs of identical place names lying on North-South lines, but two of them are also aligned North-South to within a degree - within one part in 400. This strange 'evidence' did not at the time seem to fit at all within a book about the megalith builders, and so I filed it away, and gave it no more of my attention. But like the Devil when ignored, unresolved aspects of research tend to come back to haunt us. As a result of working with Paul on his landscape Bear this mysterious 'twin towns' material was once again taken off the shelf, given a good dusting and used as the second test of the emerging *Theory of Arthurian Northness*. The obvious next stage was to look for Arthurian connections entwined within these sites and their alignments.

SITE	DISTANCE APART	BEARING (Az)	LATITUDE (N)	LONGITUDE (W)
Trefdraeth (Newport)	114 miles	357° 46'	52° 00'	4° 50'
Tywardreath			50° 21'	4° 43'
St Clears	92 miles	359° 10'	51° 49'	4° 29'
St Cleer			50° 29'	4° 28'
Llanstephan	77 miles	359° 27'	51° 46'	4° 23'
Launceston			50° 39'	4° 22'
Arthur Stone	50 miles	000° 48'	51° 36'	4° 11'
Shebbear			50° 52'	4° 13'

Stone Age Surveys 2009

Two Towns on the Beach

To visit Newport in Pembrokeshire, West Wales, requires patience. The town is a long way from any motorway, and the nearest railway station is Fishguard, some twelve miles away. The Preseli region has thereby avoided the worst excesses of industrialisation and, as a consequence, sports more fine megalithic sites than it would take a well lived lifetime to investigate. The only satisfactory answer for somebody who does want to study them is to move to the area, and in 1985 I did just that. For me it has been the University of Megalithia.

The North-South line connecting Newport, West Wales, with Tywardreath, Cornwall could be explained as an act of imagination, for no such 'line' exists in reality connecting the two sites. Separated by 114 miles, and falling 2.5 degrees off being truly North-South, Trefdraeth (Newport) and, Tywardreath (Cornwall) apart from sharing the same name, form an alignment which turns out to possess important Arthur related sites at both ends and these monuments are sufficiently historically important to warrant roadside heritage signs.

Newport is a quaint and charming village that lies tucked away under the brooding dark peak of what is now known as Carningli - Angel Mountain. The peak is a long extinct volcanic plug, a windswept and highly distinctive feature visible for tens of miles. A Bronze Age 'fort' was once built around the conical summit. A much earlier and much better known site lies out of town. Four miles to the east may be found the most famous dolmen in all of Wales, the magnificent horned chambered tomb of Pentre Ifan. Also on the east side of Newport town may be found a second dolmen sitting all alone and seemingly completely out of place in the midst of a recently built housing estate. It is called Carreg Coetan Arthur, or in English, Arthur's Stone Quoit (*see Figure 3.2. below*). Up until now Coetan Arthur has remained mute concerning any connection it holds either with Cornwall or North-South alignments. But viewed through the lens of archaeoastronomy this is seen to not be the case at all.

Figure 3.2.

Carreg Coetan Arthur is located near the estuary of the river Nyfer in Newport, Pembrokeshire. Its axis of symmetry is oriented to the midsummer sunset, and the monument also acts as a backsight for detecting and observing when the moon has reached its major standstill in the south, every 18.6 years.

A theodolite is needed to confirm the precision with which the monument is astronomically located, and yet this aspect of the design of megalithic monuments is currently considered to be of no interest within modern archaeology.

A splendid dolmen, Arthur's Stone Quoit stands almost on the beach along the estuarial waters of the river Nyfer. One of the so-called Newport Group, the monument is the prominent prehistoric site in this charming West Wales town. Carreg Coetan Arthur has a further connection with northness, holding two astronomical secrets that have escaped archaeologists and remained hidden from human understanding until very recently.

I first undertook a theodolite survey of the site in 1995, which revealed that the axis of symmetry of the entire monument was constructed to align to the midsummer sunset position around 3000 BC. A later survey in 2005 refined my earlier results. Whether or not the massive capstone was once covered with a mound of earth protecting this hidden secret is neither here nor there. The astronomical secret contained within the monument was tucked away safely and it has endured the passage of the years.

During my initial survey, Coetan Arthur revealed a second astronomical secret that also connected it with both the Moon and southness. Once every 18 years and seven months, the moon slowly reaches what astronomers call the major standstill, a time when the Full Moon reaches its maximum ever height in the sky during the midwinter months, and its lowest ever elevation in the heavens during the midsummer months. The last time the Moon did this was in 2006/7, and I was on hand with theodolite at 2 am to confirm and then photograph something that I had known about for some years - Coetan Arthur is perfectly sited to detect and observe when the major standstill of the Moon has been reached (*see Figure 3.3. below*).

Directly South of the monument lies the spine of Carningli Common, a flat mountain top plateau placed to the right of the extinct volcanic outcrop with its Bronze Age 'fort'. During the midsummer Full Moon, at the standstill in 3000 BC, the disc of the Full Moon would have slid up the left hand slope of the mountain, disappeared into the volcanic peak only to then emerge from its right hand side onto the common. It would then be seen to roll along the curved horizon, like a luminous silver wheel,

Figure 3.3.

The Major Standstill Moon seen at its lowest transit in the South, photographed from Coetan Arthur on 13th June 2006 at 2:15 am. The event was clearly being enjoyed by the sundry other luminescences captured on this photograph!

In 2500 BC the lower limb of the Moon's disc would have been slightly lower, and after emerging from the peak of Carningli mountain would have appeared in full in the dip before rolling along the curved incline to the right.

reaching its culmination (maximum height) exactly South of Coetan Arthur and marked by a hut circle and enclosure. Today, because the astronomy has changed somewhat from 3000 BC, this Full Moon-wheel no longer touches the summit of the Common, it leaves a small gap.

After the major standstill is over, the Moon, full or not, is *always* higher in the sky above Carningli. For only two midsummer periods every 19 years the Moon comes down to Earth and rolls along the flat spine of the hill south of the monument. After just two hours this spectacular show is all done, and in the succinct words of Alexander Thom, referring to the lunar observatory at Temple Wood, a similarly set up monument in Argyll "...if you missed it, well... you'd just have to wait!" Well... I didn't miss it, and the photographs (*Figure 3.1. page 308 and Figure 3.3. page 313*) confirm the matter.

It is possible to calculate the difference in position between the Moon's position now and for any epoch in the past. This confirms what the photograph suggests - that Coetan Arthur is located at a supremely ideal location by which to observe and detect this important standstill of the Moon. It is the housing estate and not the dolmen that is badly located and out of place here. The natural curiosity of wanting to observe those rare times when the Moon descended and then touched Carningli, the sacred mountain of the area, provides a tangible reason why prehistoric people would have wished to build such an elaborate monument in this most suitable position to observe the lunar standstill.

Without knowing when these periodic lunar standstills occur, it is not possible to predict when eclipses may occur. Alexander Thom found much evidence, as I have, that prehistoric astronomers had grasped the mechanism by which eclipses occur. It appears this was one of the high points of their culture. It cannot of course be proved that prehistoric astronomers built this site to monitor either the lunar cycle or predict eclipses, yet there stands Coetan Arthur at the north end of this supremely fit for purpose observatory. Sadly, one cannot yet find any of this information either in the tourist guide nor in any archaeology book.

In earlier times astronomers called this periodic cycle of the Moon's risings and settings the Draconic cycle, because it was believed that people once thought that the Moon or Sun were swallowed up by a giant dragon during eclipses. Today it more commonly has the less dramatic name of the lunar nodal cycle, although the 18.61 year period continues to be referred to as the Draconic year.

Cultural Continuation suggested within the Celtic Church

Being located at the northern end of the North-South line that connects Tywardreath with its namesake, Trefdraeth (Newport), both Carreg Coetan Arthur and Pentre Ifan manifest 'Arthur' as northness within a prehistoric monument, suggesting that the alignment is much much older than traditional Dark Age and medieval Arthurian sources. The Cornish sites at the southern termination of the alignment are also prehistoric, yet as we shall shortly investigate, these sites are today wholly identified with Dark Age and medieval Arthurian sources.

What is particularly exciting is a second twinning between Trefdraeth and Tywardreath that supports knowledge of the alignment into the time of the Celtic Church. Both towns are connected with the Celtic saint, *St Samson*. Pentre Ifan, in the Parish of Newport and Nevern, stands in a field called *Corlan Samson*, 'Samson's fold' while his alleged grave, *Bedd Samson*, lies nearby on the banks of the river Nyfer. At the southern end of the line, in Cornwall, lies Tywardreath, a coastal village within the Parish of *St Sampson* which also encompasses the huge henge at Castle Dore and the now-resited Tristan Stone, both prehistoric monuments, but also very much linked to the Arthurian romances in Cornwall (*see pages 271-2*).

The Two Llansteffans

Today, there are only two obvious similarities between Launceston in Cornwall and Llansteffan, near Carmarthen, in West Wales. The first is their identical name, in the earlier languages of their respective territories, another is that both Llansteffan and Launceston sport prominent Norman castles perched on top of fearsomely steep mounds. There are differences too. The Cornish town has become a bustling regional centre (for more information on Launceston, see pages 216-20) while the former has slipped into peaceful obscurity, a place where modern well-shod Welshmen seek second homes and tourists seek sanctity within an incredibly beautiful coastal environment, endowed with a magic light from the reflected sunlight from hundreds of square miles of estuarial beaches washed twice daily by huge tidal flows.

Nearby the ruined castle lies St Anthony's well (*N 51 deg 45 min 49 sec ; W 4 deg 23 min 54 sec*), a stone plaque beside the arched opening reads,

'*St Anthony of Egypt (c 251 - 356), the first Christian hermit, had a powerful influence on the Celtic Church in South Wales. According to local tradition a Welsh hermit, Antwn (Anthony), who had taken the name of his great Egyptian predecessor, settled near this spot, probably in the sixth century*'.

From the headland a splendid panorama encompasses the North Devon coast, the Gower Peninsula and the Pembrokeshire coastline past Caldey Island and Tenby. From the castle, on a clear day, it is also possible to see Lundy to the south west. A connection between the two sites will be made in chapter four.

St Clears and St Cleer

St Clears, also in Carmarthenshire, has kept up with the passage of time and has become a typical Welsh market town close to the busy A40 road that takes traffic east-west between the other market towns of the shire capital, Carmarthen and Haverfordwest. The modern town has a population under 3000 and is built around a motte-and-bailey castle, at the confluence of the Taf and Cynin rivers, both once navigable from the coast for boats of up to 500 tons.

The motte mound of the castle is an impressive 26 feet high and its flattish top is an oval 63 feet by 33 feet and it lies on the north side of the site and is well preserved. The large, rectangular bailey extends 160 feet south of the motte to a modern house. Reports of stonework being visible on the summit of the motte suggest a masonry structure at some stage in the monument's history.

A priory was established at St Clears around 1100, probably after the foundation of the castle. The early history of the castle is obscure. Giraldus Cambrensis mentions St Clears Castle by name as the home of twelve archers who had murdered a young Welshman who was 'devoutly hastening to meet the Archbishop' presumably to offer himself as a crusader. A terrible sin, the twelve Englishmen themselves later took the cross as penance.

It may be the castle called Ystrad Cyngen which we know was captured in 1153 by Rhys ap Gruffydd, of the south-west Royal house of Deheubarth. Soon after the English (Normans) took it, and the tables were turned when the Lord Rhys again took the castle from the English a year later in 1189. Thereafter the castle swapped hands between the Welsh princes and Norman barons, ownership oscillating back and forth in sundry conflicts in typical medieval fashion until the Earl of Pembroke took matters in hand in the early part of the thirteenth century. Then, in the fourteenth century, when the feuding was all done, the castle then fell into a state of disrepair. St Clears does however figure briefly in the Glyndwr uprising in 1405, when it was besieged and presumably captured along with the castle at Carmarthen, after which English rule was eventually and resentfully reimposed.

There is little surviving of prehistoric interest around St Clears, perhaps because of the extensive medieval buildings and subsequent development of the region. Of significance is that the Church is dedicated to Mary Magdalene, a signature of the Templars. Opposite the church gate is a fine Town Hall with an equally fine Boar on the town crest, situated above the entrance.

The sleepy town of St Cleer in Cornwall is well known to earth mysteries enthusiasts. The now well publicised St Michael line runs right through the town, directly through the flamboyant and somewhat pompous Victorian superstructure built above the holy well of St Clarus. The nearby church, also dedicated to St Clarus, is typically much more impressive than one might have expected the local population could support (for more information on St Cleer and environs, see pages 196-7).

Gateway to the southern edge of Bodmin Moor, St Cleer lies near to the prehistoric sites of the Cheesewring, the Hurlers stone circles and within a mile of standing stones, carved and decorated during the Dark Ages.

More significantly, St Cleer is the nearest town to the curious slab-roofed dolmen, Trethevy Quoit, just a mile to the north-east, which is again known as Arthur's Quoit. (*N 50 deg 29 min 35 sec ; W 4 deg 27 min 20 sec*).

While I was drawing the three pairs of North-South lines on a diagram, I found a further pair of sites which supported the theory that I was investigating, and these are described below and included in the earlier table on page 311.

Arthur and a She Bear

On the Gower Peninsula near Swansea may be found The Arthur Stone (*N 51 deg 36 min ; W 4 deg 11 min*), a heavily quartzed capstone dolmen supported by small upright stones. Thought to be a glacial erratic, it is aligned North-South and stands conspicuously on a flat plateau near to a huge cairn known as Cefyn Bryn. The site enjoys spectacular panoramic views to the South, and on a clear day you can see Morte Point near Ilfracombe, in North Devon. There are two ruined burial chambers on Morte Point, whose name is thought to derive from the many deaths of unfortunate mariners whose vessels were wrecked in medieval times.

The Arthur Stone has a quintessentially Arthurian legend attached to it. Across the water in nearby Carmarthenshire, it is said that King Arthur removed a troublesome pebble from his boot and flung it across the wide tidal inlet from Mynydd Sylen to where it stands today. Now Sylen Mountain lies directly North of Arthur's stone, identified by the modern transmitting aerials festooning its summit, which is just under a thousand feet high. The dolmen connects a North-South alignment with an Arthurian legend, involving a superhuman Arthur with boots to match his size - the 'pebble' weighs over 30 tons!

This same line projected directly south from the Arthur Stone cuts the Devon coast near Morte Point, a curious reminder of the title of perhaps the most famous of the Arthurian romances, *Le Morte d'Arthur*. Continuing southward, it passes directly through the curiously named small village of Shebbear in North Devon (*N 50 deg 51 min 37 sec ; W 4 deg 13 min 10 sec*). The distance between the Arthur Stone and Shebbear is just 50 miles and the alignment falls within one degree of exactitude, at 0.8 degrees east of True North. Shebbear is 10 miles from the River Tamar, the traditional boundary of Cornwall, and this alignment was found interesting enough to include here.

To find Arthur and a She-bear connected within this emerging arrangement between both Wales and Cornwall is enough to make any-one smile. Coincidental it may be, but dancing along with the words, King Arthur and the Queen of Shebbear would have made quite a formidable alliance, and the Queen had made a grand if unexpected entry!

During this research I decided to look at all the sites on the western side of Wales whose name mentioned the word Arthur, based on those given in the Ordnance Survey Historical map of Ancient Britain. I knew the two sites well, and they both responded to analysis.

Arthur's Quoit, St David's Head, Pembrokeshire

This particular Coetan Arthur resembles a stone grand piano lid (*Figure 3.4. below*). Known to archaeologists as an 'earthfast' cromlech, one side of the large capstone slab is dug into the ground and supported at its other end by upright stones. The monument has endured in a position of unbelievable exposure on the receiving end of Atlantic gales, and has done so for over 5000 years. Four miles from St David's Cathedral, a walk along this magnificent headland offers one the feeling that the Neolithic period has lingered on here, the landscape much the same as when Coetan Arthur was first erected.

Directly south of this monument one can see Skomer Island, just 11 miles distant. Now a famous and important nature reserve, in prehistoric times there were two settlements on the island, both near the only sources of fresh water. A prehistoric standing stone, the Harold Stone, may also be found here.

Geodetic calculations revealed that these settlements have the following relationship to Arthur's Quoit:

From Settlement 1 to Arthur's Quoit: Azimuth 358° 26'

From Settlement 2 to Arthur's Quoit: Azimuth 359° 41'

Arthur's Quoit coordinates: N 51° 54' 15" ; W 5° 18' 26"

These both satisfy the criteria of falling on a North-South line containing an 'Arthur' named site to the North. From those settlements on Skomer, St David's Head is seen directly to the North, and the cromlech precisely so from settlement two. Skomer's Scandinavian name suggests that the Harold stone should in fact be called the Harald stone, after Harald Hardrada, a Norwegian hero-king from the eleventh century, the period when much of Pembrokeshire was subject to repeated Viking attacks. Harold was the hapless king who was shot in the eye and killed at the Battle of Hastings during the Norman invasion. Renaming this stone the Arthur Stone would of course be better still, although another one in the eye for Harold!

Figure 3.4. Arthur's Quoit, St Davids Head, Pembrokeshire. *This 'earth-fast' dolmen resembles a grand piano lid made from rock. It is located North of two settlements on Skomer Island, some 11 miles away.*

Bwrdd Arthur (Arthur's Table), Anglesey

Finally, I wanted to investigate a site that in the 60s had been one of my favourite haunts to visit on dreamy summer days. During my student days at Bangor, North Wales, I came to know and love the magical island of Anglesey, *Ynys Mon* in Welsh. As if I needed the excuse to revisit an old friend, it seemed entirely appropriate to widen the landscape spread of the theory of Arthurian northness by again sitting at Arthur's Table.

Almost on the northernmost tip of the Penmon peninsula, on Anglesey, may be found a limestone outcrop. On the flat top of this outcrop is sited Bwrdd Arthur (Arthur's table), commanding a fabulous panoramic view of the North Wales coastline, including the Great Orme, Puffin Island and across to Benllech, Point Lynas and, overland, to Holy Island. The folklore surrounding this site contains reference to a table and 24 chairs, and with imagination the small limestone outcrops emerging from the frail topsoil vegetation can indeed create the image of a round table surrounded by chairs. The pressing question on this visit was to establish what, if anything, may be found North or South of this point.

Northwards from Arthur's Table (N 53° 18' 37" ; W 4° 07' 27") leads to the East of the Isle of Man and on to the Scottish coast near Castle Douglas. The South line is much more interesting, crossing the Menai Strait, past Bangor Garth and Bangor's Victorian pier, and then on and through the original site of the Celtic Cathedral in Bangor. It then runs onwards to the summit of Bangor Mountain (328'), a narrow ridge that runs longitudinally parallel to the city and which defines its whole topology. The large area of Bwrdd Arthur means that a true North-South alignment may be found over a band of longitudes. However, to the trig point at Bwrdd Arthur gives a bearing of 359° 39' 12". The range is 5.7 miles.

Again an 'Arthur' site defines the north end of a significant North-South line connecting with Bangor's most important ancient religious site. The present Bangor Cathedral is built over the original site of the foundation of the Christian Church in North Wales, in the sixth century. In the time of King Maelgwyn Gwynedd, around 525 BC, the church had been founded by St Deiniol on this same site who became the first Bishop of Bangor. The original church was completely demolished in 633-4 and the rebuild was sacked just after the Norman invasion in 1073. The first Dean of the Cathedral following the Norman invasion was Arthur de Bardsey.

The present red sandstone building is Victorian and it now stands amidst the worst excesses of postwar vernacular style. In recent times the first ever Tesco in Wales was opened across the road from the Cathedral, in 1967, and within a year the Britannia Bridge connecting Wales to Ireland via Anglesey and the Holyhead ferry was destroyed in a spectacular fire. In addition the Beatles turned up with the Maharishi and I spent four years living on this alignment as an undergraduate student in the Department of Engineering Science, Dean Street, Bangor. These events are not however thought to be connected.

Arthur's Table spectacularly satisfies the criteria of connecting Arthur with a polar alignment associated with other significant medieval monuments. The site presents very similar conditions to Tintagel Island (*see page 96-7*), being a north facing plateau overlooking the sea, and it is interesting to compare the Welsh pronunciation of Bwrdd Arthur to that of the English 'Birth Arthur', which is almost exactly the same.

Summary: The results of this little experiment now lay in front of me on my desk top. Collating the evidence and data had embraced all the sites which bore the name Arthur in Cornwall and West Wales marked on the Ordnance Survey map of Ancient Britain. That there was a connection between prehistoric sites, northness and the legends surrounding Arthur seemed no longer to be in any doubt, and the twin towns clinched it! It is of course up to the reader to determine their own conclusions from the evidence presented here, but I was happy that I had answered Paul's requirement for a tangible and quantitative source of evidence that connected the Great Bear, the polar axis and northness with prehistoric sites associated with the legend of King Arthur.

However, as so often happens when focussing in on this kind of research into ancient landscape, my involvement did not stop with this first exploration into Arthur's kingdom. There were other astonishments emerging from the growing piles of data and site plans accumulating on my desk. The next step was to be a giant leap, and it was to take the whole matter into a new dimension.

Figure 3.5.

Two Precision Instruments. Carreg Coetan Arthur, Newport, Pembrokeshire.

'Arthur's Quoit' is probably the most common name for a dolmen, and in the following chapter we investigate why this may be so. Although assumed to have been built as burial chambers, these enigmatic monuments are also shown to reveal astronomical and geodetic secrets indicative of high cultural achievement, long before the main structures at Stonehenge were erected. A modern theodolite is needed to reveal their astronomical secrets because the Earth's axial tilt has changed since the monuments were erected and the rise and set positions of Sun and Moon have are now significantly different. This change can be accounted for - the theodolite accurately measures from the monument, and independent calculations can reveal the rise and set positions for the time the monument was built.

4

REVEALING THE PREHISTORIC ARTHUR

It is often the case that in our speech as in writing we fail to appreciate the deeper meanings that lie behind the words and phrases that we utter, pen, or more commonly in modern times, type out on a computer keyboard. In the story of Arthur as Arth Fawr and the Great Bear, we can reconnect to a hidden and deeper meaning behind these words, the cosmological truths of northness, the polar axis, the rotation of the Earth and having in our earthly life to bear the cycles of time that spring from that rotation - the day, the year, lunar months and even the Great Year of the precessional cycle.

There are many words and expressions that resonate with this theme. It is common to talk about laying the bearings when engaged in surveying work, or commencing a new project or setting out in a direction, always referred to True North and the polar axis. In receiving directions we are told to bear right or to bear left. Our ancestors are our forebears. Our vehicles have wheels mounted on axles and rotating in bearings. The millwheel grinds flour mounted on great bearings and connected to an axial pole which, in the case of the windmill, points vertically upwards towards the sky. We complain about the daily grind, and of arguments being off-axis, and of people we cannot bear, who are poles apart from ourselves. The meaning lies in the concept of accepting a weight or task, a strain or inheritance within cycles of rotation or recurrence. In human terms this often relates to our experience of duality and fate.

Great writers have always known all about the underlying meanings of words, polarity and human fate. The earliest texts that survive, the Rig Veda, refer constantly to the turning of the sky, the wheel of fate, in poetic verses that can still move us today,

> *A seven-named horse does draw this three naved wheel,*
> *Ageless and irresistible as well,*
> *Which props all worlds.*

> *RV 1.164.1-2*

Upon this five-spoked wheel revolving ever
all living creatures rest and are dependent.
Its axle, heavy laden, is not heated: the
nave from ancient times remains unbroken.
The wheel revolves, unwasting, with its felly:
ten draw it, yoked to the far-stretching car-pole.

RV 1.164.13-14

Shakespeare wrote extensively about this theme in Hamlet, perhaps the most potent text he ever wrote concerning the burden of human fate. A pioneering and classic work on the subject, *Hamlet's Mill* (de Santillana and von Dechend, 1969), deals extensively with the historical legacy and mythology of the precessional cycle and the turning of the polar axis through time, relating it to cosmological models that can be traced back into the Stone Age.

Hidden within the complexites of modern life are terms, phrases, idioms and adages that concern themselves with the present era yet hark back to the most ancient references of bears, setting, grinding, axes, the pole and turning of the Earth. These have been retained and remain in everyday use, integrated within the more recent overlays, despite their original context fading into obscurity. If our words carry this cargo of meaning from the dawn of language, then perhaps so too might many other aspects of modern culture.

Taking Jung's axiom that, 'Everything born of a moment in time has the properties of that moment in time' might one expect that it is not only the roots of our language that harbour the most ancient references to human life in prehistoric times? Could one reasonably expect that the aspirations and capabilities of that distant time would remain printed onto the landscape in just the same way that words remain printed within our dictionaries? And just as we do not often think enough about the underlying meaning of the words we employ, so too we do not give enough thought to the underlying meaning of a landscape, a standing stone, a stone circle or a dolmen, even a church or castle.

That this is the case is demonstrable when we study the cultural model we find described in archaeology books concerning the Neolithic and Bronze Age periods. Here, an impenetrable fog descends. This model is framed within an innate comparison between our present time as more evolved against a previous time that was less evolved, primitive. This cuts against the findings of biologists and anatomists, who long ago delivered their proof that the human brain then was to all intents and purposes identical to that of a modern man now. The begged question that naturally follows is to enquire what our ancient forebears were doing with all that brain capacity? If we are ever to move from the ethnocentricity and racism-through-time of classifying our ancestors as primitive and less evolved by our standards, then our first step is surely to investigate the possibility that something more was going on in their world, something with which we have so far failed to connect.

One obvious way to connect with these distant people is through their surviving artefacts. Language is recognised as one important, non-physical, artefact. If language has recorded and stored an insight into cultural priorities relating to hunting, navigating, astronomy, time cycles and the importance of the polar axis, then logic dictates that we might also profitably look for these things within the more tangible artefacts left behind on the landscape. The stones and their locations are almost all we have left from this culture. Confirming what they are telling us is only possible to someone who understands the 'language' of both their astronomy and geometry. None of the material here is incomprehensible, nor need be seen as other than a welcome addition to our knowledge of the past. Celebrity archaeologists have been appearing on our television screens on a regular basis for many years, presenting radical ideas, and this has brought an unexpected popularity boost to archaeology that it has rarely previously enjoyed. What little prehistoric astronomy has been presented to the public has been, since Thom's documentary, largely a pale and wan affair, controlled almost entirely by the archaeological establishment, and has failed to turn up much new evidence. How best to correct this failing than by using a familiar face everybody knows, Arthur, Britain's home-grown hero?

The evidence presented here is neither vague nor difficult to grasp in its implications and importance. Furthermore, it does not require the skills of a conventional archaeologist. Quantitative in nature, it centres around sites that are related to other sites through alignments on the landscape, these alignments and their geometries are readily appreciated and verified. For those who wish to check my figures, examples are to be found in my books and on www.skyandlandscape.com. The sites themselves may be found on any large scale OS map, their folklore and legends in scores of antiquarian books, their locations to the nearest second of a degree on various fine websites built to assist tourists and visitors to these sites, most notable of these being *Google Earth*, *The Megalithic Portal* and *The Modern Antiquarian*.

This chapter begins where we left off in chapter two, the 'coincidence' of identically named towns, one in Cornwall and the other in Wales, being aligned along a North-South axis. This mysterious fact convincingly demonstrated a connection between the Arthur myth and northness. But there is a further curious 'coincidence' that must now be taken into account. All three pairs of town locations lie closely equidistant from the latitude North 51 degrees and 11 minutes. So what's so important about that? Well, plenty, as it happens!

Figure 4.1.

A Fearful Symmetry.

The remarkable arrangement of the 'twin-towns' discussed in the previous chapter reveals something much more mysterious than medieval townships sharing the same name.

Each of the identically named towns is closely equidistant from the line of latitude connecting Stonehenge to the centre of Lundy Island, in the Bristol Channel, at 51°10' 42". Each pair is therefore closely equidistant from both our National Temple and Lundy Island.

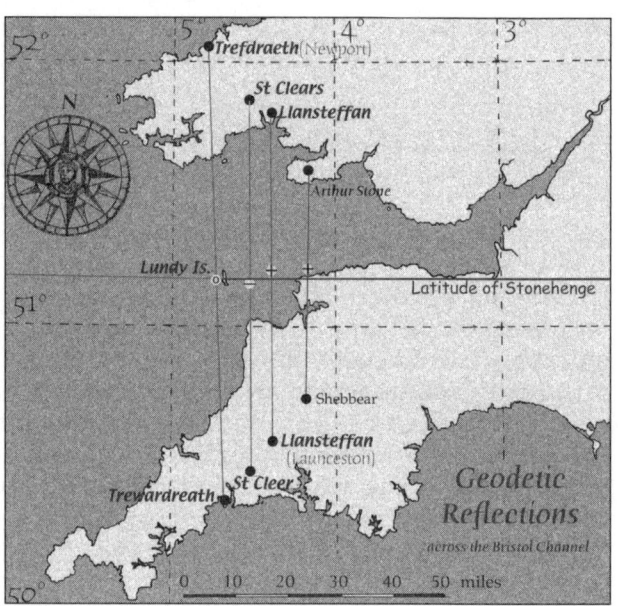

What strange coincidence is this? Although some may find this information odd, even meaningless, *this latitude happens to be the precise latitude of Stonehenge*. More specifically it is the latitude connecting the centre of Stonehenge with the centre of Lundy Island, 51 degrees, 10 minutes and 42 seconds North. It is a true East-West alignment and it is *exact*. The coupling of towns across the Bristol Channel is one curious thing. That they are aligned along North-South lines is another, but to now discover that each of these sites and their reflected 'twin towns' lie loosely equidistant from our National Temple, Stonehenge and therefore also equidistant from the East-West line of latitude connecting our most famous prehistoric monument with Lundy Island is surely beyond curious, it is truly astonishing. Stacked up, these facts show deliberate human geodetic intent.

Here is the discovered evidence:

Three pairs of towns, one from each pair located in Cornwall and the other one in Wales, are found to have the same name, each pair is aligned North-South of each other and each are equidistant from Stonehenge and hence the parallel of latitude upon which Stonehenge is built, which is also the latitude of the centre of Lundy Island.

Although modern minds come primed to reject such a discovery as incredible, the objective evidence that supports the reality of this web of geodetic connections is plainly verifiable by almost anyone. It is simple geometrical evidence that may be confirmed even if only by holding a ruler against a large map of Britain! Its revealed truth, once recognised, had the power to raise the hairs on the back of my neck. It strongly suggests that, long after the prehistoric period, people still knew all about the prehistoric significance and underlying meaning of this most ancient geodetic system, as evidenced in the matching of the modern town names. If in medieval times people had by chance just happened to have sited identically named towns on top of existing prehistoric sites or monuments that had been part of the original grid then this would be stretching coincidence beyond any acceptable limits. The later builders must have known of the ancient geodetic system. These twin-towns are sited deliberately and knowingly with respect to the earlier geodetic grid.

The implications of this discovery may be uncomfortable to some. Some questions immediately spring to mind with regard to these implications are: How was an exact East-West line between Stonehenge and Lundy set up in the first place, and when? Surely the naming of these 'twin' towns, which are named (in two examples) after Christian saints, was decided in the Dark Ages or the Middle Ages long after the megalithic culture had vanished? And why should Stonehenge or Lundy be geodetically linked to the locations of these towns anyway?

I had already run geodetic programs to ascertain the bearing between each of the Cornish towns and their similar Welsh counterparts. Their North-Southness was not in doubt. But there was more to follow. It remained for me to draw out the complete pattern from all four matched pairs of sites onto a map. What appeared before my eyes as I did this seemed entirely magical. I beheld a bigger truth connecting to the material that I had investigated twelve years previously.

Although intending to have done so, I had not yet calculated the angles of the sloping sides of the lines that connected the Welsh sites and the Cornish sites. These angles are clearly shown in the following diagram (see *Figure 4.2.*). So I ran each pair in turn through my computer program, and then ran pairs of pairs and finally the bearing between the ends of each of the putative alignments. When I calculated along their whole length, their angles were both closely matched, Cornish and Welsh, and both lay within a degree of 45 degrees, half the angle in a right angle. I have called this geodetic form the 'Arthur triangle'

Where did these alignments meet? I reached for the Ordnance Survey map of that part of North Devon, a worn old Series Seven cloth-backed map once purchased from a local charity shop for nearly nothing. What then emerged was to completely transform the scale of the work that now engaged Paul and myself, for I was stunned to discover that the respective towns I had used as data for my exploration into the validity of 'Arthur' and 'northness' were forming an arrowhead terminating at Dunster Castle, also located on the Stonehenge-Lundy line of latitude and a town profoundly steeped in the Arthurian legends. It is the place where Arthur is said to have spent his youth.

There is a legend connecting Dunster with St Caranog, a sixth century holy man who converted much of central Cornwall to the Celtic Christian faith. Originally from Wales, and having founded a church at Llangrannog on the Cardiganshire coast, directly north of St Clears, Caranog had constructed a floating altar, which he launched on the waters of the Bristol Channel, vowing to preach wherever it came to land. The altar arrived at Dunster, where Arthur lived. At that time, Arthur was looking for a huge dragon that was terrorising the inhabitants of nearby Carhampton. Caranog inquired where his altar was and Arthur told the saint that he knew its location and, if the saint would only slay the dragon, he could have his altar. The saint kept his side of the bargain, and Arthur produced the altar, saying that he had been trying to use it as a table, but that everything he placed on it kept sliding off.

Despite the small 'spread' resulting from the slight variations in the bearings from each of the eight locations in my 'Arthurian survey' of twin towns and one dolmen, the average was firmly located on Dunster Castle. These lines were now connecting me to the Arthur story directly, through monuments named in the medieval romances as well as prehistoric sites. Here are two accurate sets of alignments, each the reflection of the other, which meet at Dunster Castle and which are inclined at 45° to the horizontal. They are integrated with, and share sides with, the larger geometric form connecting Stonehenge with Lundy Island (*see Figure 2.3. page 307*).

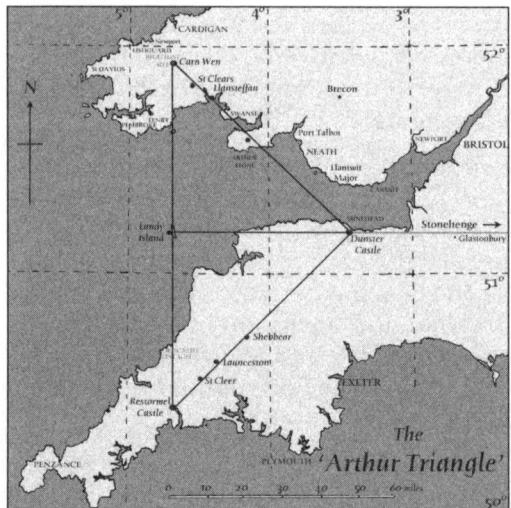

Figure 4.2.

The 'Arthur Triangle'.

The terminations of the North-South alignments of twin-towns and other sites across the Bristol Channel form a further pair of alignments which meet at Dunster, a highly significant town in the Arthurian legends.

Situated on the Somerset coast near Minehead, Dunster lies on the same latitude as both Stonehenge and the centre of Lundy. The visual symmetry shown here is confirmed by accurate geodetic calculations - the angles of the triangles are each 45 degrees and Dunster splits the line between Stonehenge and Lundy in the ratio 7:5.

These two 45 degree alignments were laid out in prehistoric times, and they reveal a once important cultural message from people who lived five thousand years before us. These people clearly understood why and how they were laying out these shapes and demonstrably possessed both the technology and the will to complete these huge expressions of their geodetic prowess. But four millennia later, who were the people who also clearly understood the importance of this prehistoric endeavour sufficiently well to have adapted it for a new purpose - naming Cornish and Welsh towns identically in order to sustain and augment the earlier geometric undertaking? It became crucial to find out the answer to this new and surprising question.

The 'Arthur Triangle' is based on a circle of radius 100,000 Megalithic yards (51.429 miles) centred on the tump at the geodetic centre of Lundy Island. Around the perimeter of this circle are many sites that were once of prime importance in the history of Britain. The bluestone site, source of the eighty-odd famous stones that were once taken to Stonehenge at huge expense of toil, is one of them and clearly prehistoric, while the majority of other sites around the perimeter are much later, and include an astonishing number of well known monastic centres. I had already dropped a hint concerning this mystery about links between monasteries and megaliths in diagrams within earlier works, in *Sun, Moon & Stonehenge* (*Fig 10.13.*), and *The Measure of Albion* (*Fig 1.3.*). It is well worth a revisit here (*Figure 4.3.*).

In Cornwall, the perimeter passes through St Columb Major (*see pages 163-7*) and Restormel Castle, just north of Lostwithiel, the one-time capital of Cornwall. In Dunster, Somerset, a large monastic settlement existed at nearby Old Cleeve, near Carhampton. By application of only a small act of imagination it is easy to see the basis of a Round Table myth in this circle surrounding its centre, Lundy Island, that remarkable rocky outcrop in between Wales and Cornwall. Lundy provided the centre of all of this geodetic activity.

In Wales, the sixth century Priory and later Cathedral of St Davids formed the foundation stone of the Roman Church in Wales. Llantwit Major was once the site of a famous college and monastery set up by St Illtud, also during the sixth century. Both sites lie on the perimeter of this

Figure 4.3. The Geodetic Habits of the Celtic Saints.

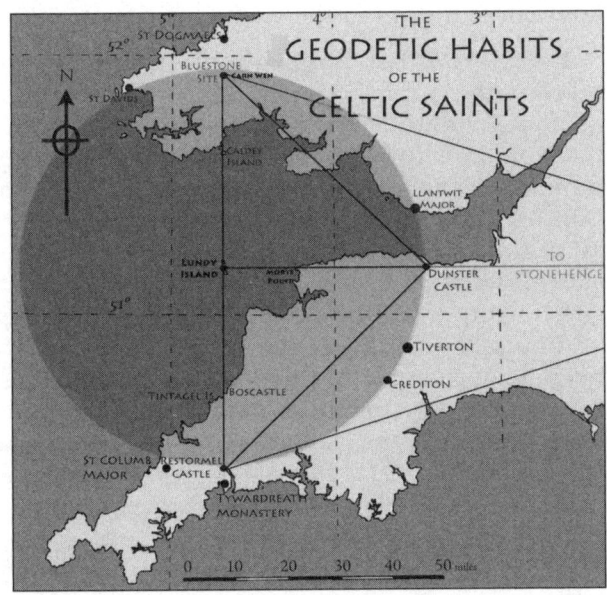

The perimeter of a circle centred on Lundy Island and of radius of 100,000 Megalithic yards passes over the sites of many of the principal monastic sites of the Celtic Church. The North-South (axis) diameter through Lundy takes in Caldey Island and, within five minutes of a degree of longitude, Tintagel Island. The projection of this diameter passes through three other important monastic sites, St Dogmaels and Mynachlog ddu in Wales, and Tywardreath in Cornwall. It passes significantly close to important monastic sites at Tiverton and Crediton, in Devon. The 5-12-13 'lunation' triangle and its 'reflection' in Cornwall is shown superimposed on the circle. Its apex is Stonehenge, not shown but off the right hand side of the diagram. The 'Lundy' axis provides the North-South side of this large geodetic construction.

circle. The North-South 'Lundy axis' runs through the monastic settlement on Caldey island, where the oldest church in Wales, dedicated to St Illtud, may still be visited. Further north and the monastery at Mynachlog ddu (*black monastery*) was sited just below the bluestone site.

Extending the North-South 'Lundy axis' northwards beyond the perimeter of the circle, it passes through the ancient monastery of St Dogmaels, near Cardigan, and finally leaves the Welsh coast at Mwnt, the one-time embarkation point for Celtic saints, both alive and recently departed, *en route* by sea to Bardsey island, and said to be the place where 20,000 saints are buried, in addition to Arthur and Merlin. Remote and wind-blasted medieval churches still stand at both Mwnt and Bardsey. Southwards, the extended diameter passes near the once important medieval monastic centre at Tywardreath, in Cornwall.

The only conclusion one can sensibly draw from all of this would be that the founding fathers of the Celtic Church were fully familiar with the use of geodetic surveying and knew of the original prehistoric template which somehow they had either discovered or inherited from the megalith builders. They also mysteriously chose, for curious reasons that we do not yet understand, to *purposefully* found their centres within the same template. That the later medieval Lords, Knights and Kings also built onto this geodetic pattern demonstrates that they too had been initiated into the rules that lay behind such an activity, despite the circumferential locations of many principal sites by the Celtic Church having been chosen several hundred years previously. This demonstrates cultural continuity over four millenia and offers some explanation for the location and naming of the secular 'twin-townships' in Wales and Cornwall. Might one refer to these later contributors to the prehistoric pattern as the Knights Template?

There are other implications lurking in the background. For a start, there is the apparent importance of Lundy Island as the vital centre for all this geodetic activity. If two pilgrimages to St Davids are decreed by the Roman Church to be worth one pilgrimage to Rome, then one might now suggest that two pilgrimages to Rome may in turn be worth one to Lundy! And the historian cannot avoid the presence of Stonehenge in all of this, a key actor in this mystery play, waiting off stage, in the wings, ever-present and very prehistoric indeed. Stonehenge and the bluestone site so important to its development belong to a much earlier period, and appear to suggest the origin of the geodetic story that is unfolding here. It becomes blindingly obvious that the whole matter begins much further back in time than monks with strange geodetic habits. So how far does it go back and exactly what lies behind all this mysterious use of the British landscape?

In order to attempt to answer this question a brief recap may be useful. In 1990, during research into the choice of siting of Stonehenge, I discovered a geometrical link between the original site of the famous bluestones, in West Wales, and the location of our national temple, Stonehenge. These two locations are accurately connected as the two opposite corners of a 5 by 12 rectangle, each unit being 20,000 of Thom's Megalithic yards. Lundy Island provides a third clearly defined 'corner' in this construction. Importantly, the rectangle is aligned to the four cardinal points of the compass. Stonehenge is the only *built* site of the three clearly identified 'corner' locations which define the three points of a 5, 12, 13 triangle, the others are *natural* landscape features (*see Figure 2.3. page 307*). Stonehenge was therefore the *human component* in defining the rectangle. We know from radiocarbon dating that the monument in its present form was sited and construction begun prior to 3000 BC. If we take account of the eponymous 'car-park post-holes', the dating retreats back beyond 5000 BC or even earlier. Time for a sit down with a cup of strong tea?

A reflection of this triangle may also be found on the landscape south of Lundy, a second similarly dimensioned triangle locates Restormel Castle as its opposite 'reflected' counterpoint to the bluestone site. The whole structure integrates itself within a display of geodetic prowess that takes the breath away. Evidence from astronomy, geometry and metrology each supports the validity of these forms on the landscape. The building of Celtic Christian and medieval buildings onto this geodetic grid further supports the reality of the original prehistoric survey.

Completing the Jigsaw

All researchers harbour the hope that their research will provide useful pieces of the jigsaw that they and other historians are trying to complete, a piece that will slot into the others and enable the bigger picture to be recognised and then constructed from the remaining pieces. For most historical research, there is an historical framework, the picture on the box that holds the pieces of the jigsaw. But here Paul and I have discovered that there is no existing historical framework for the evidence we have presented! There simply isn't a picture on the lid because there isn't a box, neither for the pieces of the jigsaw that relate to the prehistoric aspects of astronomy and surveying, nor for the pieces that derive from the historical period. What we do know is that we have found a large collection of previously missing pieces that in the distant past fell down the back of the sofa of history.

How did all of this history become lost? Or forgotten? The pieces of this puzzle assemble themselves into a picture that is comprised of components from several cultural periods, the prehistoric and megalithic right through to the Druids and then the early Celtic Church and beyond, into the later post-Norman period that defines the start of medieval history. Some pieces of the jigsaw we might have expected to have been assembled by an historian before now, yet it appears not to be the case. All of it simply disappeared, until now.

The research Paul and I have undertaken relates directly to the Arthurian story. If Arthur is indeed a cover-all term for prehistoric polar alignments, and thence surveying of the landscape, then the later monuments, legends and myths surrounding our 'Once and Future King' are derivatives drawn from this original root. If the location of Arthur's grave has never been agreed upon by any two researchers, we have now made it abundantly clear that his grave *is the landscape itself,* together with the patterns that have now been revealed upon it. Arthur has indeed been resting, laid down in the Earth for millenia and while the legends and folklore thrive, the landscape component described here has been completely forgotten and lost.

The destruction of the prehistoric sites was largely undertaken in the early seventh century, as the result of a papal edict from Rome. Pope Gregory the Great (590-604 AD) described the British as a nation 'placed in an obscure corner of the world...hitherto...wholly taken up with the adoration of wood and stones.' He dispatched St Augustine from Rome to enforce his edict throughout the British Isles. The old idols were to be destroyed and new churches were to be built on the ruins of these old 'pagan' monuments. Any practices involving the ancient stone monuments were to be considered heretical, and ruthlessly eliminated from the new form of Christianity that ultimately overtook the Celtic Church as an omnipotent Church-State. The Celtic Church was gradually and inevitably dismantled in this takeover of power.

As a consequence of this takeover the purpose and meaning of the ancient monuments and their alignments became lost from public view. It was no longer safe to say or have written anything down concerning their intended purpose, now deemed as demonic. As forbidden relics, their purpose was not even safe to investigate or discuss any more. Yet in a delicious irony, by commanding that the new Churches were to be built on the original sites of the old pagan stones, the Pope himself had inadvertently assured the preservation of many of the prehistoric patterns they made in the landscape.

To build the new churches of the Roman religion required people with the same skills as those that erected the prehistoric stone monuments - surveyors, architects, stonemovers and stonemasons. The first two professions in this list would have required education in the traditional arts, which includes geometry, astronomy, navigation and surveying. The only established centres of learning on the western side of Britain during this period capable of delivering these subjects were - guess what? - the colleges and monasteries of the Celtic Church!

People within these colleges and monasteries would have been trained in precisely the same skills needed to recognise and adapt the existing older geometrical patterns in the landscape. The view from a newly erected church tower could only have assisted this process. Evidence has previously been produced showing that the patterns of the prehistoric geometers were familiar to people within the Celtic Church, presumably the same assemblage of monks who once taught in their colleges.

Evidently there emerged from the ashes of the Celtic Church a covert group of educated and enlightened people who *understood something of the purpose* of the older pattern in the land and was able to operate despite the injunctions against the pagan ways imposed by the Roman Church. They could even operate within the Church, with its blessing, having been edicted an open ticket to build new churches on the old sites. With their roots still firmly planted in the now cut down Celtic Church, those same monks who had previously taught Euclid, Plato and Pythagoras in their colleges merely adapted to the new regime! This group quietly initiated a resurrection of the old 'pagan' processes by not only siting churches onto the destroyed pagan sites located on the original landscape pattern, but also by decorating both the inside and outside of many of these fine buildings with blatantly pagan themes. Many of the military, royal and noble buildings of the powerful Norman family dynasties similarly display the trademarks of what one might term the Celtic Church architects.

These heretical architects were the *conscious* preservers of the 'Arthurian pattern', and to have preserved it against all the personal dangers of being found out one must assume that they understood the importance of the pattern, what the pattern was *for*, its underlying meaning. The pattern is shown here to have survived, and with it so too has our prehistoric heritage. In later centuries, the Normans were to reclaim this heritage and literally continued to build on it. Paul has ably shown that architects who knew of the system emerged from the powerful families of secular local rulers and war-lords of early Norman Britain. In so doing they too preserved the story of Arthur, our most ancient 'Once and Future King'.

LAYING THE BEARINGS

In laying out a straight line across a landscape, the most fundamental decision is knowing in which direction it is required to track. "Where are you going?" is a practical question about an intended future location that must be answered prior to starting the work in hand, whereas "Where are you coming from?" is known, it is the present position from where one started.

The traditional method of laying out a straight line over short distances is by employing three people to alternately ferry rods, one in front of the other, in alignment. The first of these rods is placed vertically above the desired start point of the exercise, and a second rod is taken some distance away and placed to set the desired direction (angle) of travel of the line. If the distance apart between these two rods is sufficiently great, an accurate angle can be defined. Practical work with college students undertaken in the 1980s demonstrated to me that it is relatively easy to set an angle accurate to a sixth of one degree with the naked eye using two poles or rods placed a mile apart. No complex technology is required to meet such a standard, ropes and poles are all that is required, along with some knowledge of basic geometry.

Once the angle of direction has been determined the third pole carrier walks on and sets the third pole in alignment with the other two. Thenceforth, the rearmost pole-walker strolls up the line to repeat the process of alignment and the line (very) slowly progresses across the landscape. Again using untrained students as surveyors, it was possible on several occasions to maintain the original angle to one part in 1,000 over a twenty mile line - an angle accurate to 99.9%.

This process can additionally include an attempt to measure the length of the line as work proceeds. With care this too can be done to high accuracy, Professor Alexander Thom managed to achieve better than one part in 1,500, or three feet in a mile (0.6m in a Km). [*Megalithic Sites in Britain & Brittany*, Oxford, 1978]. Accurate determination of length and angle is all you ever need in surveying, and these traditional methods offer an impressive precision in both, a precision which can be realised in practice.

However, there's a snag. For most lines, there is a price to pay if the line becomes longer than a few miles. The Earth is not flat, and straight lines laid out on the Earth's surface begin progressively to curve, always following a huge spiral path around the North Pole. The resulting line, if continued indefinitely would resemble a giant serpent wrapping itself around the north polar axis, just as does the constellation Draco around the celestial pole. But there are two exceptions to this effect, important for the reader in understanding the message of this book. *True North-South and East-West lines are exempt from this gradual curving effect. Tracking along a meridian (North-South) or a small circle (East-West) assures that the former line will always point straight up to the pole, maintaining the same longitude, while an east-west line would always remain at the same latitude. The importance of determining True North is now appreciated as a vital part of land surveying.*

We do not know at which epoch in human history it was realised that the Earth was a globe and that its surface was curved or who had accurately measured its size and shape, also at some unknown time in the past. This knowledge, which is clearly written down in several ancient texts, appears to have been culturally embedded into the metrology, geometry and astronomy of a long gone prehistoric culture, so that ancient units of length are commensurate with the key dimensions of the Earth. Plato, Pliny, Ptolemy and other natural philosophers accurately record both the size and shape of the Earth in their written works, and such knowledge clearly pre-dates Classical Greece (see *The Measure of Albion*, Bluestone Press, 2004).

The modern myth that the ancients thought our world to be flat certainly did not originate from the great civilisations, and appears to be a product of the Dark Age Church in Europe. Today, it is only our children who are taught that the ancients thought that the Earth was flat.

5

CORRIDORS OF POWER

The subject of Arthur had now become much bigger than I had originally envisaged. It had become, in the words of Sherlock Holmes, 'a two pipe problem', and a true mystery. By now it was much more complex than demonstrating that a polar cosmology from prehistoric times had been recorded onto the landscape, and the project was raising more complex questions that demanded answers. Like Perceval, I needed to find the right questions to ask.

An answer as to when, how and from which source people acquired the skills necessary to recognise the prehistoric pattern in the Dark Ages has been attempted. Despite an over-arching religious cultural takeover, an older culture, the Celtic Church, appears to have continued to preserve the memory of a yet still older prehistoric endeavour within the later built landscape. The later Normans similarly preserved the prehistoric legacy by erecting their forts, castles, monasteries and churches onto the existing landscape patterns.

Within the cultural life of post-Roman Britain, people began to build monuments aligned to these original prehistoric patterns. Why would they have done this if they failed to understand anything of the original purposes of these artefacts or the pattern? Did they perhaps, like us, having discovered the patterns, themselves strive to discover what they might mean? Because the later Arthurian romances display a flowering of comprehension of the ancient wisdom inherent in the geodetic patterns it appears that they succeeded in this quest.

The required understanding of the geometric rules and the techniques involved in laying down these ancient 'Arthurian' lines clearly ran from the prehistoric period to the Elizabethan era. This provides a mechanism by which cultural continuity could have taken place, and this may satisfy a reader who previously had thought that later generations simply built on ancient sites *without* understanding anything of the larger landscape patterns they help define. Paul has similarly made inroads into discovering who knew about the prehistoric pattern in medieval Cornwall. Important figures of history emerge from powerful Norman families, and they appear to have known about the the purpose that lay behind the pattern.

There were enough surviving monuments aligned to the North, or involved in geometric patterns, to suggest that my initial task here was done. Evidence of a time-line of cultural continuity and connectivity stretching out from the prehistoric period to the late medieval had been produced, together with a supporting technology of astronomical, geometrical and surveying skills. It was time to move on. But because no history book mentions any of this material, this makes moving on seem like driving out into a foggy night.

But at least the questions were clear. *How* was the demonstrable level of accuracy of these geometrical patterns achieved without our modern surveying aids? *How* was the pattern surveyed? And supremely more important than these technical questions, what was the important truth that lay behind *why* these patterns were made? What was their purpose?

Evidence drawn from the later history and legends of the local environments surrounding many of these sites fully upholds the suggestion that the later builders full well understood the hidden purposes behind the patterns. They were almost certainly geomancers - and knew exactly why they needed to place their new buildings at a particular location or on top of the ruins of a previous culture's construction.

Largely on account of the Roman Church, history leaves us completely in the dark concerning geomancy, that hidden or esoteric activity involving human interaction with the power of landscape, as it also fails to explain the enduring nature of the Arthurian mythos. Arthur may indeed be sleeping within this landscape, but is it not now an irresistible question to ask how he might be woken up? Can we now discover anything of the driving force that has had the power to sustain this theme of geomantic expression through six millennia of human culture? Not even the Egyptian civilisation lasted that long. What else has endured so long? Here is one huge mystery!

Inspecting the Evidence

In searching for North-South alignments connected with Arthur, we found not one, not a few, but dozens. In the process of identifying these there were the obvious spin-offs from any surveying exercise, the East-West alignments and the 'cross-quarter' alignments of the 'Arthur triangle', running between the four Cardinal Points. Other alignments were less relevant to our unfolding story, and have been omitted.

The modern view is that there are no actual lines running across the landscape, and that there never were. Watkins's leys are dismissed robustly by archaeologists. Yet something exists, because dowsers, geomancers and psychics can and do sense the energies flowing along an alignment. But as yet, no link has been forged between the world of the scientist and that of the intuitive or sensitive.

However, we can look at the evidence from a scientific perspective. Landscape alignments may be inferred through the tangible artefacts and natural landscape features arranged along their length. In modern times, actual alignments do exist and these include motorways, railways, canals, gas and water pipes, and electricity transmission lines. These later and often ugly additions to our landscape are engineered for the transmission of energy, goods, services and people, and although it would be presumptuous to assume a similar function for the Arthurian alignments, such a possibility cannot be ruled out just because our present scientific instruments are unable to measure anything. There may have been a power cut since the alignments were set up! Even if the prehistoric system is largely inactive after five millennia, it can still be identified. Almost forgotten, and its ancient hold largely loosened on our present culture, it has now been rediscovered and this suggests it can be better understood than at any time since the Elizabethan era.

It may be possible to reactivate something of its power, as John Michell suggested in *The View over Atlantis*. The geomancer identifies the natural telluric currents of the Earth, taking this information in order to harmonise, heal or adjust in other ways their effects on the local landscape and its inhabitants. The ancient Chinese art of Feng Shui still plays an important role in oriental life, the cultural relevance of such knowledge finding application in the siting of buildings. In the West, the Goddess movement and various spiritually based 'earth-healing' groups have recently been formed to facilitate harmonisation between Humankind and the landscape. One could argue that the entire Green movement is attempting much the same thing on a secular level.

The apparent chasm between the 'hard' science of surveying and the art of the geomancer is caused by a false and limited vision of the natural world, and the megalith builders appear to have worked within a unified system. Their monuments are beginning to reveal that they were located with full knowledge and recognition of the natural energies of the Earth, as some have long suspected they were. It is now perfectly legitimate and 'scientific' to ask whether the energies that may once have coursed along these alignments may be reactivated by those with suitable knowledge of the geomancer's art.

The Arthurian lines are only identifiable insomuch as they are sprinkled throughout their length with ancient sites from various epochs. We have purposefully ignored the flash-ponds, crossroads and other evidence for leys presented by Watkins, because we have adequate evidence already without their inclusion. But an actual line connecting these points, however impressively straight and well surveyed, no longer exists, it must be inferred by a surveyor or geometer who has seen the pattern of artefacts forming alignments across the landscape. It is as though we have found ancient railway stations, signal boxes and level crossings long after the track has been lifted and the ballast removed. The rolling stock and locomotives are missing too, as is the coal to shovel in the engine.

In true Euclidian fashion, these Arthurian lines are vanishingly thin yet they do exist, in the sense that they connect two, three or more points on an alignment. For each, one finds the same prehistoric, religious, State and Royal connections in the form of built sites placed along these alignments. And from these sites one may glean firm evidence that informs us about the accuracy by which they were originally surveyed and laid out. There are tangible measurements of length and angle to be recovered from such an exercise, whereby one may enter the minds and methodologies of the original surveyors.

In the geometry of the Arab world, lines are allowed to have width. The ever practical Muslims required this concession from Euclidian geometry in order to pack together (tesselate) those incredibly beautiful mosaic patterns that decorate their mosques. The width of these lines is known as 'the Way', and this remains a familiar word used to describe a road or path, such as Peddar's Way in East Anglia, or the Pennine Way running along the mountainous spine of northern Britain.

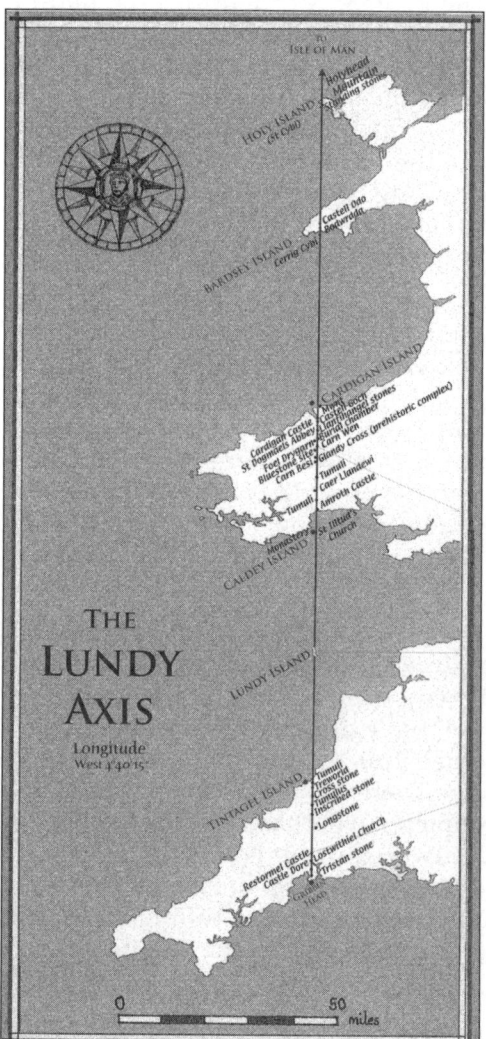

THE LUNDY AXIS

Longitude
West 4°40'15"

0   50
                miles

The abundance of 'Arthurian' North-South alignments stretching across from Cornwall to Wales suggests a 'Way', a corridor running up the west side of Britain. A remarkable number of important sites are found contained within a narrow band of longitudes between 4° 35' and 4° 45' West, and yet within this corridor may also be discovered separate 'families' of sites, connected North-South such that they are constrained within a much tighter bandwidth of longitude. This is remarkable, yet readily verifiable by anyone equipped with a 1:25000 Ordnance Survey map and ruler.

Figure 5.1. (left) & 5.2. (right).

Corridors of Power.

The two principal North-South axes passing through the centre of Cornwall and Wales. These axes are little over a mile apart, and form a corridor found to encompass much of the history of the landscape it passes over. The sites and further details, particularly concerning the Cornish section of this corridor, may be found described throughout The Secret Land. It is intended to publish a book including details of the Welsh section of these alignments in the near future, together with an investigation into the Welsh part of the 'Arthur Triangle'.

Amongst the most precise of these alignments is that now known as the 'Lundy axis', that North-South alignment that begins at Gribbin Head, on the south Cornish coast near Fowey and which can be traced as it shoots ever northwards through Cornwall, Lundy, South Wales, North Wales and on through the Isle of Man to Ayr and up to Loch Eriboll, near Cape Wrath, on the northern coast of Scotland. From a section of this axis are constructed the Stonehenge and 'Arthur' triangles and their reflections. The two maps left and right (*Figures 5.1. & 2*) show the extent and nature of this axis.

That was not the end of the matter. A secondary major axis was also identified - referred to as the 'King Arthur's Hall axis'. The two axes define a North-South corridor tracking up western Britain.

The Hall of the Moorland King

High upon Bodmin Moor may be found an enigmatic site, known as King Arthur's Hall. On a fine sunny and frosty December day I undertook a survey of the site with Paul and my partner Trish. Warmed by the effort involved in carrying the theodolite, tripod and all the other paraphernalia of surveying, the site appeared over the brow of a small knoll, about a mile from the boggy car park. With no wind and not a cloud in the sky and bolstered by some warmth from a low December sun, it was a delight to find ourselves at this spectacular example of the megalithic builder's craft.

King Arthur's Hall, (*at longitude 4° 38' 30" West*), is a rectangular bank, formed from earth dug from within its perimeter. The inside of the bank was originally set out with a rectangle of large stones. Its longer axis is aligned North-South. The central floor was apparently paved and may always have been intended to remain filled with water, as it is today, perhaps to provide a reflection of the sky to aid measuring the movement and directions of stars.

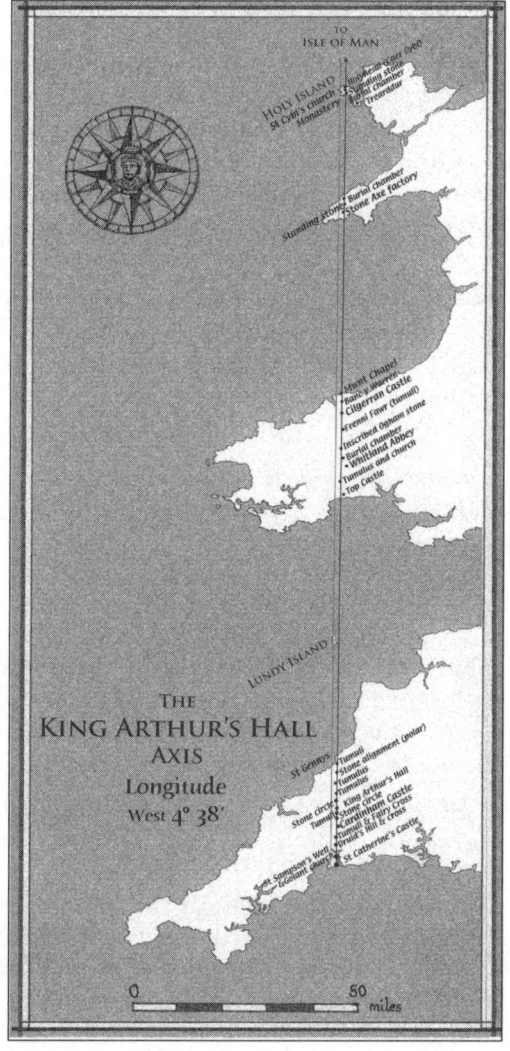

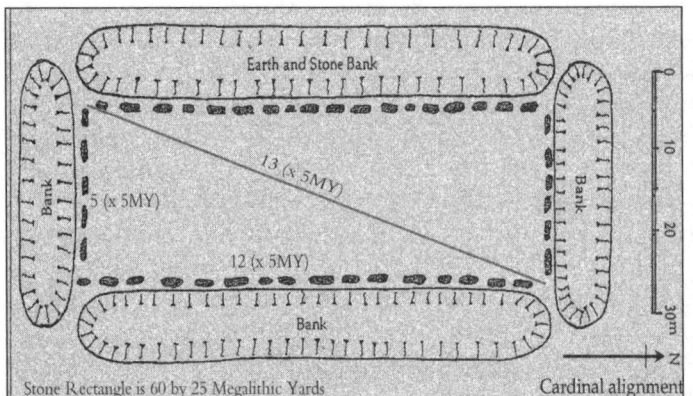

Figure 5.3.

King Arthur's Hall,
Bodmin Moor.

A survey of this site revealed the inner megalithic wall had been constructed as a 5:12 rectangle, the unit being 5 Megalithic yards. The sides of the rectangle remain closely orientated to the Cardinal Points of the compass despite the ruinous condition of the site.

The survey revealed that the rectangular stone enclosure was designed as a 5 by 12 rectangle, in units of 5 Megalithic yards (MY). For comparison, the station stone rectangle at Stonehenge is also 5 by 12, in units of 8MY. The two sites are therefore connected in both their geometry and their metrology and I consider King Arthur's Hall to be a crucially important site in providing further confirmation that the megalith builders were fully familiar with both the shape and properties of the 'Pythagorean' 5:12:13 triangle that is formed by the diagonal.

King Arthur's Hall is aligned on exactly the same line of longitude as Cardinham Castle and less than 12 seconds of longitude (840 feet) from the Boscastle stone row (*see page 100*). What is highly significant within the context of this book is that the corridor enclosed by these two axes is, near Boscastle, occupied by Paul's landscape Bear.

Prehistoric Surveying

These two polar axes demonstrate that during the prehistoric period a well informed and accurate long distance survey was undertaken along the west coast of Britain. From accurately defined North-South lines, the simple geometry of using a right angled Pythagorean triangle made up from rope divided up into twelve (the 3-4-5) or thirty (the 5-12-13) would have established similarly accurate East-West lines via the right angle inherently contained within these triangles. *The right angle forms itself naturally during the process of laying out such triangles on the ground with ropes and pegs.* Other simple geometrical techniques would have facilitated the 45 degree 'cross-quarter' angles.

There is no doubt that the megalith builders understood these things and more. Each of these techniques was plainly utilised at the sites of the monuments themselves, and long distance surveying would have emerged as a natural extension of those practices. So too would have been the use of standard units of length to cover longer distances. Having mastered at some accuracy the techniques of measuring angles and distances, the prehistoric culture was then theoretically equipped to undertake surveys to very similar standards to those of the medieval surveyors and map makers.

Their respective technologies would have been very little different. Indeed, I am certain that a prehistoric surveyor would very quickly recognise the practices and intentions of their more modern counterpart.

A remaining matter to be discussed is why long distance alignments became important to this culture. What were they trying to establish on the surface of the land?

The Power in the Land

Land mapping to establish the extent of a territory implies issues to do with ownership and boundaries, these ultimately related to *power*. Powerful tribal chiefs may well have had enough wealth and status to divert the same skills being employed by the prehistoric astronomers and navigators into this new application. *How big is the land?* is a natural question of normal human curiousity, as relevant and as natural as asking when the next Full Moon will occur, or whether that Full Moon will be eclipsed. The stones and the alignments we have uncovered here prove that the technology existed to have enabled the existing prehistoric astronomy of the period to adapt itself into land mapping. It was clearly applied.

The geodetic patterns discovered here appear to relate directly to the activities of the prehistoric astronomers. My books have revealed that the geometrical shapes which prehistoric people incorporated within their stone circles and larger landscape patterns connected land to sky in ways which would be familiar to anyone who is trained in the traditional arts. The 5, 12, 13 Pythagorean triangle possesses a geometry that facilitates integration of the solar calendar with that of the lunar month. It becomes a tool that allows the year to be calibrated into lunar months. An integrated soli-lunar calendar is a cosmic representation of the balance of masculine and feminine forces, as is the interchange of square and circular forms, or straight and curved lines.

By using just pegs and ropes, and knowing the date of the previous New or Full Moon, the 5-12-13 shape can, in just an hour or two, reveal the dates of previous or future lunations, including waxing and waning quarter Moons. This it does with precision, to the day, using 30 rods of the same length or by dividing a rope in 30 equal parts (5 + 12 + 13 = 30). Through use of these techniques, sailors could connect the Moon with the times of the tides, and also to the range of the tides, both invaluable aids to safe navigation along coastlines where the tides are very large, and the induced currents dangerously strong. If the date of the last eclipse was known, the same geometrical construction can also predict which Full and New Moons in the future are likely to be eclipsed. It is hard not to imagine that being able to forecast an eclipse would have given the astronomers enormous power amongst a populace uninitiated into this technique.

That such a simple geometry can unlock the secrets of the motion of the Sun and Moon must have appeared as magical to ancient people as perhaps it ought to us today. To perform this 'magic' a subtle interplay between the numbers twelve and thirteen is undertaken, using the number five, historically always associated with marriage, as the union of the 'male' and 'female' numbers 3 and 2. The pentangle and pentagon are amongst the most magical of ancient symbols known. Arthur, as a typical solar-hero, is associated with Jesus and a host of other solar-heros who each had twelve followers, knights or disciples respectively. The hero becomes the thirteenth, always sacrificed, and always reborn.

That the Cosmos itself is arranged to express itself in such a simple geometric form as to allow the integration of solar and lunar cycles shows us that the heavens are not chaotic, the view held by modern science. There is indeed *Cosmos* rather than chaos. This revealed truth poses important questions as to who or what 'arranged' such a simple geometrical template into which the motions of Sun and Moon are compelled to fit and through which their rhythms can be brought down onto the Earth by the simple application of a length of rope divided into 30 identical lengths. As a symbol of cosmic order, the lunation triangle would have connected an astronomer-priest directly to the Creative Force, God. It still does.

Quite a few of these geometrical forms have survived from the megalithic period. King Arthur's Hall turns out to be a 5 by 12 rectangle. In Britain there is the station stone rectangle at Stonehenge. A site near Carnac in Brittany, known as *Le Manio Quadrilateral*, is precisely laid out in contiguous stones to make the required soli-lunar calculations in order to derive the accurate calendar described above. All these sites are further related through their metrology, as is the giant geodetic triangle between Stonehenge, Lundy Island and the Bluestone site.

It should by now be becoming evident to the reader that all of these artefacts have plenty to do with Arthur. In early chapters we saw how all astronomy and all surveying starts with determining North and the Pole, and how this task invokes the Great Bear. In later chapters I suggested that North-South alignments became identified with this process and thereby naturally attracted the name Arthur or linked Arthurian myths in the towns and sites through which the alignments ran. Evidence that this practice was continued into the medieval period and how this was facilitated has also been laid out for the reader.

There is something important that has not yet been explained. The geometry of the 5, 12, 13 triangle is apparently not just a relic of a time when placing the lunar months within the year was of more significance than it is today. The form appears today in modern times, stalking the corridors of modern power within our present culture. The capital cities of Scotland, Wales and England are mysteriously but accurately arranged to form the corner points within the same geometry (*illustrated opposite in Figure 5.4.*), again aligned to the Cardinal Points of the compass. The northern apex of this huge geodetic 5, 12, 13 triangle made by connecting London, Cardiff and Edinburgh terminates directly under Arthur's Seat, a giant volcanic plug around which the entire City of Edinburgh has been built. The seat of the new Scottish Parliament has recently been expensively and inconveniently sited direct-ly on this apex. What this has to say about the knowledge and uses of hidden geomantic powers within the Modern State I leave to the reader to ponder, although an explanation is attempted in the book *Powerpoints (see bibliography)*.

There is a further aspect of this quest that connects us with the later stories concerning Arthur. In particular, it connects the esoteric and spiritual aspects of the early Christians with the later Arthurian romances of Malory, Wace and others. Arthur was the Saviour King of Britain, and most accounts find our *Once and Future King* surrounded within his court alongside twelve knights. As the Saviour King he was the thirteenth member of the group, and was sacrificed, in heroic battle, while attempting to save the Kingdom. That he is termed the once and future King

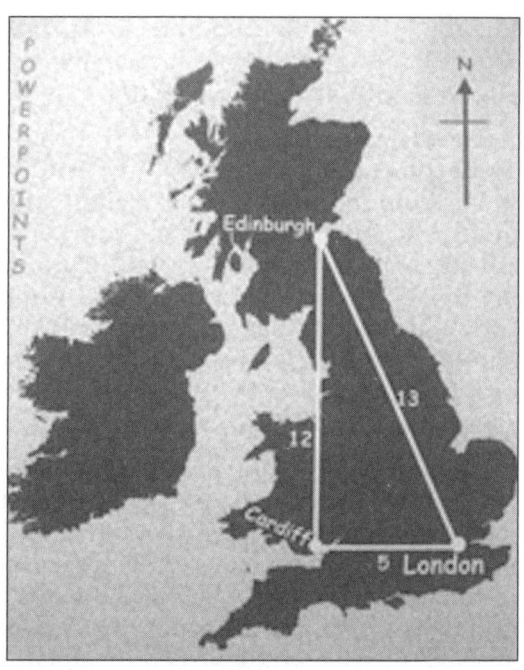

Figure 5.4. The three capital cities of the present United Kingdom are located to form the corners of an accurate 5-12-13 triangle, aligned to the Cardinal Points. Other than being an outrageous coincidence, what is suggested by such a holographic discovery, in the light of the evidence produced in this book?

implies that there will be some coming resurrection. It is transparently clear that this story in many ways carries the same mythic and numerical information as that of Jesus, who surrounded himself with twelve disciples, was destined to save his people, was sacrificed and would then rise again. For the crucifixion substitute Badon Hill. For Merlin, substitute John the Baptist or Joseph of Arimathea, for the water being turned into wine, substitute a sword being pulled from the rock, for Judas substitute Gawain, for the Magdelene substitute Gwynevere, for Second Coming substitute Future King.

Both Jesus and Arthur are classic solar-hero myths in Jungian terms and invoke the same interplay between the solar number 12 and the lunar number 13. The life of a solar-hero is an archetypal model or analogue of the journey we are all undertaking through mortal life, women too. Women are entitled to ask if they have been left out of this quest, and whether they require a complimentary ticket to ride their lives as lunar-heroines. Until recent times, women have suffered greatly within a social and religious system that has massively overvalued the male principle. Despite many centuries of the Church minimising the role and power of the feminine aspect of life the first attempts to restore feminine power, since the Roman Church attenuated it, were manifest in the time of Eleanor of Aquitaine,

Elizabeth I and within the Arthurian romances. They resurfaced with Emily Pankhurst, Marie Stopes and again in the social revolution of the 60s, where feminism was championed by Germaine Greer.

The true message of the Arthurian Romances, Courtly Love or even modern Feminism is not about reinforcing the polarity of male or female, it is about becoming more whole through integrating the qualities of male and female within each one of us, male or female, and within our culture. This was the *zeitgeist* of the medieval age, a major theme of the medieval mystics, alchemists and philosophers. And if the reader thinks that none of this has anything to do with the myth of Arthur, he or she should take a walk around Glastonbury, much of which, since the advent of the alternative culture of the late 60s has become a giant stage-set for a reinactment of the period of the Arthurian Romances.

This Holy hot-spot is a place where Early Christianity collided with the Arthurian legends, and it has consequently become the epicentre for men trying to connect with their 'feminine' side, and women learning to reconnect with their power. There are countless books about reconnection to cosmic cycles, calendars and the neglected aspects of the moon's phases. Today one sees the words *organic* and *holistic* everywhere, but they first arrived on the High Street in Glastonbury during the late 60s. There are therapies that promise to connect people to their past, present and future lives. There are courses inducing folk into the male or the female mysteries. There is the biggest music festival in Britain, every midsummer, and a children's festival. In other words, there is a questing, searching and vibrancy here that isn't to be found in such a concentration anywhere else in Britain. Here there is *permission* to explore the nature of life, whatever one thinks life is about or needs to encompass.

In prehistoric Britain, our forebears similarly embraced the need to understand the nature of life on Earth and they developed a mythology and cosmology in order to describe their world. Part of this endeavour was the need to understand the patterns and cycles of the sky, which led to the ability to survey and measure the extent of the territory under which their Cosmos revolved. This has been shown here to have played a significant role in their lives. At key moments in their cultural development star patterns were imprinted on the Earth, an early statement of 'As above, so below'. 'The Great Bear of Tintagel' and other landscape figures are simple examples of this desire to draw down the star-patterns and create huge landscape effigies, while the 'Lundy axis' and the great landscape triangles and rectangles took things a stage further, and reflect an understanding of the motions of the Sun and Moon, even the timing of eclipses.

All surveying depends on the measurement of angles and distances. To the prehistoric surveyors, the stars provided the North Point while markers placed on the distant horizon provided the degrees and minutes of modern surveying, marking the significant risings and settings of the Sun, Moon and stars. The science of geometry developed to service this need. The instrument developed through the ages to perform the task of measuring angles and distances culminated in the instrument we call the *theodolite*. According to the Oxford Etymological Dictionary, this instrument is probably named after a Greek mathematician, Theodorus. The name is most appropriate, for it means 'servant of God', from the Greek, *Theo*, God and *doulos*, servant.

The geometry of the sky and its cycles was eventually understood and the Cosmos seen to be ordered. Throughout northwestern Europe during the prehistoric period astronomer-priests were truly 'servants of God', engaged in moving huge stones in order to honour and permanently record the patterns they had observed and measured in the sky and setting up geodetic patterns on the landscape that reflected the cosmic order. This was the rich legacy of our forebears, our true history, and it has endured. It lies at the very root of our enduring fascination with the Arthurian legends and the *Matter of Britain*.

The Wheel of Heaven circles God like a mill
And it is only God encircling creation
Rumi

APPENDIX I - THE BOTTREAUX FAMILY

There has been much speculation about where the name of the Bottreaux family originates from. Some say it means 'the place above the waters' and derives from their castle set on a spur of land overlooking the village of Boscastle and its harbour, whose name is said in turn to come from *Bottreaux Castle*. Yet the name predates their occupation, and there are a number of possibilities if we consider their Norman connections. Close to the Brittany/Normandy border is a place called Les Bottereaux, and another called Tibidi Botorel (the earliest members of the family were called de Boterel in its various forms). They were related to Alan Fergant (the Red), Earl of Brittany, who became Earl of Richmond after his services at the Battle of Hastings.

He was an immensely rich and powerful character, and it was his brother Etienne and his wife Havise who gave birth to Geoffrey Botherel, who is recorded as living in Wiltshire in the early twelfth century. His son William Boterele is recorded in Cornwall from 1130 when he was the first to found the dynasty of the Boterells or the family Bottreaux which made their seat of power at Boscastle. Their crest of three toads probably came from Alan Fergant (or Ferphant), a phant being a toad.

Then again the name could come from the village near Anjou in France called Bottreaux. This would link them to the Anjou and Plantagenet dynasties, and provide much material for further speculation about the mystical driving force behind the following centuries, something beyond the scope of the present book. It is of interest, however, that Minster Church at Boscastle, the *Talkar* mentioned in the Domesday Book which, through William Bottreaux was to become an important monastery, was dedicated to St Sergius and St Dionysus of Anjou. Why should this be unless they had strong connections with the Angevins? Another possibility is that it is a name connected with the Greek *Botrus*, which means vine-cluster.

If the latter is entertained as a possibility, this could indicate followers of the Arcadian nature religion whose gods Dionysus and Bacchus were symbolised by the vine. The Bottreaux family could just as well be linked (through either the Norman or Anjou connections, or even both) to the families of the Champagne region who were so instrumental in propagating the Arthurian cycles, commissioning Chrétien de Troyes and others to write the stories down for future posterity. Or could this reference to the vine symbolise a blood line, as in the case of Jesus who was 'of the vine?'

Whatever the truth of this, the Bottreaux family tree shows they were descended from the lineage of William the Conqueror and Rollo, the first Duke of Normandy, and were thus of the bloodline of the royal families of Britain, Europe and the Viking countries. The question remains why such an influential family should make their seat of power at Boscastle. It was certainly the only sheltered harbour on this stretch of the wild north coast, and provided an important maritime link.

And yet the land was bleak and sparsely populated and this would not have really represented a sound commercial reason for settling here. It has always been notoriously difficult to transport goods to and from Boscastle, set at the end of steep and narrow hills.

But if Leland was correct when he observed that the Bottreaux were an 'ancient Cornish family' he may have been referring to the fact that they were exiled in France during Irish or Saxon incursions and only returned when William the Conqueror came. There were no less than ten Williams in the family subsequently, emphasising the royal bloodline they belonged to. Brittany was, after all, the first British colonial settlement in history. If they were distantly descended from true Cornish stock all of this would make perfect sense from what we know, and would explain why they were most likely the builders of Tintagel Castle.

APPENDIX II - DRAKE AND THE ELIZABETHANS

The Elizabethan Court in which Drake, Raleigh, Dee and a constellation of other powerful characters operated was a hotbed of secret societies, intrigue, scheming and plotting. The origins of the secret service, with its codes, encryptions, espionage and subterfuge were laid down at this time by Francis Walsingham and a small select group of undercover agents. Dee and Drake were necessarily deeply involved in this, and the great strides forward in the science of navigation at this time were partly due to such activities. Mapping, a knowledge of the stars and these sources of covert information all contributed to the discoveries of new lands which created the beginning of the British Empire. Amongst Dee's voluminous writings was *The Perfect Art of Navigation* that convinced Drake he could circumnavigate the globe.

But beyond this adventuring and privateering (Drake was, amongst other things, a pirate, slave trader and effectively commander of his own private navy) lay the idea of the re-establishment of Britain as a rich and powerful kingdom based on Arthurian ideals. Dee was galvanised by the idea of such a restoration of British supremacy, introducing the sextant and teaching navigation and astronomy at his house in Mortlake, which reputedly had more books in its library than any other in Europe. The members of this 'Invisible College' were the prime movers of the Elizabethan court, and included Francis Bacon who wrote *The New Atlantis* urging a renaissance of the arts, sciences and higher ideals for all, as well as the Rosicrucian Robert Fludd. Alchemy and mysticism and a return to the great Age of Arthur was thus the background to this vibrant period of British history.

The fact that Drake chose to have himself elected MP for Bossiney and was inaugurated on top of the Mound (to which the Great Bear appears tethered) may point to the fact that remnants of the old wisdom persisted amongst certain members of Elizabeth's court, especially those steeped in Westcountry traditions. When Elizabeth rewarded Drake for returning to England with vast hoards of Spanish gold, she gave him the Cistercian Abbey at Buckland, just to the north of Plymouth. Buck-land means, of course, the land of Buck, Bucca or Puck, and Drake must have been as familiar with the giant turf-cut figures on Plymouth Hoe just as much as the legend of Arthur's birth at Tintagel. In local tradition, Drake was to not only become a later version of Arthur who would one day come back when his country needs him most, but he was also his own leader of the Wild Hunt, galloping across Dartmoor on stormy and moonless nights with headless horses and the Wish Hounds snapping at their heels.

If, as I have suggested, these giant effigies on Plymouth Hoe were somehow a memory of the annual battle between Gwyn (or Puck) and Gwythyr, then it is possible that Drake and/or Dee (who mentions the tradition of the Glastonbury Zodiac and was immersed in the mystical lore of Britain) also knew of the Cornish Grail material and wished to align themselves with it. The two giants, which could be seen on the Hoe during Drake's time (he was, after all, inclined to go there for a game of bowls!) may even have been incorporated into popular culture. Michael Drayton, in *Polyolbion* of 1622 describes Cornish soldiers going into battle at Agincourt flying a banner featuring two wrestlers. Could this have been a folk memory of the battle of the old giants of British prehistory, invoked to ensure victory? Was Cornish wrestling itself a symbolic re-enactment of this heroic fight between the old gods of Light and Dark, deeply embedded in folk culture? It may seem an extraordinary idea, but many such games and pastimes are known to have had a symbolic function relating to ancient ritual.

Drake, Mayor of Plymouth and public benefactor, must have had an abiding interest in these traditions, being a Westcountryman born and brought up surrounded by such ideas. He is said to have often stayed at *The Ship* in the port of Fowey, at the southern end of the Polar Axis of the Great Bear. Did Drake, Raleigh and their seagoing compatriots, all students of star-lore for practical navigational purposes, understand something of its mystical dimension in an age when Science, Magick (as it was spelt in Elizabethan times), Astronomy and Astrology were all believed to be closely related? Were they actively involved in seeking to fulfil some prophetic vision, empowering ancient Albion to be restored to its legendary glory days? It is a very curious fact indeed that Drake's home, Buckland Abbey, lies precisely due North of Plymouth Hoe where the giants were located, the site of the mythical founding of ancient Britain.

Another distinguished Elizabethan who was a member for a Cornish constituency was Sir Henry Neville who represented Liskeard from 1597 to 1598. He was married to a Cornishwoman, Anne Killigrew from Falmouth and therefore had many family connections in the Westcountry. He was also a friend of Richard Carew whose *Survey of Cornwall* has often been referred to in this book. In fact Sir Henry was so close a friend to Carew that the two travelled together to France along with Carew's son when Sir Henry was sent by Queen Elizabeth to Paris as English ambassador in 1599.

Sir Henry Neville was an important aristocrat descended from John of Gaunt and from the Nevilles of Warwick, but that is not the main reason for modern interest in him. In 2005 two academic writers, Brenda James and William D.

Rubinstein published a book called *The Truth Will Out* in which they convincingly argued the case for Sir Henry being the true author of the Shakespeare plays. (The actor William Shakespeare agreed to let his name be used to conceal Neville's true identity). Since then other books have developed the initial idea and its implications, but without seeing much significance in Neville's Cornish connections.

Richard Carew was married to an Arundell, whose distinguished family with its wolf crest was likely to have known about the shapes carved into the countryside in their local area and, as Carew spent time travelling with Neville, it is certainly possible that he would have shared some of this knowledge on the secret land of Cornwall with his friend. Neville might also have heard stories about Cornwall through his in-laws.

The potential implications of this for Shakespearean studies are immense. To be initiated into the powerful encoded images in the Cornish landscape would have made an extraordinary impact on a literary genius who based many of his plays on ancient legend as well as the history of Britain in which his own family had played such an important part. The secret of the images would also have appealed to a man who had to publish his plays under the pseudonym of Shakespeare and keep his own identity hidden. The Elizabethans frequently used codes to conceal their secrets, both in serious espionage and in literature, so they would have felt an affinity with hidden meanings in the landscape. Neville was also a good astronomer and would have been very interested in theories about the circumpolar stars and Arthurian legends. It seems quite remarkable under the circumstances that the Neville family crest originally depicted two Bears dancing around a central pole, just like Ursa Major and Ursa Minor. Later this was adapted into the 'Bear and Ragged Staff' of the Nevilles, known as the *Kingmakers* because of their royal influence.

The last group of Shakespeare's plays (including Pericles, Cymbeline, The Winter's Tale and The Tempest) seem especially to be in the spirit of the Cornish countryside with its ancient myths and country traditions. One Shakespeare critic, Edward Dowden, in his introduction to Cymbeline, said that in these last plays 'Divine Oracles, benign enchantment, visions, supernatural beings stand as shadows or symbols of those higher powers that encircle human existence'.

The ancient landscape of Cornwall with its pagan past and history of Celtic saints, together with the mysteries outlined in this book, could certainly be described in a similar way. If Neville is one day accepted as the author of the plays then the Cornish landscape images and legends, and the menagerie of animals on family crests and in local churches, could become a rich mine for the Shakespeare scholars of the future. As a starting point the famous stage direction in The Winter's Tale — 'Exit, pursued by a Bear' — would certainly have some fresh light thrown on it by the Great Bear of Tintagel!

APPENDIX III - THE HUNT OF VENUS

The planet Venus is the brightest 'star' in the sky and is a close companion to the Sun, never straying more than 48° from it. It also approaches Earth closer than any other heavenly body except the Moon, with which it is especially associated, hence it was known in earlier times as the 'daughter of the Moon'. As it is so strongly connected with both Moon and Sun it is also the planet of love and attraction, a very ancient goddess of fertility whose names are many, including Inanna, (the Sumerian 'Queen of Heaven') Isis (in her role as companion to Ra), Astarte, (from which the word *star* derives) Ashtaroth, Aphrodite and Diana. Its movements between one and the other, sometimes as the morning star and sometimes as the evening star, made it appear as if it were being hunted, and this Hunt of Venus came to be known as a metaphor for the hunt for love.

From Earth it traces a perfect pentagram in the sky over an eight-year cycle, and because of this the five-pointed star has come to be one of the most ancient and enduring symbols of the perennial wisdom concerning the rhythms of Nature. The bright star in the crescent of the new Moon, as if being cradled in its arms, has always been a symbol of mystical power, hence its adoption by a number of religions. In prehistoric times Venus, as the planet of love, was especially important for the increase of population, and the famous rock carving of the Venus of Laussel (about 20,000BC) has the goddess holding a horn marked with thirteen notches, the number of the months in a lunar year, and holding her pregnant belly. Venus and its association with the Moon came to stand for the Divine Feminine principle transmitted from age to age, and its occult power is behind the Adam and Eve story and the Tree of Knowledge.

The Hunt of Venus became absorbed into classical mythology in the story of Diana, where she carries a Moon-like crescent bow with which to shoot her prey. She is attended by hares, the archetypal lunar animal. The Anglo-Saxon and Celtic goddess Oestre whose special time became the Christian Easter combines all three elements; the rebirth of the Sun in the spring, the first full Moon after the vernal equinox, and the rampant lascivious behaviour of the Mad March Hare which epitomises the awakening energy of the Earth Goddess. The motif of the three hares chasing each other around in a circle (the *Tinners' Hares*) symbolises these three aspects and the way they are locked together in a continuous dance, hence its alternative name the *Hunt of Venus*. Venusian imagery can be seen

in many churches, including Lewannick, to the North of the effigy of the Great Hare. Under the stone seats inside the porch is the very worn carving of a hunting scene where a hare is being chased. Inside, the magnificent font, one of the finest in Cornwall, is carved with maze patterns and a pentagram.

RECENT ARCHAEOLOGICAL DISCOVERIES
AT THE GREAT BEAR OF TINTAGEL

As this book was being prepared for publication a number of discoveries have been made that are of particular interest. Engineers working for South West Water on the last phase of the 'Clean Sweep' project to improve the quality of the local coastal waters found a collection of about forty graves which may date back as early as the fourth century. The site is not far from 'Paradise' at Boscastle and indicates that this area was thought to be of special sanctity. Where better to be buried than at the top of the Bear's Head?

These cist graves—stone-lined boxes covered with large slabs—were empty because their contents had been eaten away by the acid soil. A rare example of a Gwithian style jar dating from the sixth to the eighth centuries was also recovered. The site has now been given special protection pending further investigation.

Probably the most interesting aspect of this find is that the graves were a mix of Pagan and Christian; that is, they were oriented North-South and East-West respectively, demonstrating two things. The first is that Pagans and Christians apparently lived (and died) side by side during the 'Arthurian' period of the Dark Ages when Celtic Christianity was at its apogee. The second is that the transition from a preoccupation with North (the cosmic centre) to East (the rising Sun) is quite graphically demonstrated.

In June 2009 they also discovered, whilst digging the foundations for a treatment plant, a remarkably large Bronze Age roundhouse at Trevalga near Tintagel, very close to the remains of King Arthur's Quoit. This unique structure has so far brought to light a number of associated artefacts including moulds for casting metals. The style of its construction is quite extraordinary for its age, the walls being lined with large slate slabs. Since nothing as large and sophisticated as this has ever been found before, archaeologists are naturally baffled. The area around it has revealed nothing, so it was not part of a settlement. Standing alone in this exposed position, its entrance was on the South away from the prevailing wind, with a paved area on the North whose purpose is unknown. The site is right on the outline of the Great Bear, near the bridge of its snout.

Another site that has been excavated is the 'lost village' of Old Melorne at Slaughterbridge, right at the centre of the Bear's Polar Axis (access is through The Arthurian Centre where there is an excellent exhibition of Arthurian legend). Previously a collection of tumps and hummocks beside an earthwork, the foundations of the buildings underneath are notable for their unexpectedly fine finishing, with flag slate floors and hearths. The site is unfortunately marred by electricity pylons, but is interesting for its length of occupation. It is thought to have been occupied as far back as the thirteenth century as a medieval farm and was still in use up until the nineteenth. The concentration of remains in this small area, with Old Melorne, the possibility of two battle sites, one where Arthur and Mordred reputedly fought and another, the supposed site of the

Battle of Gafulford mentioned in the Saxon Chronicle as taking place in 823, the Elizabethan Worthyvale Manor and 'King Arthur's Stone' seems indicative of its one-time singular importance. The Arthurian Centre has now provided a focus for these disparate elements of historical interest and its existence here, almost exactly on the Polar Axis, seems a continuation of a long and eventful history, as well as a response to awakening interest in these matters.

APPENDIX V - THE KING OF LOSTWITHIEL

In J.G. Frazer's *The Golden Bough* there occurs a curious remnant of ancient ritual concerning kingship and the Cornish Town of Lostwithiel. The passage is worth quoting in full:

'A custom of annually appointing a mock king for a single day was observed at Lostwithiel in Cornwall down to the sixteenth century. On little Easter Sunday the freeholders of the town and manor assembled together, either in person or by their deputies, and one among them, as it fell to his lot by turn, gaily attired and gallantly mounted, with a crown on his head, a sceptre in his hand, and a sword borne before him, rode through the principal street to the church, dutifully attended by all the rest on horseback. The clergyman in his best robes received him at the churchyard stile and conducted him to hear divine service. On leaving the church he repaired, with the same pomp, to a house provided for his reception. Here a feast awaited him and his suite, and being set at the head of the table he was served on bended knees, with all the rites due to the estate of a prince. The ceremony ended with the dinner, and every man returned home.'

This intriguing glimpse of an annual ceremony taking place at Easter appears to have overtones of the Christian myth of Jesus mixed with archaic mock kingship rites like those occurring at the Winter Solstice. Its survival into the sixteenth century suggests that Lostwithiel retained its ancient connections with the kingship traditions of far earlier times and may have also have kept alive a memory of the royal associations of the Polar Axis, on which the Church of St Bartholemew's with its unique font is built.

APPENDIX VI - A FLIGHT TO THE EAST?

One last possible figure should be mentioned before this current book draws to its close. I spotted it some years ago but it took some time before realising that it was probably a genuine effigy. I noticed what appeared to be a giant Bird, or rather its head and the leading edge of its wings, flying towards the East. It was drawn by the roads running around the base of Kit Hill near Callington, the most outstanding feature of the district and a striking landmark, topped by its distinctive old mine stack. From the tip of its beak ran a dead straight road Eastwards to Drakewalls, and beyond, Dartmoor.

The reason for my reticence was that despite consulting a number of illustrated bird books I could come to no firm conclusion as to exactly what type it might be. Various possibilities presented themselves; too many, for the shape of its head and beak could be said to represent a great variety of birds, especially as juveniles often exhibit this characteristic look before reaching maturity. It could also be a species that has since died out or evolved into something else. Another complication was that the roads at the base of the Hill had been disturbed by centuries of industrial activity.

Yet the figure seems convincing. It is exactly due East of the Great Hare's head and is also flying in the same direction—towards the rising Sun at the equinoxes. It is rich in history and ancient sites which cluster around it. These include Dupath Holy Well, a Gothic oratory and healing spring built by the monks of St Germans, Castlewitch Henge, in Neolithic times a sort of wooden version of Stonehenge, and the great earthworks of Cadsonbury. Kit Hill, from which Lundy Island can be seen on a clear day, is topped by an 'ancient British Camp' according to the Old Cornwall Society, although the area has suffered greatly from mining and quarrying, just like Stowes Hill to the West. The fine granite from here has gone to build at least six bridges in London as well as the Thames Embankment. It is a curious thing to stroll along the Thames and think of the stone under your feet as coming from these Cornish power centres.

Kit Hill's mineral wealth was legendary, being for some centuries one of the richest places in Cornwall for tin. Carew quotes a country saying of the time; 'Hengsten downe, well ywrought, Is worth London towne, dear ybought'. He also recorded it was a place noted for its 'Cornish Diamonds' or pure quartz crystals found during mining operations.

The railway which runs around the top of the Bird's head has probably changed the character of the lower slopes too. Certain names though, may point to its importance in the past. There is *Monkscross* where the beak joins the head and *Sevenstones* at the tip of its beak, just above a place called *Rising Sun*. Where its eye may once have been is now an unseemly scattering of loose stone or 'clitters' left over from quarrying.

Callington has a number of Arthurian and historical associations of relevance. It was thought in the past to be one of the prime candidates for King Arthur's great Cornish stronghold of Celliwic, together with Castle Killibury, whether because of its closeness to Kit Hill or Stowes Hill is not clear. The old church of St Mary's in the town has much of interest. It was built on the site of an ancient chapel by Nicholas Ayssheton in 1465. Ayssheton's early history is not known; it has been speculated he may have been the son of the alchemist Thomas Ashton, whose father fought at Agincourt. Then again he could have been the son of Reginald Aishton who held one of the manor farms in 1392. If so he would have been educated by the monks of Tavistock or St Germans before taking up Law. In 1433 he was appointed executor of the will of Sir John Arundell and over the next few years became highly influential, holding the patronage of many churches in Devon and Cornwall and even living for a time at St Columb.

The magnificent alabaster tomb memorial of Robert, first Lord Willoughby de Broke, one to rival Prior Vyvyan's tomb at Bodmin, can be seen near the altar. A close friend of Henry VII he was a Knight of the Order of the Garter and rose to become Lord High Steward, the highest office in government. His last official act was to escort Princess Catherine of Aragon to meet her future husband Prince Arthur, Henry's first son. Henry wished to use his power to restore King Arthur's mythical lost realm, as we have already touched on. The tragedy for him was that Prince Arthur was to die young and so the new Arthurian dynasty never materialised. In fact Henry VIII came to the throne and his reign was to finish with a wasteland of destroyed abbeys and monasteries.

A whole chapter (or even a book) could be written about the history and sites of this area, but what led me in the end to consider that this probably was indeed a giant Bird flying towards the Sun was the fact that Hingston Down (Hengest's Down), of which it forms part, is the site of the final battle between the Cornish and the Anglo-Saxons which eventually spelled the end of Cornish independence and its Celtic Christian traditions. The question is; could the Cornish have specifically chosen this place to make a last-ditch stand against the might of the Anglo-Saxon and Roman Church because of its symbolic importance to them?

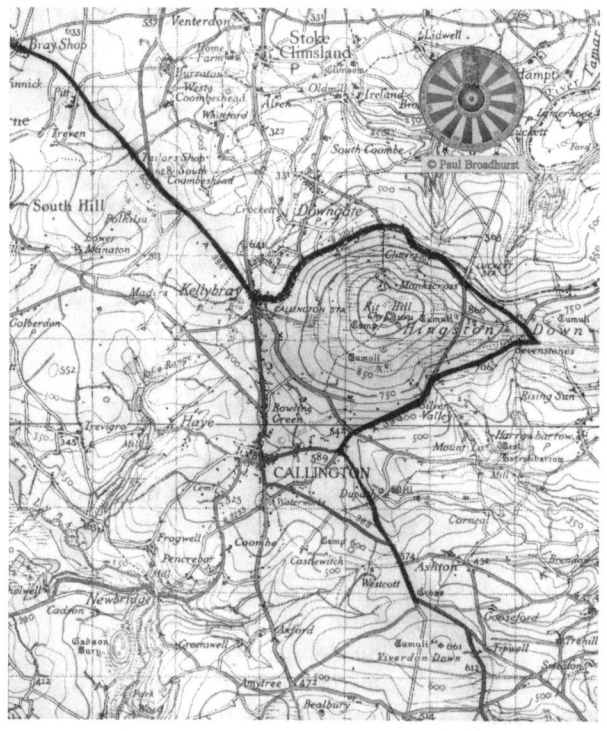

And what is the Bird? In the absence of any definite identification I like the idea of it being some sort of Hawk, since the roads that form the point of its beak could have been altered at some time in the past, like the others surrounding the Hill, thereby changing what may have once been a hooked beak. Kit Hill means Kite's Hill, and country people often use the term Kite for any large bird of prey which soars high up in the sky. If this is entertained as a possibility, then it could be an early symbol for Gawain, the 'Hawk of May'. Many cultures use the Hawk as a glyph of the Sun.

It could also explain why the mounted Knight on the Lostwithiel font has a Hawk on his arm, symbolically empowering the Lord of the Animals, his companions and the land in which they reside with the force of the rising Sun and the changing ages of the precessional cycle.

THE SECRET LAND

Material for this book has been gleaned from many different sources, and it would be impossible to point the reader to each individual reference. The regional daily paper for the Westcountry, *The Western Morning News*, has proved invaluable through book reviews and articles on local history over the years, and continues to be a source of well-researched material. Second-hand bookshops have also been a treasure trove of useful information, since copies of *Old Cornwall*, the journal of the Old Cornwall Society, can be bought for very little yet contain considerable scholarship. Similarly, the series of booklets *Devon and Cornwall Notes and Queries* contains much that is of interest, especially in the fields of archaeology and genealogy. The Cornish magazine *Meyn Mamvro* is probably the best source concerning megaliths and other ancient sites in Cornwall. And it is probably true to say that without the excellence of the wealth of Church Guides, many of the connections which have proved so valuable to this quest may not have become apparent. Always buy one, and be generous with your donation!

Other books referred to are as follows, arranged under headings that should prove useful to anyone wishing to follow up on any matters arising from the main text:

PREHISTORIC BEAR CULTS AND BEAR MYTHOLOGY
Ashe, Geoffrey *The Ancient Wisdom*, Abacus London 1979
Baring, Anne and Cashford, Jules *The Myth of the Goddess* Arkana, London 1991
Brunner, Bernd *Bears A Brief History* Yale University Press 2007
Campbell, Joseph *The Way of the Animal Powers* Times Books, London 1984
Campbell and Loy *Humankind Emerging* HarperCollins New York 1996
Chauvet, Jean-Marie *The Dawn of Art* Thames and Hudson London 1996
Frank, Roslyn M. *Hunting the European Sky-Bears: When Bears ruled
    the Earth and guarded the Gate of Heaven* Astronomical traditions in past
        Cultures, Sofia: Institute of Astronomy 1996
Michell, John New *Light on the Ancient Mystery of Glastonbury* Gothic Image 1990

CORNISH HISTORY AND MYTHOLOGY
Baring Gould, Sabine A Book of Cornwall Methuen, London 1925
Borlase William *Antiquities Historical and Monumental
    of the County of Cornwall* Bowyer and Nichols 1769
Broadhurst, Paul *Tintagel and the Arthurian Mythos* Pendragon Press 1992
Broadhurst, Paul *Secret Shrines* Pendragon Press 1988
Broadhurst, Paul, and Miller, Hamish *The Sun and the Serpent* Mythos 2006
Canner, A.C. *The Parish of Tintagel* Friary-Clark Ltd. 1982
Carew, Richard *The Survey of Cornwall* Andrew Melrose London 1969
Deane, Tony and Shaw, Tony *Folklore of Cornwall* The History Press 2009
Dexter, T.G.F. *Cornish Names* Bradford Barton Truro 1968
Doble, Gilbert *The Saints of Cornwall* Llanerch Felinfach 1997
Gilbert, Davies *The Parochial History of Cornwall* J.B.Nichols and Son London 1838
Hawker R.S. *Footprints of Former Men in Far Cornwall*
    Westaway Books London 1948
Henderson, Charles *Cornish Church Guide* Bradford Barton Truro 1964
Hockin, J.R.A. *Walking in Cornwall* Methuen and Co. London 1944
Hole, Christina *English Folk Heroes* Batsford, London 1948
Irving Little, Roger *Boscastle* Camelot Pottery Cornwall 1985
James, Beryl *Tales of the Saint's Way* Dyllansow Truran 1993
John, Catherine Rachel *The Saints of Cornwall* Lodenek Press Padstow 1981
Knight, Rod and Anne *The Book of Boscastle* Halsgrove Tiverton 2004
Langdon, Arthur G. *Old Cornish Crosses* Cornwall Books 1988
Lightbody, Sheila *The Book of Callington* Barracuda Buckingham 1982

Pevsner, Nikolaus, and Radcliffe, Enid *The Buildings of England*: *Cornwall*
    Penguin 1990
Redding, Cyrus *An Illustrated Itinerary of Cornwall* How and Parsons, London 1887
Rowse, A.L. *Tudor Cornwall* Truran Books, Truro 2005
Thomas, Charles *Tintagel, Arthur and Archaeology* Batsford London 1993
Venning, Arthur Bate *The Book of Launceston* Barracuda Books Chesham 1976
Warden Page, John Lloyd *The North Coast of Cornwall* Joseph Pollard Truro 1897
Weatherhill, Craig *Cornish Place Names and Language* Sigma, Wilmslow 1995
Whetter, Dr. James *Cornwall in the 13th Century* Palace Printers Lostwithiel 1998

ARTHURIAN MYTHOLOGY

Anderson, J.J. *Sir Gawain and the Green Knight* J.M.Dent London 2002
Ashe, Geoffrey *The Quest for Arthur's Britain* Academy Chicago 1987
Bédier, J and Belloc, Hilaire *The Romance of Tristan and Iseult*
    DoverPublications New York 2005
Evans, Sebastian *The High History of the Holy Grail* James Clarke
Fitch, Eric L. *In Search of Herne the Hunter* Capall Bann 1994
Jenkins, Elizabeth *The Mystery of King Arthur* Michael Joseph 1975
Jones, Gwyn and Thomas *The Mabinogion* J.M.Dent & Sons London 1950
Knight, Gareth *The Secret Tradition in Arthurian Legend* Aquarian
    Press Northants 1983
Loomis, Roger Sherman The Grail - *From Celtic Myth to Christian Symbol*
    Constable, London 1992
Maltwood, Katherine *Enchantments of Britain* James Clarke, Cambridge 1982
Matthews, Caitlin and John *King Arthur's Raid on the Underworld*
    Gothic Image, Glastonbury 2008
Matthews, John *Gawain, Knight of the Goddess* Aquarian Press Northants 1990
Seddon, Richard *The Mystery of Arthur at Tintagel* Rudolf Steiner
    Press London 1990
Senior, Michael *Sir Thomas Malory's Tales of King Arthur* Guild Publishing 1980
Spence, Lewis *The Mysteries of Britain* Aquarian London 1970
Stein, Walter Johannes *The Death of Merlin* Floris Edinburgh 1989
Weston, Paul *Mysterium Artorius* Avalonian Aeon Glastonbury 2007
Wilson, Joy *Cornwall Land of Legend* Bossiney Books Cornwall 198

PREHISTORIC CORNWALL

Barnatt, John *Prehistoric Cornwall* Turnstone Press, Wellingborough 1982
Henwood, Philip *Prehistoric East Cornwall* Henwood, Callington 2007
Payne, Robon, and Lewsey, Rosemarie *The Romance of the Stones*
    Alexander Associates Fowey 1999
Straffon, Cheryl ed. *Meyn Mamvro* magazine St Just

ASTRONOMY

Cornelius, Geoffrey *The Complete Guide to the Constellations*
Duncan Baird London 1997
De Santillana, Giorgio and Von Dechund, Hertha *Hamlet's Mill*
    David R. Godine, Boston 1977
Hinckley Allen, Richard *Star Names Their Lore and Meaning*
    Dover NewYork 1963
Lockyer, Sir Norman *Stonehenge and other British Stone Monuments Astronomically
    Considered* Macmillan London 1909
Michell, John *At the Centre of the World* Thames and Hudson 1994
Temple, Robert *The Sirius Mystery* Century London 1998 (Since *The Sirius Mystery*
    Robert Temple, along with his wife Olivia, have published *The Sphinx Mystery*
    detailing how the Sphinx was originally a huge statue of Anubis standing in
    the middle of a lake, guarding the Giza pyramid field, the entrance to the
    Egyptian Underworld).

NORMANS AND VIKINGS
Denholm-Young, N. *Richard of Cornwall* Basil Blackwell Oxford 1947
Bellingham, Whittaker and Grant *Myths and Legends* Quintet London 1992
Harvey, John *The Plantagenets* B.T.Batsford London 1948
Leitch, Yuri *Gwyn* Temple Publications, Somerset 2007
Montgomery, Hugh *The God-Kings of Europe* The Book Tree, California 2006
Savage, Anne *The Anglo-Saxon Chronicles* BCA London 1984

SAINTS AND CELTIC LORE
Spencer, Ray *A Guide to the Saints of Wales and the Westcountry* Llanerch 1991
Stewart, R.J. Ed. *The Book of Merlin* Blandford Press Dorset 1987
Stewart, R.J. *The Mystic Life of Merlin* Arkana 1986
Stewart, R.J. *The Prophetic Vision of Merlin* Arkana 1986
Stewart R.J. ed. *The Book of Merlin* Blandford Press Dorset 1987
Stewart, R.J. and Matthews, John *Merlin Through the Ages* Blandford Dorset 1995
Taylor, Thomas *The Life of St Samson of Dol* Llanerch Felinfach 1991

LUNDY ISLAND
Chanter, John R *Lundy Island a monograph* Westwell Publishing
     Appledore reprinted 1997
Farrah, Robert *'There was a Holy Race of Men on Lundy': A Speculative Literature
     Search for the Otherworld Island* Time and Mind: The Journal of Archaeology,
     Consciousness and Culture Vol 2 Issue 2 July 2009 Berg
Langham, A and M *Lundy* David & Charles Newton Abbot 1970
Petherton, Col. P.T. and Barlow, Vernon *Lundy- the Tempestuous Isle*
     Lutterworth Press London 1960
Thomas, Charles *And Shall These Mute Stones Speak?* University of Wales
     Press 1994

OTHER BOOKS OF INTEREST
French, Peter *John Dee The World of an Elizabethan Magus* RKP London 1972
Friar, Stephen *Heraldry* Alan Sutton, Stroud 1997
Matthews, John *Healing the Wounded King* Element Dorset 1997
Stewart, R.J. *The Underworld Initiation* Aquarian Press Northants 1985

*Books by Paul Broadhurst, published by MYTHOS can be obtained
from www.mythospress.co.uk. Books by Robin Heath published by
Bluestone Press may be purchased from www.skyandlandscape.com.
(Some titles are out of print and only available secondhand).*

THE QUEST FOR THE PREHISTORIC ARTHUR

Sun, Moon & Stonehenge, Robin Heath, Bluestone Press 1998
The Measure of Albion, Robin Heath & John Michell, Bluestone Press 2004
Sun, Moon & Earth, Robin Heath, Wooden Books 1999
Stonehenge, Robin Heath, Wooden Books 2000
Powerpoints, Robin Heath, Bluestone Press 2005
Alexander Thom: Cracking the Stone Age Code, Robin Heath, Bluestone Press 2007
The View over Atlantis, John Michell, Garnstone Press 1969
The Old Straight Track, Alfred Watkins 1925
The Key to the Temple, David Furlong, Piatkus 1996
Megalithic Sites in Britain, Alexander Thom. Oxford 1967
Megalithic Remains in Britain & Brittany, A Thom & A S Thom, Oxford 1978
Landscape & Memory, Simon Schama, Harper Collins 1995
Before Civilisation, Colin Renfrew, Pimlico 1999
A History of Pagan Europe, Prudence Jones & Nigel Pennick, Routledge 1995

Alchemy 206, 250-8
Annwn 71, 155, 248, 276, 278-9
Anubis 171-5
Arcadia 33, 38-40
Arcturus 38-40
Arianrhod 248, 250
Artemis 32, 34
Arthur as title 42
Arthur Stones, the 100-1
Arundell family 166-70, 176-81, 220
Athelstan 108-9
Atkinson, Richard 98
Ashe, Geoffrey 71, 148, 278

Baptism 145
Baring Gould, Sabine 199,213, 261
Basques 25, 29, 31
Bear and Ragged Staff 35
Bearah Tor 224, 274
Bear Cult, prehistoric 18-40
Bear etymology 31-2, 37
Bears as healers 31
Bear, Little 19, 25, 33-4
Bear, Mother 20, 34, 36-9, 61
Bear people 30
Beheading Game 122-4
Berserkers 49
Bishop, George 215
Blaise 229
Black Prince 125-6
Blisland 152
Boars 150
Boconnoc 235-243, 256-8
Bodmin Beacon 108, 111
Bodmin font 144-5
Bodmin Gospels 109
Bodmin Priory 106-9
Boscastle 15, 53-64, 67
Bossiney 15, 17, 72
Bossiney Mound 73-6, 81
Botelet 253-4
Bottreaux family 15, 17, 56-8, 65, 75, 120, 213, 215, 253-4, 288
Braddock 237-8, 240-2
Brauron 34
Brittany 45-7, 200, 271
Brutus 103
Brychan, King 81, 154, 254, 281
Bucca 223-4
Bury Down 232

Callisto 32
Camelford 16-7, 64-6, 236
Canis Major 26, 174-6, 222
Caradon Hill 194, 196
Caradon Town 211
Carew, Richard 65, 83, 106 -7, 114-5, 127, 176-7, 259-60
Cardinham 157, 160
Cardinham family 109, 117, 122, 127-8, 133-4, 157, 160, 162
Carminow family 236
Castle-an-Dinas 192
Castle Canyke 108
Castle Dameliock 148, 192
Castle Dore 99, 158, 238, 271
Celliwic 149, 157
Celtic Christianity 45-6, 48-9, 143-151
Cheesewring 102, 198, 223-4
Civil War 237-8
Corona Borealis 248
Creiddylad 247-8

Darley Oak 211
Dee, John 67, 74, 80, 85
Devil 209, 214, 234
Devil's Doorway 214
Dexter T.G.F. 218
Diodorus Siculus 172, 265
Dobwalls 195
Dormarth 248-9
Draco 19, 26, 40, 213-4, 229
Drachenloch 21-2
Drake, Sir Francis 68, 73-4
Druids 45-6, 48-9, 143, 151, 182-3, 199, 211, 244
Druid's Hill, Boconnoc 235, 37, 239
Dunster Castle 184

Earendel 186-7
Earth Energy 132-3, 148, 219
Easter Fire 212
Edmund, Prince 124-5
Egloskerry Church 57, 213
Eleanor of Aquitane 221
Excalibur 41

Farrah, Robert 278
Fogous 83-4
Footprint stones 86-8
Fowey 129, 232, 239, 266
Frank, Roslyn M. 25, 27, 29, 31

Fraser, Barbara 106
Freemasonry 37
Garden of Eden 263-6
Gawain 122, 135, 264
Geoffrey of Monmouth 13, 42, 45, 47, 75, 79, 103, 150, 157
Giants 232-61, 284-5
Giant's Hedge 232, 239
Gibbs, Kevin 64, 101
Gildas 13
Glastonbury 53-5, 64, 245, 250-1
Glastonbury Zodiac 106, 248
Gogmagog 103, 261
Grail legends 49, 71
Graves, Robert 244, 279
Great Bear 18-21, 33, 40, 72, 97, 103-4, 161, 277
Great Bear of Tintagel 15-18, 27, 55-78
Great Dog or Wolf of St Columb 163-188
Great Hare of Bodmin Moor 194-226, 256
Guinevere 158, 229, 247, 264
Gumb, Daniel 225-6
Greek Bear myth 32-5
Green Knight 122
Grenville Sir Bevill 191, 237-8
Grenville, Sir Richard 288
Grylls family 252-3
Gwythyr ap Greidawl 247-8, 261, 274
Gwyn ap Nudd 240, 242-4, 247-51, 255-61, 273-4, 275-9, 284, 290

Hallwell nr. Launceston 215
Hamlet's Mill 186-7, 250, 321
Hares 26, 201-222
Hawker R.S. 53, 62-3, 225
Higgins, Sharon 278
High History of the Holy Grail 243
Hingston Down 45, 109
Helland 152-3
Helman Tor 193
Henderson, Charles 63, 182, 221
Henwood, Philip 194, 196
Herne 188
Horns 140-1, 155, 232

Hospitallers, Knights 197, 211
Hurlers 199, 222-3

Isles of Scilly 114

Jennings, Pete 49

Kay Sir 184
Kelliwic 149, 157
Killibury, Castle 148-9, 157
King Arthur's 'chair' and 'oven' 110
King Arthur's Footprint 86-8, 91
King Arthur's Grave or Stone, Slaughterbridge 16, 65, 100, 127
King Arthur's Grave, Rillaton 199
King Arthur's Hall, Bodmin Moor 160-162
King Arthur's Head, Tintagel 90
King Arthur's Hunting Lodge 192
King Arthur's Quoit nr Castle-an-Dinas 192
King Arthur's Quoit, Trethevy, St Cleer 196
King Arthur's Quoit, Trethevy, Tintagel 69
King Arthur's Seat 84-5
King Arthur's Wain 38
Kingbeare 213
King Doniert's Stone 194
Kipling, Rudyard 233
Knight, Gareth 141, 231
Knight, Rod and Anne 57
Knights Templar 128-9, 145, 166, 205-6, 216-7, 220, 278, 286

Labyrinths 71-2, 277
Lanherne 168, 180-3, 220
Lanivet 111-2
Langdon, Arthur 151
Lanhydrock 106, 190
Lanlivery 120-3, 127-8, 247
Lanreath 251-3
Launceston 47, 57, 73, 216-20
Lawhitton 220
Leitch, Yuri 225
Leodegrance, King 229
Lepus 26, 222
Lesnewth 16-7, 63
Lenkiewicz, Robert 260
Lewannick 211-3

Lezant 215, 220

Lockyer, Sir Norman 163, 197
Lostwithiel 106, 115
Lostwithiel font 127-41, 221-2, 233-4
Lundy Island 98-9, 277-89
Lyonesse 113-4, 229

Mabon 154-6
Mabinogion 154, 157
Malory, Sir Thomas 65, 219, 229
Massey, Gerald 274, 277
Marisco family 286-7, 289
Matthews, Caitlin 155
Matthews, John, 124, 156
Major Standstill Moonrise 207, 211, 215, 256-7, 273-4
Maltwood, Katherine 105-6
Manilius 5, 176
Marlborough, Wiltshire 68
Mary Magdalene 130, 215-20
McCloud, Fiona 182
Merlin 13-4, 68-9, 74, 80, 99, 155-7, 184-5, 229, 236
Merlin's Cave 81, 88-90
Michell, John 91, 99, 258, 260, 279, 282
Minions 194
Minster Church 15, 17, 61
Minster Cross 100
Montgomery, Hugh 43, 49
Mordred 65, 114, 158
Morganwg, Iolo 243-4
Murray, Margaret 143-4, 234

Nennius 13
Nine Maidens stone row 163-4
Norden, John 163, 197, 273
North Doors 214
North Hill 213
North Petherwin 213
Nudd 244, 247, 259

Orion 137-41, 145, 164, 175-6, 186-7, 222-3
Owls 249

Palomides, Sir 130-1
Payne, Robin 164, 199
Pan 33, 40, 259
Pellinore, King 230-1

Penheale Manor 57
Pentargon 17, 60, 100
Perceval/Parzifal 48, 81, 205, 227-8, 231
Pesh-en-kef 37
Phoenicians 171-2, 206
Pigs 152-8
Pipers 223-4
Pitt family 236-7, 257-9
Plymouth Hoe 103, 261
Prayerbook Rebellion 179-80, 220
Preseli Mountains 98
Port Eliot 258-60
Puck 233-4

Questing Beast 230-1

Ralegh Radford 82, 199
Raleigh, Sir Walter 68, 110
Richard of Cornwall 42-3, 57, 73, 81, 119, 130
Rillaton Cup 199-200
Restormel Castle 99, 107, 115, 117-9, 120, 129
Robert de Mortain 47, 116, 217
Robin Goodfellow 233-4
Roche Rock 193, 271
Rocky Valley Mazes 15, 17, 71-2, 277
Rollo, Duke of Normandy 43-5, 56
Rufus the Red 143-4

Samford Courtenay 180, 206
Santillana, Giorgio de 32, 187
Seven Rishis 36
Shamanism 24, 26-7, 29-30, 49-51, 151, 246
Sheen, Brian 223
Sirius 174-6, 187-8
Slaughterbridge 16-7, 65-6, 265
Solstice Axis 102-3
Somerton, Somerset 105
Spence, Lewis 275
Spica 39
Spoils of Annwn 71, 275, 279
Steiner, Rudolf 290
Stewart, R.J. 155
Stonehenge 98-100
Stowes Hill 198-201, 223-4, 274
Straw Bear 35-6
Synod of Whitby 204

St Bartholemew's Church,
   Lostwithiel 118
St Blazey 229
St Catherine 128-9
St Columba 182-3
St Columb Major 163-7,
   178, 188
St Corentin (Cury) 46
St Dunstan 250
St Eval 189
St Germanus 261
St Germans 259
St George's Island 225
St Guron 108
St Helen's Churchyard,
   Lundy 280, 283-4
St Kew 148-51
St Mabyn 152, 154
St Madryn 61-2
St Mawgan-in-Pydar 164,
   167, 178, 181
St Materiana 61, 93-4
St Martin 23, 40
St Meubred 118, 157, 160
St Michael 23, 47, 173,
   273-4, 290
St Michael Line 55, 131,
   235, 257, 273
St Michael's Mount 47
St Nectan 76-7, 254-5, 2
   81-2, 287
St Nectan's Kieve 16-7, 52,
   70, 76-7
St Newlyn East 186
St Peter 31
St Petroc 69, 109-10
St Piran 70, 178
St Pinnock 251
St Ursula 23, 252
St Samson 46, 149,
St Veep 249
St Winnow 249-50, 267-8

Temple, Bodmin Moor 263
Temple, Robert 174-5
Tennyson, Alfred Lord 53
Thom, Alexander 163
Thomas, Charles, 42, 62,
   82, 281-2
Tintagel 13-5, 53, 79-104,
   246
Tintagel Castle 42-3, 57,
   81, 88
Tintagel Church 92-7, 163
Tintagel Ware 82, 103
Tintagel monolith 94-7
Tinner's Hares 204-7
Tokenbury Fort 194
Tolkien J.R.R. 187

Totemism 146, 185
Trecarrell 215, 217
Tregeare Rounds 148
Trethevy Quoit, St Cleer
   196-7, 225
Trethevy, Tintagel 15, 17,
   19
Trevalga 68
Treworld 16-7, 100
Tristan Stone 271-2
Tudor Pole, Wellesley 290

Upton Cross 194
Uther Pendragon 79-80,
   229

Venus 202-3, 205-6
Vikings 43, 47-51, 108-9,
   118-20, 218
Von Dechend 187
Von Eschenbach, Wolfram
   48, 81, 129, 263
Vortigern 99
Vyvyan, Prior 190-1

Western Morning News
   176, 222
Welltown Manor 65
White Goddess 227, 229,
   255
Whittlesea 35-6
Wild Hunt 138-41, 155,
   185-6, 188, 204, 230, 258
Willapark, Boscastle 59, 67
   William, Duke of
Normandy 56, 62, 116
Winchester 247
Withiel 190
Wolves 33-4, 69, 169-76,
   182-3
Worthyvale 16, 65

Ygdrassil 121

Aberaeron 305
Aberarth 305
Abraham 300
Admiral Somerville 310
Age of Aquarius 300
Age of Aries 300
Age of Pisces 300
Age of Taurus 300
Anglesey 306, 310, 319
Arbor Low 305
Archangel Michael 304
Aries 300
Arthur' Quoit, St David's Head, 319
Arthur's Cross 306
Arthur's Grave 331
Arthur's Quoit, Newport 303
Arthur's Quoit, Trevethy 317
Arthur's Table 319-20
Arthur as The Bear 300
Arthurian Romances 315, 317, 333
Arthur Triangle 326, 341-2
Astrology 300-1
Astronomer Royal 309
Atkinson, Richard 309
Aveni, Anthony 309

Badon Hill 341
Bangor 319
Bangor Cathedral 319
Bangor Mountain 319
Bardsey Island 310, 328
Bishop of Bangor 319
Blake, William 310
Bluestones 307
Bluestone site 307, 327-329, 340
Bodmin Moor 336
Boscastle 338
Bryn Celli Ddu 305-7, 309

Caldey Island 315, 328
Callanish 310
Cape Wrath 337
Cardiff 340
Cardigan 305, 329
Cardigan Island 310
Cardinham Castle 338
Carhampton 326-7
Carmarthen 306, 311, 315
Carningli, 'Angel Mountain' 308, 313-4
Carningli Common 308, 313
Carreg Coetan Arthur 314
Castle Dore 315
Castle Douglas 319
Cefyn Bryn 317

Celtic Church 291, 314-5, 328-30, 333
Cheesewring 316
Cistercian abbeys 306
Classical Greece 299
Criccieth Castle 306

Dark Ages 303-4, 306, 308, 317-8, 325-26, 333
Draco (The Dragon) 299
Draconic cycle 314
Dragon of Radnor Forest 304
Dunster Castle 325-26

Edasich 300-1
Edinburgh 340
Egypt 301
Eleanor of Aquitaine 341
Elizabeth I 342
Euclid 331, 336

Fishguard 311
Fowey 311, 337

Gawain 341
Giraldus Cambrensis 316
Glastonbury 342
Glyndwr uprising 316
Gower Peninsula 317
Great Bear 295 onwards
Great Year 300
Gwynevere 341

Hamish Miller 304
Hamlet's Mill, 322
Harald Hardrada 320
Harold Stone 318
Heyerdahl, Thor 298, 300
Holy Island 297-8, 310

Ilfracombe 293, 317
Iron Age 300
Isle of Man 310, 319, 337

Jesus 304, 340
John the Baptist 341
Joseph of Arimathea 341
Journal of Archaeoastronomy 297
Judas 341

King Arthur's Hall 337-38, 340
King Arthur's Hall axis 337
King Maelgwyn Gwynedd 319
Kochab 299

Launceston 311, 315
Lethbridge, T C 295
Liskeard 311
Llanarth 306
Llanfihangel ar Arth 304-6
Llangrannog 325
Llansteffan 311, 315
Llantwit Major 327
Loch Eriboll 337
Lostwithiel 327
Lunar eclipses 298
lunar nodal cycle 314
Lundy axis 328, 336, 342
Lundy Island 293, 305, 307, 324, 326-9, 340

Major standstill 308, 313
Mary Magdelene 341
Megalithic yards 307, 327,329, 338
Menai Strait 321
Merlin 306-7, 328, 341
Merlin's Hill 306
Merlin's Stone 306
Michell, John 294, 309, 335
Morte Point 305-7, 317
Mynachlog ddu 328

Newport in Pembrokeshire 311
Nyfer, river 312-13, 315

Old Cleeve 327

Pentre Ifan 312, 314-5
Plato 331-2
Platonic Year 300
Pliny 332
Pole Star 292, 296-7, 299-302
Pope Gregory the Great 330
Powerpoints 341
Preseli region 307, 311
Ptolemy 332
Pythagoras 307, 331

Records in Stone 309
Restormel Castle 327, 329
Rhys ap Gruffydd, 316
Rig Veda 321
Royal Astronomical Society 310

Shebbear 317
Sir Norman Lockyer 309
Skomer Island 318
Small Bear (Ursa Minor) 299
Solar-hero 340
St Caranog 325
St Anthony's well 315

St Augustine 330
St Clarus 316
St Clears 293, 311, 315-6, 325
St Cleer 311, 316-7
St Columb Major 327
St David's Cathedral 318
St Davids 305, 327-8
St Deiniol 319
St Dogmaels 327
St Illtud 328
St Mary 304
St Michael 304
St Michael line 316
Stonehenge 304-5, 307, 320,
        324, 3260-9, 338, 340
Stonehenge-Lundy line 325
Strata Florida 306
St Samson (& St Sampson)
        315
Sun, Moon & Stonehenge
        311, 327
Sylen Mountain 317

Temple Wood 314
Tennyson 297
The Ancient Sage 295
The Arthur Stone 306, 317,
        318
The Enlightenment 301
The Great Bear 301-2, 304,
        320-1, 340
The Matter of Britain 3423
The Measure of Albion 327,
        332
The Megalithic Portal 323
The Modern Antiquarian 323
Theodolite 312, 340
Theodorus 343
The Old Straight Track (1925)
        309
The Precessional Cycle 321-2
The Tristan stone 315
The View Over Atlantis 309,
        335
Thom, Alexander 295, 309,
        314, 333
Thuban 299
Tintagel Island 320, 327
Trefdraeth (Newport) 311-2
Tregaron 306
Trethevy Quoit 317
Tywardreath, in Cornwall
        308, 327-8

Underwood, Guy 295
Ursa Major 295-6, 301
Uther Pendragon 301

Watkins, Alfred 295,
        309, 334
William Stukeley 309
Woolacombe 305
World Age 300

Zodiac 301

KING   ARTHUR